D1245075

The Cold War

David G. Williamson

HODDER
EDUCATION
AN HACHETTE UK COMPANY

To Sue

The material in this title has been developed independently of the International Baccalaureate®, which in no way endorses it.

The Publishers would like to thank the following for permission to reproduce copyright material:

Photo credits   **p.18** The Granger Collection, NYC/TopFoto/Cartoon by C. Berryman published in the Washington Star, 9 October 1939; **p.34** © Hulton-Deutsch Collection/CORBIS; **p.45** British Cartoon Archive, University of Kent/artwork © Alex Marengo; **p.77** © dpa/Corbis; **p.89** Press Office of the Government of Germany; **p.111** Xinhua News Agency/Eyevine; **p.114** TopFoto; **p.115** © Bettmann/CORBIS; **p.122** Xinhua News Agency/Eyevine; **p.131** AFP/Getty Images; **p.143** Press Office of the Government of Germany; **p.155** Jack Esten/Picture Post/Getty Images; **p.170** Press Office of the Government of Germany; **p.180** TopFoto; **p.189** © Bettmann/CORBIS; **p.199** © Bettmann/CORBIS; **p.208** © Bettmann/CORBIS; **p.249** Keystone/Getty Images; **p.261** Sahm Doherty/Time Life Pictures/Getty Images; **p.264** © Pascal Manoukian/Sygma/Corbis; **p.289** culture-images/TopFoto.

Acknowledgements   **Norman Davies:** Table: Statistics of Poland's trade balance from 1950–76 in millions of convertible zloty from *God's Playground – A History of Poland*, Volume 2 (Oxford University Press, 2005), reproduced by permission of the publisher; **C.S. Maier:** Tables: 'Numbers of visitors from the GDR to the FRG' and 'Total indebtedness to the West' from *Dissolution: The Crisis of Communism and the End of East Germany* (Princeton University Press, 1997), © 1997 Princeton University Press, reprinted by permission of Princeton University Press; **Christian Ostermann:** 'The United States and the East German Uprising of 1953 and the Limits of Rollback' from *Cold War International History Project* (Woodrow Wilson Center for Scholars, 1994), reproduced by permission of the author; **Richard Sakwa:** Table: 'Republics of the USSR' from *Soviet Politics in Perspective* (Routledge, 1998), reproduced by permission of Taylor & Francis Books (UK); **G. Swain and N. Swain:** Tables: 'State control of industrial output and trade in 1952' and 'Collectivization of agriculture in eastern Europe' from *Eastern Europe since 1945* (Palgrave Macmillan, 1993), reproduced by permission of the publisher; **M. Walker:** Table: 'Numbers of US and Soviet nuclear launchers and warheads, 1962–80' from *The Cold War* (Vintage, 1993).

Every effort has been made to trace all copyright holders, but if any have been inadvertently overlooked the Publishers will be pleased to make the necessary arrangements at the first opportunity.

Although every effort has been made to ensure that website addresses are correct at time of going to press, Hodder Education cannot be held responsible for the content of any website mentioned in this book. It is sometimes possible to find a relocated web page by typing in the address of the home page for a website in the URL window of your browser.

Hachette UK's policy is to use papers that are natural, renewable and recyclable products and made from wood grown in sustainable forests. The logging and manufacturing processes are expected to conform to the environmental regulations of the country of origin.

Orders: please contact Bookpoint Ltd, 130 Milton Park, Abingdon, Oxon OX14 4SB. Telephone: +44 (0)1235 827720. Fax: +44 (0)1235 400454. Lines are open 9.00a.m.–5.00p.m., Monday to Saturday, with a 24-hour message answering service. Visit our website at www.hoddereducation.co.uk

Cover photo © The Granger Collection/TopFoto
Illustrations by Barking Dog Art
Typeset in 10/13pt Palatino and produced by Integra Software Services Pvt. Ltd., Pondicherry, India
Printed in Dubai

A catalogue record for this title is available from the British Library

ISBN 978 14441 56478

Contents

Dedication

Dedicated to Keith Randell (1943–2002)

The original *Access to History* series was conceived and developed by Keith, who created a series to 'cater for students as they are, not as we might wish them to be'. He leaves a living legacy of a series that for over 20 years has provided a trusted, stimulating and well-loved accompaniment to post-16 study. Our aim with these new editions for the IB is to continue to offer students the best possible support for their studies.

Introduction

This book has been written to support your study of Topic 5: The Cold War for IB History Diploma Route 2 Paper 2.

This first chapter gives you an overview of:

✪ the content you will study for the Cold War

✪ how you will be assessed for Paper 2

✪ the different features of this book and how these will aid your learning.

What you will study

The late twentieth century witnessed the Cold War. The end of the Second World War brought two superpowers, the United States (US) and the Union of Soviet Socialist Republics (USSR), to the fore of international relations. Both states had vast territories, with large populations, tremendous national resources and major industrial complexes. They both fielded large militaries that had defeated Axis states in the Second World War and each represented a specific governing and economic structure. The US generally stood for democratically elected governments that espoused free trade or capitalism, while the USSR was a communist state in which there was only one political party, the Communist Party, and the economy was primarily directed by the state. These competing economic and government models, along with the need for each to create alliances for their security and the security of their allies, had worldwide consequences as each state attempted to gain further allies, spread their economic and governing systems and competed militarily, both in terms of quantity and technology.

The Cold War is an interesting topic of study. The competition between the US and the USSR and their allies had economic consequences for Europe and many other parts of the world. Various wars, such as those in Korea, Vietnam and Afghanistan resulted, in part, from the desire to either limit or spread communism or capitalism. While the Cold War may often be seen as a period in which the world was often seemingly on the threshold of nuclear warfare, it may also be interpreted as an era in which the search for peace and security were paramount concerns for many nations' leaders.

This book addresses East–West relations from 1945. It:

- begins by looking at the origins of the Cold War and the ideological differences which underpinned it (Chapter 1)
- examines the early years of the Cold War, including how Truman's policy of containing Communism developed, and the development of the 'Iron Curtain' (Chapter 2).

- covers the division of Germany from 1948 to 1952 and the consolidation of the division of Europe into a Soviet bloc and a Western bloc (Chapter 3)
- traces how communism spread in Asia and its impact on different conflicts in the region (Chapter 4)
- considers the advent of *détente* and its subsequent breakdown during various crises, culminating in the Berlin Crisis (Chapter 5)
- covers the global Cold War from 1953 to 1961, looking at conflict in Africa, Vietnam and the Middle East (Chapter 6)
- looks in detail at the politics of *détente*, 1963 to 1979 (Chapter 7)
- concludes by examining the end of the Cold War and the collapse of communism in eastern Europe and the USSR (Chapter 8).

How you will be assessed

The IB History Diploma can either be studied to Standard or Higher Level. It has three papers in total: Papers 1 and 2 for Standard Level and a further Paper 3 for Higher Level. It also has an internal assessment which all students must do.

- For Paper 1 you need to answer four source-based questions on a prescribed subject. This counts for 20 per cent of your overall marks at Higher Level, or 30 per cent of your overall marks at Standard Level.
- For Paper 2 you need to answer two essay questions on two different topics. This counts for 25 per cent of your overall marks at Higher Level, or 45 per cent of your overall marks at Standard Level.
- For Paper 3 you need to answer three essay questions on two or three sections. This counts for 35 per cent of your overall marks at Higher Level.

For the Internal Assessment you need to carry out a historical investigation. This counts for 20 per cent of your overall marks at Higher Level, or 25 per cent of your overall marks at Standard Level.

Topic 5: The Cold War is assessed through Paper 2. There are five topics on Paper 2 and you will answer two questions in total, each from a different topic. Questions for Topic 5 may ask you to discuss the origins and development of the Cold War, the importance of specific policies or leaders, about various crises or treaties and their effects, the impact of proxy conflicts such as those in Korea, Vietnam or Afghanistan, the final years of the Cold War, and so forth.

Examination questions

You will answer only one question out of the six questions you will find on Topic 5: The Cold War. Your answer will take the form of an essay. These questions are not in any particular order. There will be questions that your teacher has prepared you to answer, but others that you will not be able to address. This is normal and expected. Topic 5 has many areas of the Cold War which may be studied and your teacher has selected various periods, covering different regions, such as Asia, Africa, Europe or the Americas. Each question on the exam is worth 20 points, making Paper 2 worth a total of 40.

There are several types of questions, some of which may be as follows.

Questions about the importance of a single event

Your examination will possibly contain questions regarding a single event or issue. This event or issue may be named, or the examination paper may allow you to choose one to address.

Example 1

To what extent was the Potsdam Conference responsible for the Cold War?

Example 2

For what reasons, and with what results, did the Suez Crisis in 1956 affect Cold War relations?

Example 3

Which event in eastern Europe in 1989 contributed most significantly to the collapse of communism in that region?

Example 4

Analyse the importance of the Cuban Missile Crisis on Cold War diplomacy.

Questions that involve more than one region

Your examination will have questions regarding more than one region during the Cold War.

Example 1

With reference to two Cold War communist leaders, each from a different region, compare and contrast their relationship with the Soviet Union.

Example 2

Examine the difference between the Soviet Union's relationships with communist governments from two different regions.

Example 3

Analyse the origins of communist government in two different states, each from a different region.

Example 4

Assess the importance of the Cold War for Africa and Asia.

Questions that involve quotations

Examinations often have questions that begin with a quotation that must be analysed.

Example 1

'The Cold War began as the result of Soviet provocations at the end of the Second World War.' To what extent is this statement true?

Example 2

'The United States was responsible for the Cuban Missile Crisis.' Assess the validity of this statement.

Example 3

'Gorbachev's policies, and not those of the United States, were responsible for bringing the Cold War to an end.' Examine the accuracy of this statement.

Example 4

'*Détente* was not the exception to international diplomacy during the Cold War between the United States and the Soviet Union, but the norm.' To what extent is this statement valid?

The appearance of the examination paper

Cover

The cover of the examination paper states the date of the examination and the length of time you have to complete it: 1 hour and 30 minutes. Please note that there are two routes in history. Make sure your paper says Route 2 on it. Instructions are limited and simply state that you should not open it until told to do so, answer only two questions, each from a different topic, and to make sure that you understand what the paper means by regions. A map indicates the regions for you.

Topics

Once you are allowed to open your examination paper, you will note that there are five topics, each numbered and titled. Topic 5 obviously comes last and six questions will follow below this title. Again, the questions are in no particular order, so a question on a more recent event or issue may come before one that deals with something or someone that occurred earlier in time.

Questions

You are required to answer only one of the six questions. Make sure you have read through all the questions before starting, selecting the question you know the most about and feel the most comfortable with. It is important to understand that you need to answer the question fully in an essay format. We will discuss more about answering questions at the end of each chapter.

 # About this book

Coverage of course content

This book addresses the key areas listed in the IB History Guide for Route 2: Twentieth-century world history Topic 5: The Cold War. Chapters start with an introduction outlining the key questions that will be addressed. Chapters are then divided into a series of sections and topics covering the course content. Throughout the chapters, you will find the following features to aid your study of the course content.

Key and leading questions

Each section heading in the chapter has a related key question which gives a focus to your reading and understanding of the section. These are also listed in the chapter introduction. You should be able to answer the questions after completing the relevant section.

Topics within the sections have leading questions which are designed to help you focus on the key points within a topic and give you more practice in answering questions.

Key terms

Key terms are the important terms you need to know to gain an understanding of the period. These are emboldened in the text and are defined in the margin. They also appear in a glossary at the end of the book.

Sources

Each chapter contains several sources including speeches, quotes by historians, photographs, and charts. These sources have questions for you to practise your knowledge and are similar to questions found on Paper 1 examinations.

Theory of Knowledge (TOK) questions

It is important to understand that there are strong links between IB History and Theory of Knowledge (TOK) issues. Each chapter has a Theory of Knowledge question that makes this link.

Summary diagrams

At the end of each section is a summary diagram which gives a visual summary of the content of the section. It is intended as an aid for revision.

Chapter summary

At the end of each chapter is a short summary of the content of that chapter. This is intended to help you revise and consolidate your knowledge and understanding of the content.

Skills development

We have included instruction at the end of each chapter on the meanings of the various command terms used on IB examinations. Examples of outlines, introductions, conclusions, and body paragraphs will be presented and discussed as well. In addition, this chapter provides:

- examination practice in the form of Paper 2 style questions
- suggestions for learning activities, including ideas for debate, essays, displays, and research which will help you develop a deeper understanding of Topic 5 content.

End of the book

The book concludes with the following sections.

Glossary

All key terms in the book are defined in the glossary.

Timeline

This gives a timeline of the major events covered in the book which is helpful for quick reference or as a revision tool.

Further reading

This contains a list of books, websites, films and other resources which may help you with further independent research and presentations. It may also be helpful when further information is required for internal assessments and extended essays in history. You may wish to share the contents of this area with your school or local librarian.

Internal assessment

All IB History diploma students are required to write a historical investigation which is internally assessed. The investigation is an opportunity for you to dig more deeply into a subject that interests you. There is a list of possible topics at the end of the book that could warrant further investigation to form part of your historical investigation.

CHAPTER 1

The origins of the Cold War, 1917–45

The Cold War was a period of political hostility between capitalist and communist countries, in particular between the US and the Soviet Union, which, from its onset in 1945, lasted for over 40 years. It brought the world perilously close to another global war several times. This chapter looks at the origins of the Cold War, which can be traced back to the Russian Revolution of 1917. You need to consider the following questions throughout this chapter:

✪ How significant were the ideological differences between the opposing sides as a cause of the Cold War?

✪ To what extent did the USSR's foreign policy in the interwar years reflect its priorities of defence and regaining territory lost at the end of the First World War?

✪ In what ways were the war aims and ambitions of the USSR, US and Great Britain conflicting?

✪ How far did the liberation of Europe, 1943–45, intensify the rivalry and distrust between the 'Big Three'?

✪ What was achieved at the Yalta Conference?

 KEY TERM

USSR Union of Soviet Socialist Republics, the name given to communist Russia and states under its control from 1922, also known as the **Soviet Union**.

Communism A political and economic system in which all private ownership of property is abolished along with all economic and social class divisions.

Capitalism An economic system in which the production of goods and their distribution depend on the investment of private capital with minimal government regulation and involvement.

 # The ideology of the Cold War

▶ *Key question: How significant were the ideological differences between the opposing sides as a cause of the Cold War?*

The term 'cold war' was used before 1945 to describe periods of extreme tension between states stopping just short of war. In May 1945, when the US and the **USSR** faced each other in Germany, this term rapidly came back into use to describe the relations between them. The writer George Orwell, commenting on the significance of the dropping of the atomic bomb by the US on Japan in 1945 during the Second World War (see page 44), foresaw 'a peace that is no peace', in which the US and USSR would be both 'unconquerable and in a permanent state of cold war' with each other.

The Cold War was a fundamental clash of ideologies and interests. Essentially, the USSR followed Karl Marx's and Vladimir Lenin's teachings (see pages 9–11) that conflict between **communism** and **capitalism** was unavoidable, while the US and its allies for much of the time saw the USSR, in the words of US President Reagan in 1983, as an 'evil empire', intent on the destruction of democracy and civil rights.

Capitalism and communism

Communism

In the nineteenth century, two Germans, Friedrich Engels and Karl Marx proposed communism as an idea for radical social change. This system provided the foundations of **Marxism–Leninism** which, in the twentieth century, became the governing ideology of the **Soviet Union**, much of central and eastern Europe, the People's Republic of China, Cuba, and several other states.

Marx argued that capitalism and the **bourgeoisie** in an industrial society would inevitably be overthrown by the workers or 'proletariat' in a socialist revolution. This initially would lead to a '**dictatorship of the proletariat**' in which the working class would break up the old order. Eventually, a true egalitarian communist society would emerge in which money is no longer needed and 'each gives according to their ability to those according to their need'. In this society all people would be completely equal and economic production would be subordinated to human needs rather than profit. Crime, envy and rivalry would become things of the past since they were based on greed and economic competition. So, in its essence, communism is profoundly hostile to capitalism.

Marxism–Leninism

In the early twentieth century, Vladimir Ilych Lenin developed Marx's ideas and adapted them to the unique conditions in Russia. Russia's economy was primarily agricultural and lacked a large industrial proletariat which would rise in revolution. Lenin therefore argued that communists needed to be strongly organized with a small compact core, consisting of reliable and experienced revolutionaries, who could achieve their aims of undermining and toppling the Tsarist regime. In 1903 Lenin and his followers founded the **Bolshevik Party**, which seized power in Russia in October 1917.

Just before the Bolsheviks seized power Lenin outlined his plans for the creation of a revolutionary state in an unfinished pamphlet, *State and Revolution*. It would be run by 'the proletariat organized as a ruling class' and would use terror and force against any organization or person who did not support it. In fact the state would be the 'dictatorship of the proletariat', and would 'wither away' only once its enemies at home and abroad were utterly destroyed. Then, of course, the promise of communism would dawn where there would be no economic exploitation, crime, selfishness or violence.

Under the leadership of first Lenin, and then Josef Stalin, the USSR became an authoritarian, communist state where the state was in charge of all aspects of the economy; there were no democratic elections and freedom of speech was limited.

← In what ways did the ideologies of the opposing sides differ?

 **KEY TERM**

Marxism–Leninism Doctrines of Marx which were built upon by Lenin.

Soviet Union See **USSR**.

Bourgeoisie The middle class, particularly those with business interests, whom Marx believed benefited most from the existing capitalist economic system.

Proletariat Marx's term for industrial working-class labourers, primarily factory workers.

Dictatorship of the proletariat A term used by Marx to suggest that, following the overthrow of the bourgeoisie, government would be carried out by and on behalf of the working class.

Bolshevik Party The Russian Communist Party which seized power in a revolution in October 1917.

Capitalism

Capitalism is an economic system in which the production of goods and their distribution depend on the investment of private capital with a view to making a profit. Unlike a **command economy**, a capitalist economy is run by people who wish to make a profit, rather than by the state. By the 1940s western economies such as the US, Canada and Britain were mixed – with the state playing an increasingly major role in key sections of the economy, but with private enterprise playing a large part as well.

What were the clashes between the two ideologies?

Ideological clashes

Opposition to Marxism–Leninism in the USA and the western European states in 1945 was reinforced, or – as Marxist theoreticians would argue – even determined by the contradictions between capitalism and the command economies of the communist-dominated states.

Political systems

In the west there was a deep mistrust of communism as a political system, particularly its lack of democracy. The USSR dismissed democracy as a mere camouflage for capitalism and its politicians as its puppets. For Marxist–Leninists, democracy meant economic equality where there were no extremes between wealthy capitalists and poor workers and peasants. However, for the **parliamentary governments** of western Europe and the US, democracy meant the liberty of the individual, equality before the law and **representative government**, rather than economic equality under the dictatorship of the proletariat. Liberal or parliamentary democracy challenges the right of any one party and leader to have the permanent monopoly of power. It is, at least in theory, opposed to dictatorship in any form.

Religion

Marxism–Leninism was bitterly opposed to religion. One of its core arguments was that it was not an all-powerful God who influenced the fate of mankind, but rather economic and material conditions. Once these were reformed under communism, mankind would prosper and not need any religion. For Marxists religion was merely, as Marx himself had said, 'the opium of the masses'. It duped the proletariat into accepting exploitation by their rulers and capitalist businessmen. During the revolution in Russia, churches, mosques and synagogues were closed down, and religion was banned.

In Europe, Christian churches were amongst the leading critics and enemies of communism. After 1945, Catholic-dominated political parties in western Germany and Italy played a key role in opposing communism. In 1979, the election of Pope John Paul II of Poland as head of the Roman Catholic Church led many in Poland to oppose communist government (see page 260).

KEY TERM

Command economy
An economy where supply and pricing are regulated by the government rather than market forces such as demand, and in which all the larger industries and businesses are controlled centrally by the state.

Parliamentary government A government responsible to and elected by parliament.

Representative government A government based on an elected majority.

SOURCE A

An excerpt from *The Cold War, 1945–1991*, by John W. Mason, published by Routledge, London, UK, 1996, p. 71.

Fundamentally the cold war was a confrontation between the United States and the Soviet Union, fuelled on both sides by the belief that the ideology of the other side had to be destroyed. In this sense ... co-existence was not possible ... The Soviet Union held to Lenin's belief that conflict between Communism and Capitalism was inevitable. The United States believed that peace and security in the world would only emerge when the evil of Communism had been exorcised [expelled].

What does Source A reveal about the nature of the Cold War? **?**

Marxism–Leninism

- Believes that economic factors determine reality
- Perceives capitalism to be immoral as it exploits labour
- Foresees its overthrow by the workers

↓

Dictatorship of the proletariat

↓

After abolition of profit and economic exploitation, a communist society would evolve

The enemies of Marxism–Leninism

- Capitalism
- Liberal democracy
- Religion

↓

Capitalism
Belief in private ownership of land and business

↓

Liberal democracy
Belief in parliamentary democracy

↓

Religion
Belief that ultimately God determines the fate of mankind, not economic factors

SUMMARY DIAGRAM

The ideology of the Cold War

The Soviet Union and the Western powers, 1917–41

> ▶ **Key question:** *To what extent did the USSR's foreign policy in the interwar years reflect its priorities of defence and regaining territory lost at the end of the First World War?*

The Bolshevik Revolution in Russia succeeded against the odds but Lenin was initially convinced that victory within Russia alone would not ensure the survival of the revolution. An isolated Bolshevik Russia was vulnerable to pressure from the capitalist world; its very existence was a challenge to it. If communism was to survive in Russia, it had also to triumph globally. This belief had a large influence on Soviet relations with the rest of the world.

SOURCE B

?
What is the importance of Source B for understanding the aims of Russian foreign policy after the Bolshevik Revolution?

An excerpt from 'Farewell Address to the Swiss Workers' by Lenin, April 1917, quoted in *Lenin's Collected Works*, Vol. 23, English edition (trans. M.S. Levin, *et al.*), Progress Publishers, Moscow, 1964, p. 371.

To the Russian proletariat has fallen the great honour of beginning the series of revolutions which the imperialist war [the First World War] has made an objective inevitability. But the idea that the Russian proletariat is the chosen revolutionary proletariat is absolutely alien to us. We know perfectly well that the proletariat of Russia is less organised, less prepared and less class conscious than the proletariat of other countries. It is not its special qualities but rather the special conjuncture of historical circumstances that for a certain, perhaps very short, time *has made the proletariat of Russia the vanguard of the revolutionary proletariat of the whole world.*

Why was there hostility between the US and Russia 1917–20?

→ The US and Russia

One historian, Howard Roffmann, has argued that the Cold War 'proceeded from the very moment the Bolsheviks triumphed in Russia in 1917'. There was certainly immediate hostility between Bolshevik Russia and the US which, along with Britain, France and Japan, intervened in the Russian Civil War (1918–22) by helping the Bolsheviks' opponents, the Whites (see page 15).

This hostility was intensified by the ideological clash between the ideas of US President Woodrow Wilson and Lenin. Wilson, in his **Fourteen Points** of January 1918, presented an ambitious global programme that called for the

 KEY TERM

Fourteen Points A list of points drawn up by US President Woodrow Wilson on which the peace settlement at the end of the First World War was based.

self-determination of subject peoples, creation of democratic states, free trade and **collective security** through a **League of Nations**. Lenin preached world revolution and communism, repudiated Russia's foreign debts and nationalized all businesses in Russia, including those owned by foreigners.

However, the rivalry between these two embryonic superpowers which was to give rise to the Cold War after 1945, had not yet become acute. Despite playing a key role in negotiating the Treaty of Versailles, the US Congress refused to allow President Wilson to sign the peace treaty or for the US to join the League of Nations. Instead, the US retreated into **isolation** until 1941.

The Russian Revolution and Allied intervention

The Russian Civil War

Although the Bolsheviks had seized power in the major cities in 1917, they had to fight a bitter civil war to destroy their opponents, the Whites, who were assisted by Britain, France, the US and Japan. These countries hoped that by assisting the Whites, they would be able to strangle Bolshevism and prevent it spreading to Germany which, after defeat in the First World War in November 1918, was in turmoil and vulnerable to communist revolution by its own workers. If Germany were to become communist, the **Allies** feared that the whole of Europe would be engulfed in revolution. However, Allied intervention was ineffective and in 1919 French and US troops withdrew, and British troops were withdrawn in 1920. Only Japan's troops remained until the end of the Civil War in 1922. Intervention in the USSR did inevitably fuel Soviet suspicions of the Western powers.

The Polish-Russian War, 1920

At the **Paris Peace Conference** in 1919, British Foreign Minister Lord Curzon proposed that the frontier with Russia should be about 160 kilometres to the east of Warsaw, Poland's newly-created capital; this demarcation became known as the Curzon Line. Poland, however, rejected this and exploited the chaos in Russia to seize as much territory as it could. In early 1920, Poland launched an invasion of the Ukraine. This was initially successful, but, by August 1920, Bolshevik forces had pushed the Poles back to Warsaw. With the help of military supplies and advisors from France, Poland rallied and managed to inflict a decisive defeat on the **Red Army**, driving it out of much of the territory Poland claimed. In 1921, Poland signed the Treaty of Riga with Russia and was awarded considerable areas of the Ukraine and Byelorussia, in which Poles formed only a minority of the population.

KEY TERM

Self-determination Giving nations and nationalities the right to be independent and to form their own governments.

How did Allied intervention after the Russian Revolution have an impact on subsequent Soviet foreign policy?

KEY TERM

Collective security An agreement between nations that an aggressive act towards one nation will be treated as an aggressive act towards all nations under the agreement.

League of Nations International organization established after the First World War to resolve conflicts between nations to prevent war.

Isolation A situation in which a state has no alliances or close diplomatic contacts with other states.

Allies In the First World War, an alliance between Britain, France, the US, Japan, China and others, including Russia until 1917.

Paris Peace Conference The peace conference held in Paris in 1919–20 to deal with defeated Germany and her allies. It resulted in the Treaties of Versailles, St. Germain, Neuilly and Sèvres.

Red Army The army of the USSR.

The extension of Poland so far east helped to isolate Russia geographically from western and central Europe. The creation of Finland, Estonia, Latvia, and Lithuania helped further this, leading to the creation of a *Cordon Sanitaire*, a zone of states to prevent the spread of communism to the rest of Europe. The recovery of these territories of the former Russian Empire became a major aim of the USSR's foreign policy before 1939.

SOURCE C

? What information about the situation in Europe in 1921 is conveyed by Source C?

Central and eastern Europe in 1921.

Soviet foreign policy, 1922–45

Once the immediate possibility of a world communist revolution vanished, the consolidation of communism within the USSR became the priority for Lenin and his successors. This did not stop the USSR from supporting subversive activities carried out by communist groups or sympathizers within the Western democracies and their colonies. These activities were co-ordinated by the **Comintern**, which was established in 1919 to spread communist ideology. Although foreign communist parties had representatives in the organization, the Communist Party of Russia controlled it.

In the 1930s, the USSR increasingly concentrated on building up its military and industrial strength.

Hitler and Stalin, 1933–41

The coming to power of Hitler and the Nazi Party in Germany in 1933 led to a radical change in Soviet foreign policy. Nazi Germany, with its hatred of communism and stated goal of annexing vast territories in the Soviet Union for colonization, presented a threat to the USSR's very existence. To combat this, Stalin, despite the ideological differences between the USSR and Britain and France, attempted to create a defensive alliance against Nazi Germany:

- In 1934, the USSR joined the League of Nations, which Stalin hoped to turn into a more effective instrument of collective security.
- In 1935, Stalin also signed a pact with France and Czechoslovakia in the hope that this would lead to close military co-operation against Germany. French suspicions of Soviet communism prevented this development.
- In September 1938, in response to Hitler's threat to invade Czechoslovakia, Stalin was apparently ready to intervene, provided France did likewise. However, Hitler's last-minute decision to agree to a compromise proposal at the Munich Conference of 29–30 September, which resulted in the **Munich Agreement**, ensured that Soviet assistance was not needed. The fact that the USSR was not invited to the Conference reinforced Stalin's fears that Britain, France and Germany would work together against the USSR.

Anglo-French negotiations with the USSR, April–August 1939

In March 1939, Germany invaded what was left of Czechoslovakia and, in April, the British and French belatedly began negotiations with Stalin for a defensive alliance against Germany. These negotiations were protracted and complicated by mutual mistrust. Stalin's demand that the Soviet Union should have the right to intervene in the affairs of the small states on her western borders if they were threatened with internal subversion by the Nazis, as Czechoslovakia had been in 1938, was rejected outright by the British. Britain feared that the USSR would exploit this as an excuse to seize the territories for itself.

Stalin was also suspicious that Britain and France were manoeuvring the Soviets into a position where they would have to do most of the fighting against Germany should war break out. The talks finally broke down on 17 August over the question of securing Poland's and Romania's consent to

To what extent was Soviet foreign policy based on the aim to consolidate the Soviet state?

KEY TERM

Comintern A communist organization set up in Moscow in 1919 to co-ordinate the efforts of communists around the world to achieve a worldwide revolution.

Munich Agreement An agreement between Britain, France, Italy and Germany that the Sudetenland region of Czechoslovakia would become part of Germany.

the passage of the Red Army through their territory in the event of war; something which was rejected by Poland.

The Nazi-Soviet Pact

Until early 1939, Hitler saw Poland as a possible ally in a future war against the USSR for the conquest of **lebensraum**. Poland's acceptance of the **Anglo-French Guarantee** forced him to reconsider his position and respond positively to those advisors advocating temporary co-operation with the Soviet Union.

Stalin, whose priorities were the defence of the USSR and the recovery of parts of the former Russian Empire, was ready to explore German proposals for a non-aggression pact; this was signed on 24 August. Not only did it commit both powers to benevolent neutrality towards each other, but in a secret protocol it outlined the German and Soviet **spheres of interest** in eastern Europe: the Baltic states and Bessarabia in Romania fell within the Soviet sphere, while Poland was to be divided between them.

On 1 September 1939, Germany invaded Poland, and Britain and France declared war on Germany on 3 September. The Soviet Union, as agreed secretly in the Nazi-Soviet Pact, began the invasion of eastern Poland on 17 September, although by this time German armies had all but defeated Polish forces. By the beginning of October, Poland was completely defeated and was divided between the Soviet Union and Germany, with the Soviets receiving the larger part.

? What message is conveyed in Source D about the Nazi-Soviet Pact?

SOURCE D

'Wonder How Long the Honeymoon Will Last?' A cartoon printed in US newspaper, the Washington Star, 9 October 1939.

WONDER HOW LONG THE HONEYMOON WILL LAST?

Territorial expansion, October 1939–June 1941

Until June 1941, Stalin pursued a policy of territorial expansion in eastern Europe aimed at defending the USSR against possible future aggression from Germany. To this end, and with the dual aim of recovering parts of the former Russian Empire, Stalin strengthened the USSR's western defences:

- He signed mutual assistance pacts with Estonia and Latvia in October 1939. The Lithuanians were pressured into agreeing to the establishment of Soviet bases in their territory.
- In March 1940, after a brief war with Finland, the USSR acquired the Hanko naval base and other territory along their mutual border.
- Stalin's reaction to the defeat of France in June 1940, which meant German domination of Europe, was to annex the Baltic states of Estonia, Latvia, and Lithuania and to annex Bessarabia and northern Bukovina from Romania.

In June 1941, Germany invaded the Soviet Union, and the USSR became allies with Britain against Nazi Germany, soon to be joined by the US.

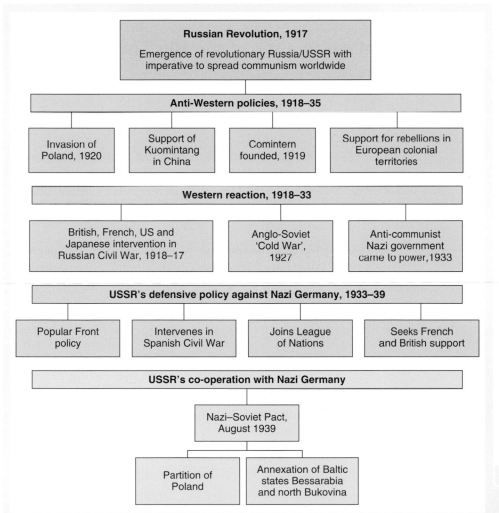

SUMMARY DIAGRAM

Russia and the Western powers, 1917–41

Axis The alliance in the Second World War that eventually consisted of Germany, Italy, Japan, Slovakia, Hungary, Bulgaria, and Romania, as well as several states created in conquered areas.

Reparations Materials, equipment or money taken from a defeated power to make good the damage of war.

③ The Grand Alliance, 1941–45

▶ **Key question:** In what ways did the war aims and ambitions of the USSR, US and Great Britain conflict?

In the second half of 1941, the global political and military situation was completely transformed. Not only were Britain and the USSR now allies against Germany but, on 7 December 1941, Japan's attack on the naval base at Pearl Harbor, Hawaii, brought the US into the war, as the US immediately declared war on Japan, an **Axis** power. In response, Germany and Italy both declared war against the US on 11 December. Germany was now confronted with the Grand Alliance of Britain, the US and the USSR, the leaders of which became known as the Big Three. The USSR was to suffer the brunt of the German attack and effectively destroyed the German army by 1945, but in the process suffered immense physical damage and some 25 million casualties.

What were the aims of the Big Three?

The conflicting aims of the Big Three

As victory over the Axis powers became more certain, each of the three Allies began to develop their own often conflicting aims and agendas for post-war Europe.

The USSR's aims

By the winter of 1944–45, Stalin's immediate priorities were clear. He wanted security for the USSR and **reparations** from the Axis powers to help rebuild the Soviet economy. To protect the USSR against any future German attack, Stalin was determined to regain the land the USSR had annexed in 1939–40 and lost during the course of the war, including:

- land that the Soviet Union had annexed from Poland in 1939 (see page 16); in compensation, Poland would be given German territory that lay beyond the Oder River
- the Baltic provinces of Estonia, Latvia and Lithuania
- territory lost to Finland in 1941
- Bessarabia and northern Bukovina from Romania.

Eastern Europe

In eastern Europe, Stalin's first priority was to ensure that regimes friendly to the USSR were established. By 1944, Stalin seems to have envisaged a post-war Europe, which for a period of time would consist of three different areas:

- An area under direct Soviet control in eastern Europe: Poland, Romania, Bulgaria and, for a time at least, the future Soviet zone in Germany.

- An 'intermediate zone', which was neither fully communist nor fully capitalist, comprising **Yugoslavia**, Austria, Hungary, Czechoslovakia and Finland. The communists would share power there with the liberal, moderate socialist and peasant parties. These areas would act as a 'bridge' between Soviet-controlled eastern Europe and western Europe and the US.
- A non-communist western Europe, which would also include Greece.

Continued co-operation

Stalin wanted to continue close co-operation with Britain and the US even after the end of the war. In 1943, he dissolved the Comintern (see page 15) as a gesture to convince his allies that the USSR was no longer supporting global revolution. The British government saw this as evidence that Stalin wished to co-operate in the reconstruction of Europe after the end of the war.

US aims

In the 1950s, Western historians, such as Herbert Feis, argued that the US was too preoccupied with winning the struggle against Germany and Japan to give much thought to the political future of post-war Europe, since it assumed that all problems would in due course be solved in co-operation with Britain and the USSR. Yet this argument was sharply criticized by **revisionist** historians in the 1960s and 1970s, who insisted that the US very much had its own security agenda for the post-war period.

More recently, historian Melvyn Leffler has shown that the surprise Japanese attack on Pearl Harbor in 1941, and the dramatic developments in air technology during the war, made the US feel vulnerable to potential threats from foreign powers. Consequently, as early as 1943–44, US officials began to draw up plans for a chain of bases which would give the USA control of both the Pacific and Atlantic Oceans. This would also give US industry access to the raw materials and markets of most of western Europe and Asia. Leffler argues that the steps the USA took to ensure its own security alarmed Stalin and so created a 'spiral of distrust', which led ultimately to the Cold War.

SOURCE E

An excerpt from an article by Melvyn Leffler, 'National Security and US Foreign Policy' in *Origins of the Cold War*, ed. M.P. Leffler and D.S. Painter, published by Routledge, London, 1994, pp. 37–38.

The dynamics of the Cold War … are easier to comprehend when one grasps the breadth of the American conception of national security that had emerged between 1945 and 1948. This conception included a strategic [military and political] sphere of influence within the western hemisphere, domination of the Atlantic and Pacific oceans, an extensive system of outlying bases to enlarge the strategic frontier and project American power, an even more extensive system of transit rights to facilitate the conversion of commercial air bases to military use, access to the resources and markets of Eurasia, denial of these resources to a prospective enemy, and the maintenance of nuclear superiority.

KEY TERM

Yugoslavia In 1918, the kingdom of Serbs, Croats and Slovenes was formed. In 1929, it officially became Yugoslavia. The Serbs were the dominating nationality within this state.

Revisionist In the sense of historians, someone who revises the traditional or orthodox interpretation of events and often contradicts it.

How important is Source E in explaining the cause of the Cold War?

Tariffs Taxes placed on imported goods to protect the home economy.

Economic nationalism An economy in which every effort is made to keep out foreign goods.

Autarchic economy An economy that is self-sufficient and protected from outside competition.

Decolonization Granting of independence to colonies.

Atlantic Charter A statement of fundamental principles for the post-war world. The most important of these were: free trade, no more territorial annexation by Britain or the USA, and the right of people to choose their own governments.

Economic aims

Much of US President Roosevelt's policy was inspired by the ideas of his predecessor Woodrow Wilson (see page 12), who in 1919 had hoped eventually to turn the world into one large free trade area. This would be composed of democratic states, where **tariffs** and **economic nationalism** would be abolished. The US government was determined that there should be no more attempts by Germany or Italy to create **autarchic economies**, and that the British and French, too, would be forced to allow other states to trade freely with their empires. Indeed, the US commitment to establishing democratic states meant that they supported the **decolonization** of the European colonial empires.

The United Nations

These ideas were all embodied in the **Atlantic Charter**, which British Prime Minister Churchill and US President Roosevelt drew up in August 1941, four months before the US entered the war. This new, democratic world order was to be underpinned by a future United Nations Organization (UN). By late 1943, Roosevelt envisaged this as being composed of an assembly where all the nations of the world would be represented, although real power and influence would be wielded by an executive committee, or Security Council. This would be dominated by the Soviet Union, Britain, China, France, and the US. For all his talk about the rights of democratic states, he realized that the future of the post-war world would be decided by these powerful states.

Britain's aims

The British government's main aims in 1944 were to ensure the survival of Great Britain as an independent Great Power still in possession of its empire, and to remain on friendly terms with both the US and the USSR. The British government was, however, alarmed by the prospect of Soviet influence spreading into central Europe and the eastern Mediterranean where Britain had vital strategic and economic interests. The Suez Canal in Egypt was its main route to India and British industry was increasingly dependent on oil from the Middle East. As Britain had gone to war over Poland, Prime Minister Churchill also wanted a democratic government in Warsaw, even though he conceded that its eastern frontiers would have to be altered in favour of the USSR.

> To what extent had the Great Powers agreed on dividing up Europe into spheres of influence by the end of 1944?

→ Inter-Allied negotiations, 1943–44

Churchill and Roosevelt held several summit meetings to discuss military strategy and the shape of the post-war world, but it was only in 1943 that the leaders of the USSR, US and Britain met for the first time as a group.

The foreign ministers' meeting at Moscow, October 1943

In October 1943, the foreign ministers of the US, USSR, and Britain met in Moscow, the Soviet Union's capital, in an effort to reconcile the conflicting ambitions of their states. They agreed to establish the European Advisory Commission to finalize plans for the post-war Allied occupation of Germany. They also issued the 'Declaration on General Security'. This proposed the creation of a world organization to maintain global peace and security, Roosevelt's United Nations, which would be joined by all peaceful states. US **Secretary of State** Cordell Hull insisted that the Chinese President Chiang-Kai-shek, as head of a large and potentially powerful allied country, should also sign this declaration. Stalin also informed Hull, in the strictest secrecy, that the USSR would enter the war against Japan after Germany's defeat in Europe.

KEY TERM

Secretary of State
The US foreign minister.

Tehran Conference, 28 November–1 December 1943

At the Tehran Conference, Churchill, Roosevelt and Stalin met for the first time to discuss post-war Europe, the future organization of the UN and the fate of Germany. Stalin again made it very clear that he would claim all the territories which the USSR had annexed in Poland and the Baltic in 1939–40, and that Poland would be compensated with German territory. To this there was no opposition from either Churchill or Roosevelt.

The key decision was made to land British, Commonwealth and US troops in France (Operation Overlord) rather than, as Churchill wished, in the Balkans in 1944. This effectively ensured that the USSR would liberate both eastern and south-eastern Europe by itself, and hence be in a position to turn the whole region into a Soviet sphere of interest. It was this factor that ultimately left the Western powers with little option but to recognize the USSR's claims to eastern Poland and the Baltic States.

SOURCE F

An excerpt from *Alliance* by Jonathan Fenby, published by Simon and Schuster, London, UK, 2008, pp. 246–247.

On 29 November Roosevelt told his son Elliot, who accompanied him to Tehran that:

'Our Chiefs of Staff are convinced of one thing, the way to kill the most Germans, with the least loss of American soldiers is to mount one great big invasion and then slam 'em with everything we have got. It makes sense to me. It makes sense to Uncle Joe. It's the quickest way to win the war. That's all.

Trouble is, the PM [Churchill] is thinking too much of the post-war, and where England will be. He's scared of letting the Russians get too strong in Europe. Whether that's bad depends on a lot of factors.'

According to Source F, what were the political implications of Operation Overlord?

The Churchill–Stalin meeting, October 1944

A year later, in an effort to protect British interests in the eastern Mediterranean (see page 22), Churchill flew to Moscow and proposed a division of south-eastern Europe into distinct spheres of interest. This formed the basis of an agreement that gave the USSR 90 and 75 per cent predominance in Romania and Bulgaria respectively, and Britain 90 per cent in Greece, while Yugoslavia and Hungary were to be divided equally into British and Soviet zones of interest.

After reflection, this agreement was quietly dropped by Churchill as he realized that it would be rejected outright by Roosevelt once it was brought to his attention. This, Churchill feared, would only lead to unwelcome tension in the Anglo-US alliance. Roosevelt had informed Stalin shortly before Churchill arrived in Moscow that there was 'in this global war … no question, either military or political, in which the United States [was] not interested'. However, it did broadly correspond to initial Soviet intentions in eastern Europe, and Stalin did recognize Britain's interests in Greece, even denying the local communists any Soviet support (see page 30).

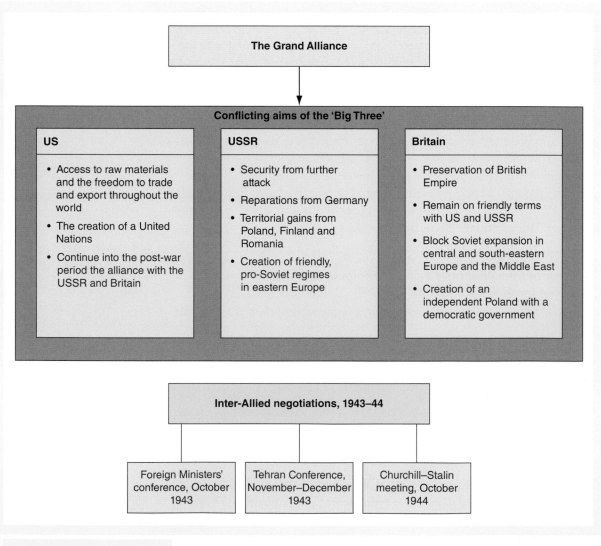

The Grand Alliance

Conflicting aims of the 'Big Three'

US

- Access to raw materials and the freedom to trade and export throughout the world
- The creation of a United Nations
- Continue into the post-war period the alliance with the USSR and Britain

USSR

- Security from further attack
- Reparations from Germany
- Territorial gains from Poland, Finland and Romania
- Creation of friendly, pro-Soviet regimes in eastern Europe

Britain

- Preservation of British Empire
- Remain on friendly terms with US and USSR
- Block Soviet expansion in central and south-eastern Europe and the Middle East
- Creation of an independent Poland with a democratic government

Inter-Allied negotiations, 1943–44

| Foreign Ministers' conference, October 1943 | Tehran Conference, November–December 1943 | Churchill–Stalin meeting, October 1944 |

The Grand Alliance, 1941–44

The liberation of Europe, 1943–45

▶ *Key question: How far did the liberation of Europe, 1943–45, intensify the rivalry and distrust between the 'Big Three'?*

The liberation of eastern Europe by the Soviet army and western Europe by predominantly Anglo-American forces in 1944–45, created the context for the Cold War in Europe. It was indeed in Europe where the Cold War both started and ended.

Eastern Europe, 1944–45

 What were the key sources of political power in liberated eastern Europe, 1944–45?

To understand the complex political situation created by the end of the war, it is important to understand the significance of the Allied Control Commissions, the tension between the governments-in-exile and the local partisan groups, and the close links between the communist parties and the USSR.

Allied Control Commissions

Bulgaria, Finland, Italy, Hungary and Romania were Axis states. Although they were allowed their own governments after their occupation by the **Allied powers**, real power rested with the **Allied Control Commissions** (ACC). The first ACC was established in southern Italy in 1943 by Britain and the US after the collapse of the fascist government there. As the USSR had no troops in Italy, it was not represented on the ACC. Similarly, as it was the USSR that liberated eastern Europe from Germany, Soviet officials dominated the ACCs in Romania, Bulgaria, Finland and Hungary. In this respect, Soviet policy was the mirror image of Anglo-American policy in Italy.

Governments-in-exile and partisan groups

In the states actually occupied by the Germans and Italians in eastern and south-eastern Europe (Poland, Czechoslovakia, Greece and Yugoslavia), governments-in-exile were established in London during the war. They were made up mainly of politicians who had managed to escape the German occupation; yet, being in London, they lost control of the **partisan groups** fighting in the occupied territories. Except for Poland, communist partisan groups emerged as the strongest local forces and their leaders were not ready to take orders from their governments-in-exile. Sometimes this suited Stalin, and sometimes, as in Greece (see page 30), it did not.

Communist parties

In the liberated territories, Stalin advised the local communist parties to form popular fronts or alliances with the liberal, socialist and peasant parties.

KEY TERM

Allied powers Commonly referred to as the Allies during the Second World War, this group first consisted of Poland, France, Britain and others, with the Soviet Union and the United States joining in 1941.

Allied Control Commissions These were set up in each occupied territory, including Germany. They initially administered a particular territory in the name of the Allies.

Partisan groups Resistance fighters or guerrillas in German- and Italian-occupied Europe.

Eventually these fronts became the means by which the communists seized power in eastern Europe (see map on page 147).

To what extent was Stalin's concern about post-war Poland prompted by the needs of Soviet security?

Poland

The Polish question was one of the most complex problems facing the Allies. Britain, together with France, had gone to war in September 1939 as a result of the German invasion of Poland. The British government therefore wanted to see the emergence of a democratic Poland once Germany was driven out by the Red Army. On the other hand, Stalin was determined not only to regain the territories that fell into the Soviet sphere of interest as a result of the Nazi-Soviet Pact (see page 16), but also to ensure that there was a friendly pro-Soviet government in Poland. In effect, this meant forcibly establishing a communist dictatorship, as the majority of Poles were strongly anti-Soviet and anti-communist.

In principle, Britain and the USA had agreed at Tehran to the Soviet annexation of eastern Poland up to the Curzon Line (see page 13), and that Poland would eventually be compensated for this by acquiring territory on her western frontiers from Germany. Both hoped optimistically that Stalin would tolerate a democratically elected government in Warsaw.

The Soviet advance into Poland

Once the Red Army crossed Poland's eastern frontier in early January 1944, the Soviet Union annexed the territory it had claimed in September 1939. By July, Soviet troops had crossed the Curzon Line and moved into western Poland. As they advanced, they systematically destroyed the **nationalist** Polish resistance group known as the **Polish Home Army**. Stalin fatally undermined the authority of the Polish government-in-exile in London by establishing the Committee of National Liberation, based in Lublin in Poland, which became known as the Lublin Committee. The task of the committee was to administer Soviet-occupied Poland, and eventually to form the core of a future pro-Soviet government in Poland.

KEY TERM

Nationalist Someone devoted to the interests and culture of their nation, often leading to the belief that certain nationalities are superior to others.

Polish Home Army The Polish nationalist resistance group that fought German occupation during the Second World War.

? What does Colonel Sanders' report in Source G reveal about the activities of the Lublin Committee in Soviet-liberated Poland?

SOURCE G

An excerpt from a report by Colonel T.R.B. Sanders who was in command of an Allied mission, which visited the V2 missile site at Blizna in central Poland in September 1944 after it had been captured by the Red Army. National Archives (NA HS4/146), London, UK.

Everywhere we went (except in the forward areas) there were posters with portraits and short descriptions of the nine or ten chief members of the Lublin Committee. Other posters dealt with conscription, giving up of wireless sets, giving up of arms and payment of social insurance instalments. In addition all along the roads, there were numerous billboards with slogans in Russian and Polish such as 'Long live the Red Army!' 'Glory to our Great Leader Stalin!'

The Warsaw Uprising

The Soviet Union's policy was revealed when the Polish Home Army rose in revolt against the Germans in Warsaw in August 1944 in a desperate attempt to seize control of parts of Poland before the Red Army could overrun the whole country. By capturing Warsaw, the Home Army calculated that it would be able to set up a non-communist government in the capital, which would be recognized by the Western Allies as the legal government of Poland. It was hoped that this would then stop Stalin from creating a communist Poland. Not surprisingly, Stalin viewed the uprising with intense suspicion. Although Soviet troops penetrated to within 20 kilometres of Warsaw, the Polish insurgents were left to fight the Germans alone and were defeated by 2 October.

The German defeat of the Warsaw Uprising effectively destroyed the leadership of the Home Army, and inevitably this made it easier for Stalin to enforce his policy in Poland. As Soviet troops moved further west towards the Oder River in the remaining months of 1944, the **NKVD**, assisted by Polish communists, shot or imprisoned thousands of participants in the Home Army in a determined attempt to eliminate the anti-Soviet Polish opposition.

Britain, the USA and Poland

Despite all that had happened, Roosevelt and Churchill still clung to the hope that it would be possible to reach a compromise with Stalin about the future of Poland. In the interests of post-war Allied unity, they were both determined to avoid a premature break with the USSR over Poland. In January 1945, the USSR formally recognized the communist-dominated Committee for National Liberation as the **provisional government** of Poland. Britain and the US, although they still supported Poland's government-in-exile in London, played down the significance of this in the interests of the unity of the Grand Alliance.

> **KEY TERM**
>
> **NKVD** Soviet security organization responsible for enforcing obedience to the government and eliminating opposition.
>
> **Provisional government** A temporary government in office until an election can take place.

Romania and Bulgaria

On 20 August 1944, the Soviets launched a major offensive to drive the German army out of the Balkans. The immediate consequence of this brought about the collapse of the pro-German regimes in both Romania and Bulgaria. Like Poland, both states were vital to the military security of the USSR, since, if they were under friendly pro-Soviet governments, they would protect the USSR's south-western frontiers from any future attack. Soviet control of Romania would also allow access to Yugoslavia and central Europe, and enable it to strengthen its strategic position in the Black Sea. Control of Bulgaria would give the USSR a naval base from which to dominate the approaches to the Turkish Straits and the Greek frontier (see the map on page 147).

> How did the USSR consolidate its position in Romania and Bulgaria?

Romania

The Soviet Union was also determined to re-annex the Romanian territories of Bessarabia and northern Bukovina, which it had occupied in 1940, and launched an offensive against Romania on 20 August 1944. In a desperate attempt to take command of Romania in the face of the Soviet invasion, Romania's king deposed the pro-German government on 23 August. The king hoped, like Italy (see page 31), that Romania would be allowed to negotiate a ceasefire with the Western Allies and then form a new government in which communists would only be a minority. This idea was an illusion based on the false assumption that Britain and the US would begin a second front in the Balkans which would give these two allies more say in Romania's affairs. The king had no alternative but to negotiate an **armistice** on 12 September, with the Soviets who now occupied the country.

The National Democratic Front

Britain and the US already tacitly accepted that Romania was in the Soviet sphere of influence, and gave no help to the Romanian government which was anxious to obtain a guarantee that Soviet troops would be withdrawn as soon as the war with Germany was over. An Allied Control Commission (ACC) was created and dominated by Soviet officials. A coalition government composed of communists, socialists, National Liberals and the left-wing National Peasants' Party, the so-called Ploughmen's Front, was formed. This was paralysed by disagreements between the National Liberals and the three other parties. Supported by Soviet officials on the ACC, communists and their allies formed the National Democratic Front and incited the peasants to seize farms from landowners and the workers to set up communist-dominated production committees in the factories.

In March 1945, Stalin followed the precedent of Britain, which had intervened in December 1944 in Greece (see page 29), to establish a new government friendly to the Soviet Union. With the help of the Red Army, Romanian communists orchestrated a coup which led to the creation of the pro-Soviet communist-dominated National Democratic Front government.

Bulgaria

Although Stalin did not want a break with Britain and the US, Western observers noted the anti-Western bias of Soviet policy in Romania and how Soviet officials actively supported the workers and peasant parties. The occupation of Romania allowed the Soviets to invade Bulgaria in early September 1944 and establish an ACC on 28 October.

Local communists, including several thousand partisan troops, had already established the Patriotic Front, an alliance of anti-German **left-wing** forces. The Front seized power from the pro-German government of Konstantin Muraviev and established a government in Sofia shortly before the Red Army arrived. Inevitably, this success strengthened local communists who attempted a communist revolution in the country. The country's former ruling class were eliminated with over 10,000 people executed. The trade unions and police were dominated by communists and large farms were taken over by peasants.

KEY TERM

Armistice The official agreement of the suspension of fighting between two or more powers.

Left-wing Liberal, socialist or communist.

Soviet response

This enthusiasm for revolution did not, however, fit in with Stalin's overall strategy. Essentially, he was determined to safeguard Soviet control over Bulgaria, yet not antagonize his Western Allies any more than necessary while the war with Germany was still being fought, and at a time when Poland was becoming an increasingly divisive issue. Since the USSR's position was guaranteed through the key role of the Soviet chairman of the ACC, and the strong position of the local communist party, Stalin could afford to be conciliatory. Consequently, he attempted in the autumn of 1944 to persuade the Bulgarian communists to pursue a more moderate policy. He wanted them to tolerate a certain degree of political opposition and to work within the Patriotic Front coalition. This was difficult to achieve as local communists, sometimes backed by Soviet officials on the ACC, were determined to gain complete power regardless of Stalin's instructions or the diplomatic consequences.

Yugoslavia and Greece

Why were Tito's ambitions viewed with suspicion by Stalin in 1944 and early 1945?

Josip Broz (Tito) was one of the most successful partisan leaders in German-occupied Europe. As a communist, he looked to the USSR as a model for the state he wished to create in Yugoslavia, but his very independence and self-confidence caused Stalin considerable problems.

Yugoslavia

After the occupation of Bulgaria, Soviet troops joined with partisan forces in Yugoslavia, launching an attack on Belgrade on 14 October 1944. By this time, Tito had created an effective partisan army which not only fought the Germans but also waged civil war against non-communist Serbs and Croat nationalists. Tito's position had been strengthened when Britain decided in May 1944 to assist him rather than the nationalists, as his partisans were more effective opponents of the German army. With British weapons and equipment, they effectively dominated the struggle against the Germans and nationalists, laying the foundations for a communist take-over in 1945 in both Yugoslavia and in neighbouring Albania. Whenever Tito's partisans occupied an area, they formed communist-dominated committees which took their orders from him rather than the Yugoslav government-in-exile in London.

To the Soviets, the key to controlling south-eastern Europe was to create a military and political alliance between Yugoslavia, Bulgaria and the USSR. Tito was not, however, an easy ally and tried to carry out his own policies independently of the USSR. Despite Stalin's reluctance to provoke a crisis with Britain and America on the eve of the Yalta Conference (see pages 33–35), Tito established communist governments in both Yugoslavia and Albania, which his forces controlled by November 1944.

Stalin was able to exercise a firmer control over Tito's foreign policy. In January 1945, he vetoed Tito's scheme for a federation with Bulgaria which would have turned it into a mere province of Yugoslavia. He made it very clear that Yugoslavia would have to subordinate its local territorial ambitions to the overall foreign policy considerations determined by the Soviet Union, although this displeased Tito.

Greece

Tito and Stalin also clashed over the attempts by the communist-controlled People's Liberation Army (ELAS) in Greece to set up a National Liberation Government on the Yugoslav model. During the war, ELAS emerged as the most effective resistance force in Greece and, like Tito's partisans, fought the Germans and non-communist **guerrilla groups**. By 1944, ELAS was able to launch a communist take-over of Greece. Yet, as Greece was an area regarded by the USSR as being well within the British sphere of influence, Stalin urged ELAS to join a moderate coalition government with non-communist parties. When a revolt encouraged by Tito broke out in Athens on 3 December 1944, Stalin, true to his agreement with Churchill (see page 22), stopped him from helping Greek communists and raised no objection to their defeat by British troops.

What was Stalin's policy in Hungary and Czechoslovakia?

→ Hungary and Czechoslovakia

In neither Czechoslovakia nor Hungary did Stalin have any immediate plans for a communist seizure of power. He wanted to keep alive the possibility of co-operation with non-communist parties in order to protect Soviet interests. Local communist parties were consequently ordered to enter into democratic coalition governments and to work within these to consolidate their position.

Hungary

The decision taken at the Tehran Conference not to start a second front in the Balkans (see page 23) ensured that the Red Army would decide Hungary's fate. When Soviet troops crossed the Hungarian frontier in September 1944, Head of State Admiral Miklós Horthy appealed to the Soviets for a ceasefire, but Germany took Horthy's son prisoner and encouraged Hungarian ultra-nationalists, the **Arrow Cross Party**, to seize power in western Hungary. It was not until early December 1944 that Red Army units reached the outskirts of Budapest, Hungary's capital.

In the Soviet-occupied section of the country, the Hungarian Communist Party was initially too weak to play a dominant role in politics, and it therefore had little option but to co-operate with the Socialist Party, the Smallholders Party (a peasants' party), and several other middle-class parties. In December 1945, when elections took place for the National Assembly, the Communist Party, despite the presence of the Red Army, gained only 17 per cent of votes cast, but they were given three key posts in the provisional national government. Throughout 1945, Stalin's immediate aim was to remove anything from Hungary that could be used as war reparations by the USSR since Hungary had been a German ally. In the longer term he was not sure if Hungary should be integrated into the emerging **Soviet bloc** where it would be dominated militarily, politically, and economically by the USSR.

KEY TERM

Guerrilla groups Fighters who oppose an occupying force using tactics such as sabotage and assassination.

Arrow Cross Party A Hungarian ultra-nationalist political party that supported Germany in the Second World War.

Soviet bloc A group of states in eastern Europe controlled by the USSR.

Czechoslovakia

Of all the eastern European states, Czechoslovakia had the closest relations with the USSR. The Czechoslovaks felt betrayed by Britain and France over the Munich Agreement of 1938 (see page 17) and looked to the USSR as the power that would restore their country's pre-1938 borders. In 1943, the Czechoslovak government-in-exile in London under Edvard Beneš, the former president, negotiated an alliance with the USSR, although this still did not stop Stalin from annexing Ruthenia in eastern Czechoslovakia in the autumn of 1944 (see the map on page 47).

As the Soviet army occupied more and more of Czechoslovakia in the winter of 1944–45, the balance of power tilted steadily away from the democratic parties represented by the government-in-exile in London to the Czechoslovak Communist Party led by Klement Gottwald, who was a refugee in Moscow. Stalin nevertheless forced Gottwald to accept Beneš as President and work within a coalition government. In turn, Beneš followed a conciliatory policy and was ready to co-operate with the Communist Party, enabling Stalin to achieve a harmony that had been impossible to reach in Poland. When the Provisional Government was formed in 1945, the Communist Party was able to demand eight seats in the cabinet including the influential Ministries of the Interior and Information, although Gottwald skilfully camouflaged the Communist Party's powerful position by not demanding the position of Prime Minister.

Finland

In the summer of 1944 when Soviet troops invaded, Finland was granted an armistice on unexpectedly generous terms. The Finns had to:

- declare war on the Germans
- cede part of the strategically important Petsamo region on the Arctic coast, and
- pay reparations.

However, politically they were allowed a considerable degree of freedom. Marshal C.E.G. Mannerheim, who had co-operated closely with Germany during the war, remained president until 1946 and there was only one communist in the first post-war cabinet. Finland was in a position to give the USSR vitally needed reparations, such as barges, railroad equipment and manufactured goods. A repressive occupation policy would have disrupted these deliveries. In addition, the Finnish Communist Party was weak and unpopular, and the USSR had little option but to rely on the non-communist parties.

> **Why did Stalin pursue such a moderate policy in Finland?**

The liberation of Italy and France

Italy and France were liberated by the Western Allies. Italy was a leading Axis state, while France, until its defeat in 1940, had played the main part in the war against Germany. In both states, resistance to German occupation and

> **How influential were the Communist Parties in Italy and France?**

puppet governments helped legitimize the Communist Party and enhance its popularity.

Italy

After the Allied landings in Sicily in July 1943, Mussolini, the Italian Fascist dictator, was overthrown and imprisoned, and in September an armistice was signed. This did not prevent German troops from seizing Italy's capital, Rome, and occupying most of the Italian peninsula. The Allies were then forced to fight their way up the peninsula, and it was only in April 1945 that northern Italy was finally conquered. Italy was the first Axis state to sign an armistice, and the way it was administered by the Allies set important precedents for the future. All Soviet requests to be involved were firmly rejected by Britain and the US which later gave Stalin an excuse to exclude them from eastern Europe. An Italian government was established and it was gradually given responsibility for governing the liberated areas. This government was closely supervised by the Anglo-American Allied Control Commission (ACC).

Palmiro Togliatti

Stalin had little option but to accept these arrangements, although he was determined that Italian communists should not be excluded from participating in the new government. Palmiro Togliatti, the leader of the Italian Communist Party, was ordered to form a coalition with the Socialist Party. He was to avoid any aggressive actions, such as an uprising or a civil war, which would cause tension between the USSR and the West and so make it more difficult for Stalin to consolidate the Soviet position in eastern Europe. Togliatti was also to draft a popular programme for reforming the Italian economy which, by promising measures that would help the workers and peasants, would prepare the way for later Communist Party electoral successes.

Togliatti carried out these instructions as well as he could, joining the new government that was formed when Rome was occupied by the Allies in June 1944. In the north in the winter of 1944–45, communists played a key role in the resistance against the Germans. Togliatti, only too aware of how the British had crushed the Greek revolt, managed to keep his more radical partisans in check. By the time the war had ended, this resistance won the communists considerable support throughout Italy and made them an essential partner in coalition government. This was seen when Togliatti himself became Minister of Justice in the Italian government, which was formed in April 1945. At this stage, then, Stalin's policy in Italy was to push the Italian Communist Party into joining a governing multi-party coalition.

France

When Paris was liberated in August 1944, General Charles de Gaulle, the leader of the **Free French**, immediately established an independent government.

His aim was to rebuild French power and to create a powerful French-led western European bloc. To counter the predominance of the Anglo-Americans, he looked to the Soviet Union, and in December 1944 signed the Franco-Soviet Treaty of Alliance and Mutual Assistance, which committed both states to co-operate in any future defensive war against Germany.

As in Italy, the French Communist Party, having played a prominent part in the resistance, became a major force in French politics. Its leader, Maurice Thorez, was instructed by Stalin to support the Soviet–French alliance and work towards creating a left-wing coalition with socialists, which, it was hoped, would eventually be able to form a government.

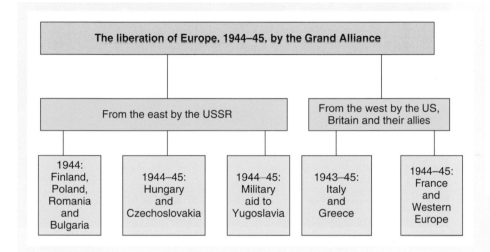

The liberation of Europe, 1944–45, by the Grand Alliance

From the east by the USSR — **From the west by the US, Britain and their allies**

1944: Finland, Poland, Romania and Bulgaria | 1944–45: Hungary and Czechoslovakia | 1944–45: Military aid to Yugoslavia | 1943–45: Italy and Greece | 1944–45: France and Western Europe

SUMMARY DIAGRAM

The liberation of Europe 1943–45

The Yalta Conference, February 1945

▶ *Key question: What was achieved at the Yalta Conference?*

The Yalta Conference, attended by Stalin, Roosevelt and Churchill, was, to quote the journalist and historian Martin Walker, 'the last of the wartime conferences … [and] the first of the post-war summits'. Besides creating plans for finishing the war in Europe and eastern Asia, it also attempted to lay the foundations of the coming peace. Plans were finalized for the occupation of Germany by the victorious powers, amongst whom, on Churchill's insistence, France was to be included because he feared that the US might withdraw its troops from Europe soon after the end of hostilities. Each power was allotted its own zone, including a section of Berlin, which was placed under **Four-Power Control** (for details of the zone divisions, see map on page 47). The decision was also taken to establish the United Nations.

 **KEY TERM**

Four-Power Control
Under the joint control of the four occupying powers: Britain, France, the US and USSR.

The 'Big Three': Churchill, Roosevelt and Stalin (front row, left to right) at the Yalta Conference.

> **?** What message is conveyed by Source H about inter-Allied relations?

How was an agreement on Poland reached?

Poland

Poland again proved to be the most difficult subject on the agenda, and the Allies were only able to reach agreement through a series of ambiguous compromises, which could be interpreted differently by the USSR and the Western powers:

- They confirmed that Poland's eastern border would run along the Curzon Line.
- They agreed in principle, as they had at Tehran, that in compensation for the land lost to the USSR, Poland would receive a substantial increase in territory in the north and west from land to be removed from Germany. The exact details of this were not stated.
- The decision was also taken to reorganize the provisional government by including democratic politicians from both Poland and the London government-in-exile.
- Elections would be held as soon as possible.

Superficially this seemed to be a success for Britain and the US, but in fact, the terms were so vague that Stalin could easily manipulate them. First, the exact amount of land that Poland would receive at the cost of Germany was not fixed and secondly, democracy meant very different things to the participants. For Stalin it essentially meant the domination of Poland by the Communist Party, while for Britain and the US it meant effectively the domination of the non-communist parties.

SOURCE I

An excerpt from *God's Playground: History of Poland*, Vol. 2, by Norman Davies, published by OUP, Oxford, UK, p. 205.

Given the relentless character of Soviet diplomacy over the Polish problem, it must be recognized, however, that Stalin's views had changed fundamentally. In 1939–41, the Soviet dictator had showed a willingness to trample on every vestige of Polish nationality or independence. From 1941 onwards he constantly reiterated his desire to restore 'a strong and independent Poland'. His understanding of 'strength' and 'independence' differed considerably from that which was held in Britain and America, or indeed in Poland, but was no less substantive for that. Anyone who has any doubts concerning the genuineness of Stalin's commitment should compare the post-war history of Poland with that of the Baltic states or the Ukraine. Stalin was the author not only of post-war Polish independence, but also of the peculiarly stunted interpretation of that concept which prevailed in the post-war era.

> What information is conveyed by Source I on Stalin's Polish policy?

Declaration on Liberated Europe

> **How significant was the Declaration on Liberated Europe?**

To underpin the right of the liberated states to determine their own governments, Roosevelt persuaded Stalin and Churchill at Yalta to agree to the Declaration on Liberated Europe which committed the three governments to carry out emergency measures to assist the liberated states and to encourage democratic governments.

With the start of the Cold War, this became, as historian Martin Walker observed, a key text 'upon which all future accusations of Soviet betrayal and bad faith were made'. Yet such accusations completely ignored the reality of the situation in eastern Europe. Stalin saw Poland, and indeed the other eastern European countries, as corridors for an attack from Germany or western Europe on the USSR. He was therefore going to ensure that friendly governments, which in most cases were to mean communist ones, were in place.

SOURCE J

An excerpt from 'Declaration on Liberated Europe', quoted in *The Cold War and the Making of the Modern World*, by Martin Walker, published by Vintage, London, UK, 1994, p. 14.

… The three governments will jointly assist the people in any liberated state or former Axis satellite state in Europe where in their judgement conditions require: (a) to establish conditions of internal peace; (b) to carry out emergency measures for the relief of distressed peoples; (c) to form interim governmental authorities broadly representative of all democratic elements in the population and pledged to the earliest possible establishment through free elections of governments responsive to the will of the people; and (d) to facilitate where necessary the holding of such elections.

> How reliable is Source J as a guide to the immediate post-war policies of the 'Big Three'?

When did the war in
Europe end?

→ The end of the war in Europe

Three months after the Yalta Conference, the war in Europe ended. In the final weeks of the war British and US forces raced to Trieste, Italy, in an attempt to stop Yugoslav forces seizing the port, while the British army in northern Germany crossed the River Elbe to prevent the Soviets from occupying Denmark (see map on page 47).

Churchill urged the US to make special efforts to take Berlin and Prague to pre-empt a Soviet occupation. But the US generals were not ready to see their soldiers killed for what they regarded as political reasons, and so both capitals fell to Soviet troops.

When the war ended with the surrender of Germany on 8 May 1945, Anglo-American forces occupied nearly half the area that was to become the Soviet zone in Germany (see the map on page 47). It was not until early July that these troops were withdrawn into the US and British zones, which had been agreed upon at Yalta.

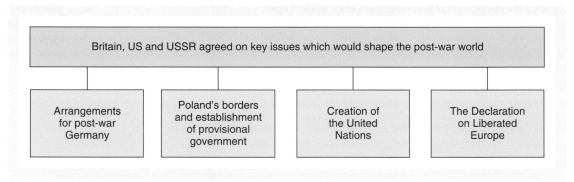

SUMMARY DIAGRAM

The Yalta Conference, February 1945

Chapter summary

The origins of the Cold War, 1917–45

The origins of the Cold War are complex. On the one side it is impossible to ignore the teachings of Marxism–Leninism and the sense of righteousness which they instilled in the Soviet regime that established itself in Russia in 1917. On the other side this was countered by the US's intention to open up the world to free trade, democracy and self-determination in the firm belief that this would lead to global peace. To the USSR this was merely a camouflaged attempt by the US to pursue its own economic, capitalist interests, which were fundamentally hostile to Marxism–Leninism.

During the inter-war years the Soviet government focused on internal issues rather than foreign policy. Nevertheless, through the activities of the Comintern, Soviet agents attempted to stir up trouble in the capitalist states of western Europe and their empires.

Through the Nazi-Soviet Pact of August 1939 the USSR regained the land she had lost to Poland.

The German attack on the Soviet Union in June 1941 led to a massive shift in diplomatic relations. The USSR was now allied to the very states it so distrusted. While the Second World War lasted the USSR and its Western Allies had no option but to co-operate to defeat Germany.

The military campaigns that defeated Germany in 1944–45 dictated the immediate post-war situation in Europe. Eastern Europe was under the ultimate control of the Red Army, while western Europe was firmly within the sphere of the British and US.

At the Yalta Conference of February 1945 the 'Big Three' agreed:

- Germany was to be placed under Four-Power Control
- in Poland the USSR would retain her gains of September 1939, while there would be democratic elections as soon as possible
- that democratically elected governments should be set up in liberated Europe.

✓ Examination advice

How to answer 'analyse' questions

When answering questions with the command term 'analyse', you should identify key elements and their relative importance.

Example

Analyse the origins of the Cold War before 1945.

1. To answer this question successfully you need to investigate the origins of the Cold War before the end of the Second World War. With the use of the plural word 'origins', it is expected that you will review more than one origin. The question does not ask you to discuss the impact of the Cold War or any issues after 1945.

2. Take at least five minutes to write a short outline. An example of a focused outline to this question might be:

- Political and economic ideological differences – capitalism versus communism.
- Western-Soviet political relations 1917–41:
  - Russian Civil War 1918–22
  - Comintern and communist revolts 1919–onward
  - Paris Peace Conference 1919
  - the Polish-Russian War 1920
  - isolationism and pre-Second World War negotiations
  - Nazi-Soviet Pact, Soviet expansion.
- Conflicting aims and actions during Second World War and at its conclusion.

3. In your introduction, set out your key points about the origins of the Cold War. An example of a good introductory paragraph for this question is given below.

Many issues led to the development of the Cold War before 1945. The economic and political system of communism employed by the Soviet Union conflicted with the representative governments of much of the Western world that also followed a capitalist economic system. These divergent economic and political systems led to isolation of the Soviet Union, both imposed and by choice, although the Soviets initially supported communist revolts just after the First World War in Europe and supported communist groups, such as those in China. Soviet and Western relations were beset by mistrust as a result of these actions and by the diplomacy preceding the Second World War when the Soviet Union felt it was being manoeuvred into fighting Germany for the benefit of Poland, Britain and France. Furthermore, during the Second World War, the Soviets felt that its allies, primarily Britain and the USA, delayed in creating a significant Western Front while these allies believed that the Soviets worked to expand their control of much of Europe, violating various war-time agreements.

4. For each of the key points you outline in your introduction, you should be able to write two to three paragraphs with supporting evidence. Be sure to indicate how each point related to the origin of the Cold War. An example of how one of the key points could be expanded is given below.

A critically important issue in the development of the Cold War was the conflicting nature of the two systems of capitalism and communism. Communism, based on the teachings of Marx and Lenin, held that a classless society was the ultimate goal, where money was not needed, all means of production would belong to the entire society, and there would be no such thing as profit, greed, crime, religion or want. In order to create this system, a dictatorship would be required to represent the working classes that would replace all other groups and personal freedoms, such as those of speech, religion and association. Non-working classes would have to be removed as they were considered the enemies of the working classes. Communism was also opposed to the concept of nationalism since it taught that the idea of nationality was created to divide workers so that they would not unite to overthrow the existing economic and social order which existed on the labour of impoverished and politically impotent workers. This meant, of course, a conflict with capitalism.

Capitalism was based on the concept of trade and the accumulation of wealth. In theory, those that worked hard or invested well could gain major profits and improve their lives through the accumulation of more money, property and political power. Since profit was the goal of business owners and investors, workers rarely benefited to any great extent since sharing with workers would mean less profit for the owners and investors. While those controlling the economic system might feel some effects of any economic downturns or turmoil, *poorly-paid workers would often suffer the most, losing their jobs and therefore their ability to pay rent, purchase food or improve their economic or social position. Yet, this economic system was usually accompanied by representative governments and democratic freedoms. Workers had the right to vote, form unions to advocate for improved conditions, as well as freedom of speech, press and more. Some workers were able to become business owners and investors themselves, proving to others that those who were dedicated to working, saving their money and investing wisely could improve their condition and vindicate the social and economic divisions of society. The tenets of capitalism meant it opposed, and worked against, communism which sought to replace it.*

5. In the final paragraph, you should tie your essay together stating your conclusions. Do not raise any new points here, or make reference to events after 1945. An example of a good concluding paragraph is given below.

There were several origins to the Cold War before 1945. The two systems of communism and capitalism were in conflict and therefore the Soviet Union, as the world's only communist state, was opposed by capitalist nations, not the least because the Soviets attempted to spread their philosophy through communist rebellions in other states after the First World War. As capitalist nations limited their economic and political dealings with the Soviets and as the Soviets concentrated on industrializing their state and eliminating social divisions, the Soviet Union was isolated from international affairs. The Second World War forced the co-operation of the communist Soviet Union with the capitalistic USA and Britain after the invasion of the Soviet Union by Germany in 1941. The two groups continued to mistrust the other, although there was significant economic and military co-operation. Finally, the Soviet Union's need to end its economic and political isolation, as well as prevent future invasion from the west led to renewed tensions, and therefore the Cold War, between the Soviets and capitalist nations, led by the USA, that worked to limit the spread of communist government in 1945.

6. Now try writing a complete answer to the question following the advice above.

Examination practice

Below are exam questions for you to practise using content from this chapter.

1. Explain the importance of the Second World War in the development of the Cold War.
   (For guidance on how to answer 'explain' questions, see page 134.)

2. Assess the importance of the Yalta Conference.
   (For guidance on how to answer 'assess' questions, see page 256.)

3. Why was Poland a central issue in the development of the Cold War?
   (For guidance on how to answer 'why' questions, see page 228.)

 # Activities

1. In groups, compare and contrast capitalism and communism in the form of a chart for classroom display. Be sure to include overviews of governmental structures, economic policies, and more. Consider extending this activity by conducting research in a library to learn more about how each of these systems viewed gender issues, poverty, and colonialism.

2. Create a timeline of the ten most significant events for the Soviet Union between 1917 and 1945. This will require you to make judgments about which events were the most important. Be sure to indicate the event on the timeline and add a short explanation as to why that event was important.

3. Divide the class into two groups. Debate the validity of the following statement: 'The Soviet Union was to blame for poor international relations between it and the international community between 1917 and 1941'. One group should argue that the statement is accurate, while the other argues that it is not. Both groups should use evidence to support their argument.

CHAPTER 2

From wartime allies to post-war enemies, 1945–47

This chapter considers reasons for the break-up of the Grand Alliance from 1945–47. During this period there were tensions between the Western Allies and also between them and the Soviet Union. Much of the tension arose from the problems of dealing with Germany, which was under the control of four different states. Neither the Western powers nor the USSR could agree on joint measures for its economic and political reconstruction.

You need to consider the following key questions throughout this chapter:

✪ In what ways did the friction between the members of the Grand Alliance increase during 1945–46?

✪ Why did the four occupying powers fail to work out a joint programme for Germany's future?

✪ To what extent was the Truman Doctrine and Marshall Plan designed to contain Soviet power?

✪ How far had an 'Iron Curtain' descended across Europe by the end of 1947?

✪ Did the US or the USSR start the Cold War, 1945–47?

1 Transition from war to fragile peace, 1945–46

▶ *Key question: In what ways did the friction between the members of the Grand Alliance increase during 1945–46?*

All three members of the victorious Grand Alliance – Britain, the US and the USSR – wished to continue their alliance, yet for this alliance to survive there needed to be either a common danger or agreement between its members on key principles. In post-war Europe this was no longer the case. Publically, Roosevelt had stressed the importance of the Declaration on Liberated Europe (see page 35), but had privately recognized that Britain and the US had little option but to accept Soviet predominance in eastern Europe. When, only two weeks after the Yalta Agreement, the Soviets imposed a puppet government on Romania (see page 27), Roosevelt made no complaint to Stalin.

What initial impact did Truman have on US policy towards the USSR?

US President Harry Truman

Roosevelt died on 12 April 1945 and was replaced by Harry Truman. The new President, like his predecessor, wanted the USSR to declare war against Japan, which would potentially save the US hundreds of thousands of casualties if it became necessary to invade Japan. Truman was both more aggressive and decisive, but less experienced than Roosevelt. He became President at a point when the government of the US was becoming increasingly concerned about Soviet policies in Poland, and was considering curtailing **lend–lease** shipments to the USSR, except for material to be used for the war on Japan. The US hoped that this might persuade Stalin to become more co-operative in carrying out the Yalta Agreement. In fact, the policy had the opposite effect and, unsurprisingly, merely succeeded in giving Stalin the impression that the US was trying to extract political concessions through crude economic pressure.

SOURCE A

An excerpt from *Shattered Peace* by Daniel Yergin, published by Houghton Mifflin, Boston, USA, 1977, p. 72.

Truman could not believe that Russia's quest for security had a rationality. When he was finally confronted with foreign policy questions, all he had as a background was a storybook view of history and a rousing Fourth of July patriotism. He tended to see clearly defined contests between right and wrong, black and white. Neither his personality nor his experience gave him the patience for subtleties and uncertainties.

KEY TERM

Lend–lease The US programme begun in March 1941 that gave over $50 billion ($650 billion in today's terms) of war supplies to Allied nations.

What does Source A tell us about Truman's assessment of Soviet foreign policy?

The creation of the United Nations

To what extent did the Allies disagree about the constitution of the United Nations?

In August 1944, the representatives of Britain, the US, the USSR and China met at Dumbarton Oaks near Washington to discuss the future structure of the United Nations. They agreed on the establishment of the General Assembly of the United Nations in which all member nations would be represented, and on the Security Council. Britain, the US, the USSR and the China would be permanent members of this, with the right to veto any decision decided upon by the Assembly. In 1945, it was decided that France, too, should became a permanent member on the Security Council.

There were disagreements with the USSR over whether a permanent member of the Security Council, if it were involved in a dispute with another member of the United Nations, should have the right to veto a decision by the Council of which it disapproved. The Soviets also attempted to increase their influence by demanding that the sixteen member republics of the USSR should also become members of the UN. At the subsequent conference in San Francisco in April 1945, the right of each individual permanent member to exercise a veto was conceded but only two of the Soviet republics – the Byelorussian Soviet Socialist Republic (Belarus) and the Ukraine – were given seats in the Assembly, in addition to one for the whole of the Soviet Union.

The impact of the atomic bomb

Why did the UN fail to gain control over nuclear weapons?

The atomic bomb was tested successfully at Alamogordo in New Mexico in the US on 16 July 1945. Its destructive potential was much greater than expected and it was ready for immediate use against Japanese cities. On 6

August, an atomic bomb was dropped on Hiroshima, killing nearly half the population and flattening the city. Three days later, another bomb was dropped on Nagasaki, killing a further 40,000 people. The horrific destruction of these two cities, as well as a massive invasion of **Manchuria** by the Soviet Union, left Japan with little option but to surrender.

Essentially two alternatives confronted Truman's government once the atomic bomb had been shown to be effective. The first was that the US could seek to retain its nuclear monopoly as long as possible. The second was that it could hand over the control of the bomb to the United Nations. Some in the US government initially believed that a monopoly on the weapon would enable the United States to dictate the terms of the diplomatic debate to the rest of the world.

KEY TERM

Manchuria A region in the far north-east of China, occupied by the Japanese in 1931 until the end of the Second World War.

? According to Source B what impact did the atomic bomb have on international relations?

SOURCE B

An excerpt from _The United States and the Cold War, 1941–1947_ by John Lewis Gaddis, published by Columbia University Press, New York, USA, 2000, p. 245.

But the bomb had more than purely military implications. American possession of this revolutionary new weapon drastically altered the balance of power, making it at least technically feasible for the United States to impose its will upon the rest of the world. 'God Almighty in his infinite wisdom [has] dropped the atomic bomb in our lap', Senator Edwin C. Johnson proclaimed in November 1945; now for the first time the United States 'with vision and guts and plenty of atomic bombs [could] compel mankind to adopt the policy of lasting peace … or be burned to a crisp'.

Truman's advisors were much more cautious. Dean Acheson, Under Secretary of State, pointed out that the US lead in nuclear science was only temporary and that the Soviets would rapidly catch up. Indeed the temporary nature of the US lead was revealed when a Soviet espionage network was discovered in September 1945 operating in both Canada and the US, which had already sent a considerable amount of information about the atomic bomb to the Soviet Union.

The United Nations Atomic Energy Commission

Truman, therefore, agreed in principle to the international control of atomic energy by the United Nations, providing that other nations also agreed to abide by its rules. In November 1945, the US, together with the two nations that had helped it develop the atomic bomb, Britain and Canada, called for the creation of a United Nations commission which would create rules for the control of nuclear weapons. These were:

- exchange of basic scientific information for peaceful ends between all nations
- establishing means for the control of atomic energy to ensure its use for peaceful purposes only

- the elimination from national armaments of atomic weapons
- establishing an effective system of inspection to prevent the clandestine manufacture of nuclear bombs.

At the Moscow Conference of Foreign Ministers in December 1945, the Soviets agreed to the establishment of the United Nations Atomic Energy Commission. They did, however, insist that it should report to the Security Council rather than the Assembly, where the Soviets could use their veto power as a permanent member if the need arose. The US countered in early 1946 by suggesting that no country should have veto power over atomic energy matters, even in the Security Council, in an obvious effort to circumvent any Soviet interference.

Breakdown of agreement

Increasingly, however, plans for the international control of nuclear energy became a casualty of the growing mistrust between the Soviets and the Western powers in the spring of 1946. When US

SOURCE C

'Christmas Card' by cartoonist Kem (Kimon Evan Marengo), 1945. It shows Truman (as the Statue of Liberty) with Stalin, British Prime Minster Clement Attlee, French President Charles de Gaulle and Chinese leader Chiang Kai-shek.

> What information is conveyed in Source C about the importance of the atomic bomb? **?**

proposals were again discussed at the United Nations in June 1946, the Soviets refused to surrender their veto on the grounds that it would enable them to be out-voted on the Security Council and instead suggested the immediate destruction of all nuclear weapons. The US rejected the plan, claiming there were no safeguards to ensure that all nuclear weapons would in fact be destroyed. The Soviets retaliated in December 1946 by vetoing the US plan in the Security Council.

Potsdam Conference: July–August 1945

To what extent did the Potsdam Conference reveal fundamental disagreements between the wartime allies?

It is possible that Truman deliberately delayed the Allied summit at Potsdam until after the successful testing of the atomic bomb on 16 July 1945. He and his officials hoped that the possession of the bomb would enable the US to force Stalin to make concessions in eastern Europe. Stalin was impressed by the weapon and ordered the Soviet development programme to make faster progress, but it did not make him any more flexible in eastern Europe or Germany. In fact, it appeared to have little effect on Soviet policy.

On 17 July, Stalin, Churchill and Truman at last met at Potsdam just outside Berlin. On 26 July, Churchill was replaced by Clement Attlee as British Prime Minister after a decisive Labour Party victory in the British general election. The conference continued, however, without interruption. The inter-linked questions of Germany and Poland dominated the agenda.

Germany

While Britain, the US and USSR could agree on the necessary measures for German demilitarization, **denazification** and the punishment of war criminals, they were only able to conclude the following minimal political and economic guidelines for the future of Germany:

The Allied Control Council

As there was no central German government, an Allied Control Council (ACC) was established, composed of the military commanders from each of the four occupying powers. To avoid being out-voted by the three Western powers, the Soviets insisted that each commander should have complete responsibility for his own zone. This decision effectively stopped the ACC from exercising any real power in Germany as a whole. A limited number of central German departments dealing with finance, transport, trade and industry were to be formed at some point in the future.

Reparations

Agreement on reparations was difficult to achieve. The USSR had suffered immense damage in the war, and was determined to extract as much as possible in reparations from Germany. Britain and the US, on the other hand, were convinced that the German economy must be left sufficiently strong so that it could pay for the imported food and raw materials that the Germans needed; they did not want the cost of this to be borne by the Allies. A temporary compromise was negotiated whereby both the USSR and the Western powers would take reparations from their own zones. In addition to

KEY TERM

Denazification The process of removing all Nazi Party ideology, propaganda, symbols, and adherents from all aspects of German of life.

this, Britain and the US would grant 10 per cent of these reparations to the Soviets and a further 15 per cent in exchange for the supply of food and raw materials from the Soviet zone.

Poland

The Western Allies had agreed at Yalta that Poland should be awarded 'substantial accessions of territory' from Germany to compensate for the land annexed by the USSR (see page 34). However, both Britain and the US considered that the new boundary between Germany and Poland lying along the Oder and Western Neisse Rivers, which the USSR had unilaterally determined, gave far too much territory to Poland. As Soviet troops occupied eastern Germany and Poland, there was little that Britain and the US could do to change the frontier. Both powers eventually recognized the Oder-Neisse Line pending a final decision at a future peace conference. They hoped that this concession would persuade the Soviets to be more flexible about German reparations and the establishment of a democratic government in Poland.

> What information about the territorial changes in Poland and Germany is conveyed by Source D? **?**

SOURCE D

Germany and Poland in 1945.

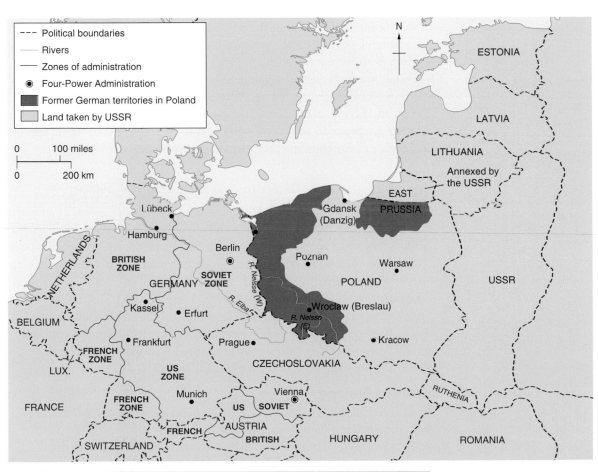

The Council of Ministers

At Potsdam, the Council of Ministers, composed of the Foreign Ministers of Britain, the USSR, China, France, and the US, was formed to negotiate peace treaties with the former Axis powers of Italy, Romania, Bulgaria, Finland and Hungary, and to prepare a peace settlement with Germany once the Allies had set up a German government able to negotiate on behalf of Germany.

Why, despite worsening relations between the USSR and Britain and the US, was it possible to negotiate the peace treaties with Italy and other minor Axis states?

The Paris Peace Treaties with Italy and the minor Axis powers, 1945–47

When the Council of Ministers met for the first time in September 1945 to discuss the details of the peace treaties, arguments erupted almost immediately. The Soviets pressed for a harsh peace with Italy, while Britain and the US argued that Italy, having broken with Germany in September 1943, deserved more lenient treatment. The USSR also insisted that the armistice agreements, which it had already signed (see pages 26–30) with Bulgaria, Finland, Hungary and Romania, should form the basis of the subsequent peace treaties. The US, on the other hand, insisted that before the peace treaties could be signed with these states, legal governments representing their people must be formed. To save the negotiations from a complete breakdown, James Byrnes, the US Secretary of State, went to Moscow in December 1945, where a compromise was reached whereby the eastern European and the Italian peace treaties would be negotiated simultaneously. Negotiations dragged on for over a year and were frequently threatened by escalating tension between the USSR and the US and its British and French allies. Nevertheless, in the final analysis, both sides wanted the peace treaties concluded, and were able to make compromises. In February 1947 the Paris peace treaties were finally concluded.

Italy

The US argued that Italy, by making peace with the Allies in 1943, had effectively joined their side by 1945, but the USSR insisted that, as a former Axis power, Italy should accept a punitive peace. The US was also alarmed by Soviet claims to a share of Italy's former colony, Libya, which would enable the USSR to extend its power into the Mediterranean Sea. Only by agreeing to a severe peace with Italy, which involved the loss of territory to Yugoslavia (see page 64), the payment of $360 million reparations ($100 million of which were to go to the USSR), and controls on the size of Italy's armed forces, was the US able to achieve agreement that Italy's former colonies would become trusteeships under the United Nations. With the signature of the treaty, Italy again became an independent state.

Eastern Europe

In eastern Europe, the Soviets wanted the conclusion of the peace treaties with the former Axis states as soon as possible as they wished to dissolve the Allied Control Commissions on which western observers participated (see page 25) and obtain reparations. Once new governments were in place in the ex-Axis states, Britain, France and the US were ready to accept the peace treaties. These were all signed on 10 February 1947, but disagreements about the value of former German property to be handed over to the USSR delayed the Austrian treaty until 1955 (see page 146). No treaty could be signed with Germany as disagreement between the four occupying powers prevented the restoration of an independent central German state until 1990.

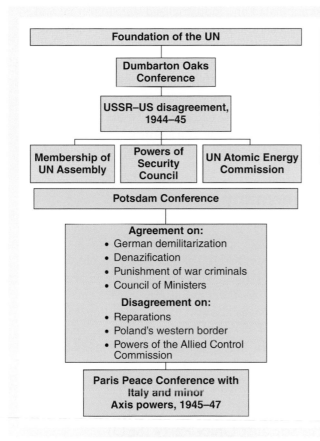

Truman	Stalin
• Ended lend–lease	• Deep distrust of the West
• Critical of Soviet policy in Poland	• Determined to install USSR-friendly government in Poland
• Failed to understand the USSR's need for security	• US possession of atom bomb made him determined to develop Soviet version

Foundation of the UN

Dumbarton Oaks Conference

USSR–US disagreement, 1944–45

Membership of UN Assembly

Powers of Security Council

UN Atomic Energy Commission

Potsdam Conference

Agreement on:
• German demilitarization
• Denazification
• Punishment of war criminals
• Council of Ministers

Disagreement on:
• Reparations
• Poland's western border
• Powers of the Allied Control Commission

Paris Peace Conference with Italy and minor Axis powers, 1945–47

SUMMARY DIAGRAM

Transition from war to fragile peace, 1945–46

Germany, June 1945– April 1947

> ▶ **Key question:** Why did the four occupying powers fail to work out a joint programme for Germany's future?

Germany was the most populated and industrialized state in central and western Europe before the Second World War and much of its economic strength, especially its highly trained workforce, remained at the war's conclusion. Germany's potential wealth and military and economic strength ensured that neither the USSR, nor the Western Allies, would allow the other to dominate it. Indeed, as tension rose, both sides began to wonder whether Germany itself could be rehabilitated to become an ally in a future conflict between the two opposing political camps. The German question became one of the central issues of the Cold War. Stalin was to appreciate this well before the US did.

Soviet aims in Germany

To what extent did the USSR aim to control the whole of Germany?

In June 1945, Stalin explained his plans for eventually bringing a reunified Germany into Moscow's sphere of influence to the leaders of the German Communist Party (KPD). The Red Army would directly control the Soviet zone of occupation, while the KPD would seek to win the support of the German workers in both the Soviet and the western zones. Once Germany was allowed to hold elections for a new parliament, he hoped that the KPD would form a governing coalition with the Socialist and Liberal Parties, eventually taking control of the German government. This may well have been the reason why the USSR was the first occupying power to allow the formation of democratic parties in its zone in June 1945.

The creation of the Socialist Unity Party (SED)

To broaden the appeal of the KPD, Stalin ordered his officials to force the merger of the Social Democratic Party (SPD) with the KPD in the Soviet zone in eastern Germany. After at least 20,000 Social Democrats had been interrogated and imprisoned and in some cases even murdered, the Central Executive of the SPD in the Soviet zone agreed in February 1946 to the formation of the new party Stalin envisaged: the Socialist Unity Party (SED).

SOURCE E

? What, according to Stalin's instructions in Source E, is the future task of the SED?

An excerpt from *Stalin's Unwanted Child: The German Question and the Founding of the GDR* by Willy Loth, published by Macmillan, UK, 1998, p. 38.

At the end of April 1946, Stalin issued an important directive to his officials in the Soviet zone:

From the standpoint of the Soviet Union, it is not yet time to establish central authorities nor in general to continue with a policy of centralisation in Germany. The first goal, organising the Soviet occupation zone under effective Soviet control, has been more or less achieved. The moment has thus now come to reach into the Western zones. The instrument is the United Socialist–Communist Party. Some time will have to elapse before the party is organised in an orderly fashion in Greater Berlin itself, and this process will take even longer in the Western zones. Only when the Soviet vision has been realised and the Unity Party has established itself in the Western zones, will the time have come to address once again the question of central administrations and of effective Soviet support for a policy of centralisation in Germany.

Reaction in western Germany

The violence in eastern German created fear and suspicion in western Germany, preventing the party's success there. When SPD voters in the western zones of Berlin were asked by the SPD leaders in Berlin to approve the merger of the two parties, it was rejected by 82 per cent. Soviet and KPD actions in eastern Germany made many in western Germany and in the western zones of Berlin, as well as the Western Allies, suspicious of Soviet intentions.

The problem of reparations

By the spring of 1946, the compromise over reparations which had been negotiated in Potsdam was already breaking down. The western zones, particularly the heavily populated British zone, were absorbing the majority of the German refugees who had been expelled by the Poles and Czechs from the former German territories that had been ceded to them at the end of the war (see map on page 47). This meant that there were now many more people to feed.

> Why could the occupying powers not agree on the reparations?

British and US economic policy in Germany

Britain and the US wanted a moderate German economic recovery so that their zones could at least pay for their own food imports. Consequently, until that point was reached, they wished to delay delivering to the USSR the quotas from their own zones of machinery and raw materials, which had been agreed at Potsdam (see pages 46–47). There were even discussions that the Soviet zone would have to deliver food to the hard-pressed western zones. The Soviets, who had suffered the most casualties and war damage during the Second World War as a result of a German invasion of their country, were very reluctant to agree to this.

General Clay, governor of the US-occupied zone, attempted to force the Soviets to agree to British and US economic policy in Germany by unilaterally announcing in May 1946 that no further deliveries of reparation goods would be made to the Soviet Union. Clay stated that there would have to be an overall plan for the German economy for deliveries to be continued, although this violated the earlier agreement.

Soviet response

The Soviets saw this as an attempt by the US to force Germany's reconstruction along capitalist lines, which would benefit both US and British industries as it would inevitably integrate Germany into their trading systems.

The Soviets responded in June 1946 by increasing eastern Germany's industrial production – the products of which went directly to the Soviet Union as reparations – while taking over control of 213 east German companies.

The Conference of Foreign Ministers, July 1946

When the Conference of Foreign Ministers returned to the question of Germany in July, Soviet Foreign Minister Molotov insisted that Germany should pay the USSR the equivalent of $10 billion in reparations. US Secretary of State James Byrnes again argued the US position that reparations could only be paid once Germany had a **trade surplus** that would cover the cost of food and raw material imports for the US and British zones. He then offered to unify the US zone economically with the other three zones. Only Britain, whose economy was under great pressure (see page 54), accepted the US proposal while both France and the USSR rejected it. France strongly opposed a united Germany, while the USSR would not tolerate a united Germany dominated by the US and restored to economic strength, and therefore potential military strength.

The creation of Bizonia, January 1947

This lack of agreement was a major step in the division of Germany into two states, which eventually took place in 1949 (see pages 79–81). When the British and US zones were merged economically in January 1947 to form what became known as Bizonia, the US argued that, far from breaking the Potsdam Agreement, the amalgamation would eventually create the economic conditions for fulfilling the Potsdam Agreement and enable reparations to be paid. The US stated that only through economic prosperity could the Soviets receive full reparation payments. Bizonia would be the first stage in restoring economic prosperity to Germany and this prosperity would mean that the French and Soviet zones would eventually merge with it.

The Soviets suspected that Britain and the US hoped to use Bizonia only to create a capitalist Germany and believed that the two countries did not have the right to form such an economic entity by themselves without consulting the USSR or France. The Soviets also feared that Britain and the US would attempt to establish a separate German state in western Germany of which Bizonia was only a first step.

The Moscow Conference of Foreign Ministers, March–April 1947

The Moscow Conference was one of the turning points in early post-war history. The Soviets made a determined effort to destroy Bizonia by demanding that a new central German administration under Four-Power control should be

KEY TERM

Trade surplus The situation that occurs when a country sells more than it buys from other countries it trades with.

immediately created in line with earlier agreements that all Four Powers should rule Germany together (see page 32). They ran into strong opposition from Britain's Foreign Secretary Ernest Bevin who feared that this would slow up the economic recovery of the British zone and, indeed, the whole of Bizonia.

Britain proposed a plan for revising the reparation clauses of the Potsdam Agreement, which involved the USSR returning some of the reparations it had seized from eastern Germany to the western zones so that the zones of the Western Allies would be better able to pay for their imports. This plan further stated that the Soviet Union would receive no coal or steel from any part of Germany as reparations until Germany could pay for all its imports of food and raw materials. The Soviets rejected the proposal outright – it appeared to them that they were the only ones making economic sacrifices for the benefit of Germans and the Western Allies, while their own nation was in ruins and in need of coal and steel.

The lack of unity at the Moscow Conference on the part of the Four Powers regarding Germany's economic future gave Britain and the US an excuse to continue operating independently in their zones with little regard for Soviet views. Bizonia was strengthened economically and given more political independence while France slowly began to accept British and US views on German economic development. The divisive issue of reparations, and the future of Germany's government, was to be discussed in November 1947 in London (see page 74).

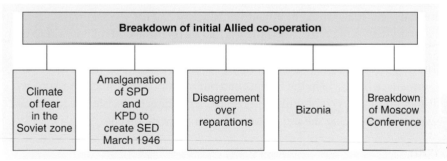

SUMMARY DIAGRAM

Germany, June 1945– April 1947

The Truman Doctrine and the Marshall Plan

> ▶ **Key question:** *To what extent was the Truman Doctrine and Marshall Plan designed to contain Soviet power?*

The Truman Doctrine and Marshall Plan marked the real beginning of the Cold War and of US military and economic engagement in western Europe. Together they helped ensure capitalism and democratic governments in much of western and southern Europe while limiting the political and economic influence of the Soviet Union and its satellite states.

What was the significance of the Truman Doctrine?

The Truman Doctrine

In June 1945, the US assumed that Britain would continue to play a major role in the eastern Mediterranean, but Britain faced a crippling economic crisis. As a result of political unrest in areas Britain controlled, such as India, Palestine and Egypt, and the long delay in completing post-war peace treaties, Britain had to keep a large number of troops in Germany, Italy, the Middle East and Asia. This was, of course, enormously expensive, and by January 1947 the post-war US loan of £3.75 billion had been nearly exhausted. The situation was made worse by heavy blizzards and exceptionally cold weather that had brought transport, industry and coal mining in Britain virtually to a halt for several weeks. On 21 February 1947 Britain informed the US that its financial and military aid to both Greece and Turkey would cease on 31 March as a result of financial problems. The US, meanwhile, faced deteriorating relations with the Soviet Union over Germany, while in 1946 the Soviets had put military and political pressure on Turkey and Iran. A communist-led rebellion, not directly assisted by the USSR, was also threatening the pro-Western government in Greece.

Iran

Early in 1942, Britain and the Soviet Union moved troops into Iran to safeguard its oil supplies from threats from Italy and Germany, and agreed to remove their troops six months after the end of hostilities. At the war's end, however, the Soviets increased their troop numbers in Iran; this was seen as a threat to both neighbouring Turkey and Iraq. The US protested against Soviet moves and Iran appealed to the Security Council of the United Nations in order to have the Soviets withdraw their forces. This was accomplished in March 1946.

Turkey

In August 1946, a new crisis arose when the Soviets suggested a plan for a joint Turkish-Soviet defence of the **Dardanelles**. The US suspected that this was an attempt by the Soviets to establish naval bases in Turkey and make it a Soviet satellite state. In response, the US government encouraged Turkey to resist Soviet demands, and dispatched units of the US naval fleet to the

  KEY TERM

Dardanelles Strait connecting the Mediterranean and Aegean Seas with the Black Sea, separating Europe from Asia Minor.

eastern Mediterranean in a demonstration of military strength. The Soviets soon dropped their demands on Turkey.

Greece

In Greece, Stalin proceeded with caution as he had agreed with Churchill in 1944 (see page 22) that the country was in Britain's sphere of interest. The Soviets gave little direct aid to the communist guerrillas who were fighting a civil war there. Instead, Stalin allowed Yugoslavia, Bulgaria and Albania to assist the Greek Communist Party with both soldiers and money in the campaign against the British-backed Greek government (see page 62).

This communist-led rebellion threatened to topple the Greek government just as the British withdrew their troops. Truman regarded the rebels as an instrument of Soviet policy and feared that their success in Greece would lead to a **domino effect** that would force Turkey and other countries in the region into the Soviet sphere of influence.

The announcement of the Truman Doctrine

Truman felt that he had to act quickly to strengthen non-communist forces in areas that were vulnerable to Soviet pressure. This required money which had to be approved by Congress, the US parliament.

On 12 March, Truman appealed to Congress by outlining his views on the state of international politics, highlighting the increasing divide between the US and the Soviets Union (see Source F). He outlined plans for financially assisting states like Greece and Turkey, which were perceived to be threatened by communism.

KEY TERM

Domino effect The belief that the fall of one state to communism would result in a chain reaction leading to the fall of other neighbouring states.

SOURCE F

An excerpt from Truman's speech to Congress, 12 March 1947, quoted in *The Soviet Union in World Politics*, by Geoffrey Roberts, published by Routledge, London, UK, 1999, p. 22.

One way of life is based upon the will of the majority, and is distinguished by free institutions, representative government, free elections, guarantees of individual liberty, freedom of speech and religion, and freedom from political oppression. The second way of life is based upon the will of a minority forcibly imposed upon the majority. It relies upon terror and oppression, a controlled press and radio, fixed elections and the suppression of personal freedoms.

I believe that it must be the policy of the United States to support free peoples who are resisting attempted subjugation by armed minorities or by outside pressures. I believe that we must assist free peoples to work out their own destinies in their own way … The seeds of totalitarian regimes are nurtured by misery and want. They spread and grow in the evil soil of poverty and strife. They reach their full growth when the hope of a people for a better life has died.

What information does Source F convey about US policy towards states perceived to be threatened by communism?

Initially Stalin dismissed this speech as an exercise in propaganda. It was soon clear, however, that this was the beginning of a new US policy which was rapidly supplemented by substantial economic aid through the **Marshall Plan**.

What were the aims
of the Marshall Plan
and why did the
USSR reject it?

KEY TERM

Marshall Plan US
economic aid programme for
post-war western Europe,
also known as Marshall Aid.

Supranational
Transcending national limits.

? What information does
Source G convey about the
conditions that were attached
by the US to the granting of
Marshall Aid?

The Marshall Plan

Since 1945, the US had granted funds to governments in western Europe to
prevent economic collapse and starvation. In 1947, influential US journalists
and politicians argued that only through political and economic integration
would western Europe solve the complex economic problems which it was
believed contributed to the world wars, the Great Depression, and the rising
appeal of communism. If Bizonia and eventually all Germany could enter
this economically integrated Europe, Germany would be less likely to
dominate Europe politically and militarily in the future as it would have no
incentive to do so.

Marshall's offer

In June 1947, US Secretary of State George Marshall made his historic offer
of aid for Europe. The key to it was that the Europeans must help themselves
while the US would provide the money. The Europeans were to set up a
supranational organization that would plan how US aid should be spent.

SOURCE G

**An excerpt from General Marshall's speech to Harvard University on 5
June 1947, quoted from *US Department of State Bulletin*, XVI, 15 June
1947, p. 1160.**

*It is already evident that before the United States Government can proceed further
to alleviate the situation and help start the European world economy, there must
be some agreement among the countries of Europe as to the requirements of the
situation and the part those countries themselves will take in order to give proper
effect to whatever action might be undertaken by this Government. It would be
neither fitting nor efficacious for this government to undertake to draw up
unilaterally a programme to place Europe on its feet economically.*

Paris negotiation on Marshall Aid

After Marshall's speech, the British and French called for a conference in
Paris to formulate plans for the acceptance of US aid. Stalin suspected that
the Marshall Plan masked an attempt by the US to interfere in the domestic
affairs of the European states, but he sent Soviet Foreign Minister Molotov to
Paris to discuss further details with Britain and France. The Soviets certainly
wanted financial aid from the US, but without any conditions attached.
Britain and France, however, argued that the European states should draw
up a joint programme for spending the aid, as the US had demanded, rather
than each individual state sending in a separate list of requests. Molotov
rejected this and left the Paris talks as Stalin feared that an economic
programme involving cooperation with the western European nations would
enable US economic power to undermine Soviet influence in eastern Europe.

On 16 July, detailed negotiations on the Marshall Plan began at the
Conference of European Economic Co-operation, where sixteen western
European nations, including Turkey and Greece, were represented. Eastern

European states were invited too, but were prevented from attending by Stalin. Czechoslovakia initially accepted in defiance of Stalin's command, but the government soon bowed to Soviet pressure and declined to attend (see page 64).

For the Western powers, this simplified the negotiations, but agreements were still difficult to achieve. Each western European state had its own agenda. France wanted to ensure that its own economy had preference in receiving US aid over the economic needs of Bizonia. France was, however, ready to consider the formation of a European **customs union** as long as it enabled France to control the western German economy. Britain wished to safeguard its national **sovereignty** and was opposed to creating powerful supranational organizations.

By mid-August, the US was disappointed to find that western Europeans had not made any plans for economic integration and co-operation. Each country had instead merely drawn up a list of requests with its own needs in mind, rather than planning on a more regional level. Jefferson Caffery, the US Ambassador in Paris, complained that this simply re-created pre-war economic conditions with all the 'low labour productivity and mal-distribution of effort which derive from segregating 270,000,000 people into … uneconomic principalities [small countries, with their own separate economies] '.

Western European states asked for $29 billion, far more than Congress was ready to grant. To avoid the conference ending in failure, Bevin called another meeting in Paris to allow the US to propose cuts to the proposals which European states wanted the US to fund. US officials immediately established an Advisory Steering Committee which worked to bring European states into line with essential US requirements, but this achieved only limited success by September with:

- seventeen states agreeing to allow imports from countries involved in the Marshall Plan
- all agreeing that Germany needed to recover economically while also still being controlled
- all agreeing to develop hydroelectric power sources together and to facilitate cross-frontier railway freight services
- all agreeing to establish overall production targets for coal, oil, steel, and agricultural products.

However, there were to be no supranational organizations that could force the individual states to carry out these policies. At most, the states promised to create a joint organization to review how much progress was being made.

In spring 1948, the US Congress approved a programme for $5 billion as the first instalment of Marshall Plan aid. To administer and distribute this, the Organization for European Economic Co-operation (OEEC) was created, although each nation involved did not surrender any of its own authority to the OEEC.

KEY TERM

Customs union An area of free trade.

Sovereignty National political independence.

? What information is
conveyed by Source H about
the granting of Marshall Aid?

Graph showing how much Marshall aid was given to each western European country, including the Federal Republic of Germany (West Germany), which was formed by the Western Allies in 1949.

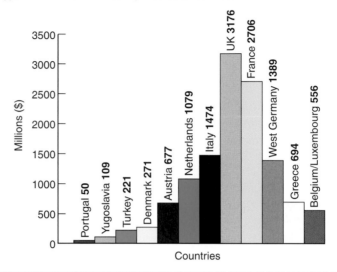

SUMMARY DIAGRAM

The Truman Doctrine and the Marshall Plan

Truman Doctrine, March 1947
Reasons for its announcement
• Britain unable to defend eastern Mediterranean • Yugoslavs assisting Greek Communists
The Doctrine
• Truman offered US support to countries resisting Communist subversion • Stressed need to improve economic conditions in Europe
The Marshall Plan
• Offer of aid package • Funds to be distributed by supranational organization
• Accepted by Western European states • Rejected by USSR, which set up Cominform

The 'Iron Curtain'

> ▶ **Key question:** *How far had an 'Iron Curtain' descended across Europe by the end of 1947?*

Stalin's decision to pressure eastern European states to boycott the talks on the Marshall Plan in Paris in July marked the end of his attempts to co-operate with the USA and maintain the Grand Alliance. In September 1947, he invited the leaders of eastern Europe and the leaders of the French and Italian Communist Parties to a conference in Poland to discuss establishing the Communist Information Bureau (**Cominform**). This organization would co-ordinate policies and tactics of communist parties in both the satellite states and in western Europe. Andrei Zhdanov, Chairman of the Soviet Union, told the delegates that the world was now divided into two hostile camps: the imperialist bloc led by the US, intent on the economic 'enslavement of Europe', and the 'anti-imperialist and democratic camp' led by the USSR.

In order to prevent the spread of US economic and political influence, communist governments were to be fully supported where possible. This meant that co-operating with moderate socialists and liberals in the governments of Hungary, Czechoslovakia and other eastern European states would now end, and local communist parties, following the Soviet model, would work to take over all political power in the region.

KEY TERM

Cominform The Communist Information Bureau established in 1947 to exchange information among nine eastern European countries and co-ordinate their activities.

SOURCE I

An excerpt from Winston Churchill's speech at Fulton, Missouri in the United States on the 'Iron Curtain' on 5 March 1946, quoted in *The Unsettled Peace* by R. Morgan, published by BBC, London, UK, 1974, pp. 67–68.

From Stettin in the Baltic, to Trieste, in the Adriatic, an iron curtain has descended across the continent. Behind that line lie all the capitals of the ancient states of Central and Eastern Europe – Warsaw, Berlin, Prague, Vienna, Belgrade, Bucharest and Sofia. All these famous cities, and the populations around them, lie in the Soviet sphere, and all are subject in one form or another, not only to Soviet influence, but to a very high and increasing measure of control from Moscow. Athens alone … is free to decide its future … The Russian dominated Polish government has been encouraged to make enormous and wrongful inroads upon Germany … The Communist parties, which were very small in all these eastern states of Europe, have been raised to pre-eminence and power far beyond their numbers, are seeking everywhere to obtain totalitarian control. Police governments are prevailing in nearly every sense, and so far, except in Czechoslovakia, there is no true democracy … An attempt is being made by the Russians in Berlin to build up a quasi-Communist party in their zone of occupied Germany by showing special favours to groups of left-wing leaders.

Compare and contrast the views expressed in Sources I and J about Soviet influence in Europe.

An excerpt from Stalin's interview with the Soviet newspaper, *Pravda*, on 13 March 1946, quoted in *Origins of Cold War, 1941–1949*, third edition, by M. McCauley, published by Longman, Harlow, UK, 2003, pp. 142–43.

… The following circumstances should not be forgotten. The Germans made their invasion of the USSR through Finland, Poland, Romania and Hungary. The Germans were able to make their invasion through these countries because at the time governments hostile to the Soviet Union existed in these countries. As a result of the German invasion the Soviet Union has lost irretrievably in the fighting against the Germans, and also through the German occupation and the deportation of Soviet citizens to German servitude, a total of about seven million people. In other words, the Soviet Union's loss of life has been several times greater than that of Britain and the United States of America put together. Possibly in some quarters an inclination is felt to forget about these colossal sacrifices of the Soviet people which secured the liberation of Europe from the Hitlerite [Nazi] yoke. But the Soviet Union cannot forget about them … And so what can there be surprising about the fact that the Soviet Union, anxious for its future safety, is trying to see to it that governments loyal in their attitude to the Soviet Union should exist in these countries? How can anyone, who has not taken leave of his senses, describe these peaceful aspirations of the Soviet Union as expansionist tendencies on the part of our state?

Opposition from the French and Italian Communist Parties

How did the Communist Party in France and Italy react to the Truman Doctrine and Marshall Plan?

In both Italy and France, there were strong Communist Parties, which, as in the eastern European states, had been members of coalition governments. Cominform instructed them that they were to oppose their countries' support for the Marshall Plan.

France

In January 1947, a new coalition government was formed by the Communist Party with the Radical and Socialist Parties. The Communist Party held 186 seats in the Assembly but the government was soon paralysed by divisions between the Communists and the other groups in the coalition over economic, foreign and colonial policies; the Communist Party was expelled from the government in May.

Following Cominform instructions to protest against the Marshall Plan, the French Communist Party began a series of strikes in major French cities and in coal mines which soon led to violent riots and street battles with police. By 24 November, nearly 2 million workers were on strike but the Communist Party was weakened when many strikers joined separate political groups. Communist Party action failed to prevent the government from accepting

Marshall Plan aid. Another mass strike to protest against the Marshall Plan in October 1948 also failed. As the Cold War intensified, the Communist Party remained in opposition until 1981.

Italy

In January 1947, the Italian Communist Party (PCI) was a key member of the coalition government. As tension grew between the US and USSR in 1946–47, hostility between PCI and the **Christian Democrats** within the cabinet increased. In May, a new government was formed which the PCI did not join. This cleared the way for the government to accept the Marshall Plan and to align itself diplomatically with the **Western bloc**. The PCI was ordered by the Cominform to oppose the Marshall Plan and US capitalism both politically and through strikes. This action was seen by the Italian public as preventing US aid which the economy desperately needed. In April 1948, the PCI suffered a heavy defeat in a general election while the pro-Marshall Plan Christian Democrats took 307 seats out of 574, giving them control of the government. The Italian Communist Party remained in opposition until its dissolution in 1991, but as late as the 1960s it was still the largest communist party in western Europe.

The formation of the Soviet bloc, 1946–47

By the end of 1947, eastern Europe, with the exception of Finland, had fallen under Soviet control (see map, page 147). The US and Britain, despite Truman's declaration to Congress, were not ready to risk the outbreak of war with the USSR by intervening directly in the affairs of eastern Europe. Their priority was to prevent the spread of communism to western Europe.

Poland

To deflect Western criticism from his policies in Poland, Stalin followed the Yalta Agreement (see page 33) and established the Provisional Government of National Unity in June 1945 to govern until elections could be held. It included four representatives of democratic, non-communist parties, while the other seventeen were pro-Soviet politicians. The large non-communist majority in Poland pinned its hopes on winning power in the coming elections. The Yalta Agreement promised 'free and unfettered elections', but in reality the likelihood of genuinely free elections taking place was virtually nil, as they would have resulted in the overwhelming defeat of pro-Soviet politicians and communists.

Many in Poland resented the annexation of the eastern provinces by the Soviets, and the brutal attempts by the NKVD to impose a pro-Soviet dictatorship on occupied Poland (see page 26). In large parts of Poland, a guerrilla war was waged by members of the former Home Army against the Soviet-dominated provisional government. It was defeated in 1947 by government security forces assisted by the NKVD.

 **KEY TERM**

Christian Democrats Moderately conservative political party seeking to apply Christian principles to governing the country.

Western bloc An alliance of western European states and the USA.

How did the USSR consolidate its grip over the eastern European states, 1946–47?

Stalin was determined to ensure a friendly government in Poland in order to give the Soviet Union security from another attack from the west such as happened in both world wars. Stalin believed that only a Polish communist state could provide this security. After the announcement of the Truman Doctrine and the lack of agreement about the future of Germany, the future of Poland became even more important to the Soviets as a reconstructed Germany, controlled by the US, was an implicit threat to Soviet security.

Poland's national elections, held on 19 January 1947, took place in an atmosphere of fear and intimidation, with 2 million potentially anti-communist voters struck from voter rolls by the Provisional Government; voters were pressured to vote for approved candidates. Officially 80.1 per cent voted for the pro-Soviet Democratic Bloc, while the anti-Soviet Peasants' Party won only 6.9 per cent. Britain and the USA complained about the lack of free elections, but eventually accepted the results as they had no means by which to force the Soviets to change their policy or actions in Poland. In fact, the new **doctrine of containment** being formulated by Truman accepted, unofficially, that Poland was within the USSR's sphere of interest and that the US would not intervene in its domestic affairs.

Romania

Like Poland, Romania was a vital security zone for the USSR, protecting it from attack on its south-west border while it also possessed valuable oil supplies. In March 1945, the Soviet chairman of the Allied Control Commission, with the support of the Red Army, ordered the King to dismiss his government and appoint a National Front Democratic Government, which contained socialist, communist and liberal representatives who were ready to co-operate with them, under the leadership of Petru Groza. Although there were only two communists in the cabinet, Soviet pressure ensured that the socialists co-operated closely with them, and there was no doubt that the government was dominated by the communists. Those socialists who were not ready to co-operate with the communists were forced out of the government.

After the Potsdam Conference (see page 48), at which it was decided that peace treaties could only be signed when governments recognized by the wartime allies had been established, Romania's King Michael called on Britain and the US not to recognize the new government as it was imposed by the Soviet Union. As the Council of Foreign Ministers was about to begin negotiations on the Romanian peace treaty, Stalin decided to call on Groza to appoint two more non-communists to the government. In reality, however, this made little difference. Groza was able to strengthen the National Democratic Front in March 1946 when the Romanian Socialist Party merged with the Communist Party. As in the Soviet zone of Germany, this effectively ensured communist domination

 KEY TERM

Doctrine of containment
A policy of halting the USSR's advance into western Europe. It did not envisage actually removing Soviet control of eastern Europe.

of the party. In May, the Front was further extended to include the National Popular Party, the National Peasant Party, as well as representatives from the communist-organized trade unions, youth and women's organizations.

In November 1946, the communist-dominated Front went to the polls. As in Poland, abuses did occur during the election: opposition newspapers were closed down and leading members of the opposition were murdered. It was therefore unsurprising that the Front won more than 80 per cent of the vote. Nevertheless, it did represent a broad spectrum of the population and would have won the national elections even without these aggressive and undemocratic tactics. The Front opposed the supporters of the former government, which had allied with Germany in the Second World War, and it also carried out popular social reforms such as the redistribution of land from the great land owners to the peasantry.

In February 1947, with the signature of the Paris Peace Treaties (see page 48), the ACC was dissolved. Under Soviet pressure, Romania refused Marshall Aid and joined the Cominform. In December 1947, the King was forced to abdicate and, in April 1948, a communist People's Republic was declared.

Bulgaria

The Soviets applied similar techniques and policies in Bulgaria to those used in Romania, although Stalin hoped to avoid unnecessary friction with the Western powers until a peace treaty was signed. In December 1945, the Bulgarian government, which was dominated by the Communist Party, was forced by the Soviets to include two members of the opposition although they were given no real power. The Bulgarian Communist Party was also ordered to allow the creation of a new Labour Party in September 1946 which would have a broader appeal to the public, as yet another measure to alleviate Western concerns of communist domination of Bulgaria.

In October 1946, elections took place for a national assembly. Opposition parties managed to win one-third of the total votes, but Western hopes that this would form the basis of an effective parliamentary opposition were soon dashed. The Truman Doctrine and increasing US involvement in Greece meant that Bulgaria became a frontline state in the defence of communism. Consequently, Stalin allowed the Communist Party to remove its opponents. Nikola Petkov, the leader of the popular Agrarian Party, was executed and, in April 1947, all opposition parties were outlawed. Soon **agriculture** was **collectivized** and all industries nationalized, imitating Stalin's actions in the Soviet Union twenty years earlier.

Yugoslavia

Yugoslavia occupied a unique position among the Soviet-dominated states in eastern and south-eastern Europe, as its Communist Party had effectively won power independently of the Red Army. The People's Front, a bloc of

 **KEY TERM**

Collectivization of agriculture Abolishing private farms in favour of large, state-owned farms where peasants work together.

parties dominated by the Yugoslav Communist Party, won 90 per cent of the votes in November 1945 elections. Tito, Yugoslavia's communist leader, restricted the activity of political parties outside this alliance, arresting their members and suppressing their newspapers.

In southern Europe, Tito had ambitious aims which clashed with British and US policy. Yugoslavia assisted Greek communists in their attempts to seize power in Greece (see pages 29 and 55), while also claiming border territories from Italy – specifically Venezi Giulia and Trieste, an important port on the Adriatic Sea. In May 1945, Yugoslav partisans occupied both territories after German troops were withdrawn, but were forced out of Trieste by British and US troops.

The USSR broadly supported Tito and argued that Trieste belonged historically, as well as geographically and economically, to the regions that now formed Yugoslavia, but Stalin was not ready to risk confrontation with Britain and the USA over these claims. In the end, an agreement was reached in the Paris peace negotiations in 1947 (see page 48) where Trieste was divided into two separate parts; one under Anglo-American, the other under Yugoslav control.

Czechoslovakia

Soviet troops were withdrawn from Czechoslovakia by December 1945. The elections in May 1946, in which Communists won 38 per cent of the vote, occurred without any violence or attempt to manipulate the vote and the coalition government under President Beneš (see page 30) remained in power. Although Klement Gottwald, the communist leader, controlled the key ministries of the Interior, Agriculture and Information, he had no plans for a coup and was ready to wait and to gain power peacefully through elections. Without the intensifying Cold War, Czechoslovakia might have remained a link between communist and non-communist Europe, as Beneš had hoped, but the Marshall Plan and the subsequent creation of the Cominform effectively created a divided Europe, which made this impossible.

The Czechoslovak cabinet voted unanimously in July 1947 to send representatives to attend the Paris Conference on the Marshall Plan (see page 56), but were soon dissuaded by the Soviets from doing so. Jan Masaryk, Czechoslovakia's Foreign Minister, later told Britain's Ambassador: 'I went to Moscow as the Foreign Minister of an independent sovereign state; I returned as a lackey of the Soviet government.' In February 1948, the Communist Party seized power in Czechoslovakia.

Hungary

Hungary, like Czechoslovakia, was treated as a special case by Stalin. The elections of November 1945 were free and transparent. Two years later, the press was still free as were debates in parliament, the borders with Austria were open, and smaller businesses were privately owned. The Soviets, however, retained control of the Allied Control Commission, which was the real governing force in Hungary. Stalin was able to insist on the Communist Party participating in a coalition government and having authority over the vital Ministry of the Interior which controlled the nation's security forces.

In spring 1947, the most powerful opposition to the Communists was shattered when the Minister of Agriculture and General-Secretary of the powerful Smallholders' Party, Béla Kovács, was arrested by Soviet troops for conspiring against the Soviet occupation. Yet, even this did not lead to an overwhelming Communist Party success in the August 1947 elections when the left-wing bloc only won 45 per cent of the vote. As late as autumn 1947, it still seemed possible that Hungary might retain some independence, although its membership of Cominform and rejection of Marshall Plan aid meant it was increasingly being drawn into the Soviet bloc. In March 1948, as a result of Soviet pressure, the Hungarian Communist and Socialist Parties merged. The following February, the Communist-dominated Hungarian People's Independence Front was formed, and in the elections of May 1949, only candidates from the Independence Front were allowed to stand.

Finland

Finland still remained the exception to the pattern developing in the other eastern European states. Its government was headed by a conservative politician and supported by the Democratic Bloc, a coalition composed of the Communist, the Social Democrat and the Agrarian Parties. The Communist Party was relatively weak and received no assistance from the Soviet Union. The historian Adam Ulam argues that Finland escaped being integrated into the Soviet bloc merely by chance, as Zhdanov, the Soviet chairman of the Allied Control Commission in Finland, was away most of the time in Moscow. Yet, another historian, Jukka Nevakivi, argues that Stalin simply wanted to neutralize Finland, and once the peace treaty with Finland was concluded in 1947, which committed Finland to paying $300 million in reparations and ceding the strategically important naval base of Petsamo to the USSR (see map, page 147), he was ready to leave them alone. He was convinced that, unlike Poland, Finland was no threat to the USSR and the threat of invasion through Finland into the Soviet Union was considered highly unlikely.

Finland's neutrality was emphasized in 1947 when its government declined an invitation to the Paris Conference on the Marshall Plan on the grounds that it wished 'to remain outside world political conflicts'. On the other hand, it did not become a member of Cominform, and received financial assistance from the USA outside the Marshall Plan.

Divisions caused by Soviet response to Marshall Aid

Cominform set up by Stalin

Eastern Europe

Poland
Communist-dominated electoral bloc won January 1947 elections

Romania
Communists in control by March 1946

Bulgaria
Enemies of Communist Party liquidated

Yugoslavia
Communist Party dominant under Tito

Hungary and Czechoslovakia
By December 1947 these countries had ceased to be a 'bridge' to the West

OECC set up in Paris

Western Europe

France
Communists expelled from coalition in May 1947 and oppose Marshall Plan

Italy
Communists in opposition to government and against Marshall Plan

Finland
Remained neutral but not under communist control

The 'Iron Curtain'

Key debate

▶ *Key question: Did the US or the USSR start the Cold War, 1945–47?*

The Cold War divided Europe until 1989. Why this happened and who was responsible are topics much debated by historians. To the conservative or traditionalist historians in the West, there is no doubt that it was Stalin; while revisionists look more sympathetically on the USSR and blame the US and, to a lesser extent, Britain. With increased access to Soviet archives after 1990, historians from both 'the West' and the former Soviet bloc, such as Leonid Gibianski, argue that Stalin's policy in Europe was more varied than had been originally assumed by Western historians.

The origins of the Cold War

> **Who started the Cold War?**

Traditionalist interpretations

Traditionalist Western historians, such as Herbert Feis who wrote in the 1950s, firmly put the blame for starting the Cold War on Stalin. These historians argued that Stalin ignored promises given at the Yalta Conference in February 1945 to support democratically elected governments. Instead, over the next three years, he proceeded to put his own communist puppets in power in the eastern European states. Once it was clear that Britain and France were too weak economically and politically to defend western Europe, the US intervened and made the following key decisions which marked the beginning of the Cold War:

- creation of Bizonia
- Truman doctrine of containment
- Marshall Plan.

This interpretation of the start of the Cold War depicted the USA responding defensively to aggressive Soviet moves. In the US, the leading Cold War historian John Gaddis, writing after the end of the Cold War, gave a new slant to this interpretation by arguing that the Cold War was an unavoidable consequence of Stalin's paranoia, and was an extension of the way he dealt with opposition within the USSR.

SOURCE K

An excerpt from 'Origins of the Cold War' in *Foreign Affairs*, by Arthur Schlesinger, Vol. 46, 1967, pp. 22–52.

An analysis of the origins of the Cold War which leaves out those factors – the intransigence of Leninist ideology, the sinister dynamics of a totalitarian society and the madness of Stalin – is obviously incomplete. It was these factors which made it hard for the West to accept the thesis that Russia was moved only by a desire to protect its security and would be satisfied by the control of eastern Europe; it was these factors which charged the debate between universalism [the belief that mankind can only be saved through a particular belief – in this case Marxism–Leninism] and spheres of influence with apocalyptic [prophetic] certainty.

> According to Source K, what was the cause of the Cold War? **?**

Revisionist historians

Revisionist historians argued that the USA pursued policies that caused the Cold War in Europe. For instance, William Appleman Williams claimed in 1959 that the US aimed to force the USSR to join the global economy and open its frontiers to both US imports and political ideas, which would have undermined Stalin's government. Ten years later another historian, Gabriel Kolko, summed up US policy as aiming at restructuring the world economically so that American business could trade, operate, and profit without any restrictions.

? What, according to Source L, was the USA's role in causing the Cold War?

SOURCE L

An excerpt from *The Tragedy of American Diplomacy*, by William Appleman Williams, published by Delta Books, New York, USA, 1962, pp. 206–7.

*American leaders had … come to believe the theory, the necessity and morality of open door [free trade] expansion … As far as American leaders were concerned the philosophy and practice of open-door expansion had become in both its missionary and economic aspects, **the** view of the world …*

Particularly after the atom bomb was created and used, the attitude of the United States left the Soviets with but one real option; either acquiescence in American proposals or be confronted with American power and hostility. It was the decision of the United States to employ its new and awesome power in keeping with the Open Door policy, which crystallized the Cold War.

Post-revisionist historians

Post-revisionist historians have the advantage of being able to use Soviet archive material. Historians like John Lewis Gaddis, Vladislav Zubok, Constantine Pleshakov and Norman Naimark have shown that local communists in the Soviet zone in eastern Germany, Bulgaria, Romania and elsewhere, had considerable influence on policies which sometimes ran counter to Stalin's own intentions. They have also shown that Stalin's policy in eastern Europe was more subtle than traditionally viewed. While he was certainly determined to turn Poland, Romania and Bulgaria into satellite states, regardless of what the West might think about the violation of democracy or human rights, he also had flexible views. For two years this allowed Hungary and Czechoslovakia to retain connections to the West and for Finland to remain a neutral non-communist Western-style democracy.

? What information does Source M give about Stalin's post-war goals?

SOURCE M

An excerpt from *The Cold War*, by John Lewis Gaddis, published by Allen Lane, London, UK, 2006, p. 11.

Stalin's post-war goals were security for himself and his ideology in precisely that order. He sought to make sure that no internal challenges could ever again endanger his personal rule, and that no external threats would ever again place his country at risk. The interests of communists elsewhere in the world, admirable though these might be, would never outweigh the priorities of the Soviet state as he had determined them. Narcissism, paranoia and absolute power came together in Stalin …

Conclusion

Is it an exaggeration to say that Stalin pursued a relatively moderate line in eastern Europe up to 1947, and that his German policy was more a clumsy attempt to neutralize Germany and gain the vital reparations needed by the USSR, rather than a result of deep-laid plans to take control of territory occupied by Germany during the Second World War? Historian Michael McGwire has argued that Stalin was actively seeking to preserve what was left of the wartime co-operation between the Britain, the US and the USSR and, as a consequence of this, had by 1947 lost his chance to control Greece. By mid-1947, Stalin was pushed on the defensive first by the Truman Doctrine and then by the Marshall Plan.

Does this mean that Truman in fact started the Cold War? The Truman Doctrine and the Marshall Plan were certainly important stages reached in the escalation of the Cold War, but the context in which the US acted is also important. The seismic events of early 1947 – Britain's near bankruptcy and withdrawal from the eastern Mediterranean, growing economic paralysis in Germany, civil war in Greece and China (see pages 109–114) and the strength of the Communist parties in Italy and France – galvanized the US government into announcing first the Truman Doctrine and then the Marshall Plan. This was the turning point in the immediate post-war period and provoked the USSR into tightening its grip on eastern Europe and creating the Cominform.

> **T O K**
>
> It is often held that Stalin or Truman was responsible for the beginnings of the Cold War. Can any single event or person be responsible for anything in history? (History, Reason, Emotion)

Chapter summary

From wartime allies to post-war enemies, 1945–47

After the Second World War ended, the Grand Alliance between Britain, the US and the USSR came under increasing pressure as all three powers had diverging aims. The abrupt termination of Lend-lease supplies, disagreement over the United Nations and the control of nuclear weapons increased the tension between the three former allies. The Potsdam Conference temporarily produced compromise agreements on Germany and Poland. Four-Power control in Germany rapidly exposed divisions between the powers. There was disagreement on reparations, and in January 1947 Britain and the US took the first step towards the partition of Germany by establishing Bizonia.

The year 1947 was pivotal in the collapse of the Grand Alliance and the start of the Cold War. In March 1947, in response to a communist rebellion in Greece, pressure on Turkey, and Britain's growing economic weakness, US President Truman announced the Truman Doctrine. This was followed in June by the Marshall Plan, which offered financial aid to Europe. Fearing that the Plan would enable the US to interfere with the economies of eastern Europe, Stalin created the Cominform and vetoed any acceptance of the Marshall Plan by the eastern European states. The USSR also began to consolidate its grip on these states. In reaction to this, western European states looked increasingly to the US for economic aid and military protection.

✅ Examination advice

How to answer 'compare and contrast' questions

For compare and contrast questions, you are asked to identify both similarities and differences. Better essays tend to approach the question thematically; simple narrative should be avoided.

Example

> Compare and contrast US and Soviet policies in Germany between 1945 and 1947.

1. You are being asked to describe the similarities and differences in US and Soviet policies regarding Germany between 1945 and 1947. Policies are different from actions, although policies may lead to actions; be sure to discuss the policy before discussing any actions. Do not discuss any issues after 1947 or those of any nations other than the US and the Soviet Union, although you may wish to indicate when other nations supported various policies if appropriate. Do not discuss policies that do not specifically involve Germany.

2. For at least five minutes before writing your essay, create a chart to show the similarities and differences between US and Soviet policies regarding Germany between 1945 and 1947. When you write your essay, check off each item. Below is an example of a possible chart for this question.

	US	Soviet Union
Differences	Limit/end reparations to USSR, ostensibly to pay for food imports to Western-occupied zones of Germany; wanted overall economic plan for all Germany. Economic integration of Western zones of Germany; Bizonia. Marshall Plan to build economic integration and sharing of European resources which would benefit Germany.	1945 agreements to be followed, including reparations, Four-Power government, etc. Worked to create a single communist party for all Germany which would ally to the USSR. Opposed Germany's economic integration with western Europe.
Similarities	Initial policies in 1945: 1 German demilitarization, denazification, punishment of war criminals.	

> **2** *Germany to be ruled by Allied Control Council, divided into four zones.*
> **3** *Reparations to Allies from zones under their control, plus 10 per cent for Soviets from non-Soviet controlled zones.*
> **4** *Both US and USSR wanted unification but under their own economic/political systems.*

3. In your introduction, begin by explaining that Germany was occupied by the Soviet Union, United States, Britain and France at the end of the Second World War in Europe by May 1945. Furthermore, explain that as Europe's most industrialized economy and with one of the largest populations of any European state, it was economically and politically important. You then need to generally introduce the idea that there were similarities and differences in the policies of both the Soviet Union and the US regarding Germany and that these developed over time. An example of a good introductory paragraph for this question is given below.

Germany was defeated and occupied by the Allied powers at the conclusion of the Second World War in Europe. As Europe's most industrialized nation and one of its most populated, it was viewed as critically important to the economy and stability of the region. The Allies, which included the Soviet Union and the US, agreed to implement various economic and political policies upon Germany's defeat. While some of these policies were implemented, such as dividing Germany into zones and removing elements of the former government, others were altered or abandoned, such as reparations or overall Allied control of the zones. The US and the Soviet Union both developed policies between 1945 and 1947 dealing with Germany that contrasted with the other, exacerbating tensions between these world powers. Some of these contrasting policies dealt with the economic integration of the zones of occupation and western Europe and Soviet control of its zone's economic production, ostensibly for reparations. There were similarities and differences in US and Soviet policies regarding Germany between 1945 and 1947.

4. The bulk of your essay will discuss the various points outlined in your introduction. Your argument should focus on both similarities and differences in their policies and it is important that you make it clear that you understand that there were both. It is fine if you suggest that the differences far outweighed the similarities (or vice versa) but explain the reasons this might have been the case and support with evidence.

5. Write a concluding paragraph which states your conclusions. Be sure not to include new information here. An example of a good concluding paragraph is given below.

Initial policies in 1945, such as agreements on reparations and Four-Power control over a Germany divided into four zones, were similar but were soon altered so that they were no longer in agreement. This was partly because both the US and Soviet Union desired a united German state that would economically benefit and pose no military threat to themselves. The policies of each of these superpowers to achieve this goal, however, led to contrasting policies. The US initiated policies such as the integration of its zone with that of Britain to form Bizonia, an entity that would create an overall economic area and therefore, according to the Soviet view, a separate, western German state. The Soviets, in contrast, refused to integrate their zone with Bizonia and instead increased the economic production of eastern Germany to make reparations to the Soviet Union for the damages of the Second World War. The Soviets also insisted that the US return to the earlier-agreed Four-Power control of all Germany and that reparations from the Western-occupied zones be resumed. While the US continued to integrate western Germany into the economic system of western Europe through the Marshall Plan, the Soviets refused to allow eastern Germany's participation in the US economic plan. While the aims of the US and the USSR were similar, their efforts to achieve these were different.

6. Now try writing a complete answer to the question following the advice above.

Examination practice

Below are three exam-style questions for you to practise regarding this chapter.

1. Analyse the policies of the Soviet Union in Europe between 1945 and 1947.
   (For guidance on how to answer 'analyse' questions, see page 38.)

2. Evaluate the significance of Germany on US and Soviet relations.
   (For guidance on how to answer 'evaluate' questions, see page 98.)

3. Compare and contrast Soviet policies regarding Romania and Yugoslavia between 1945 and 1947.
   (For guidance on how to answer 'compare and contrast' questions, see page 70.)

 # Activities

I Each student in class should create a 'True or False' quiz with 25 questions for someone else in the class, using information found in this chapter. This quiz should be taken after the chapter has been read or reviewed by the group; the chapter should not be reviewed while the quiz is in progress. Once all have completed a quiz, papers should be exchanged between individuals and marked, again without referring to the chapter.

2 Students should access the University of Kent, UK, cartoon archives at www.cartoons.ac.uk. Each student should use the search engine located at this site to find at least one cartoon regarding information found in this chapter, such as the Potsdam Conference, US President Harry Truman, Marshall Plan, communist revolt in Greece, etc. After cartoons have been selected, analyse the content of the cartoon. Be sure to indicate the cartoon reference number, the artist responsible for this artwork, what information it is trying to convey, and what symbols or pictures are used. This may be presented in class or simply shared with other students.

3 This chapter helps you to understand how to answer 'compare and contrast' questions. Create three questions of this type based on information located in this chapter and exchange with others in your class. Each student should select one of the questions and answer it according to the advice presented above. Students should mark each other's work, pointing out appropriate elements and ones that are either incorrect or need further supporting evidence.

CHAPTER 3

The division of Germany and Europe, 1948–52

This chapter covers the key period from 1948 to 1952 during which two German states, the Federal Republic of Germany (FRG) and the German Democratic Republic (GDR), were created and the division of Europe was consolidated into a Soviet bloc and a Western bloc.

You need to consider the following questions throughout this chapter:

✪ Why and how were the FRG and GDR created?

✪ Why was Western European military power strengthened, 1948–52?

✪ How did the polarization of Europe into two rival blocs accelerate during the years 1950–52?

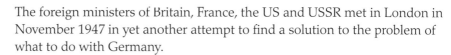

1 The division of Germany

> ▶ Key question: Why and how were the FRG and GDR created?

The foreign ministers of Britain, France, the US and USSR met in London in November 1947 in yet another attempt to find a solution to the problem of what to do with Germany.

By the time the conference opened in London, the chances of any agreement on Germany seemed remote. The US vigorously supported the idea of **Western European integration** and was at least temporarily resigned to the division of Germany. The USSR still wished to avoid the partition of Germany, as this would result in the great industrial complex of the **Ruhr** becoming a part of a US-dominated Western European bloc.

The Soviets had tried hard to rally public opinion across Germany against the policy of the Western Allies. Walter Ulbricht, the leader of the SED (see page 50), was instructed to organize a 'German People's Congress for Unity and a Just Peace'. Representatives from all parties throughout Germany were invited to attend its meetings on 6–7 December 1947 in Berlin. The intention was then to send a delegation to the London Conference to support the Soviet demand for the formation of a German central government. Roughly one-third of the 2225 delegates came from the West, but these were overwhelmingly communists from areas like the Ruhr and the big industrial towns. The movement did not therefore genuinely reflect West German opinion and the British Foreign Secretary Ernest Bevin refused to allow its delegation permission to enter Britain.

No agreement emerged and the London Conference ended on 15 December. The Soviets accused Britain and the US of violating the Potsdam Agreement and of denying the USSR its fair share of reparations, while the Western

KEY TERM

Western European integration The process of creating a Western Europe that was united politically, economically and militarily.

Ruhr The centre of the German coal and steel industries and at that time the greatest industrial region in Europe.

powers rejected Soviet proposals for forming a German government, which would govern a united Germany, as they feared the Soviets would gain control of it. All hope of Four-Power co-operation now disappeared, and instead for Britain, France and the US, the alternatives of a Western alliance, closer economic co-operation in western Europe and the creation of a west German state appeared to be the only practical options.

The decision to create a west German state

The failure of the London Conference of Foreign Ministers in December 1947 strengthened the Western allies in their resolve to form a separate west German state. A second London conference was then held from February to June 1948 where Britain, France, the US and the **Benelux states** met to discuss the establishment of this new state.

At the conference, US and British plans met with considerable hostility from France which dreaded the revival of a Germany with the potential to invade France yet again. French fears were gradually eased by a US pledge to keep troops stationed in western Europe to maintain peace and prevent a revival of an aggressive Germany. Britain and the US also promised to control tightly the new German government that they were resolved to establish. The production of the great industrial centre of the Ruhr, for example, was to be regulated by the **International Ruhr Authority** which would be controlled by the Western allies. West Germans would also have to accept the **Occupation Statute** which would give Britain, France and the US far-reaching powers over trade, foreign relations, economic issues and disarmament.

On 7 June, Germans in the western zones were granted permission to create a constitution for a democratic, **federal** West Germany.

Currency reform

On 20 June, the Western allies, without consulting the Soviet Union, introduced a new currency for western Germany, the *Deutschmark*, or German mark. Four days later, the Soviets responded by introducing a new currency for their eastern German zone, the *Ostmark*, or East Mark. With the introduction of new currencies, two separate German states began to take shape.

The Soviet response: The Berlin Blockade

The Soviets believed that they could force the Western allies to abandon their plans for a west German state by applying pressure to West Berlin, which was controlled by the Western allies but separated from the rest of Germany due to its location in the Soviet zone in eastern Germany. West Berlin was totally dependent on the rail and road links running through the Soviet-controlled zone for its supplies of food and new materials from western Germany. Starting in March 1948, Soviet forces began to restrict the movement of people and goods between West Berlin and western Germany.

The blockade begins

The Soviets reacted to the introduction of the *Deutschmark* into West Berlin on 23 June 1948 by blockading West Berlin. They argued that the blockade

> How was French opposition to the establishment of the FRG overcome at the London Conference?

KEY TERM

Benelux states Belgium, the Netherlands and Luxemburg.

International Ruhr Authority Established how much coal and steel the Germans should produce and ensured that a percentage of its production should be made available to its western neighbours. It was replaced in 1951 by the European Coal and Steel Community.

Occupation Statute A treaty defining the rights of Britain, France and the US in West Germany.

> Why did the Berlin Blockade fail to prevent the creation of the FRG?

KEY TERM

Federal A country formed of several different states that have considerable autonomy in domestic affairs.

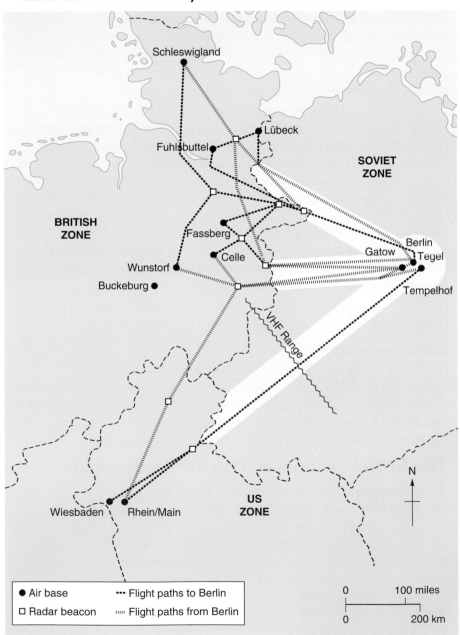

? What does Source A indicate about West Berlin's vulnerability to blockade?

was a defensive measure to stop the Soviet zone being swamped with the devalued **Reichsmark**, which the new *Deutschmark* was replacing in western Germany and West Berlin. Rail and road links to the west, as well as the supply of electricity which came from East Berlin, were cut.

SOURCE A

A diagram showing how the airlift worked. Radar beacons regulated the flow of the aircraft before they entered corridors to Berlin.

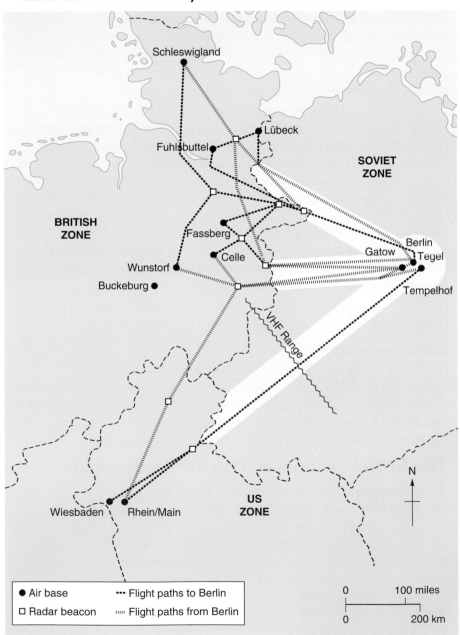

The Western response: the Berlin airlift

The Western response was initially confused and unsure of what course of action to pursue, if any. France was convinced that West Berlin could only hold out for a matter of weeks, while the US **Military Governor**, General Clay, argued that an armed convoy could force its way through from western Germay to West Berlin. Although Britain was determined to continue with the creation of a west German state, it rejected this suggestion because it could have easily provoked a clash with Soviet forces. Finally, the western Allies decided to supply West Berlin with goods transported by aircraft. This **airlift** would follow routes or corridors that the Soviet Union had granted the Western allies in 1945 (see Source A, page 76). In order to apply further, but implicit, pressure on the Soviets, the US transferred 60 long-range bombers to Britain which most governments believed held atomic bombs. This was a bluff as bombers capable of carrying atomic bombs only arrived in 1949. Nevertheless, this deterrent may have prevented the Soviet Union from aggressively countering the Berlin Airlift, as the operation is known, since the Soviets had few bombers and no atomic bombs at this time.

KEY TERM

Military Governor The head of a zone of occupation in Germany.

Airlift The transport of food and supplies by aircraft to a besieged area.

What information is conveyed by Source B? **?**

SOURCE B

West Berlin children watch a US plane, loaded with food, come in to land in early August 1948.

By the end of July 1948, British and US aircraft were flying a daily average of 2000 tons of food and raw materials into West Berlin. This was not enough, however, as in winter 5000 tons would need to be transported per day.

The Moscow talks

The three Western allies met in Moscow on 2 August with the Soviet government to try to reach an agreement whereby West Berlin could again be supplied by road and rail. The Soviets believed this indicated that their blockade was achieving its aims and decided to reject the proposals of the Western allies as they hoped to gain more concessions, perhaps in the coming critical winter months when more supplies would be needed, such as coal, to maintain West Berlin.

? According to Source C, what were Stalin's proposals towards solving the crisis in Berlin?

SOURCE C

An excerpt from the official Soviet record of a meeting of 2 August 1948 quoted in 'The Soviet Union and the Berlin Crisis' by M. Narinski, in *The Soviet Union and Europe in the Cold War, 1945–53*, ed. F. Gori and S. Pons, published by Palgrave Macmillan, Basingstoke, UK, 1996, p. 68.

Comrade Stalin spoke of two factors – the special currency in Berlin and the decisions of the London Conference. He thought that it was those decisions which gave rise to the restrictive measures under discussion …Comrade Stalin said that … simultaneously with the rescinding of the restrictions on transport applied by the Soviet Military Administration, the special currency [the Deutschmark*] … introduced by the three powers into Berlin should be withdrawn and replaced by the currency circulating in the Soviet zone …That was the first point. Secondly, assurance should be given that application of the London Conference's decisions would be postponed until representatives of the four powers had met and negotiated on all the basic questions concerning Germany.*

The Western allies would not reverse their decision to create a west German state, but they were ready to agree to the circulation of the *Ostmark* in the whole of Berlin, subject to the financial control of all four occupying powers. Yet, as further discussions between the Military Governors of the four zones in September demonstrated, the USSR wanted the *Ostmark* to be under Soviet control as the *Deutschmark* was under US, British and French control. The Western allies believed the Soviets wanted to retain control of the *Ostmark* as a step towards the full economic integration of all Berlin with eastern Germany which was already dominated by the Soviets. These talks ended on 7 September as neither side would compromise.

SOURCE D

An excerpt from the recollections of a senior Soviet official quoted in 'The Soviet Union and the Berlin Crisis' by M. Narinski, in *The Soviet Union and Europe in the Cold War, 1945–53*, ed. F. Gori and S. Pons, published by Palgrave Macmillan, UK, 1996, p. 69.

[If the USSR were to abandon the blockade, it intended] … to restore the economic unity of Berlin, to include all Berlin in the economic system of the Soviet zone and also to restore unified administration of the city. That would have served as a basis for winning over the population of West Berlin, and would have created the preconditions for completely ousting the Western powers from Berlin.

? According to Source D, what were Soviet intentions in Berlin?

 KEY TERM

Article 99 of the UN Charter 'The Secretary-General may bring to the attention of the Security Council any matter which in his opinion may threaten the maintenance of international peace and security.'

Failure of the United Nations

As early as 28 June, the UN Secretary General Trygve Lie suggested to Britain and the US that **Article 99 of the UN Charter** might be applied to the Berlin Crisis as it threatened the 'maintenance of international peace and security'.

The issue was discussed by the Security Council in October and the President of the Council created a mediating committee with Security Council representatives from Belgium, Canada, China, Columbia and Syria. On 22 October, they proposed the immediate end of the blockade followed by a meeting of the four Military Governors to arrange for the introduction of the *Ostmark* into all Berlin. This was rejected by the Soviets on the grounds that both actions should be simultaneous. The three Western allies also rejected it because it merely referred the problem of the introduction of the *Ostmark* currency into the whole of Berlin back to the Military Governors who had recently failed to agree on this very point in the Moscow conference.

In December, the UN appointed a financial committee which suggested that the *Ostmark* shoud be the sole currency in Berlin and controlled by a new German **Bank of Emission** which would have eight representatives, five of which would be appointed by the Soviet Union. This was unacceptable to the Western allies since decisions would be made by majority vote and result in Soviet control of the Bank. In March 1949, the *Deutschmark* was introduced by the Western allies into West Berlin as its sole currency, thus rejecting Soviet and UN proposals.

End of the blockade

By the end of January 1949, it became clear that Stalin's plan to force the Western allies to abandon their plans for establishing an independent West Germany was failing. The winter of 1948–49 was exceptionally mild and, thanks to the effective deployment of the large US transport aircraft, the average daily deliveries for West Berlin in January was 5620 tons. By April, this reached 8000 tons per day.

The Soviets were not prepared to go to war over Berlin and, in an interview with a US journalist on 31 January, Stalin made a considerable concession. He indicated that he would make the lifting of the blockade dependent only on calling another meeting of the Council of Foreign Ministers. The US responded and talks began between the Soviet and US Security Council representatives at the United Nations in New York. On 4 May, they finally reached agreement that the blockade would end on 12 May and that eleven days later a Council of Foreign Ministers would convene in Paris to discuss both the future of Germany and the Berlin currency question. On neither issue did the Council produce a breakthrough, but the four states approved the New York agreement on lifting the blockade and agreed to discuss how the situation in Berlin could be resolved.

The emergence of the two German states

The future shape of Germany was effectively decided by the end of 1948. Stalin failed to deter the Western allies from pressing ahead with their plans for establishing the **Federal Republic of Germany (FRG)** and in the end he had little option but to create a communist East Germany, the **German Democratic Republic (GDR)**, as a counterweight and alternative to the FRG. The division of Germany, however, was not complete. Berlin, even though it was deep inside the GDR, remained under Four-Power control and there were still no physical internal divisions within the city.

KEY TERM

Bank of Emission The bank responsible for the issue of a currency.

Federal Republic of Germany (FRG) Capitalist state established in western Germany in 1949 following the Berlin Blockade, which involved amalgamating the British, US and French zones of occupation.

German Democratic Republic (GDR) Communist state set up in eastern Germany in 1949 following the Berlin Blockade.

←
To what extent was the GDR set up in response to the creation of the FRG?

The Federal Republic of Germany (FRG)

The West German constitution was approved in the spring of 1949 by the three Western allies and elections for the new parliament, the *Bundestag*, took place in August. Konrad Adenauer became the first West German Chancellor. The FRG was, however, not fully independent. The Occupation Statute (see page 75), which came into force in September, replaced the military government in the former Western zones with a **High Commission**. This still gave Britain, France and the US the final say on West German foreign policy, security questions, exports and many other matters.

The German Democratic Republic (GDR)

In the winter of 1948–49, the Soviets were reluctant to create a separate East German state if there was still a chance of preventing the creation of West Germany. They continued to hope that a neutral or pro-Soviet Germany would be established which would never threaten the security of the Soviet Union. Stalin was initially prepared only temporarily to give the Soviet zone a greater degree of independence so that eventual Germany unity would not be prevented. He feared that the creation of an East German state would make the division of Germany final, with the larger, most industrialized, and wealthiest section under the control of the Western allies.

Throughout the spring and summer of 1949, Walther Ulbricht, the leader of the SED in East Germany, claimed that only his party was working for national unity, in contrast to the separatists in the West, whom he alleged were deliberately plotting to divide Germany. To emphasize this claim, in March 1948, the SED established a German People's Council, the *Volksrat*, of 400 delegates, a quarter of whom were Communists from West Germany, to draft a constitution for a united German state. If a unified Germany proved impossible to create, then this constitution, the SED believed, would form the basis of a new alternative Germany state: East Germany.

By March 1949, the constitution of the future East German state had been drafted by the SED and approved by the People's Council. Although it resembled the constitution of West Germany, it masked the reality that East Germany would be a single-party state. In May, a parliament, the People's Congress, was elected with voters given a pre-approved list of candidates who represented SED positions, a method used throughout Soviet-dominated eastern Europe.

At the end of May, the Congress met and approved the draft constitution, but the Soviets delayed its implementation as they still hoped that the FRG might not be formed. West German elections were held in August and the German Communist Party (KPD) won only 5.7 per cent of the vote. This led Stalin to conclude that German unity was no longer possible and the creation of the East German state, the German Democratic Republic (GDR), was needed to prevent eastern Germany from uniting with the FRG. On 12 October, the government of the GDR was formed and the Soviet military occupation of the zone came to an end, although a Soviet Control Commission was set up, which, like the Allied High Commission in the West, retained considerable control over the GDR.

Berlin

The division of Germany ensured that Berlin remained a divided city within a divided state. Throughout the autumn of 1948, the SED intimidated western representatives in the Berlin City Assembly in the Soviet zone with hostile demonstrations. West Berliners responded to this in November by creating their own city government with an elected assembly that was overwhelmingly anti-communist. Once the FRG was created, Britain, France and the US permitted West Berlin to send representatives to sit in the West German parliament in Bonn, the FRG's capital, but, as the whole of Berlin was still legally under Four-Power control, they had no voting rights. Legally West Berliners were not yet citizens of the FRG. East Berlin became the capital of the new GDR. Only in 1961 was a barrier erected between East and West Berlin, the Berlin Wall (see page 168).

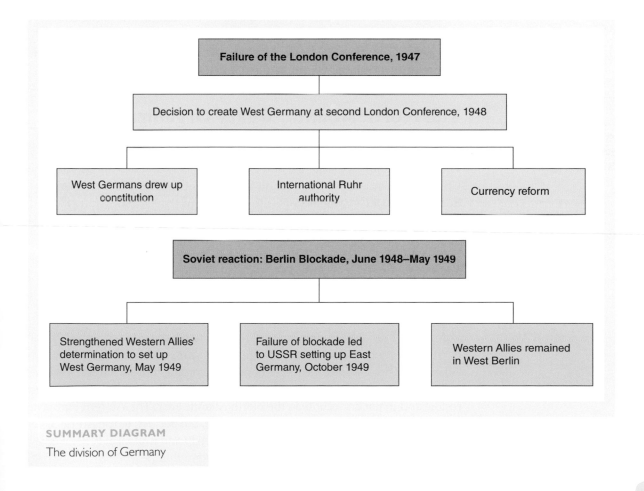

SUMMARY DIAGRAM

The division of Germany

Western European rearmament

> ▶ **Key question:** Why was western European military power strengthened, 1948–52?

KEY TERM

Consultative Council
A council on which the member states of the Brussels Pact were represented.

In January 1948, the planned creation of a West German state was viewed with deep mistrust not only in eastern Europe and the USSR, but also in many other western European countries. In an effort to calm their anxieties, Britain planned a defensive alliance against a potentially hostile Germany. In reality, as Belgian Prime Minister Paul-Henri Spaak pointed out, this defensive plan was aimed against the Soviet Union.

What were the key terms of the Brussels Pact?

The Brussels Pact

On 17 March, the Brussels Pact was signed by Belgium, Britain, France, Luxemburg and the Netherlands. The Pact promised that each of the signatory states would defend the other Pact members against any aggressor whatsoever. The treaty also contained clauses on cultural and social co-operation and a provision for creating a **Consultative Council** where Pact states could discuss mutual issues of concern. It was felt that the Pact would be more effective if the US could join it and a series of meetings led to the North Atlantic Treaty.

To what extent was NATO a compromise between European and US foreign policy aims?

The North Atlantic Treaty Organization (NATO)

The Prague coup (see page 64) and the Berlin Blockade finally persuaded the US that there was a need to commit formally to the defence of western Europe. From the spring of 1948 through to early 1949, the US gradually developed the framework for a North Atlantic–Western European military alliance with its allies in Europe. Over the course of these negotiations it became increasingly clear that the proposed North Atlantic Treaty interlocked with the plans for creating a West German state since it eased fears of a revitalized German state, particularly for France.

To persuade the US Congress to agree to commit troops to the defence of Europe, US President Truman stressed that the treaty did not oblige the US to go to war without the consent of Congress. In the end, Article 5 of the North Atlantic Treaty contained the rather imprecise wording that each treaty member 'will take such action as it deems necessary, including the use of armed force, to restore and maintain security in the North Atlantic area'. The Western European states, particularly France, found this too vague, but decided to use Article 3, which called for 'continuous and effective self-help and mutual aid', to involve the US ever more closely in the defence of western Europe.

The North Atlantic Treaty was signed on 4 April 1949 for an initial period of twenty years. It included Canada, the US, the Brussels Pact Powers, Norway, Denmark, Iceland, Italy and Portugal and it came into force in August 1949.

SOURCE E

Excerpts from the North Atlantic Treaty found at The Avalon Project of the Lillian Goldman Law Library of Yale University, US at http://avalon.law.yale.edu/20th_century/nato.asp.

Preamble:

The Parties to this Treaty … are determined to safeguard the freedom, common heritage and civilization of their peoples, founded on the principles of democracy, individual liberty and the rule of law.

They seek to promote stability and well-being in the North Atlantic area.

Article III:

In order more effectively to achieve the objectives of this treaty, the Parties, separately and jointly, by means of continuous and effective self-help and mutual aid, will maintain and develop their individual and collective capacity to resist armed attack.

Article V:

The Parties agree that an armed attack against one or more of them in Europe or North America shall be considered an attack against them all and consequently they agree that, if such an armed attack occurs, each of them, in exercise of the right of individual or collective self defence recognized by Article 51 of the Charter of the United Nations, will assist the Party or Parties so attacked by taking forthwith, individually and in concert with other Parties such action as it deems necessary including the use of armed force, to restore and maintain the security of the North Atlantic area.

Any such armed attack and all measures taken as a result thereof shall immediately be reported to the Security Council.

> According to Source E, what did the NATO require of its member states? **?**

The rearmament of the FRG

Soviet strength

Despite the foundation of NATO in April 1949, there was a strong feeling among its members in the winter of 1949–50 that they were militarily threatened by the Soviet Union and its satellite states. In August, when the USSR successfully tested its first atomic bomb, this feeling was reinforced. The Soviets, threatened by the development of NATO and the creation of the FRG, began to expand their armed forces as well. In 1948, tank production plans called for an annual increase from 1150 to 4350 tanks and production of artillery was to quadruple. Then in October, the Chinese Communist Party (CCP) drove the Nationalists, with whom they had been

> ← Why did NATO consider the rearmament of the FRG as crucial to western European security?

fighting a civil war, from mainland China to Taiwan (see page 114). China was now a communist state, and a new, powerful ally to the Soviets.

Limited western European integration

Western European integration developed only slowly. NATO was still in its infancy and there were lingering fears of eventual German domination among western European states. This stopped the US from building up the new Federal Republic of Germany's economic and military strength to a point where it could play a major role in the defence of western Europe. Until the FRG was fully integrated into a western European economic and military system, the US believed it was still possible that the Soviets might be able to persuade the West German people that a neutral, but unified, Germany was preferable to a Germany divided. If the West Germans, who now had their own parliament, voted for neutrality and reunification with the GDR, short of using military force, the Western allies would have to accept it. In such a situation, the danger for the US and its allies would be that a neutral Germany, with its economic resources and population of 80 million, would be open to Soviet influence and pressure and therefore only temporarily neutral.

The impact of the Korean War

The Korean War changed the situation dramatically. The invasion of South Korea by communist North Korean troops on 25 June 1950 (see page 120) appeared to many in western Europe and the US to be a prelude to a new global conflict in which the Soviets would finally overrun western Europe. It was assumed that North Korea acted under Stalin's orders and this fear was reinforced when East Germany's leader, Ulbricht, not only supported North Korean aggression, but appeared to recommend similar action as a way of unifying Germany. The creation of a new East German **paramilitary police force** of some 60,000 men gave some substance to these threats.

SOURCE F

An excerpt from *Geschichte der DDR [History of the GDR] 1948–1985*, by Dietrich Staritz, published by Surkamp, Frankfurt, Germany, 1985, p. 66. (translated by the author).

At the third Party Conference [of the SED] in July 1950 Pieck [President of the GDR] demanded : 'we must end the idea that certain people in our Party concentrate only on our Republic [GDR] and neglect our duties towards the whole of Germany'. And Grotewohl [Prime Minister] referred to the 'historic telegramme from Stalin' at the time of the foundation of the GDR, in which the eastern state [GDR] was defined as foundation stone for a united … Germany: [he continued] 'it is therefore obvious that we should not limit ourselves to the successes of the GDR. Rather it must be the whole of Germany'. Ulbricht [Head of the East German Communist Party] stressed that this campaign had a good chance of succeeding: 'In West Germany', he insisted, 'a situation is developing in which all sections of the population are coming together in opposition to the colonization policies of US imperialism'.

KEY TERM

Paramilitary police force
Police force that is armed with machine guns and armoured cars.

?

What information does Source F convey about the intentions of the GDR leadership towards the FRG?

The European Defence Community

← **Why did it take so long for the EDC treaty to be signed?**

In light of the Korean War and Ulbricht's statements, West German rearmament was viewed as essential to strengthen the defences of western Europe. France, however, continued to have reservations about creating a strong and independent FRG. Consequently, on 24 October 1950, the French Prime Minister, René Pleven, proposed the formation of the European Defence Community (EDC); this was known as the Pleven Plan. Its purpose was to create a European army under supranational control with a European Minister of Defence responsible to a European Assembly which would be appointed by the participating governments. To ensure that the FRG was kept under control its troops would join not in divisions (units of about 10,000 troops) but instead in battalions (much smaller units composed of only about 800 troops).

SOURCE G

An excerpt from *Memoirs, 1945–1950*, by Konrad Adenauer, published by Weidenfeld and Nicholson, London, UK, 1965, pp. 274–275.

Chancellor Adenauer's account of a conference with the three Allied High Commissioners on 17 August 1950:

I raised the subject of security … I … begged the High Commissioners to intercede with their governments for some demonstration of military strength that might restore people's confidence in the possibility of resistance …

I noted that Pieck and Ulbricht had repeatedly declared their intention of 'liberating' West Germany, and if these statements were taken in conjunction with military preparation currently being carried out by the Soviet Zone [GDR] police, there could be no doubt about their purpose.

What information is conveyed by Source G about Adenauer's assessment of the East German threat? **?**

The Spofford Compromise

Militarily, the first version of the Pleven Plan was unworkable. It was essentially a French plan aimed more at controlling German rearmament than at military effectiveness. The British refused to join and only Belgium and Luxemburg showed any real interest, while the US felt that it was military nonsense. However, after prolonged discussions, a workable compromise was realized that would ultimately enable German troops to be recruited. Charles Spofford, the deputy US representative on NATO's Atlantic Council, suggested that, while the political problems caused by the EDC proposal were being sorted out, certain practical steps to strengthen defences in Western Europe, 'upon which there already exist large measure of agreement', should be taken immediately. This was accepted by both France and Britain and the other NATO members, and from this emerged the Spofford Compromise. This proposed that, parallel with the creation of a European army, NATO itself would create an integrated force in Europe. In it would serve medium-sized German units, which would be subject to tight supervision by the Western allies.

Strains within NATO, December 1950–June 1951

At first it seemed as though the Spofford Compromise had broken the deadlock over German rearmament. Preliminary negotiations about establishing the EDC began in Paris in February 1951, and at the same time Adenauer began to discuss plans with the Western allies for creating twelve West German divisions for NATO. The Western powers also began to normalize relations with the FRG. They officially terminated the state of war with Germany and opened negotiations to replace the Occupation Statute (see page 75) with a more appropriate treaty which recognized the FRG's new status.

Throughout the first half of 1951, the West German rearmament question and US policy in Korea (see page 122) put an immense strain on the unity of the alliance. France and many other of the smaller western European states dreaded German rearmament, while the US's allies in NATO were worried that it would use nuclear weapons in Korea and so trigger a third world war.

West German rearmament

In Western Germany, the Social Democrat Party bitterly attacked Adenauer's intention to join the EDC on the grounds that this would permanently divide Germany. He therefore attempted to negotiate for more independence with the Western allies in order to convince his electorate that rearmament would lead to the FRG being given equality of treatment by its former occupiers. This, of course, frightened French public opinion, which would not allow their government to make any more concessions to the Germans.

Disagreements about Korea and China

The escalating conflict in Korea put further pressure on the Alliance. When troops from the communist People's Republic of China (PRC) came to the assistance of North Korea in November 1950, western Europeans were alarmed by rumours that the US would retaliate by dropping nuclear bombs on the PRC, and feared that this would lead to an all-out war and the withdrawal of US troops from Europe. Britain's Prime Minister Clement Attlee, with the support of the French government, tried to persuade the US to open negotiations with the PRC. President Truman refused on the grounds that he could not **appease** communism in Asia while containing it in Europe, but he did reassure him that the atomic bomb would not be used.

Once the PRC had sent troops into North Korea, it was clear that the war would continue into the indefinite future. This strengthened the Republican Party in the US Congress; they believed that the US should take a more aggressive stance against both the USSR and the PRC. This forced Truman, a Democrat, to make rearmament his government's overriding priority so that the Korean War could be ended and further action as called for by Republicans would not be necessary.

KEY TERM

Appease To conciliate a potential aggressor by making concessions.

Franco-German agreement on the EDC

In October 1951, as a result of US pressure, detailed negotiations on the EDC started in Paris. Simultaneously, talks began in Bonn, the capital of the FRG, between the High Commissioners and the West German Chancellor, Konrad Adenauer, on replacing the Occupation Statute with a treaty which recognized the FRG's new status as a semi-independent state. Both sets of negotiations proved complicated and continued slowly until May 1952.

In Bonn, the negotiations centred on how much independence the Western allies were ready to give the FRG. In Paris, the key issue was still French determination to prevent Germany from becoming a major military power again. France vetoed German membership in NATO and insisted on restricting the size of German units that could be integrated into the EDC. The General Treaty that replaced the Occupation Statute was signed on 26 May 1952, and the EDC Treaty a day later in Paris. Afterwards, there was a long, unsuccessful struggle to have the treaties **ratified** by the national parliaments of France and West Germany (see page 144).

Financing West European rearmament

As we have seen, the Korean War and the Soviet development of the atomic bomb forced US President Truman to make rearmament his government's overriding priority in Europe. The US began to develop the **hydrogen bomb** shortly after the outbreak of the Korean War and tripled military spending. Marshall Aid was at first diverted to those western European industries that were vital for rearmament and then, in 1951, stopped altogether in favour of a direct military assistance programme. The sheer expense of rearmament threatened to destabilize NATO at a time when the threat from the Soviet bloc appeared to be growing.

The economic and political costs of rearmament

In western Europe, NATO states increased their expenditure on rearmament from \$4.4 billion in 1949 to \$8 billion in 1951. This initially triggered a boom in industrial production, but expensive raw materials such as coal, copper and rubber had to be imported in considerable quantities causing inflation and serious **balance of payments** problems. Between July 1950 and June 1951, inflation caused a significant increase in the cost of living. Costs rose by 20 per cent in France and 10 per cent in Italy, Britain, and the FRG, while wages did not increase as significantly.

There was also evidence that the shift in investment from civilian to defence production and the higher taxes to pay for this were undermining political stability. In Britain, a serious split developed in April 1951 in the Labour cabinet over the cost of rearmament, while in the French and Italian elections of May and June 1951, both communists and the conservative nationalist parties made a strong showing against incumbent governments. In the FRG, there were signs that ultra-nationalists were strengthening as a result of this economic stress, particularly during the state elections in Lower Saxony.

KEY TERM

Ratify When an international treaty has been signed, it can come into effect only after the parliaments of the signatory states have ratified (i.e. approved) it.

Hydrogen bomb A nuclear bomb hundreds of times more powerful than an atomic bomb.

Balance of payments The difference between the earnings of exports and the cost of imports.

How were the economic problems caused by the rearmament programmes of 1950–51 overcome?

T O K

States competing in the Cold War spent huge sums on their militaries while neglecting, in varying amounts, public health care, education and better living conditions. To what extent can any government act ethically? (Ethics, History, Emotion, Language, Reason)

KEY TERM

Guns and butter Phrase used initially in the US press in 1917 to describe the production of nitrates both for peaceful and military purposes; now usually used to describe the situation when a country's economy can finance both increased military and consumer goods production.

Why did the USSR fail to stop West German rearmament?

Guns and butter

The Organization for European Economic Co-operation (OEEC) was convinced that western Europe faced a great economic crisis that could only be solved by a second Marshall Plan. While it was unrealistic to expect any help on this scale from the US as it was spending vast sums on its own rearmament programme, the OEEC and NATO did co-operate in a successful attempt to ensure that rearmament did not stifle the economic recovery of western Europe. In August, the OEEC called for a dramatic 25 per cent expansion of western Europe's industrial production over the coming five years. It proposed financing both rearmament and increased consumer goods production. This was summarized as a policy of the production of both '**guns and butter**'. Steadily growing demand for industrial goods and vehicles helped make this plan successful. For the next twenty years, western Europe enjoyed a period of unparalleled prosperity which in turn encouraged further economic and political integration and consolidated the Western bloc.

Stalin's response to rearmament

Stalin attempted to counter the threat of NATO and German rearmament in two ways. He:

- launched the communist-led World Peace Movement, which campaigned for disarmament and world peace (see page 92)
- offered the FRG the prospect of joining a neutral united Germany.

From the autumn of 1950, until the spring of 1952, Stalin put forward a series of initiatives aimed at achieving a united but neutral Germany. In March 1952, in a note to Western allies, he made a far-reaching proposal for free elections in Germany supervised by a commission of the four former occupying powers. This would lead to the establishment of an independent Germany. The new, reunified Germany would be neutral, and so would not be able to join the EDC or NATO. It would also not be burdened with reparations and could have a limited military force.

This offer was rejected by the US and its allies, including Adenauer, as they believed that a neutral Germany would eventually fall into the Soviet sphere of influence, which would then benefit from Germany's industrial resources and large population.

SOURCE H

An excerpt from 'Stalin's Plans for post-War Germany' by Wilfried Loth in *The Soviet Union and the Cold War, 1945–53*, ed. F. Gori and S. Pons, published by Palgrave Macmillan, Basingstoke, UK, p. 31.

The leadership of the GDR's Socialist Unity Party (SED) met the Soviet government in Moscow in April 1952 to discuss the response of the Western allies to Stalin's note. Stalin was reported by one of the SED leaders as saying:

? According to Source H, why was Stalin's proposal for free elections in Germany rejected?

Comrade Stalin considers that irrespective of any proposals that we can make on the German question, the Western powers will not agree with them and will not withdraw from Germany in any case. It will be a mistake to think that a compromise might emerge or that the Americans will agree with the draft of the peace treaty. The Americans need their army in West Germany to hold Western Europe in their hands. They say that their army is to defend [the Germans]. But the real goal of this army is to control Europe. The Americans will draw West Germany into the Atlantic Pact. They will create West German troops. Adenauer is in the pocket of the Americans … in reality there is an independent state being formed in West Germany. And you must organize your own state. The line of demarcation between East and West Germany must be seen as a frontier and not as a simple border but a dangerous one. One must strengthen the protection of this frontier.

SOURCE I

The SED celebrating its second party conference in July 1952.

> What information is contained in Source I that is important for a historian? **?**

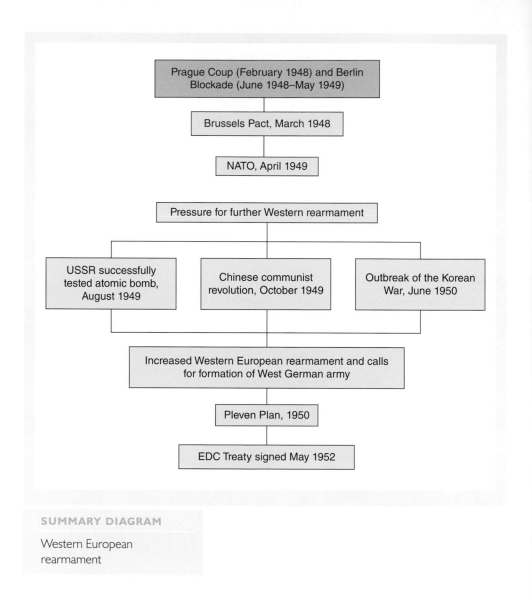

Prague Coup (February 1948) and Berlin Blockade (June 1948–May 1949)

Brussels Pact, March 1948

NATO, April 1949

Pressure for further Western rearmament

USSR successfully tested atomic bomb, August 1949

Chinese communist revolution, October 1949

Outbreak of the Korean War, June 1950

Increased Western European rearmament and calls for formation of West German army

Pleven Plan, 1950

EDC Treaty signed May 1952

SUMMARY DIAGRAM

Western European rearmament

The consolidation of the rival blocs

▶ *Key question: How did the polarization of Europe into two rival blocs accelerate during the years 1950–52?*

> **What was the political and economic significance of the ECSC?**

Western economic integration

Western integration was determined by two key factors. On the one hand, the US intended, as historian Michael Hogan has argued, to rebuild western Europe in the image of the US; they hoped that a European political and economic union would create a United States of Europe. The US government was convinced that once an economically integrated and politically united western Europe existed, it would rapidly become as wealthy as the US. This would:

- deter people from wanting communist government
- significantly boost world trade
- provide valuable markets for US exports
- eventually draw the eastern European states out of the Soviet bloc.

On the other hand, France and the smaller European states saw Western political and economic integration as providing the key to harnessing the great industrial resources of the FRG to the defence of western Europe against communism and the USSR, without running the risk of resurrecting a strong Germany.

Britain, however, refused to commit itself to further integration with Europe and, instead, insisted on cultivating its close links with the US and the British **Commonwealth**. The British government put forward the alternative strategy of using NATO as a means of rearming West Germany and of aligning it firmly with the Western powers within NATO, rather than within an integrated western European political and economic framework. France was unconvinced by this argument. It feared that within NATO, West Germany would be able to develop its vast economic strength unchecked and, once the Cold War was over, France would once again be confronted with a strong Germany which had invaded it twice already in the twentieth century.

 **KEY TERM**

Commonwealth
Organization of states formerly part of the British Empire.

The European Coal and Steel Community (ECSC)

In May 1950 France's Foreign Minister Robert Schuman announced a plan to create the European Coal and Steel Community (ECSC). The Schuman Plan, as it was called, would enable the Western allies to exploit Germany's coal and steel resources for their own rearmament programmes without running the risk of simultaneously building a strong and independent West Germany. It was received enthusiastically by Adenauer, the West German Chancellor, as he realized that only through integration could West Germany forge a partnership with the Western allies and gain security from the Soviet threat. Italy and the Benelux states also welcomed it, but Britain, not wishing to lose control of its own coal and steel industries (which the Labour government had only just nationalized), was not willing to join.

The ECSC was formed in July 1952 and replaced the International Ruhr Authority (see page 75) with a new supranational organization, controlled by the six member states: the Benelux countries, France, Italy and the FRG. The ECSC regulated all their coal and steel industries, guaranteeing that the economic needs of each member for these vital raw materials would be met. The ECSC laid the foundations for western European economic, and ultimately political, integration. Together with the military security that NATO provided, it immeasurably strengthened the Western bloc.

The consolidation of the Eastern bloc, 1948–52

From 1948, communists dominated the governments of what became known as Eastern bloc states (see Chapter 2, pages 61–65). Theoretically each state within the Soviet bloc remained independent, but all adopted identical cultural, military, economic and social policies. To further encourage and support closer relations between the various communist states in the Eastern bloc, the Soviets created two supranational organizations: Cominform and COMECON.

Cominform

Cominform, the Communist Information Bureau (see page 59), was established in September 1947 to promote ideological unity among the communist parties in Europe. All the Soviet bloc communist parties joined, as did the French and Italian parties. Its main task was to complete the **Sovietization** of the Soviet satellite states, to co-ordinate the activities of the communist parties in both the Soviet bloc and throughout the world, and to combat what was termed 'Titoism'.

Cominform and the Peace Movement

In November 1949, Cominform was given the task of mobilizing a Soviet-backed peace movement. At a time when rearmament was causing severe strains on the western European economies, Stalin intended to use the peace movement to appeal to the fears of many in western Europe, who dreaded the outbreak of a third world war. He hoped that this would lead to a backlash against NATO and Adenauer's government in the FRG.

In 1949, with assistance from Cominform, the World Committee for the Partisans for Peace was created to organize the Peace Movement. In early 1951, it handed this task to a World Peace Council elected by the Soviet-dominated Congress of the Partisans of Peace. In March 1950, the Council launched its Stockholm Appeal demanding the banning of the atomic bomb and the condemnation as war criminals of whichever government used it first in conflict. The campaign was supported mainly by Soviet bloc countries. NATO governments viewed it with considerable suspicion. The British Prime Minister Attlee, for instance, called it 'a bogus forum of peace with the real aim of sabotaging national defence'. Because of its strong links with the USSR, it had little impact on NATO states.

COMECON

The Council for Mutual Economic Assistance (COMECON) was founded in 1949 by the USSR, Bulgaria, Czechoslovakia, Hungary, Poland and Romania and joined in 1950 by the GDR. In western Europe and the US, it was seen as the Soviet response to the Marshal Plan. Its main task was to integrate the economies of eastern Europe with the USSR, but initially the organization existed only in name. It was not until 1954 that a secretariat was established and only in 1959 was the organization given more authority and became better organized. Although there was no effective economic integration in the Soviet bloc until after 1959, the individual states broadly followed the Soviet pattern of economic development:

KEY TERM

Sovietization
Reconstructing a state according to the Soviet model.

Titoism Communism as defined by Tito in Yugoslavia.

- Agriculture was collectivized.
- Centralized economies were established.
- **Five Year Plans** laid the foundations for large-scale industrialization.

What information do the tables in Sources J and K convey about the economies of eastern Europe?

SOURCE J

Collectivization of agriculture in eastern Europe, compiled from *Eastern Europe since 1945* by G. Swain and N. Swain, published by Palgrave Macmillan, Basingstoke, UK, 1993, p. 101.

Country	Started	Slowed/halted	Completed
Albania	1948	1953–57	1966
Bulgaria	1945	1953–55	1958
Czechoslovakia	1948	1953–55	1958
GDR	1952	1953–55	1960
Hungary	1948	1953–58	1961
Poland	1948	1956	–
Romania	1948	–	1962
Yugoslavia	1945	1953	–

SOURCE K

State control of industrial output and trade in 1952, compiled from *Eastern Europe since 1945* by G. Swain and N. Swain, published by Palgrave Macmillan, Basingstoke, UK, 1993, p. 102.

Country	Industry (% controlled by state)	Trade (% controlled by state)
Albania	98	88
Bulgaria	100	98
Czechoslovakia	98	97
GDR	77	54
Hungary	97	82
Poland	99	93
Romania	97	76

Soviet control of Eastern Europe

The only effective ties strengthening the bloc were the network of **bilateral** treaties of friendship, co-operation and mutual assistance signed between the USSR and the individual satellite states and also between these states themselves. Each of these treaties contained the following agreements:

- a mutual defence agreement
- a ban on joining a hostile alliance, such as NATO
- recognition of equality, sovereignty and non-interference in each other's internal affairs (although in practice this did not deter the USSR from intervening in the domestic policies of its satellites).

The Soviets achieved obedience by frequently summoning the leaders of the Eastern bloc states to Moscow for talks and instruction, and also through the

KEY TERM

Five Year Plan Plan to modernize and expand the economy over a five-year period.

Bilateral Between two states.

direct participation of Soviet ambassadors and advisors in the internal affairs of the satellites. Red Army garrisons were maintained throughout eastern Europe to provide defence, as well as to ensure that governments remained under Soviet control. The armed forces of the satellite states, unlike the NATO armies, also formed a completely integrated system controlled by the Soviets. Each army was issued with Soviet equipment, training manuals and armaments. Military uniforms and equipment in the Eastern bloc were identical and Soviet military commanders were placed in charge of all forces.

The cult of Stalin

The **Stalin cult** was also a unifying factor in the Eastern bloc. He was celebrated everywhere as the builder of Socialism in the USSR and the liberator of eastern Europe in the Second World War. Political leaders were expected to model themselves on Stalin and the societies and economies of the satellite states had to follow the Soviet example.

KEY TERM

Stalin cult The propaganda campaign vaunting Stalin as the great ruler and saviour of the USSR.

? What does Source L suggest about the Stalin cult?

SOURCE L

An excerpt from *God's Playground. A History of Poland*, by Norman Davies, published by OUP, Oxford, UK, 2005, p. 436.

The habits of Stalinism penetrated into every walk of life [in Poland]. Statues of Stalin appeared in public places. The Republic's leading industrial centre, Katowice, was renamed 'Stalinogrod'. Everything and anything from the Palace of Culture in Warsaw downwards was dedicated to 'the name of J.V. Stalin'. Soviet civilization was upheld as the universal paragon [model of excellence] of virtue … Nonconformity of any sort was promptly punished. The militiaman and the petty bureaucrat walked tall.

What caused the Yugoslav–Soviet split?

The Yugoslav–Soviet Split

By 1949, not only was Europe divided into two blocs, but within the Eastern bloc there also emerged a split between the USSR and Yugoslavia. Although Tito, the communist ruler of Yugoslavia, had been publically praised in September 1947 as one of the USSR's most loyal and effective allies, Stalin had reservations about him. Stalin was critical of Yugoslavian attempts to play an independent role in the Balkans.

In the course of the winter of 1947–48, the friction between the Soviets and the Yugoslavs increased as Tito alarmed Stalin with talk of forming a Balkan Federation which would include Greece, Bulgaria and Romania. The leaders of both Bulgaria and Romania responded enthusiastically to these proposals. Tito also stationed Yugoslav troops in Albania to protect Greek communist guerrilla camps without consulting either Stalin or Enver Hoxha, the communist Albanian leader. Stalin feared that not only would Tito's activities make the Yugoslav Communist Party the strongest force in the Balkans, which the USSR would be unable to manipulate, but they would also provoke the US at a time of escalating tension over Germany.

The break with Stalin

Communist Party officials from Bulgaria and Yugoslavia were summoned to Moscow in February 1948. Stalin specifically vetoed the stationing of Yugoslav troops in Albania and, instead of the wider federation favoured by Tito, proposed a smaller Bulgarian–Yugoslav union. The two states were required to commit themselves to regular consultations with Soviet officials on foreign policy questions in an effort to prevent independent action. Tito, however, refused to subordinate his foreign policy to the Soviet Union and rejected union with Bulgaria on these terms. He feared that, given Soviet influence there, the union would merely be a way for the Soviets to take control of the Yugoslavian government. Stalin reacted to this open defiance of his leadership by withdrawing Soviet advisors and personnel from Yugoslavia and accused its leaders of being political and ideological criminals.

Stalin pressured other Eastern bloc states to support the Soviet decision to isolate Yugoslavia and in June 1948, at the second Cominform meeting, the entire Eastern bloc, along with western European communists, expelled Yugoslavia from the organization. Yugoslavia was the first communist state to act independently of the Soviet Union.

Soviet attempts to remove Tito

Initially Stalin hoped that the Yugoslav Communist Party would overthrow Tito, but Tito rapidly purged the Party of pro-Cominform suspects. Soviet attempts to assassinate Tito were also unsuccessful, as were attempts to apply economic pressure through a **trade embargo**. Finally, Stalin started to apply military pressure by concentrating troops on Yugoslavia's borders. According to a Hungarian general who fled to the West, plans were actually created for a Soviet invasion of Yugoslavia, but abandoned when the outbreak of the Korean War indicated that the US and NATO might respond in force.

Tito and the West

These threats led Tito to turn to the West for assistance. Tito abandoned his support for Greek communist rebels and in return received arms and financial assistance from Britain and the US. Close links developed between the **CIA** and the Yugoslavian secret service. In 1954, Yugoslavia, Greece and Turkey, both of whom were NATO members, signed the Balkan Mutual Defence Pact aimed at the USSR and its allies.

Yugoslavia also distanced itself ideologically from the USSR. Tito broke with the Soviet model of centralized control over the economy, and instead in 1950 began to experiment with workers' self-management of factories. This, in theory, enabled the workers to manage and operate their own factories through elected workers' councils. Prices were no longer fixed by the government after 1952 and businesses were able to export their products without government involvement. The state did, however, retain control of the banking system and industrial investment.

 **KEY TERM**

Trade embargo
A suspension of trade.

CIA The Central Intelligence Agency was established by the US in 1947 to conduct counter-intelligence operations outside the United States.

How successful were
Western attempts to
destabilize the Soviet
bloc in the period
1949–52?

→ Western attempts to destabilize the Soviet bloc

Tito's break with the USSR in 1948 demonstrated that the unity of the Soviet bloc was more fragile than it appeared to many observers. This encouraged NATO to explore various ways of weakening the USSR's position in eastern Europe:

- The US and Britain gave military and economic assistance to Yugoslavia (see above).
- Between 1949 and 1952 there was a series of unsuccessful operations by the US and Britain to remove Albania's communist leader Enver Hoxha as a step towards replacing its Soviet-sponsored government.
- Attempts were made to undermine Soviet authority by constantly filing complaints to the United Nations about human rights abuses in the Eastern bloc.
- Eastern European refugees were helped financially, so as to encourage others to flee from the Soviet bloc.
- Radio Free Europe, which broadcasted anti-Soviet propaganda to eastern European states, was sponsored by the US government.

All these measures were aimed at weakening Soviet power in eastern Europe over the long term. Neither the USSR, nor the US and its NATO allies, were ready to risk war. It was the Far East where the triumph of communism in China posed new and dangerous challenges to the US and the European colonial powers, as we will see in the next chapter.

SUMMARY DIAGRAM

The consolidation of
the rival blocs

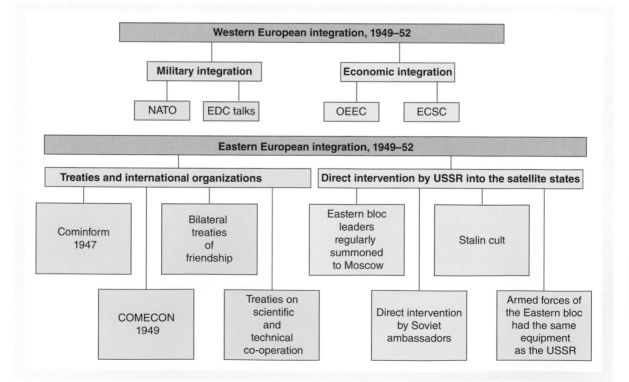

Chapter summary

The division of Germany and Europe 1948–52

After the failure of the Conference of Foreign Ministers in London in December 1947, Four-Power co-operation on the future of Germany disappeared. By June 1948, the US and its allies had decided to:

- allow the Germans in the three western zones of occupation to draft a constitution for a West German state
- strengthen this future state by introducing a new currency – the *Deutschmark*, and
- place the Ruhr industries under the control of the International Ruhr Authority.

Stalin was determined to halt the plans of the Western allies for creating an independent West Germany by blockading West Berlin. He assumed that it would be impossible to supply Berlin during the winter months. The blockade was, however, broken by the airlift, and called off on 12 May 1949. The constitution of the FRG was agreed in May 1949, and in August its first government was formed. In response, the GDR was created in October. Berlin remained under Four-Power control.

The division of Germany intensified the Cold War. The Western powers created NATO and began the process of western European integration which aimed to strengthen western Europe:

- The USA began to develop the hydrogen bomb and its allies increased their armed forces.
- The EDC Treaty was agreed but not ratified.
- The ECSC was formed.

These last two measures aimed to strengthen the Atlantic alliance by integrating the FRG firmly into a western European economic and military structure.

The USSR also responded to the growing hostility between the Western and Eastern blocs by:

- successfully testing an atom bomb and increasing its armed forces
- tightening its grip on the Soviet bloc through COMECON and Cominform, and
- launching the communist-led World Peace Movement.

In 1952, Stalin appeared to offer the prospect of German reunification, provided Germany remained neutral. The Western allies rejected the proposal because they feared a neutral Germany would be vulnerable to Soviet pressure. Consequently, Europe remained divided into two blocs. In the Western bloc, it can be argued that the US, to quote the historian Geir Lundestad, created 'an empire by invitation' to defend the western European states from the Soviet threat. The Eastern bloc was controlled by Soviet military power. Only Yugoslavia was able to establish a regime, which although communist, was independent of the USSR. It received covert financial and military aid from the US.

✓ Examination advice

How to answer 'evaluate' questions

For questions that contain the command term 'evaluate', you are asked to make judgements. You should judge the available evidence and identify and discuss the most convincing elements of the argument while also explaining the limitations of other elements.

Example

> Evaluate the impact of the North Atlantic Treaty Organization (NATO) on the Cold War from 1948 to 1952.

1. For this question you should aim to make a judgement about the degree to which the North Atlantic Treaty Organization impacted on the Cold War between 1948 and 1952. You will need to evaluate the various aspects of the Cold War that NATO affected. These should be in order of the degree to which they made an impact, with the most important coming first. Since the Cold War involved the Soviet Union and its allies as well as the US and its allies, you will need to make sure that you cover the impact of NATO's creation on each bloc. Remember, the impact could be political, economic, military or others.

2. Before writing the answer you should write an outline – allow around five minutes to do this. For this question, you need to come up with at least three to four different issues that NATO's creation affected. Among them could be:

Effects on US/allies
- *Integration of W. European economy, incl. W. Germany.*
- *Creation of W. Germany and rearmament generally.*
- *Tensions within NATO alliance:*
  - *fear that US will drag Europe into war over Korea, etc.*
  - *France/others anxious about rearming Germany.*

Effects on USSR/allies
- *Integration of E. Europe and USSR militaries:*
  - *mutual defence treaties*
  - *ban on joining NATO*
  - *Soviet troops stationed in E. Europe.*
- *COMECON.*
- *Yugoslavia resists increased Soviet control.*

---

3. In your introduction, you should introduce what NATO was, such as its membership and purpose, as well as when it was created. Then, briefly review the key ideas that you will present in the essay. An example of a good introductory paragraph for this question is given below.

The North Atlantic Treaty Organization (NATO) was created in 1948 to defend western Europe from a possible attack by the Soviet Union and its allies in eastern Europe. Many nations joined the military alliance, but it was dominated by the US, with significant participation by France, Britain, and western Germany. The creation of NATO affected its members, as well as the Soviet Union and its allies, to a great extent. To strengthen this new alliance, West Germany was organized and rearmed, a controversial decision among NATO participants. To prevent West Germany from leaving the alliance and to help pay for general rearmament throughout the alliance, the economy of western Europe was further integrated. The Soviet Union responded to NATO's creation by further integrating its economy with communist-dominated eastern European states to help pay for its own rearmament. In conjunction with this, the Soviet Union assumed more control over eastern European military forces and stationed large numbers of its own troops throughout the region. Increasing Soviet control was resisted by Yugoslavia which soon operated with greater independence than any other communist state and which refrained from participation in any military alliances. NATO's formation had a profound impact on the Cold War from 1948 to 1952.

4. You may wish to address the impact of NATO on the Cold War thematically instead of addressing the issues of each bloc separately. The following paragraph concerns the economic effects of NATO's rearmament on western Europe. If you were to continue dealing with the economic impact of NATO's creation, you would next address the economic effects of NATO on the Soviet-led bloc in eastern Europe.

NATO's creation significantly affected western Europe economically. In order for NATO to be an effective military organization, it needed modern weaponry in large quantities in order to counter the huge number of troops the Soviets would be able to field with their allies. Military expense of NATO grew from $4.9 billion in 1949, the year after its official creation, to $8 billion just two years later in 1951. Much of western Europe had already begun to receive US financial assistance through the Marshall Plan which began in 1948 and advocated multinational economic ventures and sharing of resources. The financial stress of rearmament added further impetus to western European economic *integration so that western Germany, France, Belgium, The Netherlands, Luxembourg, Britain and others could share resources such as coal, iron, food and electricity which would reduce and end import duties on many of these goods. In addition, more industry was developed throughout the alliance in order to provide more consumer goods as well as military equipment. This development was supported financially by the Organization for European Economic Co-operation (OEEC) and led to a 25 per cent expansion of western European industry in five years, helping to meet NATO's arms requirements while also providing more consumer goods. Increased armament by NATO, as well as the actual formation of the military alliance, caused the Soviet Union and its allies to also increase military spending and the size of their armed forces, exacerbating Cold War tensions.*

5. Your conclusion should include a judgement regarding the impact of NATO's creation on the Cold War. You may conclude that there was little impact, some impact, or a great impact. Whatever your conclusion may be, be sure to make it clear in the conclusion and that this was supported with evidence in your essay. Stronger essays will explain *why* and *how* the supporting evidence you use ties into your overall thesis. An example of a good concluding paragraph is given below.

The creation of NATO had a tremendous impact on the Cold War. In order for NATO to be successful, West Germany had to be officially formed and rearmed which led to the political and economic division of Germany and therefore the inclusion of East Germany in the Soviet bloc. The financial burden of NATO led to further integration of the western European economy which led to increased prosperity and political co-operation. The formation of NATO led the Soviets to increase their economic, political and military control of eastern Europe while also fully integrating the Soviet army with those of their allies. Soviet troops were stationed throughout eastern Europe, giving the Soviets the ability to enforce their political will on the region. NATO's creation was one of the most significant events of the Cold War from 1948 to 1952.

6. Now try writing a complete answer to the question following the advice above.

Examination practice

Below are exam questions for you to practise using content from this chapter.

1. Why was the Soviet Union unable to dominate Yugoslavia as it did other communist European states? (For guidance on how to answer 'why' questions, see page 228.)

2. Analyse the importance of the Berlin Blockade and Airlift. (For guidance on how to answer 'analyse', questions, see page 38.)

3. To what extent was the US responsible for the division of Germany into two separate states? (For guidance on how to answer 'to what extent', questions, see page 172.)

Activities

I History is about making arguments using supportive evidence. Divide into three groups. Each group should take one of the three statements below and find evidence in the chapter to support the statement.

- The Soviet Union was responsible for the division of Germany into two states by 1952.
- The United States and its allies were responsible for the division of Germany into two states by 1952.
- Both the Soviet Union and the Western allies were responsible for the division of Germany into two states by 1952.

Using the evidence you have located in support of your statement, the entire class should address the question: To what extent was the problem of Germany responsible for the Cold War?

2 Create a chart or poster that indicates the differences and similarities between US/allies and Soviet/allies regarding Europe and Germany after the Second World War up to 1952. You may wish to do this in the form of a Venn diagram.

3 Answer the following question in class or for homework: What was the importance of the atomic and hydrogen bombs in international diplomacy up to 1952?

CHAPTER 4

The spread of communism in Asia, 1945–54

This chapter investigates the spread of communism in Asia from the end of the Second World War until the Geneva Conference which brought the Indochinese War to a conclusion in July 1954.

You need to consider the following questions throughout this chapter.

✪ How did the US occupation of Japan from 1945–52 increase Cold War tensions?

✪ To what extent did the US and USSR influence the Chinese Civil War?

✪ What caused the Korean War and how did it affect the Cold War?

✪ To what extent did the communist triumph in China help Hồ Chí Minh in Indochina?

1 Japan and the Cold War, 1945–52

> ▶ Key question: How did the US occupation of Japan from 1945–52 increase Cold War tensions?

KEY TERM

KMT (Kuomintang) Chinese Nationalist Party led by Chiang Kai-shek.

CCP Chinese Communist Party led by Mao.

French Indochina A French colony consisting of today's Laos, Cambodia, and Vietnam.

Dutch East Indies A Dutch colony that became Indonesia.

The defeat of Japan in the Second World War eliminated a power that had dominated east Asia since the early twentieth century. In China, the Second Sino-Japanese War (1937–45) weakened China's Nationalist Government (**KMT**) led by Chiang Kai-shek but strengthened the Chinese Communist Party (**CCP**). While Chinese government forces did fight the Japanese invaders, the CCP was seen by many Chinese as having fought more consistently and aggressively. Japanese occupation of former European colonies such as Malaya, **French Indochina** and the **Dutch East Indies** weakened colonial government and led to the formation of independence movements, many of which were associated with communism and called for an end to imperialism.

Why was Soviet influence in east Asia limited during the US occupation of Japan?

The US occupation of Japan

In Europe, the Soviet Union destroyed the German army, but remained uninvolved in the concurrent war in Asia and the Pacific until August 1945. At the Yalta Conference it was agreed that the USSR would declare war on Japan three months after the surrender of Germany in order to assist a likely US invasion of Japan. In return for Soviet assistance, the US consented to the restoration of land and commercial rights that Russia had possessed before its defeat by Japan in the Russo-Japanese War fought between 1904 and 1905. This meant the:

- return of the Kuril Islands and southern part of Sakhalin Island
- restoration of Port Arthur (Lushun) as a Soviet naval base, and
- control of two key railroads: the Chinese Eastern Railroad and the South Manchurian Railroad.

SOURCE A

What information is conveyed by Source A? **?**

Map of east Asia at the end of 1945 with dates of states' independence.

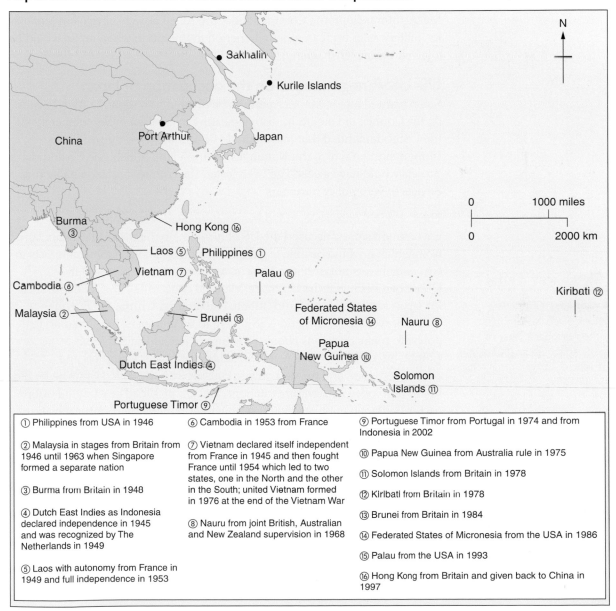

① Philippines from USA in 1946

② Malaysia in stages from Britain from 1946 until 1963 when Singapore formed a separate nation

③ Burma from Britain in 1948

④ Dutch East Indies as Indonesia declared independence in 1945 and was recognized by The Netherlands in 1949

⑤ Laos with autonomy from France in 1949 and full independence in 1953

⑥ Cambodia in 1953 from France

⑦ Vietnam declared itself independent from France in 1945 and then fought France until 1954 which led to two states, one in the North and the other in the South; united Vietnam formed in 1976 at the end of the Vietnam War

⑧ Nauru from joint British, Australian and New Zealand supervision in 1968

⑨ Portuguese Timor from Portugal in 1974 and from Indonesia in 2002

⑩ Papua New Guinea from Australia rule in 1975

⑪ Solomon Islands from Britain in 1978

⑫ Kiribati from Britain in 1978

⑬ Brunei from Britain in 1984

⑭ Federated States of Micronesia from the USA in 1986

⑮ Palau from the USA in 1993

⑯ Hong Kong from Britain and given back to China in 1997

The dropping of atomic bombs on the Japanese cities of Hiroshima and Nagasaki on 6 and 9 August (see pages 43–44) by the US rendered Soviet military assistance to defeat Japan unnecessary. The Soviets, however, were unaware of US plans to attack Japan with these weapons and began the invasion of Japanese-held Manchuria in China's north-east on 9 August. The combination of the destruction of Nagasaki and the Soviet invasion in Asia on 9 August led Japan to announce its readiness to negotiate with the Allies.

While Japan announced its unconditional surrender to the Allies on 15 August, the Soviets continued to advance into Manchuria until 26 August when northern Korea was occupied. On 28 August, US General Douglas MacArthur as Supreme Commander of the Allied Powers, arrived in Japan as its military ruler until an indefinite period in the future when Japan would be allowed to rule itself again.

US–USSR negotiations on the occupation of Japan

Stalin wanted Japan, like Germany, to be divided into separate Allied zones. At the Council of Foreign Ministers meeting in London in September 1945, the USSR demanded that Japan should be administered by an Allied Commission on which the Nationalist Chinese, the British, the US and the Soviets would have a seat. The US rejected the plan as it would enable the Soviets to veto policy decisions.

The London Conference ended in complete deadlock and the Soviet government's press accused the US of turning Japan into a US military base from which it would be able to protect its military and economic interests in east Asia. It was not until the Moscow Conference (see page 45) in December 1945, that the US made a limited concession. The Allied Council for Japan was established and Britain, **Nationalist China**, the British Commonwealth, the US and USSR were to be members, but it had no real power to make decisions about the future of Japan. The Supreme Commander, General MacArthur, retained the power to control and administer Japan and needed only to consult with the Allied Council; he did not have to obey its recommendations. The US provided most of the troops occupying Japan and was therefore able to dominate the country, dictating all policies.

KEY TERM

Nationalist China The regions of China controlled by the Nationalist Party of China led by General Chiang Kai-shek.

? What information is contained in Source B that helps the historian understand American policy in Japan, 1945–52?

SOURCE B

An excerpt from a US government document entitled 'The United States Initial Post-Surrender Policy for Japan' published on 6 September 1945, quoted in *US Department of State Bulletin*, 23 September 1945, pp. 423–427.

Although every effort will be made by consultation and by constitution of appropriate advisory bodies, to establish policies for the conduct of the occupation and control of Japan, which will satisfy the principal Allied Powers, in the event of any differences of opinion among them, the policies of the United States will govern.

US policy in Japan, 1946–52

The US transformed much of Japan's government and economy during the occupation into a liberal capitalist democracy:

- The Japanese Emperor was retained with very limited powers, while a multi-party parliamentary system of government was established.
- Large agricultural estates were dissolved and land was transferred to the peasantry to create a class of small independent farmers.
- Large industrial conglomerates, the *Zaibatsu*, were divided into separate, smaller businesses as the US believed that the Zaibatsu had encouraged and supported Japan's aggression in south-east Asia.
- Independent trades unions were developed.

In 1947, US policy in Japan changed both because the Cold War in Europe intensified and the Chinese Nationalist Government was increasingly threatened by communist forces in the Chinese Civil War, which had erupted again after Japan's defeat in 1945 (see page 112).

The emphasis was now on transforming Japan into an economic ally of the US. In 1948, a new plan for the development of the Japanese economy was unveiled and US assistance was granted to rebuild Japan's industry, despite Soviet protests that this would restore Japan's military strength. The US's intentions were to strengthen Japan's economy so that it would help prevent the formation of communist governments elsewhere in south-east Asia by encouraging regional trade and increasing prosperity.

The Treaty of Peace with Japan

Two years later, on 4 September 1951, the Treaty of Peace with Japan was signed in San Francisco between Japan and its former adversaries in the Second World War. This came into force in April 1952 and some of the clauses included:

- termination of military occupation
- end of Japanese claims to territory, rights or property in Korea, Taiwan, or China
- the right of the US to continue to use the island of Okinawa as a military base
- agreement that Japan would provide compensation to Allied civilians and prisoners-of-war who had lost property or suffered as a result of Japanese internment and human rights abuses
- reparations by Japan would be made to states affected by the war, including Vietnam, the Philippines, Burma, and Indonesia.

The USSR attended the San Francisco Conference but refused to sign the treaty. Soviet Deputy Foreign Minister Andrei Gromyko protested that the treaty aimed to transform Japan into an American military base while drawing Japan into a military alliance against the USSR. Gromyko was partly right. Japan was indeed in the US sphere of influence; only four days after the Treaty, a bilateral agreement was signed between Japan and the US which permitted the US to station troops in Japan for the purpose of defending it against a possible attack from the newly created People's Republic of China (see page 111). Japan, however, was not developed into a military power.

? What is the importance of Source C in understanding the reaction of the USSR and China to US plans to create a pro-Western and independent Japan?

SOURCE C

An excerpt from a 'Treaty of Friendship and Mutual Assistance', signed between the USSR and the People's Republic of China on 14 February 1950, quoted in *Uncertain Partners*, by S.N. Goncharov, J.W. Lewis and Xue Litai, published by Stanford University Press, Palo Alto, US, 1993, p. 260.

Article 1:

Both … Parties undertake jointly to adopt all necessary measures at their disposal for the purpose of preventing the resumption of aggression and violation of peace on the part of Japan or any other state that may collaborate with Japan directly or indirectly in acts of aggression. In the event of one … [Party] being attacked by Japan or any state allied with her and thus being involved in a state of war, the other … Party shall immediately render military and other assistance by all means at its disposal.

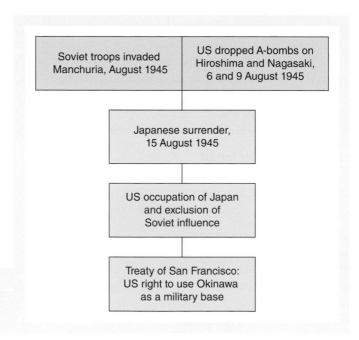

SUMMARY DIAGRAM

Japan and the Cold War, 1945–52

The Chinese Civil War

▶ **Key question:** To what extent did the US and USSR influence the Chinese Civil War?

The triumph of communist forces in China under Mao Zedong dramatically altered the character of the Cold War. The USSR gained a new and potentially powerful ally in eastern Asia which could put pressure on the US and its allies.

Nationalists and Communists in China, 1927–45

> **How did Mao seek to undermine Chiang's claim to be the leader of China?**

In 1927, General Chiang Kai-shek, the leader of the Chinese Nationalist Party, attempted to consolidate his position as the ruler of China by crushing the Chinese Communist Party (CCP) in their main stronghold in Shanghai. After this, Chiang was able to maintain a government that lasted until 1949. He did not, however, eliminate the CCP. Led by Mao Zedong, the CCP managed to establish bases in the countryside in southern China. These rural bases were eventually overrun by the government in 1934 and, in order to survive, the CCP embarked on the **Long March**, a retreat from southern to north-western China. When Japan launched a large-scale invasion of China in 1937, the CCP and the Nationalists (**KMT**) formed an uneasy anti-Japanese alliance which lasted until Japan's defeat in August 1945. At the Cairo Conference of 1943, Chiang was recognized by Britain and the US as China's leader and a key ally in their war against Japan.

The Wannan Incident, 1941

Despite the anti-Japanese alliance with the CCP, fighting between the two parties continued to erupt occasionally. Early in 1941, when troops of the Communist Fourth Army were moving their headquarters from Wannan to the north of the Yangtze River, they were attacked and destroyed by KMT forces. Only pressure from the US and USSR prevented the incident from escalating into outright civil war. The attack intensified distrust between the CCP and KMT. In 1943, Chiang published a pamphlet called 'China's Destiny' in which he argued that the CCP would have no role to play in post-war China. The CCP responded angrily by calling on the Chinese people to resist KMT dictatorship.

Mao's strategy, 1944–45

By late 1944, the strength of the CCP had greatly increased. It had an army of nearly a million people supported by an additional force of about 900,000 **militia** men, while party membership was over a million. The KMT, on the other hand, had suffered a series of devastating defeats at the hands of the Japanese in the spring and summer of 1944, which, combined with high inflation and governmental corruption in the areas it controlled, undermined Chiang's claims to be China's national leader.

> 🔑 **KEY TERM**
>
> **The Long March** A retreat by the Chinese Communist Party from southern to north-western China, covering 12,500 kilometres in approximately one year, and in which 90 per cent of all participants died.
>
> **KMT** (Kuomintang) Chinese Nationalist Party led by Chiang Kai-Shek
>
> **Militia** Part-time military reservists.

Exploiting this unpopularity at the end of 1944, the CCP decided on two new strategies:

- The CCP's best troops would penetrate into the area south of the Yangtze River to establish bases from which they would be able to confront the KMT after the war.
- In a political manoeuvre to challenge Chiang's claim to be the leader of China, Mao developed the idea of replacing Chiang's one-party dictatorship with a coalition government that included the CCP, which would then attempt to take control of key ministries.

To bring about the coalition, Mao attempted to forge links with the US which was considering using bases in China for operations against Japan. To overcome US suspicions of the CCP, he contrasted its discipline and organization with the corruption and incompetence of the KMT. The point of this was to persuade the US to bring pressure to bear on Chiang to form a coalition government with the CCP. The US initially agreed with this policy as it believed that this would stabilize China and lead to a more effective campaign against Japan.

SOURCE D

An extract from *Mao The Unknown Story*, by Jung Chang and Jon Halliday, published by Jonathan Cape, London, UK, 2005, p. 304.

In mid-1944, Roosevelt sent a mission to Yenan [where Mao was based]. Just after the Americans arrived, Mao floated the idea of changing the Party's name: 'We've been thinking of renaming our Party', he told the Russian liaison [officer] in Yenan on 12 August: 'of calling it not "Communist", but something else. Then the situation … will be more favourable, especially with the Americans …'

… Molotov [Soviet Foreign Minister] fed the same line to Roosevelt's then special envoy to China, General Patrick Hurley, telling him that in China 'Some … people called themselves "Communists" but they had no relation whatever to Communism. They were merely expressing their dissatisfaction.'

? According to Source D, why did Mao contemplate a change in the Communist Party's name?

TOK In studying the People's Republic of China, we rely on many sources of evidence. What gives any evidence value? (History, Language, Reason, Emotion)

Chiang's response

In June 1945, Chiang observed that 'Japan is our enemy abroad and the CCP is our enemy at home'. He would enter a coalition with Mao only if he were given complete control of the CCP's armed forces, a condition which Mao could hardly accept. Chiang began to blockade the areas liberated from Japanese rule in China by the CCP and sought to negotiate an agreement with Stalin, which would strengthen his position as China's leader.

The surrender of Japan, August 1945

When the USSR declared war against Japan on 8 August, Mao ordered his forces to co-operate closely with the Soviet army and occupy key cities and rail links in central and northern China, particularly the north-east. He was convinced that the Soviet entry into the war had created a new international dimension which would favour the CCP in its struggle with the KMT. He also instructed his generals and the party leaders to prepare for renewed conflict with the KMT once Japan had surrendered.

It was vital for Chiang, as the leader of China's internationally recognized government, to stop Mao from illegally occupying territory liberated from Japan by the USSR. On 12 August, he ordered the CCP forces to remain where they were and not to accept the surrender of Japan's troops. As his own army was still in southern China, he was not in a position to enforce this without Soviet and US assistance.

Soviet and US policy in China, 1945

Why were the US and USSR unable to achieve a peaceful settlement in China, 1945–46?

Initially, both Soviet and US policies in China coincided. Both assumed that the KMT would eventually reassert control over China once Japan surrendered. Both also wanted Mao to accept this and ultimately join a coalition government with Chiang. Neither the USSR nor the US understood that Mao and Chiang were not ready to compromise, and that the CCP would ultimately be much more successful than the KMT in gaining popular support for its cause in China.

The USSR

Mao and other CCP leaders were convinced that Stalin, as a communist, would never tolerate a victory by the KMT as it would benefit the US. Stalin's priority, however, was the defence of Soviet interests in China. At Yalta, in exchange for entering the war against Japan, he was promised by Churchill and Roosevelt the restoration of the economic rights which Russia had enjoyed in north-east China and Manchuria before 1905 (see page 103). He believed that only the KMT, as China's legal government, could deliver these concessions. On 14 August, Stalin signed the Sino-Soviet Treaty of Friendship and Alliance in which Chiang acknowledged the independence of Outer Mongolia, the Soviet military occupation of Port Arthur and agreed to joint control with the USSR of the Changchun Railway (formerly the Chinese Eastern Railway). In return, Stalin agreed to:

- recognize Chiang as China's leader
- recognize China's sovereignty of the former Chinese provinces conquered by Japan, and
- not assist the CCP against the KMT.

This agreement was a serious blow to Mao; it completely undermined his assumption that the USSR would prove to be a loyal ally in the struggle against the KMT.

On the same day as the Sino-Soviet treaty was signed, Chiang invited Mao to Chongqing to discuss, as he put it, 'questions related to re-establishing peace in China'. Under pressure from Stalin, Mao had little option but to agree. Stalin feared that renewed civil war would lead to Mao's defeat and ever greater involvement of the US in China.

The US

Now that the war with Japan was over, the US was concerned about the spread of Soviet influence in the Far East. It put pressure on both Chiang and Mao to negotiate a compromise agreement to stabilize China to avoid a damaging civil war which might provide the USSR with further opportunities to strengthen its position in China. When Chiang asked for assistance in taking over the territory surrendered by the Japanese, the US responded immediately by airlifting KMT troops to Nanking, Shanghai, Beijing and later to Manchuria.

The Chongqing negotiations, August–October 1945

Under the joint pressure of the US and USSR, the CCP's **Politburo** authorized Mao to meet Chiang in Chongqing on 26 August 1945. The negotiations turned out lengthy and complex. The main stumbling block continued to be whether the CCP should maintain an independent army. Chiang insisted that Mao should place all troops under the command of the government. Mao rejected this, but he was ready to reduce the number of his troops, provided the KMT did likewise. The two sides also failed to agree on a constitution for a new democratic China. By October, it was clear that the gap between the two sides was as wide as ever.

Even while the talks continued, clashes between the KMT and CCP escalated. In northern and north-eastern China, where the US had succeeded in transporting large numbers of KMT troops, several major battles took place. At this stage, it seemed as if the better equipped KMT had the upper hand.

Soviet–US tension in Manchuria

Despite the Sino-Soviet Treaty, Mao received news in late August and early September that the Soviet army of occupation in Manchuria was unofficially ready to help the CCP. After discussions between CCP commanders and a representative of Marshal Rodion Malinovsky, Commander of the Soviet forces in the region, it was agreed on 14 September that CCP forces could occupy the countryside and the smaller towns of Manchuria as long as they did not enter the cities. Significantly, the Soviets also conceded that when the time came for Soviet troops to leave Manchuria, they would not automatically hand the region over to KMT forces, but would allow the two Chinese political factions to resolve the issue themselves. Since the CCP already controlled much of Manchuria, this was a formula for allowing the CCP to establish itself in the region.

In early October, the Soviet army began to halt the movement of KMT troops into Soviet occupied areas of Manchuria, while advising the CCP to move another 300,000 troops into Manchuria. On 19 October, Mao decided to launch a campaign to control the whole of the north-east of China.

In response, Chiang informed US President Truman that the USSR's violations of the Sino-Soviet Treaty were a serious threat to peace in east Asia, and asked the US to mediate. Meanwhile, Chiang accelerated the transfer of his troops to the north-east and seized control of the Shanhaiguan Pass, a major route into Manchuria from the rest of China. US naval ships also patrolled the sea off Port Arthur which was under Soviet occupation. This appeared to the Soviets to be a deliberate provocation and there now seemed not only a danger of a full-scale civil war in China, but also of a confrontation between the US and the Soviet Union. In the face of these dangers, the USSR reduced its support to the CCP and insisted that it withdraw from the areas bordering the Chinese-Changchun railway. The CCP temporarily suspended its aim of seizing the whole of the north-east and instead concentrated on occupying the countryside and the smaller cities.

> What information does Source E relay about the relations between the Red Army and the Chinese Communist Party? **?**

SOURCE E

Soviet Red Army soldiers with CCP soldiers in Manchuria, August 1945.

The Marshall Mission

The escalation of the Chinese Civil War in the autumn of 1945 confronted the US with a major dilemma. It wanted to halt the expansion of Soviet influence in China, yet it did not want to risk military confrontation through direct intervention. US President Truman announced in December 1945 that he would continue to grant assistance to the KMT, but categorically stated that he would not intervene militarily. He also sent General Marshall, former Chief of Staff of the US army during the Second World War and later Secretary of State, to mediate between Mao and Chiang. His aim was to establish a Nationalist-dominated government in which the CCP would be represented as a minority party. Truman and Marshall continued to cling to the illusion that the CCP was not really communist and that it would rapidly become more moderate once the Chinese economy began to improve. The talks, however, achieved no break-through because both the CCP and the KMT were unwilling to compromise. Marshall left China in January 1947, but it was clear long before then that his mission would achieve nothing.

However, Marshall's insistence on a truce in the spring of 1946, just at the time when the KMT were on the verge of victory in Manchuria, enabled the CCP, with the help of the Soviets, to regroup its forces. The Soviets also made available a vast amount of captured Japanese weapons to the CCP when they left Manchuria in May 1946, while also providing officer training.

Why was the Chinese Communist Party able to win the civil war?

Defeat of the Nationalists, 1946–49

With the failure of the Marshall Mission, the civil war erupted again. In July 1946, Chiang launched a major assault, taking the key city of Zhangjiakou, and in October swept the CCP out of the Yangtze region (see map on page 113). The KMT failed to capture Manchuria where the CCP had, with Soviet assistance, established a strong base, but in the spring of 1947 the Nationalists resumed the offensive and seized Yenan, the CCP's capital. By autumn, however, the war began to favour the CCP. From December to March 1948, Mao ordered a series of offensives in Manchuria and northern China, and by autumn the CCP had advanced into central China.

Soviet assistance to the CCP, 1948–49

By spring 1948, Stalin decided that the CCP had a genuine chance of success and he sent I.V. Kovalev, the Soviet Commissar for Transportation, to oversee the repair of bridges and railways to facilitate the advance of CCP forces and to act as his contact with Mao's headquarters. However, he still kept in contact with the KMT. He was worried that a possible victory by the **Republican Party** in the US in the November 1948 elections would bring to power a president who might intervene militarily in China. Consequently, when Mao's forces moved into central and southern China where the US and Britain had strong economic interests, Stalin responded positively to a request from Chiang to mediate between the two sides. He informed Mao of

 **KEY TERM**

The Republican Party
One of the two main US political parties.

SOURCE F

Map of China showing the major battles of the Chinese Civil War.

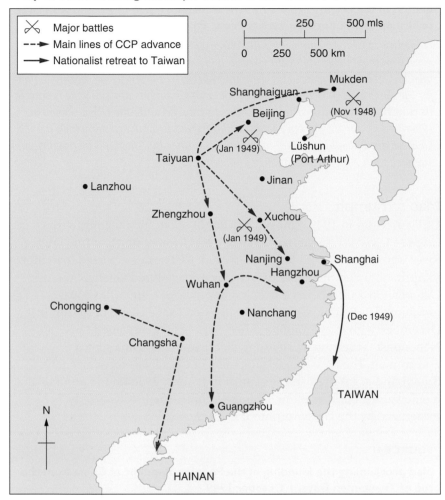

his concern about possible US intervention, but Mao, confident of victory,
firmly rejected any mediation by the USSR.

The US

In 1947, the US reviewed its policy towards China. Many US diplomats,
as well as the **Joint Chiefs of Staff** and the Secretaries of Defence and
the Navy, urged greater commitment and substantially more military aid
to the KMT. Marshall, who was now Secretary of State, and Truman
rejected this on the grounds that such a policy would both prove
prohibitively expensive and possibly lead to war with the USSR. The US,
therefore, limited its assistance to giving Chiang financial aid which
allowed him to purchase arms from the US. This policy continued even
when Chiang, defeated on the mainland, withdrew to Taiwan in
December 1949.

 **KEY TERM**

Joint Chiefs of Staff
Committee of senior military
officers who advise the US
government on military
matters.

? How accurate an assessment does Source G give of US policy in China, 1945–49?

SOURCE G

An extract from 'Soviet Assessments of US Foreign Policy, 27 Sept. 1946', quoted in *Uncertain Partners* by S.N. Goncharov, J.W. Lewis and Xue Litai, published by Stanford University Press, Palo Alto, US, 1993, pp. 229–30.

US policy in China is aimed at fully bringing that country under the control of American monopoly capital [the power of US money]. In pursuing this policy, the US Government goes so far as to interfere in China's internal affairs … how far the American government's policy towards China has already gone is seen in its current attempts to control the Chinese army. Recently the US government submitted to Congress a draft law on military aid to China under which the Chinese army would be totally reorganized, trained by American instructors, and supplied with American weaponry and ammunition …

Mao's triumph

CCP successes in 1949 removed any doubt about the outcome of the Chinese Civil War. In January 1949, the KMT forces north of the Yangtze River were defeated and Beijing captured. CCP armies crossed the Yangtze in April, occupied Shanghai in late May and captured Guangzhou in October. On 1 October, the People's Republic of China (PRC) was proclaimed in Beijing. Chiang Kai-shek fled to the island of Taiwan in December, with over 2 million others, where he maintained the Nationalist Government, claiming that it was still China's legal government. The new People's Republic of China was recognized by Britain, India, Pakistan and Sri Lanka in January 1950 on the grounds that it enjoyed the backing of the Chinese people. The PRC was only recognized by the US government in 1979.

SOURCE H

? What message does Source H convey?

Mao proclaiming the founding of the People's Republic of China from the top of Tiananmen Gate, 1 October 1949

The Sino-Soviet Pact

On 14 February 1950, Mao visited Moscow to celebrate Stalin's seventieth birthday. This was the occasion when the Sino-Soviet Pact was negotiated. It was, as Mao said, 'a big political asset to deal with imperialist countries in the world'.

> **What was the significance of the Sino-Soviet Pact, 14 February 1950?**

The Pact committed both states to:

- co-operate in terms of defence in the case of attack by Japan or its ally (meaning the US)
- conclude a peace treaty with Japan which would not be hostile to the interests of either state
- not conclude any hostile agreement with another power aimed at the other member of the Pact
- consult closely on matters of mutual interest.

Historian John Gaddis compares the Pact to the NATO Treaty of April 1949 which brought western European states and the US together to prevent a possible Soviet attack (see page 82). Similarly, it was the PRC that sought Soviet protection against the US and Japan. Nevertheless, the Pact was not signed without gains by Stalin. The USSR was to be supplied with tungsten, tin, and antimony for ten years at very low prices. Stalin, in return, provided military support for the PRC, including the establishment of air-defence installations in coastal areas near Taiwan.

> What information does Source I convey about the relationship between Mao and Stalin?

SOURCE I

Stalin and Mao Zedong at a celebration for Stalin's seventieth birthday, 21 December 1949

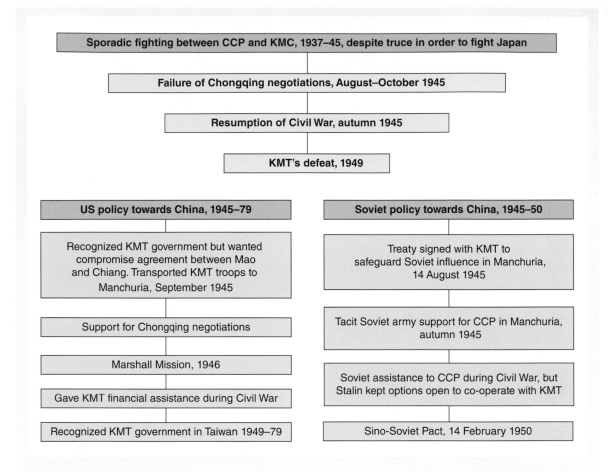

Sporadic fighting between CCP and KMC, 1937–45, despite truce in order to fight Japan

Failure of Chongqing negotiations, August–October 1945

Resumption of Civil War, autumn 1945

KMT's defeat, 1949

US policy towards China, 1945–79

Recognized KMT government but wanted compromise agreement between Mao and Chiang. Transported KMT troops to Manchuria, September 1945

Support for Chongqing negotiations

Marshall Mission, 1946

Gave KMT financial assistance during Civil War

Recognized KMT government in Taiwan 1949–79

Soviet policy towards China, 1945–50

Treaty signed with KMT to safeguard Soviet influence in Manchuria, 14 August 1945

Tacit Soviet army support for CCP in Manchuria, autumn 1945

Soviet assistance to CCP during Civil War, but Stalin kept options open to co-operate with KMT

Sino-Soviet Pact, 14 February 1950

SUMMARY DIAGRAM

The Chinese Civil War

The Korean War, 1950–53

> ▶ **Key question:** What caused the Korean War and how did it affect the Cold War?

Japan occupied Korea in 1905 and annexed it in 1910. During the Second World War, Koreans were conscripted into the Japanese army or worked as labourers. Britain, the US and Nationalist China made the Cairo Declaration in 30 November 1943, stating that Korea should become free and independent. Stalin accepted this and in May 1945 agreed that once Japan was defeated there should be a **trusteeship** for Korea with supervision by the US, the USSR, Nationalist China and Britain.

 **KEY TERM**

Trusteeship Responsibility for the government and welfare of a state handed over temporarily to other powers.

Korea, 1945–49

> **Why were there two Korean states by 1949?**

Once the Soviet Red Army arrived in North Korea on 12 August 1945, the Soviets lost little time in installing local communists in power in the areas under their control. Worried about Soviet intentions, the US immediately proposed an initial division of the peninsular at the 38th parallel (see map, page 124). In the north, Japanese troops would surrender to the Soviets and in the south to the US. This was accepted by the USSR, but when US troops eventually arrived on 8 September, they discovered that a young communist named Kim Il-sung had established a committee in the Korean capital of Seoul, announcing its intention to rule Korea as a Communist People's Republic. A rival anti-communist group under Syngman Rhee, a fervent Korean nationalist who had spent most of his life in the US, had also established a committee which claimed to be the Provisional Government for the whole nation. Kim and Rhee were each determined to unify Korea and exclude the other in the process.

The creation of North and South Korea: ROK and DPRK

Initially the US rejected the claims of both groups, and in December 1945, at the Moscow Conference of Foreign Ministers, the US and USSR went ahead with their plans for creating a trusteeship for Korea. A joint commission of Soviet and US officials were to advise the Koreans on creating a democratic government, but disagreements with the Soviets about which political parties should be allowed to participate led the US, in November 1947, to refer the problem to the United Nations.

Despite Soviet opposition, the United Nations General Assembly agreed in January 1948 to send a commission to supervise elections in both north and south Korea. When it arrived to start its work, its members were not allowed by the Soviets to enter the north. In the south, Syngman Rhee's Nationalist Party won an overwhelming majority and created the independent Republic of Korea (ROK), more commonly known as South Korea. In the north, under

Soviet protection, Kim Il-sung created the communist Democratic People's Republic of Korea (DPRK) in September 1948. Each state claimed to represent the entire nation and was hostile to the other. Each worked to unite Korea on its own terms.

Soviet withdrawal

Soviet troops were withdrawn from northern Korea by the end of 1948, but they left behind them much military hardware, which included not only their own equipment but also armaments seized from the defeated Japanese. These were regularly supplemented by further arms deliveries from the USSR. Indeed, according to one Soviet official these were on a far more generous scale than those given to the CCP in China. In the winter of 1948–49, Stalin was still not entirely confident that the CCP would win the civil war in China. In the event of their defeat, North Korea would be a useful base for protecting Soviet interests in Manchuria.

US withdrawal

With the creation of the ROK, US policy makers were divided about whether the 45,000-strong US occupation army should remain or whether these troops should be withdrawn. Military planners thought that the troops could be more effectively deployed elsewhere and that Korea should not be included within the US's **Asian defence perimeter**. Against this view was the argument that a removal of troops would weaken US prestige and result in the occupation of South Korea by a Soviet-armed North Korean army. In the end, US Secretary of State Dean Acheson and President Truman were convinced that Korea was not worth the expense of a prolonged military occupation. Consequently, when the United Nations General Assembly passed a resolution calling upon the United States and the USSR to withdraw their troops as soon as possible, the US removed its troops by June 1949.

→

Soviet and Chinese support

The two Korean states were enemies, both claiming to be the legitimate government of the whole of Korea. Alone, however, each state lacked the ability to defeat its rival. To do that they both required the support of a stronger military power. The US had no interest in supporting Rhee's ambitions since it had pulled its troops out of Korea in order to avoid costly and dangerous entanglements. Kim, however, was to gain support from both the People's Republic of China and a more cautious USSR.

Kim's talks with Stalin

Kim visited Moscow for talks with Stalin in April 1949. When he complained about southern violations of the frontier, Stalin urged him to 'strike the southerners in the teeth' (see Source J). It is probable, according to some historians, that Stalin meant that Kim should wage a guerrilla war rather than a full-scale invasion.

KEY TERM

Asian defence perimeter
A line through east and south-east Asia which the US was willing to defend against any other nation.

To what extent did both Mao and Stalin support Kim's plans to invade South Korea?

SOURCE J

An excerpt from the Stalin–Kim talks of April 1949, quoted in *Uncertain Partners* by S.N. Goncharov, J.W. Lewis and Xue Litai, published by Stanford University Press, Palo Alto, USA, 1993, p. 135.

According to Stalin's interpreter in the course of the meetings, 'Stalin asked: "How is it going, Comrade Kim?""Everything will be all right" [Kim said, but] he complained, "Only the southerners are making trouble all the time. They are violating the border; there are continuous small clashes." Stalin became gloomy: "What are you talking about? Are you short of arms? We shall give them to you. You must strike the southerners in the teeth." After thinking for a while, he repeated, "strike them, strike them".'

> According to Source J, what is the situation in Korea in the spring of 1949?

In the summer of 1949, after US troops had left, Kim sent several well-equipped guerrilla groups across the frontier to establish bases in the mountains in the south-east of the country which they failed to do. Kim decided that since guerrilla operations did not work, the only way to unite Korea under his leadership was through a major invasion. To do this he needed the support of Stalin whom he visited again in May 1950. Surprisingly, Stalin gave Kim his support because he:

- wished to dominate Korea through Kim to compensate the Soviets from having been prevented from participating in the occupation of Japan by the US (see page 102)
- believed Korea could be a useful economic and military ally as Japan had the potential to be for the US
- thought control of Korea could protect Soviet economic interests in neighbouring Manchuria
- thought the US would not assist South Korea and that the territory could be gained with little effort and little possibility of war between the superpowers.

Stalin cautiously gave his assent after consulting with Mao, but he did make his final approval of the North Korean attack dependent on Mao's consent. He told Kim that the Soviets would not fight for Korea, but that he should instead ask the PRC for assistance.

Kim's talks with Mao

When Kim visited Beijing in April 1950, Mao gave his consent based on his assessment that the US would not intervene. He was persuaded by Kim that Stalin was more enthusiastic than he was in reality.

SOURCE K

An excerpt from US Secretary of State Dean Acheson's speech to the National Press Club in Washington, 12 January 1950, quoted in *Department of State Bulletin, XXII*, 23 January 1950, p. 116.

What is the situation in regard to the military security of the Pacific area, and what is our policy in regard to it?

> What is the importance of Source K in understanding why Mao and Stalin agreed to allow Kim's forces to invade South Korea?

In the first place, the defeat and the disarmament of Japan has placed upon the United States the necessity of assuming the military defense of Japan so long as that is required, both in the interest of our security and in the interests of the security of the entire Pacific area … The defensive perimeter runs along the Aleutians to Japan and then goes to the Ryukyus. We hold important defense positions in the Ryukyu Islands, and those we will continue to hold … The defensive perimeter [then continues] from the Ryukyus to the Philippine Islands …

So far as the military security of other areas in the Pacific is concerned, it must be clear that no person can guarantee these areas against military attack. But it must also be clear that such a guarantee is hardly sensible or necessary within the realm of practical relationship. Should such an attack occur … the initial reliance must be on the people attacked to resist it and then upon the commitments of the entire civilized world under the Charter of the United Nations …

To what extent did the US provoke Chinese military intervention in Korea?

The outbreak of the Korean War

The Soviets increased the flow of weapons to North Korea and military advisors were sent in disguise so as not arouse US suspicions. By June 1950, North Korea possessed a decisive superiority over the South in terms of military strength. North Korea began its attack on South Korea on 25 June, surprising both the South Koreans and the US.

US intervention

Initially Kim's forces swept all before them, but the speed of the US reaction surprised the Soviets and their allies. Whereas guerrilla attacks might not have provoked a US response, a major military invasion was another matter. The US government reasoned that major aggression had to be countered or the lack of a US response would invite further invasions by Soviet puppet states elsewhere in the world.

The US immediately appealed to the Security Council of the United Nations to authorize a military force to force an end to fighting on the Korean Peninsula. As the USSR was boycotting the UN in protest at the exclusion of the People's Republic of China by the US, the Soviet representative was unable to veto Resolution 83 which called on member nations to assist South Korea. In response to this resolution, the US, and its allies Britain and France, ordered immediate military intervention. This decision was made less risky by the fact that Stalin had secretly informed Truman that he would not see the intervention of US troops in Korea as a cause of war between the two superpowers. At the same time, Truman sent the US Navy's 7th Fleet to patrol the Taiwan Strait to prevent either the Nationalists in Taiwan or the People's Republic of China from conducting military operations against each other. The US was determined to prevent the PRC from capturing Taiwan since aircraft based there could threaten Japan and the Philippines, both of which were in the US sphere of interest.

Impact on Mao

The appearance of the US Navy's 7th Fleet had a profound impact on Mao as it not only prevented a PRC attack on Taiwan, but was also a direct threat to the PRC. The US was also increasing military aid to the Philippines and French Indochina (see page 130). All these factors led Mao to believe that an attack on the PRC by the US was being planned. He decided that the best place to confront an aggressive US was in Korea and, on 23 July, he established the Northeast Border Defence Army. Stalin supplemented this force with an air force division of 122 fighter aircraft.

The United Nations counter-attack

By early August, Kim's forces had conquered 90 per cent of South Korea (see map, page 124) and the US-led United Nations' military task force was confined to a small area around Busan (formerly called Pusan). Supplied with equipment and reserves based in Japan, US troops were able to break out of Busan at the end of the month. A dramatic counter-attack was launched when General Douglas MacArthur, Supreme Commander of Allied Powers, who had been appointed commander of the UN task force, landed troops at Inchon on 9 September far behind North Korean lines. On 1 October, UN forces crossed the 38th parallel, and nearly three weeks later Pyongyang, the North Korean capital, was captured as US-led UN forces advanced to Korea's border with the PRC's province of Manchuria.

The PRC's entry into the war

In response to this military crisis, Kim sent an urgent request to Stalin on 29 September for Soviet military assistance. Stalin was not ready to risk war with the US, but he urged Mao to intervene, warning him that failure to do so would have grave consequences not just for the PRC's north-east provinces, but for all communist nations. The CCP's leadership hesitated until Stalin committed himself to providing further military support, which included air defences for both the main PRC cities and its troops in Korea.

SOURCE L

An excerpt from *We Now Know* by John Lewis Gaddis, published by Clarendon Press, Oxford, UK, 1997, p. 81.

Stalin … was determined to have the Chinese confront the Americans but at the same time so determined not to have the Soviet Union do so that he would have sacrificed North Korea altogether, had Mao refused to intervene. It was a simultaneous risk taking and risk avoidance, suggesting that Stalin was prepared both for a Sino-American war and an American occupation of the entire Korean peninsular. He left it to Mao to decide which it was to be …'

What, according to Source L, was Stalin's policy on the Korean War?

On 18 October, the PRC intervened in the Korean War to help North Korea. Within two weeks, PRC troops had crossed the Yalu River border and attacked UN forces whose supply lines were over-extended. By the end of the year, UN troops had been driven back across the 38th parallel.

Chinese volunteer troops crossing the River Yalu, October 1950.

What is the message of Source M?

Large-scale PRC intervention posed a major challenge to the US. At a press conference on November 30, Truman hinted that the US might use atomic bombs against PRC troops, but was dissuaded from doing so by his allies who feared that this might lead to the activation of the Sino-Soviet Pact and a much larger conflict; the Soviets now possessed atomic weapons as well. Mao, however, was undeterred by the threat and argued that atomic bombs would have relatively little impact on the PRC since it had practically unlimited manpower and could continue to field large armies. Mao may also have been confident that Soviet air defences could protect PRC cities and troops.

Why could the Korean War not be concluded until July 1953?

Attempts to end the Korean War

Although as early as December 1950 there were attempts to end the Korean War, it was not until July 1953 that a ceasefire could be agreed upon as a result of lengthy negotiations in which both North and South Koreans were determined to control the greatest amount of territory possible.

India's ceasefire proposal

On 5 December 1950, thirteen non-western states, headed by India, handed a peace proposal to the People's Republic of China and the UN.

It recommended that the PRC halt its advance at the 38th parallel, that a ceasefire should be declared and that a conference should be called to find a solution for the problem of Korea. Nine days later, the UN General Assembly approved the proposal and created a group to seek a basis on which a viable ceasefire could be arranged.

India's proposal presented the US with a dilemma. On the one hand, supporting it would lose South Korean support as well as risk the fury of the Republican-dominated Congress and much of the US press, both of which urged a tough line towards communist states. On the other hand, rejecting it would lead to the loss of support for the US in the United Nations. In the end, the US backed the proposal largely in the hope that the PRC would reject it. In this they were proved right as Mao was determined to continue the war, aiming for a crushing victory over what he termed 'American imperialism'. Consequently, after PRC military successes in December 1950, he rejected the ceasefire proposal and ordered another offensive, which resulted in the capture of Seoul on 4 January 1951.

Armistice negotiations

A spring offensive in 1951 by the PRC failed and its leadership understood that it lacked the resources to defeat the US-led UN force. The PRC, however, could still claim that the dramatic rout of the US in North Korea in December 1950 represented a major victory and that its armies commanded a strong position on the battlefield. Mao agreed to negotiations for a truce in the hope this might eventually lead to the withdrawal of UN troops from Korea. He explained this strategy as 'preparing for a long war while striving to end the war through peace negotiations'. By the end of May 1951, the US also believed that its position on the battlefield was secure enough to negotiate an end to the war, but, like Mao, the US hoped to make further territorial gains which would strengthen its position at the negotiating table.

By July 1951, fighting had stabilized along the 38th parallel. During the next two years, tortuous negotiations were conducted between the two sides, each of which constantly sought to achieve an advantage over the other. The US, for example, exploited the wishes of a large number of Chinese prisoners of war not to return to the PRC as it realized that this would make very effective anti-communist propaganda. The PRC retaliated by claiming that the US had used **biological warfare** in Korea.

KEY TERM

Biological warfare A form of warfare in which bacteria and viruses are used against an enemies, armies and civilians.

The Korean armistice

In January 1953, the Republican Dwight D. Eisenhower, formerly the general in charge the Allied forces in western Europe during the Second World War, was elected President in the US. Determined to end the war quickly, he threatened to use atomic bombs against PRC and North Korean forces. These threats had little impact on Mao who believed that the Soviets would

? According to Source N, what was the outcome of the Korean War?

Map of the Korean War.

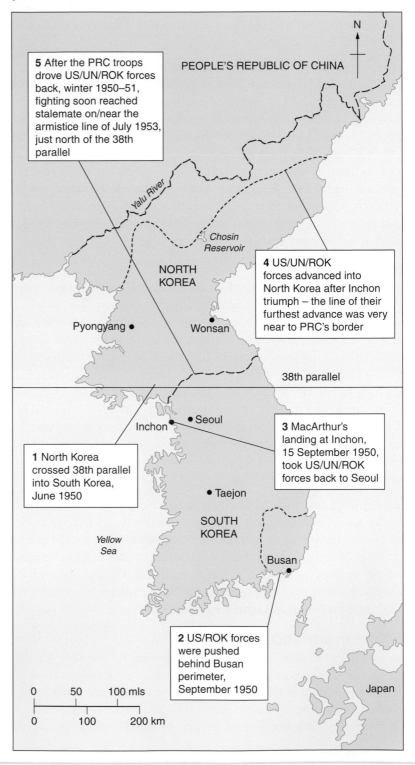

5 After the PRC troops drove US/UN/ROK forces back, winter 1950–51, fighting soon reached stalemate on/near the armistice line of July 1953, just north of the 38th parallel

PEOPLE'S REPUBLIC OF CHINA

N

Yalu River

Chosin Reservoir

NORTH KOREA

4 US/UN/ROK forces advanced into North Korea after Inchon triumph – the line of their furthest advance was very near to PRC's border

Pyongyang ●

Wonsan ●

38th parallel

Inchon ● Seoul

3 MacArthur's landing at Inchon, 15 September 1950, took US/UN/ROK forces back to Seoul

1 North Korea crossed 38th parallel into South Korea, June 1950

● Taejon

SOUTH KOREA

Yellow Sea

Busan ●

2 US/ROK forces were pushed behind Busan perimeter, September 1950

Japan

0   50   100 mls

0   100   200 km

deter the US from any such action. Stalin's death in March 1953 (see page 139) led to new Soviet leadership who wanted to end the war as soon as possible. The Soviets wanted to ease international tension, cut the USSR's military budget and divert more money to improving living standards. Mao, too, faced with persistent military stalemate in Korea, conceded that outright victory in Korea was not possible. On 27 July 1953, both sides finally agreed an armistice which recognized the 38th parallel as a temporary dividing line between North Korea and South Korea. This division has remained the frontier ever since.

The consequences of the War

The Korean War was an important turning point in the Cold War and it had important consequences for the People's Republic of China, the US, USSR and Western Europe.

What were the consequences of the Korean War?

Consequences for China

Mao used the Korean War to foment enthusiasm for revolutionary change within the PRC and to mobilize public opinion by stirring up hatred for what he termed 'American arrogance'. A national campaign aimed at suppressing 'reactionaries and reactionary activities' was unleashed across the PRC to remove any opponents of the government. By the time the Korean War ended, society and politics had been radically changed in the PRC. Agricultural land, for example, had been redistributed to the peasantry and the landlord class eliminated, ending an economic and social system thousands of years old. PRC victories in Korea in 1950 were promoted as removing over a century of humiliating defeats at the hands of European and Japanese armies, which inevitably strengthened Mao's government.

Consequences for the USSR: Sino-Soviet relations

Throughout the war, Mao consulted with Stalin on all the key decisions and was dependent on the USSR for much of the PRC's military supplies. On one level, the war brought the USSR and China closer together, but, as historian Chen Jian observes: 'on another level, the Chinese experience during the Korean War also ground away at some of the cement that kept the Sino-Soviet alliance together'. Mao resented Stalin's opportunism, such as when he demanded cheap raw materials in return for signing the Sino-Soviet Pact, and for the fact that he made China pay excessively for military supplies. The war against what Mao thought of as US imperialism in Korea also increased his feeling of moral superiority towards the Soviets which would eventually damage the Sino-Soviet alliance. At the same time, the war also accelerated both US and Western rearmament programmes to the detriment of the USSR.

Consequences for western Europe

In the long term, the Korean War did serious damage to the interests of the Soviet Union in Europe. It strengthened NATO and led to the rearmament of West Germany and the first steps towards the integration of western Europe (see pages 84–88). As the historian Norman Stone concisely stated 'the Korean War created Europe'.

Consequences for the US

The Korean War strengthened the arguments of the US National Security Council (NSC) that communism represented a co-ordinated global threat. After the outbreak of the war, US President Truman accepted the NSC's proposals for a massive rearmament programme and tripled the US military budget. It also decided to station US troops permanently in western Europe and rearm West Germany.

The Korean War convinced the US of the need to build up a system of global alliances in order to contain communism. In 1954, it formed SEATO, the Southeast Asian Treaty Organization (see page 194), and in 1955, to protect the Middle East from Soviet attack, the Central Treaty Organization (**CENTO**) or Baghdad pact.

KEY TERM

CENTO Central Treaty Organization, also known as Baghdad Pact, formed in 1955 by Iran, Iraq, Pakistan, Turkey and UK; it was dissolved in 1979.

?

According to Source O, how did the Korean War affect the Soviet Union?

SOURCE O

An excerpt from *Soviet-American Relations in Asia, 1945-1954*, by R.D. Buhite, University of Oklahoma Press, Oklahoma, USA, 1981, p. 185.

… the war spelled trouble for the Soviet Union. What had begun as a low risk Communist reply to the American programme in Japan, had resulted in the reassertion of American power and the solidification of an anti-Soviet bloc in Western Europe. Specifically the United States increased its defense budget from $13 billion to over $16 billion dollars; it doubled its draft quota; it trebled the size of the United States Air Force in Britain and augmented it with jet fighters and B-50 bombers; it began stockpiling strategic materials and stepped up aid to Southeast Asian nations; it wrote an agreement with Japan providing for United States bases and a Japanese defense force; it dispatched the seventh Fleet to the Taiwan Strait; and it successfully brought Germany into the European defense arrangement and strengthened … NATO … Although North Korea and China had borne the major burden in the fighting, the Soviet Union paid a heavy price for negligible benefit.

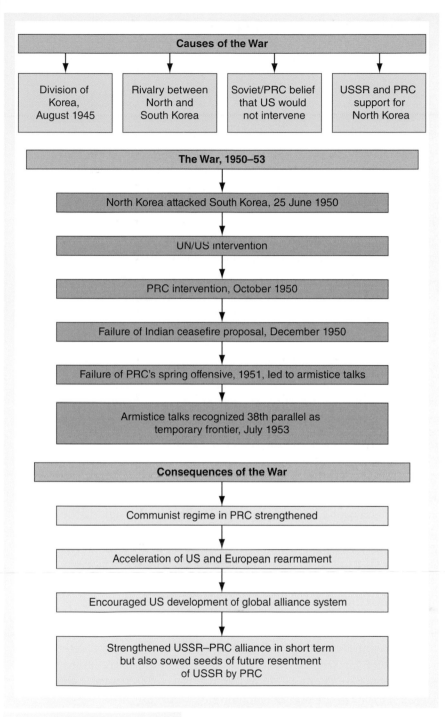

Causes of the War

| Division of Korea, August 1945 | Rivalry between North and South Korea | Soviet/PRC belief that US would not intervene | USSR and PRC support for North Korea |

The War, 1950–53

North Korea attacked South Korea, 25 June 1950

UN/US intervention

PRC intervention, October 1950

Failure of Indian ceasefire proposal, December 1950

Failure of PRC's spring offensive, 1951, led to armistice talks

Armistice talks recognized 38th parallel as temporary frontier, July 1953

Consequences of the War

Communist regime in PRC strengthened

Acceleration of US and European rearmament

Encouraged US development of global alliance system

Strengthened USSR–PRC alliance in short term but also sowed seeds of future resentment of USSR by PRC

SUMMARY DIAGRAM

The Korean War, 1950–53

Indochina, 1945–54

> ▶ **Key question:** *To what extent did the communist triumph in China help Hồ Chí Minh in Indochina?*

On 29 August 1945, Hồ Chí Minh proclaimed an independent, communist Democratic Republic of Vietnam with its capital at Hanoi. Hồ was both a nationalist and communist and aimed to free Vietnam from Japanese domination during the Second World War and from France afterwards. He created the League for the Independence of Vietnam, the **Viet Minh,** in 1941, which was commanded by Võ Nguyên Giáp, a former professor of history. Giáp would eventually unite all Vietnam in a unified communist state in 1975 after a 34-year struggle (see Chapter 6).

🔑 **KEY TERM**

Viet Minh 'League for the Independence of Vietnam' (English translation).

To what extent did the Viet Minh achieve victory in the Indochinese war of 1946–54?

The Indochinese War, 1946–54

Japan occupied French Indochina in 1940, but allowed French officials to continue to administer the region. In response to growing opposition from the Viet Minh, Japan took over complete control in March 1945. After Japan's defeat in August 1945, British troops occupied southern Vietnam while Chinese Nationalists took control of the north. Britain immediately released and rearmed French troops who had been interned by Japan, and these, reinforced by the arrival of further French military units, clashed with the pro-independence Viet Minh.

Hồ's Democratic Republic of Vietnam was isolated. While Britain supported France's attempt to regain control of Indochina, the Soviets showed little interest in the conflict; the US hoped for general decolonization in Asia, but did not challenge France over Vietnam. Chinese Nationalists in the north agreed to hand over control of the region to France after signing the Sino-French Agreement in February 1946. This agreement also meant the loss of French economic rights in China, which they had held before the Second World War. Hồ Chí Minh eventually compromised with the French government, agreeing that Vietnam should become a self-governing state within French Indochina and therefore only semi-independent.

The outbreak of hostilities

This agreement did not last as the French government was still determined to control Vietnam while Hồ wanted only the loosest of associations with France. Open conflict erupted in November 1946 when France bombarded Viet Minh forces in the port of Haiphong.

Until 1949, France had little difficulty in confining the revolt to mountainous areas. CCP guerrillas from China occasionally assisted the Viet Minh, but it was only after his victory in 1949 that Mao was in a position to offer significant military assistance. Mao believed it was the People's Republic of China's mission to encourage communist revolution throughout east

Asia, a revolution which would be based on the PRC's model. He therefore saw Hồ Chí Minh's war against France as part of the overall anti-imperialist struggle which he was waging against the US, Britain and France.

SOURCE P

Map of Indochina.

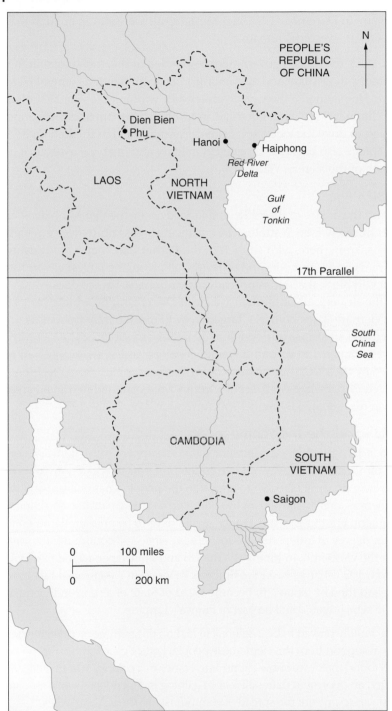

According to Source P, to what extent was the PRC's involvement likely to cause problems for France?

France on the defensive, 1950–54

In April 1950, Mao sent one of his most experienced generals, Chen Geng, to Vietnam. He organized a military campaign along the Vietnamese–PRC border where direct assistance to the Viet Minh could be provided. By November, France had lost control of the border territories and equipment and supplies flowed into Vietnam unchecked, changing the balance of power in Vietnam. In December 1952, Viet Minh troops were strong enough to seize parts of north-western Vietnam.

In mid-1953, the French government responded to this threat by sending more troops to Vietnam and appointing a new commander, General Henri Navarre. He planned a three-year strategy for winning the war. First of all, he would eliminate Viet Minh guerrillas in southern Vietnam and then launch a campaign to drive the Viet Minh from their stronghold in the Red River Delta. France also began to receive US military and financial assistance in the aftermath of the Korean War.

Điện Biên Phủ

KEY TERM

Pathet Lao Independence movement in Laos, supported by the Viet Minh.

Acting on the advice of their PRC military advisors, the Viet Minh decided to counter this new French strategy by advancing across north-western Vietnam into Laos. From there, with support of the **Pathet Lao**, they would advance southwards into Cambodia and onwards to Saigon, the largest city in south Vietnam. To block the Viet Minh's advance into Laos, France decided to fortify the strategically important village of Điện Biên Phủ which was located on the Vietnam–Laos border. A large force of French paratroopers was dropped and air strips were constructed in November 1953. The Viet Minh, however, managed to surround French positions and, with anti-aircraft guns supplied by the PRC, they prevented any further supplies from reaching Điện Biên Phủ. By late April, French troops were confined to a small area of less than two square kilometres and surrendered on 7 May 1954.

The US and the Indochinese War

The US faced a quandary in Vietnam: should it support anti-colonialism or anti-communism? One way out of this dilemma was to find a non-communist rival to Hồ who would be able to appeal to the people's nationalism and thus unite them against communism by setting up a strong, patriotic and capitalist government. For this to work, France would have to be pressured into granting a greater degree of independence to Vietnam while still continuing the war against the Viet Minh. In June 1949, the US and France persuaded Bảo Đại, who from 1925–45 had been the Emperor of Vietnam – controlled first by France and then by Japan – to become Head of State of a semi-independent Vietnam which would still be part of France's Empire.

Bảo Đại rapidly proved to be a failure. He had no programme, no ideology and little local support from the Vietnamese people; France gave him no real power. The US found that it was now supporting France in a colonial war that effectively prevented an oppressed nationality from gaining independence while its stated mission was to prevent the spread of communism to more Asian states.

SOURCE Q

Defeated French troops at Điện Biên Phủ.

What information about the war in Vietnam is conveyed by Source Q?

SOURCE R

An excerpt from *Soviet-American Relations in Asia, 1945–1954* by Russell D. Buhite, Oklahoma Press, Oklahoma, USA, 1981, p. 207.

In August 1953, the US National Security Council observed:

The loss of Indochina would be critical to the security of the US. Communist control of Indochina would endanger vital raw material sources; it would weaken the confidence of Southeast Asian states in Western leadership; it would make more difficult and more expensive the defence of Japan, Formosa [Taiwan] and the Philippines …

According to Source R, what was the danger of the loss of Indochina to communist forces?

In April 1954, faced with the imminent fall of Điện Biên Phủ, US Secretary of State John Foster Dulles recommended air strikes on Viet Minh positions from US aircraft flown from carriers in the South China Sea. If that failed to halt the Viet Minh, he contemplated the use of **tactical nuclear weapons** and the landing of ground forces. These ideas were strongly opposed by Britain and the US Military Chiefs of Staff and therefore abandoned. The US Chiefs of Staff stressed that this should only be considered if there was a full invasion of Vietnam by the PRC. The British government also feared that US intervention would provoke PRC military intervention in Vietnam.

 **KEY TERM**

Tactical nuclear weapons
Small-scale nuclear weapons that can be used in the battlefield.

Why was it possible to achieve a compromise at the Geneva Conference?

The Geneva Conference, 1954

Both the PRC and the Soviet Union were ready to compromise to end the Indochinese War. The PRC wished to avoid US military involvement in the war. After the long struggle with the KMT and the Korean War, the PRC's government needed a respite from conflict so that it could launch the first Five Year Plan to build up its economy. It was therefore ready to put pressure on the Viet Minh to negotiate a peace agreement. The Soviets, too, after Stalin's death, wished to focus on domestic issues and relax international tension. They feared that the escalating crisis in Indochina would lead to the intervention of the US and a major international crisis. Also, by being conciliatory to France, they hoped that they could weaken its support for German rearmament and the EDC (see pages 85–87).

On 28 September 1953, the Soviets suggested calling an international conference to solve the Korean and Indochinese problems.

Reaction of the US and its allies

The proposal had a mixed reception. Britain and France supported it. The French public were becoming war weary and increasingly unwilling to support the cost of maintaining the conflict. In the autumn of 1953, however, France still optimistically hoped that a victory at Điện Biên Phủ would strengthen its negotiating position. The US only reluctantly agreed in order to not offend its allies, Britain and France. US Secretary of State John Dulles feared that any compromise over Indochina would result in communist gains in south-east Asia. He was also quick to stress that the attendance of the PRC at any conference did not imply its recognition by the US.

The Conference

The Geneva Conference started on 26 April 1954. On 6 May, a massive Viet Minh attack forced French troops to surrender at Điện Biên Phủ the next day. Inevitably, the Viet Minh victory persuaded France that the Viet Minh could not easily be defeated. France consequently rejected US advice to continue fighting and, in June, a new government was formed under Pierre Mendès-France, a leading critic of the war in Indochina. He made clear that he would resign unless a peace settlement was agreed within a month. The Viet Minh were also ready to compromise, having suffered heavy casualties at the battle for Điện Biên Phủ from which they needed time to recover. The way to a compromise was now open.

Compromise reached

At the end of June, Britain, France, the USSR, and the PRC decided to support an agreement which would establish an independent Laos and Cambodia and partition Vietnam at the 17th parallel. The US government did not oppose this, but refused formally to sign the final Geneva Accords. It instead issued a declaration taking note of what had been decided and undertaking not to undermine the settlement. The PRC and the Soviet Union persuaded Hồ Chí Minh to agree and to try to unify Vietnam peacefully through future elections.

SOURCE S

An excerpt from the transcript of a meeting between Zhou Enlai (Premier of the PRC) and Hồ Chí Minh on 3 July quoted in 'Restoring Peace in Indochina at the Geneva Conference', by Li Haiwen, from paper presented at the CWIHP History Project Conference, Hong Kong, 1996.

Zhou explained to Hồ Chí Minh:

It is possible to unite Vietnam through elections when [the] time is ripe. This requires good relations with south-east Asian countries as well as among the Indochinese countries … The answer is to unite them through peaceful efforts. Military means can only drive them to the American side … Peace can increase the rift between France and the US … Peace can drive Great Britain and the USA apart … All in all peace has its advantages. It can isolate the USA.

According to Source S, why was China ready to compromise at the Geneva Conference?

The Geneva Accords

On 21 July, the Agreements were signed:

- Laos and Cambodia were made independent.
- Vietnam was divided along the 17th parallel.
- French forces would withdraw from the north of this line and Viet Minh forces from the south.
- In two years' time there would be democratic elections for a united Vietnam.
- Neither North nor South Vietnam were to conclude military alliances with foreign powers, nor to allow foreign military bases on their territory.

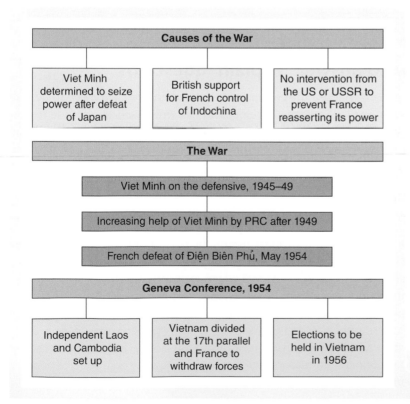

Causes of the War

| Viet Minh determined to seize power after defeat of Japan | British support for French control of Indochina | No intervention from the US or USSR to prevent France reasserting its power |

The War

Viet Minh on the defensive, 1945–49

Increasing help of Viet Minh by PRC after 1949

French defeat of Điện Biên Phủ, May 1954

Geneva Conference, 1954

| Independent Laos and Cambodia set up | Vietnam divided at the 17th parallel and France to withdraw forces | Elections to be held in Vietnam in 1956 |

SUMMARY DIAGRAM

Indochina 1945–54

Chapter summary

The spread of communism in Asia, 1945–54

In August 1945, the Soviets invaded Manchuria and northern Korea while US troops occupied Japan after its surrender. The US was unwilling to share the occupation of Japan with any other power, and over the next five years was able to ensure that Japan recovered economically to become an important part of US global defence against communist states.

The US had supplied Chiang Kai-shek with military equipment during the Chinese Civil War of 1946–49, but was not ready to intervene directly to assist him. The CCP's victory in 1949 altered the balance of power in Asia and led to PRC support for communist movements in Korea and Indochina. The signature of the Sino-Soviet Pact on 14 February 1950 seemingly established a partnership of equals between Stalin and Mao, the leaders of the two largest communist states.

Despite the withdrawal of both Soviet and US troops in 1949, Korea remained partitioned between the communist North and the anti-communist nationalist South. Kim Il-sung, the ruler of North Korea, was encouraged by Stalin to invade the south but left it to Mao to come to his rescue if the US intervened. In June 1950, North Korean troops did invade and, after initial successes, were pushed back by UN troops led by the US. Their success led to the intervention of the PRC. The war had a profound impact on western Europe, paving the way for West German rearmament and eventual economic integration.

Mao's victory in China also had a decisive impact on the war in Indochina. The PRC was able to send equipment and advisors, and by 1954, with the fall of Điện Biên Phủ, the Viet Minh had defeated France and were able to establish a communist state in northern Vietnam. At the Geneva Conference in 1954, Vietnam was partitioned into two states, while Cambodia and Laos gained independence. Elections for a united Vietnam were to be held in 1956.

 # Examination advice

How to answer 'explain' questions

For questions that use the command term 'explain', you are asked to describe clearly reasons for an event, development or a process. Each of these reasons will need to be explored fully. This means you should include evidence which supports your choice of reasons. It is best to put these explanations in order of importance.

Example

Explain the reasons for the Korean War that began in 1950.

1. This question requires you to discuss the reasons a war occurred in Korea in 1950. Please note that this requires you to do two things: explain the reason for the war in Korea and why this occurred in 1950 and not at another time. You should deal with the most important reasons for this conflict in this location and at this time first, before moving on to the less important ones. You do not need to give every possible reason, only the most convincing which you need to support with evidence. If you choose to discount certain reasons, be sure to explain why these were of minor or no importance.

2. Before writing the answer you should write out an outline – allow around five minutes to do this. Your outline will list various reasons for the conflict in order of importance. An example of an outline is given below. In this chapter you should be able to locate many facts to support each of these.

- N. Korea encouraged/supported by Soviets/PRC
- N. and S. Korea wanted to unify/rule all Korea
  - Fear of rebuilt Japan
  - Nationalism
  - Bring their forms of government to all Korea
    - Democracy v. Communism
- US wanted to defend Japan and prevent spread of communism:
  - Needed to demonstrate to Soviets/communist states that US would go to war to defend allies

3. Your introduction should indicate some of the background regarding the formation of the two Koreas after the Second World War and introduce the main points your essay is going to cover. An example of a good introductory paragraph for this question is given below.

By 1948 there were two Korean states: North and South Korea. While North Korea had been created from territory occupied by the Soviet Union at the end of the Second World War and had a communist government, South Korea was established with support from the United States and was democratic with a capitalist economy. War began between the two Koreas in 1950 after North Korea was encouraged to invade South Korea by the Soviet Union and the newly established People's Republic of China. In addition, North Korea wanted to unite all Korea under its rule, as did South Korea, in order to realize the creation of a united Korean Peninsula under a single Korean government. A united Korean government would be better able to prevent renewed domination of Korea by Japan which had annexed Korea in 1905 since it was now being quickly rebuilt by the United States. The Korean War was also the result of the US needing to demonstrate to the Soviets and the PRC that it would militarily resist the spread of communist governments, especially at the expense of their communist allies.

4. In your essay, clearly explain the importance of each of the reasons you have outlined in your introduction, using appropriate supporting evidence. As in all essays, tie your paragraphs to the question. Remember that structure in all your essays is important so fully explain each reason in separate paragraphs. An example of how one of the reasons could be addressed is given below.

> One of the most important reasons the Korean War began in June 1950 was because the Soviet Union encouraged North Korea to attack South Korea. Stalin stated that North Korea should 'strike the southerners in the teeth' in a conversation with North Korea's leader Kim Il-Sung in reference to South Korea. Although it is not clear if Stalin desired limited guerrilla warfare or a full invasion, the Soviet Union certainly increased arms shipments to North Korea and soon North Korea was better armed than South Korea. The Soviets wished to dominate the Korean Peninsula which North Korea's expansion would allow. This was partly the result of needing to protect the nearby Manchurian province of the People's Republic of China where the Soviets had economic interests. It would also build a communist counter-balance to US-reconstructed Japan which was being reorganized and industrialized to be rapidly transformed into a potential military power and ally of the US in Asia. Soviet support and encouragement of North Korea was one of the main reasons that the Korean War erupted in 1950.

5. In your conclusion you need to bring together the various threads of the reasons for the Korean War and why it broke out when it did. An example of a good concluding paragraph is given below.

> There were several important reasons that the Korean War began in 1950. Perhaps the most important was that the Soviet Union encouraged North Korea to expand its territory to include South Korea for its own foreign policy purposes and supplied it with the material to be able to do so. Both North and South Korea desired to annex the other's territory to unite the country, partly for reasons of nationalism but also for fear of a resurgent Japan that had dominated the Korean Peninsula for the entire first half of the twentieth century. The US provoked the Korean War by withdrawing its military forces from South Korea while also rebuilding Japan, which other Asian states saw as a potential and probable threat. By withdrawing its forces, North Korea, as well as the Soviet Union and the People's Republic of China, saw an opportunity to remove a US-allied government and, in the case of Korea, to replace it with their own.

6. Now try writing a complete answer to the question following the advice above.

Examination practice

Below are two exam-style questions for you to practise on this topic.

1. Evaluate the importance of the Soviet Union in the formation of the People's Republic of China in 1949. (For guidance on how to answer 'evaluate' questions, see page 98.)

2. Why did communist governments spread to many eastern Asian states after the Second World War? (For guidance on how to answer 'why' questions, see page 228.)

 # Activities

1 In order to write effective essays, it is important to be able to outline and organize your thoughts in a very timely manner. Each member of the class should create five different examination-style questions on material from Chapters 1 to 4, based on the examples already presented in these chapters. Exchange the questions. Each student should select one of the questions to be outlined. Outline the chosen question in ten minutes. Students should then exchange the question and its outline, each checking the work of the other to see if the outline addresses the question, is appropriately organized with the strongest arguments first, and if all the information is correct.

2 Repeat Activity 1, using the other questions. The timing should be reduced from ten minutes to five minutes gradually. This exercise should be repeated throughout the remainder of the course.

3 Using the question answered in Activity 1, students should write a strong introductory paragraph in ten minutes or less.

CHAPTER 5

From *détente* to the Berlin Wall, 1953–61

This chapter investigates the consolidation of the rival blocs in Europe and the initial policies of the new leadership in the US and USSR during the first period of *détente*, or thaw, in their relations. It then explores the end of the first *détente* in 1956, reviewing two major crises: an attack on Egypt by Britain, France and Israel and the suppression of the Hungarian Uprising by the USSR. A further crisis began in 1958, when the Soviet Union attempted to force the US and its allies to make concessions regarding Berlin. This crisis ended in 1961 with the construction of the Berlin Wall.

You need to consider the following questions throughout this chapter:

✪ To what extent did relations between the Soviet and Western blocs improve from 1953–55?

✪ Why did the Non-Aligned Movement cause difficulties for both the US and USSR?

✪ What caused the series of crises that shook both the Western powers and the Soviet bloc in 1956?

✪ What were the consequences of the crises of 1956 for the Soviet bloc and the Western powers?

✪ To what extent did the Soviet Union achieve its objectives during the Berlin Crisis from 1958–61?

① The thaw, 1953–55

▶ *Key question: To what extent did relations between the Soviet and Western blocs improve from 1953–55?*

The years 1953–55 witnessed an easing of the tension between the Soviet and Western blocs. The Korean War ended in 1953 and the first Indochina War in 1954 (see Chapter 4). The first summit meeting since Potsdam in 1945 was held in Geneva in 1955. The talks between Britain, France, the US and the USSR were cordial, giving rise to what became known as the 'Geneva spirit'. However, despite better relations, no solution was found to the German problem or the arms race. By the end of 1955, the division of Europe into two blocs was further consolidated (see map, page 163).

The new leaders, 1953

What were the aims of the new leaders in the US and USSR?

In 1953, there was a change of leadership in both the USSR and the US. General Dwight D. Eisenhower won the presidential election in the

US. A collective leadership took the place of Stalin in the Soviet Union after his death on 5 March.

President Eisenhower

President Eisenhower promised to take a much tougher line towards the USSR and even spoke of freeing the people in eastern Europe from Soviet control.

SOURCE A

An excerpt from *Deterrence in American Foreign Policy: Theory and Practice*, by A.L. George and R. Smoke, Columbia University Press, New York, USA, 1974, pp. 299–301.

The 1952 Republican Party platform, on which President Eisenhower had been elected, had specifically promised a policy of 'liberation' of the 'captive nations' of Eastern Europe as an alternative to Truman's policy of mere 'containment' of any further Soviet aggression. A policy of 'rolling back' communism, as it came to be known, was repeated by Dulles in his first address as Secretary of State: 'To all those suffering under Communist slavery … let us say, you can count on us'. The USSR therefore had good reason to believe that the US might actually act to implement this strategy in certain contingencies.

According to Source A, why did Eisenhower wish to remove communism from eastern Europe?

Eisenhower considered using nuclear weapons in Korea in 1953 and Indochina a year later (see pages 122 and 131). He cavalierly referred to the atomic bomb simply as 'another weapon in our arsenal'. However, like his predecessor Truman, he was not in reality ready to risk a nuclear war, aware of the damage even a few Soviet nuclear bombs would do to the US. On 1 November 1952, the US exploded the first hydrogen bomb in the Pacific Ocean and a year later the USSR also successfully tested a hydrogen bomb. By the end of 1955, both sides had long-range bombers able to drop these bombs on each other's territory. Even though the US possessed more bombs than the USSR, each superpower was in a position to inflict catastrophic damage on the other. In this situation, Eisenhower saw that the only practical alternative was the peaceful containment of Soviet power in Europe, rather than attempting to remove it; this had been the policy of Truman.

Changes in the USSR

Nikita Khrushchev, Georgi Malenkov, Vyachlav Molotov, Lavrenty Beria, and Nikolay Bulganin shared power for three years after Stalin's death. At the same time, they were political rivals, each hoping to secure sole supreme power. This group was determined to improve living standards in the USSR and to dismantle the police state created by Stalin. To implement these reforms, they needed a more relaxed international climate which would enable them to spend less on armaments. In August 1953, Malenkov declared in the **Supreme Soviet** that there was 'no disputed or unresolved question that cannot be settled by mutual agreement of the interested countries'.

 **KEY TERM**

Supreme Soviet Set up in 1936 by Stalin. It consisted of two bodies: the Soviet of the USSR and the Soviet of Nationalities. Each Soviet republic had a Supreme Soviet or parliament, as did the overall USSR.

How did the Western powers react to changes in Soviet foreign policy?

 KEY TERM

Détente A state of lessened tension or growing relaxation between two states.

Berlin's open frontier There was no physical barrier between communist East Berlin and capitalist and democratic West Berlin.

The West and *détente*

Given this desire for ***détente*** by the Soviet leadership, not only was a settlement in Korea and Indochina possible, but it also appeared as though the question of German unity might be reopened and potentially resolved.

Eisenhower's response, 1953

On 16 April 1953, Eisenhower announced that any improvement in Soviet–US relations would depend on free elections in eastern Europe. In May, Winston Churchill, who had become Prime Minister of Britain again in October 1951, suggested a Four-Power conference in which plans for German reunification and demilitarization would be discussed. This proposal was unpopular with both the West German Chancellor Adenauer, Eisenhower and indeed with Churchill's own government. They all feared a neutral Germany would be established that would then be vulnerable to pressure from the USSR and ultimately removed from the western European economic and military systems; this had consistently been the fear of Western governments. However, such was the desire for peace throughout western Europe that both Adenauer and Eisenhower reluctantly had to agree to discuss a possible agenda for talks at a preliminary conference of foreign ministers, although this did not meet until December in Bermuda.

What was the response of the USSR to the growing crisis in the GDR?

The USSR and the GDR, April–June 1953

In early 1953, the Soviet Foreign Office made proposals for German unity, submitting them to the US, Britain and France. It suggested a provisional government be created of politicians from both German states and the removal of all foreign troops of occupation.

The crisis in the GDR

As a member of COMECON (see page 92), the GDR had reorganized its economy following the model of the USSR. In 1951, its first Five Year Plan was launched with the intention of doubling Germany's 1936 industrial output. By 1952, this aim was achieved in the production of iron, steel and chemicals. Ulbricht, the GDR's leader, was, however, determined to increase heavy industry and the output of steel. In July 1952, workers' individual production targets were suddenly raised by 10 per cent, while at the same time there were steep increases in the price of food and public transport. Farmers were also threatened with collectivization of agriculture along Soviet lines.

By spring 1953, tension was further increased by the arrest of leading non-communist politicians. Church leaders warned of the possibility of a major catastrophe, while even within the GDR's Communist Party, the SED, there were indications that many were ready to challenge the government's economic plans which had severely stressed the country. Many people fled into West Berlin through **Berlin's open frontier** and this number increased daily (see Source B below). As many of these were professionals, skilled workers and farmers, their departure deprived the GDR economy of vital human resources.

Soviet concern

The growing crisis in the GDR deeply embarrassed the new Soviet leadership. If an anti-government revolt erupted, Soviet troops would have to intervene, which would threaten the USSR's new policy of *détente*. In May 1953, the **Presidium** of the Soviet Council of Ministers met to consider the problem. Beria, the head of the Soviet secret police, now called the KGB, began to reassess the value of the GDR to the Soviet bloc. It was proving an expensive and unstable state to support, as well as an area of friction with the Western bloc. Backed by Deputy Prime Minister Malenkov, he urged his more cautious colleagues in the Presidium to propose to the US, Britain and France that a united, neutral Germany be formed. He argued that to achieve reunification on such terms, Germany would be willing to pay substantial reparations to the USSR.

Although Beria and Malenkov failed to win over other Soviet ministers who still clung to the idea of working slowly and cautiously towards a unified and communist Germany, they did agree to summon Ulbricht to Moscow on 2 June. In the interests of *détente*, he was ordered to pursue a more conciliatory approach in the GDR so that various groups were not antagonized, and to abandon his programme for rapid socialization. These concessions, however, came too late and he failed to scale down the high production targets that had been set for the workers. Some contemporaries believed that by leaving the 10 per cent increase in production targets in place, Ulbricht was deliberately provoking an uprising in the GDR so that armed intervention by the USSR would be triggered. This would make it all more difficult to reunite Germany and so enable the GDR to survive as a Soviet satellite, thus keeping Ulbricht in power.

> **KEY TERM**
>
> **Presidium** Soviet inner council or cabinet.

SOURCE B

An excerpt from a document given to Ulbricht and two of his colleagues by the Soviet leadership when they visited Moscow on 2 June 1953. Quoted in 'Cold war misperceptions: The Communist and Western responses to the East German Refugee crisis in 1953' by V. Ingimundarson, *Journal of Contemporary History*, Vol. 28, 1994, p. 473.

The pursuit of a wrong political line in the German Democratic Republic has produced a most unsatisfactory political and economic situation. There are signs of bitter dissatisfaction – among broad masses of the population, including the workers, the farmers, and the intellectuals – with the political and economic policies of the GDR. The most conspicuous feature of this dissatisfaction is the mass flight of East German residents to West Germany. From January 1951 through April 1953, 447,000 people have fled alone. Working people make up a substantial number of the defectors. An analysis of the social composition of defectors reveals the following: 18,000 workers; 9,000 medium and small farmers, skilled workers, and retirees; 17,000 professionals and intellectuals; and 24,000 housewives. It is striking that 2,718 members and candidates of the SED and 2,619 members of the FDJ [Free German Youth Movement] were among the defectors to West Germany in the first four months of 1953.

> According to Source B, what were economic conditions within the GDR in 1953?

It should be recognized that the main cause of this situation is the false course adopted during the Second Party Conference of the SED – and approved by the Central Committee of the Communist Party of the Soviet Union – accelerating the pace of the construction of socialism in East Germany, without the necessary domestic and foreign policy preconditions.

What was the significance of the East German Uprising for Germany?

The East German Uprising

A series of strikes and riots broke out throughout East Germany on 16 June 1953. Workers demanded increased pay, more political freedom and the re-establishment of the German Social Democratic Party, which had been amalgamated with the KPD in 1946 to create the SED (see page 50). By the following day, waves of spontaneous and unco-ordinated strikes, demonstrations and riots had erupted across the whole of the GDR. Crowds collected outside prisons, state and party offices and called for the resignation of the government; but only in two cities, Görlitz and Bitterfeld, were there determined efforts to take over the city governments. In East Berlin, 100,000 people demonstrated on the streets.

The government, distrusting the loyalty of its own police forces, appealed to the Soviets to intervene. On 17 June, Soviet troops backed by tanks moved to suppress the uprising. Sporadic demonstrations and riots continued throughout the summer with 125 people killed, 19 of them in East Berlin.

The consequences for German unity

The uprising took both the Soviets and the Western allies by surprise, and has been called by historian Christian Ostermann 'one of the most significant focal points in the history of the Cold War' (see Source C).

According to Source C, what were the consequences of the East German Uprising for the Cold War?

SOURCE C

An excerpt from 'The United States and the East German Uprising of 1953 and the Limits of Rollback' by Christian Ostermann, published in *Cold War International History Project*, Woodrow Wilson International Center for Scholars, Washington DC, USA, Dec. 1994, pp. 2–3.

… the 1953 East German crisis has to be recognized as one of the most significant focal points in the history of the Cold War. International historians have come to corroborate this view. The uprising erupted during the crucial months after Stalin's death on 5 March 1953 at a time when the new Soviet leadership was engrossed in a fierce power struggle. In an effort to give an impression of continued strength and unity, and to gain breathing space in the international arena for domestic consolidation, the Soviet leaders displayed considerable flexibility in the foreign policy arena, raising popular hopes in the West for a relaxation of Cold War tensions. With regard to Germany, the fluidity of the situation resulted from a deep disagreement within the Soviet leadership over the future of their politically and economically weakening East German satellite. The near-toppling of the SED state in the uprising influenced the developments and decisions in Moscow.

Moreover, the USSR's massive military intervention in support of its client regime, and its visibly raised commitment to SED General Secretary [Party Leader] Walter Ulbricht and the SED dictatorship changed the dynamics of the Soviet-East German alliance. By providing SED General Secretary Walter Ulbricht with increased bargaining power, the heightened Soviet stake in the continued existence of the GDR shifted the balance within the relationship to some degree in favor of the latter. Similarly, in the West, the uprising and the resultant surge of nationalism intensified the American commitment to Adenauer and his policy of Western integration and at the same time bolstered the prospects of the Chancellor's Christian Democratic Union (CDU) in the September 1953 elections …

US reaction

Despite his pledge during the presidential election to liberate eastern Europe from Soviet control, Eisenhower did not interfere with the Soviet suppression of the East German Uprising. The US government hoped that the sight of Soviet troops on the streets of East Berlin would fuel West German fears of the USSR and persuade the voters to re-elect Adenauer in the September 1953 elections. Yet there was a danger that if the US was seen to do nothing to help the East Germans, there could, as C.D. Jackson, Eisenhower's advisor for psychological warfare, said, 'be a terrible let down in East and West Germany, which will seriously affect the American position and even more seriously affect Adenauer's position.'

SOURCE D

East German workers hurl stones at Soviet tanks on 17 June 1953.

> What information is conveyed in Source D regarding the Berlin Uprising? **?**

Eisenhower's advisors launched a two-pronged strategy. The US would respond to pressure of public opinion in West Germany for intervention in East Germany by calling for a foreign ministers' conference on the future of Germany. At the same time, through provocative broadcasts from its radio stations in West Berlin, it would do all it could to prolong the unrest in East Germany. This policy certainly strengthened support for Adenauer in the FRG; he won the election in September by a much larger margin than in the previous election.

The Berlin Conference, 25 January–18 February 1954

By the time the foreign ministers of Britain, France, the US and USSR met in Berlin in early 1954, all hope of making any progress on reuniting Germany had ended. Beria, who of all the Soviet politicians had been the most anxious to find a solution to the problems caused by a divided Germany, had been arrested and executed by his political rivals on the grounds that his 'treachery' had led to the East German uprising. In Berlin, both the USSR and the Western allies produced mutually unacceptable plans for German unity, which each side rejected. The USSR feared that the Western proposal of holding free elections in Germany would lead to a massive anti-communist vote, while the Western powers feared that a neutral disarmed Germany, not integrated into NATO or the European Defence Community (EDC), would be vulnerable to Soviet influence. The question of German reunification thus remained deadlocked.

What were the consequences of the French rejection of the EDC?

French rejection of the EDC, August 1954

On 15 May 1953, the EDC and the General Treaty (see page 87) were both ratified by the West German parliament, but the EDC was rejected by the French National Assembly on 30 August 1954. This reopened the whole question of West German rearmament and the FRG's entry into NATO, which was vital for the defence of western Europe.

FRG's entry into NATO, May 1955

The immediate priority of Britain and the US was to secure the FRG's entry into NATO. France's fears of a rearmed Germany were overcome by Adenauer's agreement to limit the West German army to the size envisaged in the EDC treaty and the FRG's renouncement of nuclear weapons. Britain's commitment to keep four divisions of troops supported by aircraft in West Germany also reassured France. In October 1954, a fresh settlement was reached that recognized the sovereignty of the FRG and its membership of NATO. The Western allies again committed themselves to work towards a united, federal Germany integrated into a democratic western Europe. Until this happened, their troops would remain in the FRG and Berlin would remain under Four-Power control. On 5 May 1955, the treaty came into force and four days later the FRG joined NATO.

These treaties effectively completed the post-war settlement of western Europe. Yet they also deepened the division of Europe. While the possibility was kept open for German unification, in reality the integration of the FRG into NATO made unity in the foreseeable future unlikely. The very success of the FRG's integration intensified what the historian Christoph Klessmann has called 'the reactive mechanism' of the Cold War: the more the FRG was integrated into the West, the more tightly bound was the GDR into the Soviet bloc.

SOURCE E

An excerpt from the General Treaty on Germany, which Britain, France, the US and West Germany signed on 23 October 1954, quoted in *Uniting Germany: Documents and Debates, 1944–1993*, ed. K.H. Jarausch and V. Gransow, published by Berg Publishers, Oxford, UK, 1994, pp.10–11.

Article 1:

(1) When this treaty goes into effect, the United State of America, the United Kingdom of Great Britain and Northern Ireland, and the French Republic … will end the occupation regime in the Federal Republic, repeal the occupation statute and dissolve the Allied High Commission and the offices of the State Commissioners in the Federal Republic.

(2) The Federal Republic will thereby have the full powers of a sovereign state over its internal and external affairs.

Article 2:

In view of the international situation, which until now prevented German reunification and the conclusion of a peace treaty, the Three Powers retain the rights and duties exercised or held by them with regard to Berlin and Germany as a whole … The rights and duties retained by the Three Powers in regard to stationing armed forces in Germany and protecting the security of these forces are determined by Articles 4 and 5 of this Treaty …

Article 7:

(2) Until conclusion of a peace treaty settlement, the signatory states will co-operate by peaceful means to implement their common goal: a reunited Germany possessing a free, democratic constitution similar to the Federal Republic and integrated into the European Community …

> To what extent does Source E recognize the Federal Republic of Germany as a fully independent power? **?**

The Warsaw Pact Treaty

> ← To what extent was the Warsaw Pact a consequence of West Germany's membership of NATO?

On 14 May 1955, the USSR and eastern European states entered the Warsaw Pact; the GDR eventually joined in January 1956. The Pact committed its members to consult on issues of mutual interest and to give all necessary assistance in the event of an attack on any one of them in Europe. Essentially, the treaty was signed for political rather than military reasons as a response to the FRG's entry into NATO, but it still kept open the option of a neutral Germany by declaring that if a 'general European treaty of Collective Security' was signed, the Warsaw Pact would lapse.

According to Source F, was the Warsaw Pact a direct response to the General Treaty of 23 October 1954?

SOURCE F

An excerpt from the introduction to the Warsaw Pact Treaty, which was signed in May 1955, quoted in *The Unsettled Peace*, by Roger Morgan, BBC Publications, London, UK, 1974, p. 75.

… the situation created in Europe by the ratification of the Paris agreements, which envisage the formation of a new military alignment in the shape of 'Western European Union', with the participation of a re-militarized Western Germany and the integration of the latter in the North Atlantic bloc … increases the danger of another war and constitutes a threat to the national security of peaceable states.

The 'Geneva Spirit' and its limitations

What was the importance of the 'Geneva Spirit' in international affairs?

In May 1956, Khrushchev and Bulganin, who had now emerged as the leaders of the USSR, accepted an invitation from the Western allies to meet in Geneva, Switzerland. This would be the first major summit conference since Potsdam in 1945 (see page 46). British Prime Minister Anthony Eden envisaged this to be the first of several summits, which would aim to reduce tension between the Soviet and Western blocs.

The Geneva Conference

When the leaders of Britain, France, the US and USSR met in July, they agreed on the following agenda:

- the reunification of Germany
- European security
- disarmament
- the development of contacts between East and West.

While conversations were conducted in an atmosphere of *détente*, and Eden invited Bulganin and Khrushchev to visit London in April 1956, the limits to the new spirit of co-existence, or 'Geneva spirit', were quickly reached. The USSR agreed to evacuate Austria, which had been divided into four zones in 1945, provided it remained neutral and did not join NATO. There was, however, still deadlock between the two sides over the future of Germany. Neither was progress made on disarmament or arms control, although it was agreed that the foreign ministers of the major powers should meet again to discuss the questions of Germany, security and disarmament.

Adenauer's visit to Moscow, September 1955

In September 1955, Adenauer visited Moscow to negotiate the return of the last German prisoners-of-war and to establish normal diplomatic relations with the USSR. Far from leading to a breakthrough in the German question, the division between the two Germanys widened still further. To reassure the GDR of continued Soviet support, the USSR acknowledged the GDR as an independent state in its own right. Adenauer, worried that an exchange of ambassadors with the USSR might be interpreted to mean that his government recognized the legal existence of the GDR, announced the Hallstein Doctrine. This stated that the FRG would consider the recognition of the GDR by any state, other than the USSR, as an unfriendly act which would lead to an immediate break in diplomatic relations. The Hallstein Doctrine deepened the divisions between the two Germanys.

> What information is conveyed by Source G about the division of Europe in May 1955?

SOURCE G

Cold War Europe in 1955.

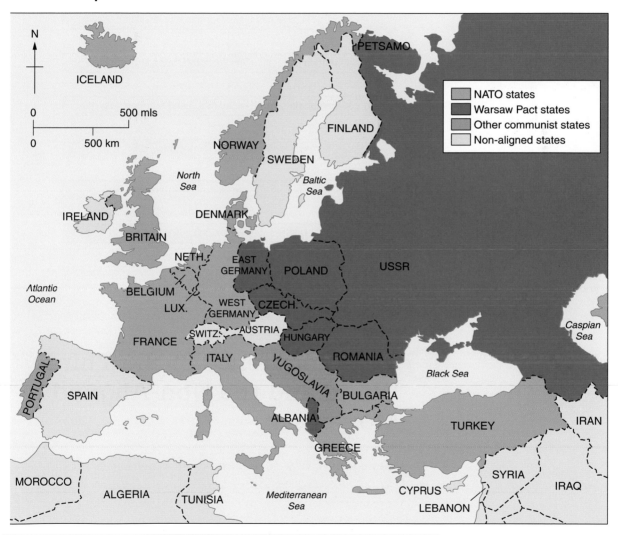

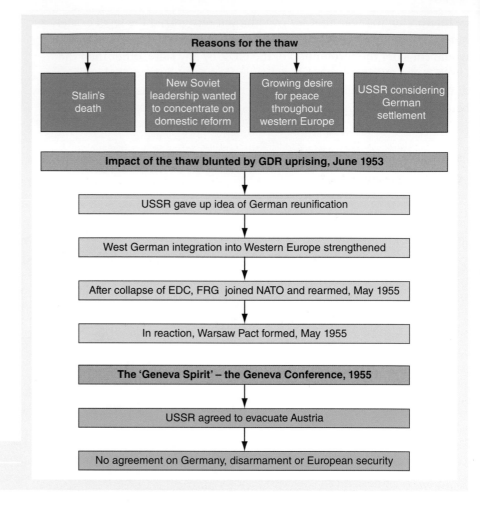

Reasons for the thaw

| Stalin's death | New Soviet leadership wanted to concentrate on domestic reform | Growing desire for peace throughout western Europe | USSR considering German settlement |

Impact of the thaw blunted by GDR uprising, June 1953

USSR gave up idea of German reunification

West German integration into Western Europe strengthened

After collapse of EDC, FRG joined NATO and rearmed, May 1955

In reaction, Warsaw Pact formed, May 1955

The 'Geneva Spirit' – the Geneva Conference, 1955

USSR agreed to evacuate Austria

No agreement on Germany, disarmament or European security

SUMMARY DIAGRAM

The thaw, 1953–55

2 The emergence of the Third World and the Non-Aligned Movement

▶ *Key question: Why did the Non-Aligned Movement cause difficulties for both the US and USSR?*

By 1955, European colonial empires were in retreat. In Asia, the Netherlands had been forced out of Indonesia, France out of Indochina and Britain out of India, Burma and Sri Lanka. In North Africa, France was under pressure to pull out of Algeria, and Britain to relinquish treaty rights in Egypt. The demand for independence was growing in sub-Saharan Africa as well.

The USSR and the Third World

How did the new Soviet leadership seek to strengthen its links with the Third World and China?

In the early 1950s, the concept of the **Third World** began to emerge to describe the global majority who claimed to have been economically depressed and enslaved by colonial powers. The Cold War divided Europe and threatened to divide the world. This confronted those countries that had achieved their independence in the post-war decade with a considerable problem. Many were predisposed to be friendly towards the USSR and to receive vital aid from the US, but had no desire to be drawn into the Cold War and to have to choose sides.

KEY TERM

Third World Developing states, many of which had been colonies or under the control of predominately European states.

Khrushchev and the Third World

Stalin had shown little interest in the Third World. The new Soviet leadership, however, was more anxious to gain influence in the recently independent states. Khrushchev realized that the USSR could exploit anti-colonialism to weaken the West. In December 1955, Khrushchev and Bulganin, during a tour of India, Burma and Afghanistan, stressed Soviet willingness to co-operate with the Third World and lost no opportunity to repeat, as Lenin had done before them (see page 14), that the main enemy was colonialism and imperialism. Khrushchev openly attacked Stalin's record of failing to understand that communism could develop in many different ways in the Third World.

PRC–Soviet co-operation

The years 1954–55 were also a period of co-operation between the People's Republic of China and the Soviet Union. In 1954, the USSR signed a series of agreements with the PRC. It agreed to return military bases in Lushun (Port Arthur) that had been occupied at the end of the Second World War (see page 103) and to increase financial and technical support. In April 1955, the USSR signed a further agreement to supply the PRC with nuclear technology.

The Bandung Conference and the creation of the Non-Aligned Movement

What was the importance of the Bandung Conference?

The Bandung Conference

The leaders of five independent Asian states – Indonesia, India, Pakistan, Burma and Sri Lanka – planned to meet in Bandung in 1955. While planning the conference, the decision was made to invite the leaders of independence movements in Africa, Asia and South America. The leaders of the PRC also attended. In the end, the conference at Bandung represented 1.5 billion people.

According to Source H, what was the importance of the Bandung Conference?

An excerpt of a description of the opening of the Bandung Conference by Richard Wright, quoted in *The Global Cold War* by Odd Arne Westad, Cambridge University Press, Cambridge, UK, 2005, p. 99.

I'd no sooner climbed into the press gallery and looked down upon the vast assembly, many of them clad in exotic national costumes, than I could sense an important junction of history in the making. In the early and difficult days of the Russian revolution, Lenin had dreamt of a gathering like this, a conglomeration of the world's underdogs, coming to the aid of the hard pressed Soviets … [But] from a strict Stalinist point of view, such a gathering as this was unthinkable, for it was evident that the Communists had no control here … Every religion under the sun, almost every race on earth, every shade of political opinion, and one and half thousand million people from 12,606,938 square miles of the earth's surface were represented here.

The conference seemed to symbolize a new era as France had just left Indochina (see page 133), the Korean War had ended and Soviet leaders were stressing peace and *détente*. The conference spent a considerable amount of time discussing the Cold War and how to avoid becoming entrapped in it.

SOURCE I

According to Source I, why did Nehru believe it was important to be neutral in the Cold War?

An excerpt from a speech by Pandit Nehru, the Prime Minister of India, to the delegates at Bandung Conference, quoted in *The Global Cold War* by Odd Arne Westad, Cambridge University Press, Cambridge, UK, 2005, p. 101.

So far as I am concerned, it does not matter what war will take place: we will not take part in it unless we have to defend ourselves. If I join any of these big groups, I lose my identity; I have no identity left, I have no view left … If all the world were to be divided up between these two big blocs what would be the result? The inevitable result would be war …

The main topic, however, was the completion of the struggle for liberation from the Western world. In the final communiqué, emphasis was placed on the importance of economic and cultural co-operation among Third World states. It was recommended that a joint policy regarding petroleum be created. This led to the creation of the Organization of Petroleum Exporting Countries (OPEC) in 1960. It also called on the states to abstain 'from the use of arrangements of collective defence to serve the particular interests of any of the big powers'.

The Bandung Conference caused concern for both the US and USSR. President Eisenhower and Dulles, the US Secretary of State, were worried about the drift towards socialism in many of the Third World states. Khrushchev welcomed this but at the same time feared that their aim of working together would make it all the more difficult for the USSR to influence them.

The Non-Aligned Movement

In 1961, India, Indonesia, Egypt, Yugoslavia, Ghana and Algeria met in Belgrade, Yugoslavia, and established the **Non-Aligned Movement** (NAM) based on the principles of self-determination, mutual economic assistance and neutrality, which had been agreed upon at Bandung. To emphasize their neutrality in the Cold War, all the heads of state of the participating counties at the conference sent identical notes to Khrushchev and US President Kennedy warning against the threat of war and appealing for a peaceful conclusion to the Berlin Crisis (see page 167). By 1964, there were over 50 members of the NAM.

 **KEY TERM**

Non-Aligned Movement (NAM) Organization of states committed to not joining either the Western or Soviet blocs during the Cold War, founded in Belgrade in 1961 and based on the principles agreed at the Bandung Conference.

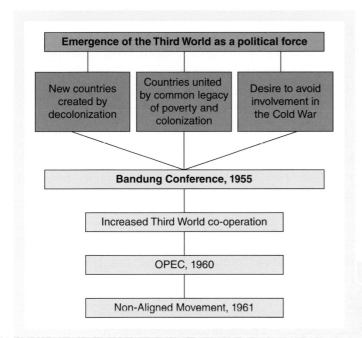

SUMMARY DIAGRAM

The emergence of the Third World and the Non-Aligned Movement

1956: The year of crises

> ▶ **Key question:** *What caused the series of crises that shook both the Western powers and the Soviet bloc in 1956?*

The year 1956 was a pivotal year in the Cold War. In the spring it seemed that the USSR would continue with the policy of *détente* and liberalization, but in the autumn Soviet leaders were confronted with the dilemma that would recur several times before the end of the Cold War: how far could they afford to relax Soviet control over eastern Europe? If concessions led to demands for ever greater political freedom, at what point would Soviet troops intervene to maintain control?

De-Stalinization

> **To what extent did de-Stalinization affect the Warsaw Pact?**

 KEY TERM

De-Stalinization The attempts to liberalize the USSR after the death of Stalin in 1953.

De-Stalinization strongly affected the relations between the USSR and its satellite states. It appeared to promise a return to the policy of 'different roads to socialism' which Stalin briefly tolerated between 1945 and 1947 (see page 68). The pace of de-Stalinization accelerated after the execution of Beria in 1953 (see page 144). Beria's secret police network, which had agents throughout eastern Europe, was dissolved and politicians such as Władysław Gomułka in Poland and János Kádár in Hungary were released from prison and returned to public life. This raised expectations in the satellite states that they would be given more independence from Soviet control.

Khrushchev's speech, February 1956

A further wave of de-Stalinization followed Khrushchev's famous speech at the 20th Party Conference of the Communist Party, February 1956. He denounced Stalin and recognized the rights of the satellite states to find their own ways to socialism. Although the speech was supposed to be secret, the Central Intelligence Agency, the US government espionage agency, acquired a copy and ensured that it was broadcast by radio to eastern Europe. By raising hopes of political change, this contributed to the unrest in Poland and Hungary later in the year.

Yugoslavia

Expectations of reform were further increased by the improvement in relations between the USSR and Yugoslavia, which was re-admitted to the Soviet bloc after Khrushchev and Bulganin, the Soviet Prime Minister, visited Belgrade in May 1955. The blame for the break in 1948 was attributed to Stalin (see pages 94–95). Khrushchev and his colleagues were, of course, primarily interested in bringing Yugoslavia back into the Soviet sphere of influence, while Tito, the Yugoslav leader, ambitiously believed that, as a result of his experience in defying Stalin, he was a role model for the new generation of Soviet bloc leaders and would now be their leader. In June 1956, after talks in Moscow, Khrushchev and Tito issued a communiqué in which they agreed that there were many different ways to achieve communism and that attempts to impose a pattern of uniformity were unacceptable. This was an optimistic doctrine which assumed that the satellite states wished to remain within the Soviet bloc.

The Polish Crisis, June–October 1956

The new doctrine's limitations were first tested in Poland in 1956. At the end of June, riots broke out in Poznań when the local factory workers protested about the imposition of increased production targets. These were suppressed with heavy casualties by the police but, to mitigate criticism of the government, the Polish Workers' Party, Poland's local communist party, recalled Gomułka, who had been recently released from prison, to lead the government as First Secretary. The Soviet government, fearing that he would seek to restore Poland's full independence, sent a delegation to Warsaw, Poland's capital, on 19–20 October, and ordered the Red Army units stationed in Poland to advance on the city in an attempt to stop his election by the Central Committee of the Polish Workers' Party. Gomułka refused to be cowed, making it clear that Poland's army would resist Soviet forces, and his election went ahead as Soviet troops returned to their barracks.

> **Why did Khrushchev not use Soviet troops to restore order in Poland?**

SOURCE 1

An excerpt of Khrushchev's comments to the Central Committee of the USSR on the political situation in Poland and Hungary, 24 October 1956, quoted in 'Hungary and Poland, 1956: Khrushchev's CPSU CC Presidium Meeting on East European Crises, 24 October, 1956' with introduction, translation and annotation by Mark Kramer, CWIHP, pp. 1–12, located at www.wilsoncenter.org/program/cold-war-international-history-project

… the discussions between the [Soviet and Polish] delegations ranged from being very warm to rude. Gomułka several times emphasised that they would not permit their independence to be taken away and would not allow anyone to interfere in Poland's internal affairs. He said that if he were leader of the country he would restore order promptly.

> What information is conveyed in Source 1 about Gomułka? **?**

The Hungarian Uprising, 1956

Just as the crisis in Poland began to be resolved, the USSR faced a more serious challenge to its power. As part of his de-Stalinization campaign, Khrushchev had, with Tito's backing, pressured the Hungarian Communist Party in July 1956 to replace its old-style Stalinist leader, Mátyás Rákosi, with the more liberal Ernö Gerö. Tito had considerable ambitions in Hungary, as he hoped that an independent communist regime would emerge there that would look to him and Yugoslavia rather than Khrushchev and the USSR and so strengthen his overall influence within the Soviet bloc.

> **To what extent was Hungary able successfully to challenge Soviet political control in 1956?**

The appointment of Imre Nagy

On 23 October 1956, there was a large demonstration in Budapest, Hungary's capital. Protestors demanded the withdrawal of Soviet troops and a new government under Imre Nagy, an independent-minded communist who advocated reforms similar to those Tito had introduced in Yugoslavia (see page 95). They attacked the state radio station and, in an attempt to avert further violence, Gerö appointed Nagy as Prime Minister.

In response to these demonstrations, the USSR initially mobilized 30,000 troops backed with tanks and artillery. Khrushchev, however, tried to reconcile his pledges to concede greater independence to the satellite states with Soviet security needs. On 30 October, he issued the 'Declaration on the Principles of Development and a Further Strengthening of Friendship and Co-operation between the USSR and other Socialist Countries'. This attempted to provide a legal and mutually agreed framework for Soviet military bases in eastern Europe. This did not, however, stop Nagy from threatening the basis of Soviet power in eastern Europe by announcing his intention to withdraw Hungary from the Warsaw Pact. If this happened, Hungary would effectively become independent of the USSR and Poland and the other satellite states would most likely follow.

Major fighting between the Hungarians and Soviet troops erupted in the countryside in north-west Hungary and, by 28 October, the rebels were in control of most of Hungary outside Budapest.

US policy

The US Radio Free Europe, a radio station sponsored by the US government to broadcast anti-Soviet and pro-US propaganda, encouraged Hungarians to revolt. They were led to believe that NATO would intervene to provide protection from the USSR, although that was in reality unlikely. US President Eisenhower, fearing that the USSR might be willing to risk nuclear war rather than lose Hungary, made it absolutely clear to the Soviet leaders that NATO would not intervene to save Nagy. He instructed Dulles to announce publically on 27 October that the 'US had no ulterior purpose in desiring the independence of the satellite countries' and would not 'look upon these nations as potential military allies'.

On 4 November, Soviet troops advanced into Hungary and, after a few days of fierce fighting with the Hungarian rebels, a new government loyal to the USSR under János Kádár was installed.

T O K

One could argue that both the US and the USSR imposed governments, or prevented real choice, during the Cold War (North and South Korea, East and West Germany, etc.). Why do we tend to believe that it is important for people to choose their own governments when no one reading this book ever has done so and likely will not? (History, Ethics, Language, Emotion, Reason)

SOURCE J

Russian officers in Budapest, Hungary, advance threateningly towards a Western photographer, November 1956.

> What does Source J reveal about the Soviet occupation of Hungary? **?**

The Suez Crisis

Soviet policy during the Hungarian Uprising cannot be fully understood without also reviewing the Suez Crisis of October 1956.

> **In what ways did the Suez Crisis influence Soviet action in Hungary?**

Nasser and the 'Bandung spirit'

Nasser, who became the President of Egypt in 1954, embodied the new independent anti-colonialist spirit of the Bandung Conference (see page 149). He recognized the PRC, forged close links with Yugoslavia and bought weapons from the Soviet bloc. He had no desire, however, to become an ally of the USSR in the Cold War. His main aim was to force European colonial powers out of the Middle East and North Africa and to return the Palestinian refugees to their homeland in what had become Israel in 1948. Throughout the Middle East, the Cairo radio station 'Voice of the Arabs' encouraged resistance to pro-British and pro-French governments in the region. Nasser was determined to play off the US against the USSR and extract concessions from both powers.

The Czechoslovakia arms deal

The US was willing to supply weapons to Egypt as long as they were to be used only for defensive purposes and accompanied by US military personnel for supervision and training. Nasser rejected these conditions, as he feared that they would tie Egypt too tightly to the US, and instead, looked to the Soviet bloc for weapon supplies. On 27 September 1955,

Nasser announced an arms deal with Czechoslovakia. Under the terms of this deal, Egypt received considerable quantities of fighter and bomber aircraft and tanks.

The Aswan High Dam

Alarmed by the arms deal, Britain and the US sought to improve relations with Egypt. They agreed in December 1955, together with the **World Bank**, to raise $270 million towards the cost of the initial stages of the construction of the Aswan High Dam to improve irrigation in the Nile valley and develop hydro-electricity. Egypt also explored Soviet offers to build a dam more cheaply as it resented the financial guarantees demanded by the World Bank, which, it argued, amounted to control of the Egyptian economy. In June 1956, the USSR offered Nasser a massive loan of $1,120,000,000 at 2 per cent interest for the construction of the dam. Egypt was therefore in a strong position to bargain with the US, but on 19 July the US and Britain lost patience with the protracted negotiations and cancelled their offer.

There are several other reasons why the US decided to withdraw the offer of funding, and not match the Soviet offer:

- Egypt regarded itself as still at war with Israel, an ally of the US.
- Nasser undermined pro-Western governments in Turkey, Iran and Iraq.
- Nasser had recognized the PRC.
- US Secretary of State Dulles believed that the Soviet Union would not be able to fulfil its commitment to build the dam, and that in time Nasser would become disillusioned with the USSR and turn again to the US.

Nationalization of the Suez Canal

Gaining control of the **Suez Canal** was a major aim of Nasser and Egyptian nationalists. The Canal was owned by an Anglo-French company, and Britain controlled a series of military bases along its shores. In 1954, Nasser and the British government negotiated an agreement whereby British troops would evacuate their bases along the Canal, leaving the Canal's operation to British and Egyptian technicians. In the event of an attack on Egypt, Britain would have the right to return to protect the Canal. To Nasser, this agreement was a step towards complete Egyptian control. The withdrawal of Anglo-US funding for the Aswan High Dam gave him an opportunity to establish complete Egyptian control of the Suez Canal. On 26 July, he **nationalized** it so that he could use its revenues, which were raised from the tolls charged to ships using the canal, to finance the construction of the Aswan High Dam.

Anglo-French collusion with Israel

Nationalization of the Suez Canal gave Britain, France and Israel an excuse to topple Nasser. All three states wanted to remove him from power. For the British and French, he was a determined enemy of their remaining colonial influence in North Africa and the Middle East. For the Israelis, Nasser

KEY TERM

World Bank International financial institution that provides loans to developing countries for large-scale engineering projects.

Suez Canal Canal located in Egypt connecting the Mediterranean and Red Sea.

Nationalize A state take-over of privately owned industries, banks, and other parts of the economy.

represented a dangerous threat as he was intent on ending what he saw as the European **Zionist** occupation of Palestine, i.e. the new state of Israel, and, to strengthen itself, Israel wished to gain control of more territory, specifically Egypt's Sinai Peninsula.

On 16 October, Britain, France and Israel created a joint plan for invading Egypt. Israeli troops would invade Egypt through the Sinai and advance towards the Canal. Britain and France would intervene in the conflict between Israel and Egypt by sending a force of 80,000 troops to protect the Canal, using the 1954 Anglo-Egyptian Agreement to justify their action. When Israel attacked on 29 October, Britain and France immediately demanded withdrawal of both the Israeli and Egyptian forces from the Canal, although Egypt had not been the aggressor and had lost control of most of the Sinai. When Nasser refused, British planes bombed Egypt's airfields on 31 October.

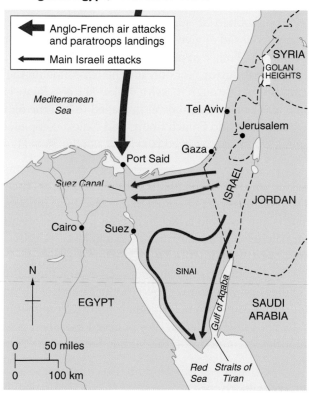

SOURCE K

Map of attacks against Egypt, November 1956.

> **KEY TERM**
>
> **Zionism** A form of Jewish nationalism that supported the foundation of a Jewish state in the historic land of Israel.

> What information is conveyed by Source K about the attack on Egypt? ?

The Suez Crisis and Hungary

Khrushchev was convinced that Nasser would be quickly defeated and that Soviet influence in Egypt would suffer a disastrous blow. If this was combined with further setbacks in Hungary, Soviet power and prestige would be greatly diminished.

? According to Source L, what was the effect of the Suez Crisis on Hungary?

An excerpt of Khrushchev's comments to the Central Committee of the USSR on Poland and Hungary, 31 October 1956, quoted in 'Cold War International History Project Bulletin' (CWIHP), Document no. 8, p. 393, located at www.wilsoncenter.org/program/cold-war-international-history-project

We should re-examine our assessment and should not withdraw our troops from Hungary and Budapest. We should take the initiative in restoring order in Hungary. If we depart from Hungary, it will give a great boost to the Americans, English and French – the imperialists. They will perceive it as a weakness on our part and will go on the offensive. We would then be exposing the weakness of our positions. Our party will not accept it if we do this. To Egypt they will then add Hungary. We have no other choice …

US intervention

On 5 November, Anglo-French forces landed along the Suez Canal. Britain assumed they would obtain US support, but Eisenhower, in the middle of an election campaign, refused to give it. The US viewed the Suez conflict as an attempt by Britain and France to prop up their disintegrating empires in the Middle East and North Africa. Not only did the US condemn the attack in the United Nations, but through massive diplomatic and financial pressure on both Britain and France, Eisenhower managed to halt the fighting on 6 November when British and French troops had almost completed capturing the whole Canal. US pressure forced Israel to leave the Sinai Peninsula in March 1957.

The main reason why the US had halted the Suez war was that it was determined to prevent Soviet attempts to increase their influence among Arab nationalists and to avoid criticism of their lack of intervention in Hungary. Khrushchev had already proposed a joint US–USSR peacekeeping operation along the Suez Canal under control of the UN and threatened to send troops to enforce the peace even if the US did not participate. Dulles and Eisenhower therefore felt that the US had to choose between supporting Anglo-French colonialism or aligning with Arab nationalism. By choosing the latter, they believed that the US would be able to counter Soviet influence in the Middle East and the Third World more effectively.

The Soviet missile threat

Khrushchev cleverly exploited this split in NATO, and on 5 November threatened nuclear missile attacks on Britain, France and Israel if they did not stop their attack on Egypt. Although it was known by the CIA that the USSR did not yet possess the missiles to propel such warheads, the ceasefire on the following day made it appear as if it was the Soviet ultimatum rather than US pressure that had saved Egypt. Khrushchev was thus able to take the credit in the Middle East and the communist world for having defeated the British and French.

Polish and Hungarian Crises

General causes
- De-Stalinization
- Impact of Khrushchev's speech at 20th Party Conference
- Tito's influence – different routes to socialism

Poland	**Hungary**
• Riots of June 1956 • Soviet objection to appointment of Gomutka • Advance of Red Army averted by Gomutka's promise to resolve order	• Stalinist leader replaced by Gerö • Tito encourages a more independent line • Riots on 28 October triggered Soviet military intervention • Nagy appointed as compromise leader • Announcement that Hungary intended to withdraw from Warsaw Pact prompted Soviet military Intervention • Khrushchev convinced that his ally in the Middle East, Colonel Nasser, would be toppled by Anglo-French action

Impact of Suez Crisis on Cold War
- Fear of Nasser's defeat strengthened Khrushchev's resolve to crush Hungarian revolt
- Khrushchev attempted to exploit Anglo-French/US split by threatening to fire nuclear missiles at London, Paris and Tel Aviv
- USSR's position in Middle East strengthened
- Khrushchev encouraged to develop policy of nuclear diplomacy

SUMMARY DIAGRAM

1956: The year of crises

The aftermath of the Hungarian and Suez Crises, 1957–58

▶ *Key question: What were the consequences of the crises of 1956 for the Soviet bloc and the Western powers?*

US intervention in Egypt showed that its interests and its allies' interests could sometimes diverge, and when that happened, the US, like any other power, would ruthlessly pursue what it perceived to be to its own advantage. In the Soviet bloc, the crushing of the Hungarian Uprising indicated that the USSR would use force to maintain its position in eastern Europe.

What were the consequences of the 1956 crises for the Soviet bloc?

The Soviet bloc

Crises in Poland and Hungary had shown how difficult it was for the USSR to encourage the satellite states to reform without creating a demand for their transformation into genuine democratic regimes. They also highlighted the problems the Soviet bloc had in the post-Stalinist era in agreeing on common policies as there was no framework for regular consultations.

Moscow Conference of International Communist Leaders, October 1957

Khrushchev attempted to remedy this at a conference attended by the international communist leaders at Moscow in October 1957 to celebrate the fortieth anniversary of the Russian Revolution. Although opposed by Poland and Yugoslavia, this conference passed a motion recognizing the USSR as 'the first and mightiest' of socialist countries, while acknowledging the legitimacy of the principle of 'different roads to socialism'. An element of diversity was still tolerated and considerable economic help was given to the satellite states by the USSR, but it was understood that they must essentially follow the Soviet political and economic model. This doctrine led to a fresh break with Tito, who now joined with India, Egypt, Indonesia and Ghana to form the Non-Aligned Movement of neutral states in 1961 (see page 151).

Growing criticism from the PRC

Outwardly, relations between Mao and Khrushchev were friendly. At the conference, Mao called on the communist world to recognize the leadership of the USSR. Yet, behind the scenes, Mao was highly critical of the whole de-Stalinization process and the way Khrushchev had handled the crises in Poland and Hungary. He argued that Stalin should still be regarded as a 'great Marxist–Leninist revolutionary leader', and implied that he, rather than Khrushchev, was Stalin's successor in the communist world.

Khrushchev and nuclear diplomacy

One of the important legacies of the Hungarian and Suez crises was that Khrushchev's position was greatly strengthened in the USSR. In 1958, he became the Soviet Prime Minister as well as remaining First Secretary of the Party. The US Secretary of State, Dulles, had perceptively warned that he was 'the most dangerous person to lead the Soviet Union since the October Revolution'. Whereas Stalin attempted carefully to calculate the consequences of his actions, Khrushchev, Dulles argued, was prepared to take dangerous risks to achieve his ends.

After his propaganda success in the Suez Crisis, Khrushchev was convinced that the mere threat of nuclear weapons would enable him to force NATO to make concessions over the status of Berlin. His policy of **nuclear diplomacy** gained more credibility when the USSR launched the world's first **intercontinental ballistic missile (ICBM)** in August 1957, and followed it up by sending a satellite, **Sputnik**, into orbit in October. Although these were impressive achievements, it was not until 1960 that the USSR had four ICBMs equipped with nuclear warheads. Meanwhile the US was developing Polaris submarines. By 1962, eight of these were at sea and were able to fire 144 nuclear missiles.

Although the overall military balance still favoured the West, Khrushchev deliberately exaggerated the extent of Soviet successes in order, as he wrote in his memoirs, 'to exert pressure on American militarists – and also influence the minds of more reasonable politicians – so that the United States would start treating us better.'

KEY TERM

Nuclear diplomacy
Negotiations and diplomacy supported by the threat of nuclear weapons.

Intercontinental ballistic missiles (ICBM) Missiles capable of carrying nuclear warheads and reaching great distances.

Sputnik Russian for 'fellow traveller', or supporter of the USSR, and the name of the world's first artificial satellite placed in the Earth's orbit.

SOURCE M

An excerpt from *We Now Know: Rethinking Cold War History*, by John Lewis Gaddis, Oxford University Press, Oxford, UK, 1997, p. 238.

… on 21 August 1957, when the Soviet Union successfully tested the world's first intercontinental ballistic missile launched from Kazakhstan, its dummy warhead splashed down in the Pacific Ocean, some 4,000 miles away. Khrushchev himself witnessed a second launch on 7 September, and was sufficiently impressed to authorize the use of a third ICBM on 4 October to send a simple satellite into orbit around the earth. Sputnik … [This] brought the Cold War quite literally close to home. One needed no Geiger counter to measure this new manifestation of potential political danger. All that was necessary was to look up, on a clear night, to see the sunlight reflecting off the spent rocket casing as it tumbled slowly in orbit over one's own house.

According to Source M, what was the significance of the successful tests of the Soviet ICBMs?

NATO, 1957–58

The Suez Crisis weakened NATO by causing profound disagreement between the three leading NATO powers: the US, Britain and France. Although good relations were restored between Britain and the US, in much of Europe distrust of the US lingered. There was an increasing awareness

To what extent did the interests of the US and its western European allies diverge in 1957–58?

that the interests of the US and its western European allies did not always coincide.

Britain

British Prime Minister Anthony Eden resigned and was replaced by Harold Macmillan in January 1957. In March, at Eisenhower's request, an Anglo-American conference was held in Bermuda. Close relations between the two powers were re-established. They agreed to base 60 **intermediate-range ballistic missiles (IRBM)** with nuclear warheads in Britain and place them under joint US–British control. In 1958, both powers co-operated to support the pro-Western regimes in the Lebanon and Jordan against subversion directed by the Egypt-dominated United Arab Republic that was temporarily formed in 1958 between Egypt and Syria (see page 211).

France

France reacted to the failure of the Suez war by seeking to make itself both militarily and economically independent of the US. To achieve this, Charles de Gaulle, who became president in June 1958, was determined that France should develop its own nuclear weapons and, through close co-operation with the FRG, make the newly created European Economic Community (EEC) independent of the US.

FRG

Fundamentally, Chancellor Adenauer did not share de Gaulle's vision of the future of the EEC. He wanted it to develop into a closely integrated community linked to the US. However, like many western Europeans, he wondered if the US would continue to defend western Europe once the USSR developed missiles capable of reaching US territory. He feared that when this occurred, and if the Soviets used this threat, the US might remove its forces from western Europe and give the GDR or the Soviet Union control of West Berlin.

EEC

The European Economic Community (EEC) was established by the Treaty of Rome which was signed by the FRG, France, Italy and the Benelux states in March 1957. Its aim was to create a common market or customs union within twelve years, while also gradually forming a more integrated political structure.

EFTA

British plans for the creation of a much larger free-trade zone were turned down by the leaders of the six powers on the grounds that it would not provide an effective basis for European economic and political co-operation. This led to Britain forming an alternative: the European Free Trade Association (EFTA) with Denmark, Norway, Sweden, Switzerland, Austria and Portugal.

SOURCE N

Map of Europe showing the EEC, EFTA and COMECON states, 1958.

According to Source N, to what extent did the three main European economic blocs reflect political divisions?

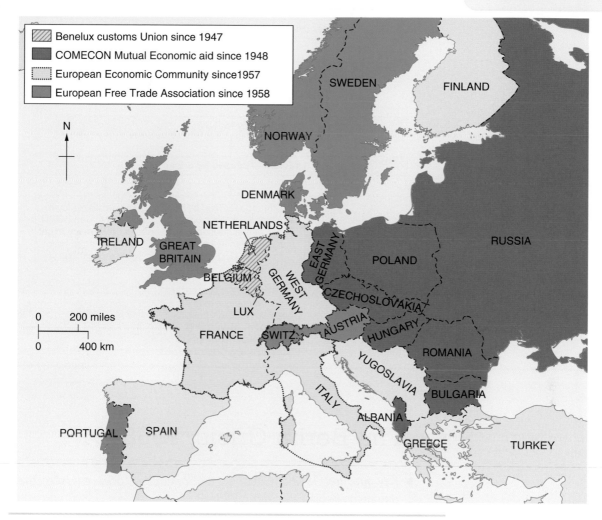

Benelux customs Union since 1947

COMECON Mutual Economic aid since 1948

European Economic Community since1957

European Free Trade Association since 1958

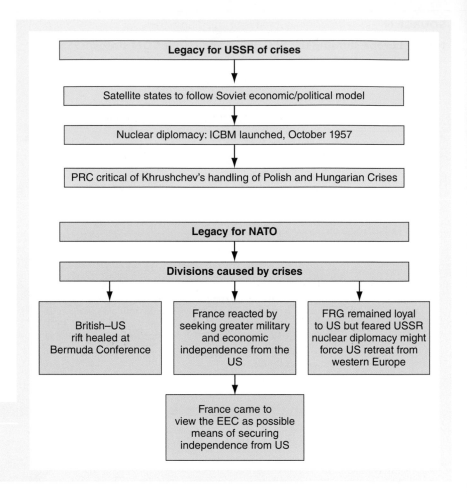

SUMMARY DIAGRAM

The aftermath of the Suez and Hungarian Crises, 1957–58

⑤ The Berlin Crisis, 1958–61

▶ **Key question**: *To what extent did the Soviet Union achieve its objectives during the Berlin Crisis from 1958–61?*

By 1958, it was clear that the Soviet aim of creating a neutral, disarmed and united Germany had failed. Not only was the FRG a member of NATO, but NATO had also decided to equip the FRG's army with tactical nuclear weapons. The priority of the USSR was now to strengthen the GDR.

What were the main weaknesses of the GDR?

The GDR

The GDR was a state unpopular with its inhabitants and totally dependent on the USSR. Unlike Poland and the other Warsaw Pact nations, it lacked a national identity, and was confronted across an artificial frontier by a prosperous West Germany, the impressive economic recovery of which inevitably attracted many of its most intelligent and ambitious citizens.

NATO states refused to acknowledge the legal existence of the GDR. They argued that its government had not been democratically elected and that it was not an independent country, but still the Soviet-occupied zone of Germany (see page 47). Although East Berlin was the capital of the GDR, legally Berlin remained under Four-Power control (see page 81). If the USSR were to close the frontier between West and East Berlin, it would be acting both unilaterally and illegally and therefore trigger a major crisis with NATO.

Through the open frontier in Berlin, it was still possible to flee from a stagnant economy, an oppressive state and rationing to the successful, capitalistic and democratic FRG. Between 1945 and 1961, about one-sixth of the whole GDR population fled to the FRG. One way of stopping this exodus was to improve the standard of living in the GDR but, to achieve this, it was essential to stop skilled workers and professionals relocating in large numbers to the FRG. This meant that the open frontier between East and West Berlin would have to be closed.

Khrushchev's ultimatum, November 1958

By grossly exaggerating the extent of Soviet nuclear power and by putting pressure on West Berlin, Khrushchev was sure that he could force Britain, France and the US to:

- withdraw from West Berlin
- recognize the legal existence of the GDR
- recognize the GDR's right to control Berlin's borders
- agree to a peace treaty with Germany, which would recognize the division of Germany and the GDR's post-war frontiers with Poland (see map, page 47).

The Berlin crisis began on 10 November when Khrushchev called for a peace treaty with the two German states.

> **How did the Western allies respond to Khrushchev's ultimatum regarding Berlin?**

SOURCE O

An excerpt from Khrushchev's speech of 10 November 1958 quoted in *The Unsettled Peace*, by R. Morgan, BBC Publications, London, UK, 1974, p. 78.

The time has obviously arrived for the signatories of the Potsdam Agreement to renounce the remnants of the occupation regime in Berlin, and thereby make it possible to create a normal situation in the capital of the German Democratic Republic. The Soviet Union, for its part, would hand over to the sovereign German Democratic Republic the functions in Berlin that are still exercised by Soviet agencies. This, I think, would be the correct thing to do.

> According to Source O, what were Khrushchev's intentions regarding Berlin? ?

KEY TERM

Free city Self-governing and independent city-state.

Land corridors Roads, railways and canals, which the USSR had agreed could be used to supply West Berlin in 1945.

Confederation A grouping of states in which each state retains its sovereignty; looser than a federation.

> **How divided was the Western response to Khrushchev's ultimatum?**

On 27 November, he followed this proposal with a six-month ultimatum demanding the demilitarization of West Berlin, the withdrawal of Western troops, and its change of status into a **free city**. If the Western allies refused to sign a peace treaty with the two German states, Khrushchev threatened to conclude a peace agreement just with the GDR and to recognize its sovereignty over East Berlin. This would then enable the GDR to control access to West Berlin and interfere at will with traffic using the **land corridors** from the FRG. The Western allies would thus be compelled to deal with East German rather than Soviet officials and so, in effect, recognize the sovereignty of the GDR, shattering the Hallstein Doctrine (see page 147).

Western reaction, 1959–60

Although the Western allies rejected the ultimatum, Khrushchev was successful in forcing them to the conference table to discuss the problem of Germany. In February 1959, they agreed that a foreign ministers' conference would meet in Geneva in the summer. Khrushchev was delighted to see divisions appearing in the Western alliance. In the preceding months, Adenauer viewed with increasing concern statements from Britain and the US signalling a desire for compromise and concession. He drew closer to de Gaulle, who urged a much tougher line against the Soviets. Adenauer was particularly alarmed by the decision of British Prime Minister Harold Macmillan to visit Moscow and by Eisenhower's invitation to Khrushchev to visit the US.

The Geneva Conference, May–August 1959

In Geneva, both sides put forward proposals for German unity, but no agreement was secured. The Western allies presented their usual demand for free elections, while the USSR suggested that the two Germanys form a **confederation** that would slowly evolve into a united state. The Soviets did succeed in persuading the West to discuss the Berlin problem as a separate issue. Khrushchev believed that his threats brought success so he continued the pressure, renewing the ultimatum in June.

Summit meetings, September 1959–May 1960

Between 1959 and 1961, there were more summits than at any time since the Second World War. When Khrushchev visited Eisenhower at Camp David, the retreat of the US president, in September 1959, the mood was friendly but, to quote historian John Gaddis, the two leaders 'got no further than an agreement to disagree'. Over the next two years, Khrushchev alternated periods of *détente*, when he temporarily allowed the ultimatum to lapse again, with phases of acute crisis during which further threats were issued to force the West into making concessions over the status of Berlin and the future of Germany.

Khrushchev's actions were not without success. Behind the scenes in Britain and the US, and at times even in France, various schemes for creating a nuclear-free zone in central Europe and legally recognizing Poland's western frontiers and the GDR were considered. Adenauer was desperate to stop any of these plans from reducing the FRG to a neutral second-rate state, but by May 1960, when the Paris Summit was to start, he had no idea what Eisenhower and Macmillan might propose. Thus, for him at least, it was 'a gift from heaven', as historian Christoph Klessmann has called it, when Khrushchev used the shooting down of an US spy plane over the USSR as an excuse to cancel the summit and wait until a new US president was elected in November.

U-2 spy planes and the arms race

In 1956, the US bought 53 Lockheed U-2 spy planes. Based in Japan, Turkey and Britain, they were able to fly over Soviet territory and photograph military bases, missile factories and launch pads. By 1961, Soviet technology caught up with the U-2s, and on 5 May a Soviet anti-aircraft missile shot down a plane that had been sent to see whether there were missile bases in the Ural Mountains. These flights established that, for all Khrushchev's boasting, the Soviets possessed very few ICBMs and no launching platforms. Indeed, the USSR had only four ICBMs based on a site near Archangel.

The construction of the Berlin Wall

Khrushchev's hopes that the new US President, John Kennedy, would make the concessions that Eisenhower had refused, proved unrealistic. Yet his response to Soviet threats to West Berlin hinted at a possible solution to the Berlin problem.

> **Why did Khrushchev agree to the construction of the Berlin Wall in August 1961?**

President Kennedy and Berlin

While Kennedy dramatically increased US forces in Europe, he also urged negotiation on the German question and pointedly stressed in a television broadcast on 25 July 1961 that the US was essentially interested in defending free access to West Berlin from the FRG, rather than maintaining the existing status of Berlin as a whole. He was, in fact, indicating that the US and NATO would fight to preserve the freedom of West Berlin, but would not intervene to stop the GDR from closing the frontier between East and West Berlin.

According to Source P, why was the US determined to keep troops in West Berlin?

SOURCE P

An excerpt from President Kennedy's 'Report to the Nation in July 1961'. 25 July 1961. *Department of State, Documents on Germany, 1944–1985,* **US Department of State Publication, no. 9446, Office of Historian, Bureau of Public Affairs, Washington, D.C., US, 1986, pp. 763–4.**

We are there [in Berlin] as a result of our victory over Nazi Germany, and our basic rights to be there deriving from that victory include both our presence in west Berlin and the enjoyment of access across East Germany. These rights have been completely confirmed … But in addition to those rights is our commitment to sustain – and defend, if need be – the opportunity for more than two million people [in West Berlin] to determine their own future and choose their own way of life.

Thus our presence in West Berlin, and our access thereto, cannot be ended by any act of the Soviet Government … An attack in that city will be regarded as an attack upon us all …

We cannot and will not permit the communists to drive us out of Berlin either gradually or by force.

Economic crisis in the GDR

Khrushchev had consistently rejected closing the East Berlin frontier. He hoped rather to uncouple West Berlin from the FRG, than to cut it off from East Germany. However, he was compelled to act by a growing economic crisis in the GDR. In April 1960, the remaining independent farmers were forced into collective farms. The immediate economic impact of this was disastrous: crop yields plummeted and within months there were serious shortages of bread, butter and meat. This led to an ever increasing number of people fleeing to West Germany. In 1960, 199,000 fled and in the six months up to June 1961, a further 103,000. There was also widespread unrest in factories.

Around the beginning of August, Khrushchev decided that the border between East and West Berlin would be closed. This decision was confirmed at a meeting of the Warsaw Pact states in Moscow on 3–5 August 1961, and in the early morning of 13 August the operation was efficiently and swiftly carried out. The border was sealed with barbed wire, and when no Western counter-measures followed, a more permanent concrete wall was built.

SOURCE Q

Berlin, 1961

What information is conveyed in Source Q about the situation in Berlin in 1961?

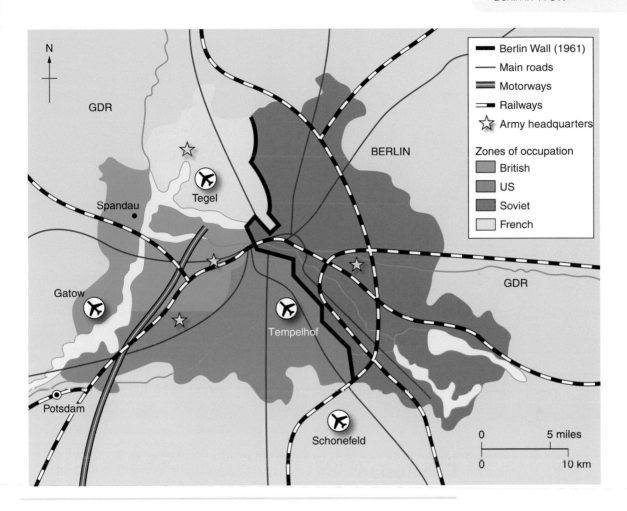

?

What information is conveyed by Source R about the construction of the Berlin Wall?

SOURCE R

Building the Berlin Wall, August 1961

Was the construction of the Berlin Wall a major success for the Soviet bloc?

→ Conclusion

The first Berlin crisis ended in complete failure for Stalin (see page 77). Like Stalin, Khrushchev failed to force the Western allies to withdraw troops from West Berlin or to compel them to negotiate peace treaties with the two German states. On the other hand, with the construction of the Berlin Wall, he achieved a limited but important success for Soviet policies. The existence of the GDR was now assured and ultimately the FRG would be forced to drop the Hallstein Doctrine and recognize its independence. By tolerating it, the Western powers, in effect, recognized East Germany. As historian Hermann Weber observed, East German communists were to look back on 13 August 1961 as 'the secret foundation day of the GDR'. With the Berlin Wall in place, the people of East Germany had no option but to remain in the GDR. This enabled Ulbricht, the GDR's leader, to develop what he called the New Economic System which was eventually supposed to revolutionize the GDR's economy and gain enthusiastic acceptance for socialism.

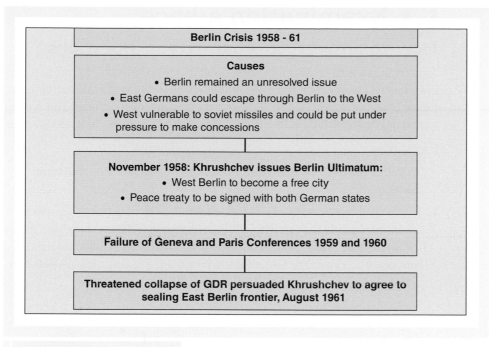

Berlin Crisis 1958 - 61

Causes
- Berlin remained an unresolved issue
- East Germans could escape through Berlin to the West
- West vulnerable to soviet missiles and could be put under pressure to make concessions

November 1958: Khrushchev issues Berlin Ultimatum:
- West Berlin to become a free city
- Peace treaty to be signed with both German states

Failure of Geneva and Paris Conferences 1959 and 1960

Threatened collapse of GDR persuaded Khrushchev to agree to sealing East Berlin frontier, August 1961

SUMMARY DIAGRAM

The Berlin Crisis, 1958–61

Chapter summary

From *détente* to the Berlin Wall, 1953–61

After the death of Stalin, the intensity of the Cold War eased. The new Soviet leadership attempted to defuse international tension by following a policy of *détente*. In practice, this policy achieved little. Germany and its capital, Berlin, remained divided. Despite the collapse of the EDC, the FRG joined NATO in 1955. The Soviet bloc responded with the creation of the Warsaw Pact, which East Germany joined in 1956. The main achievement in Europe of this period of *détente* was the Soviet agreement in May 1955 to evacuate Austria. The summit meeting in Geneva in July produced no concrete results but only the elusive 'Geneva spirit'.

In February 1956, Khrushchev shocked his comrades with a speech that openly attacked Stalin. This led to ten months of attempts to liberalize the Soviet regimes in eastern Europe, and to allow eastern European states to formulate their own policies. Riots in Poland and the Hungarian Uprising of 1956 brought these attempts to an end.

Khrushchev was more aware than Stalin of the importance of the emerging Third World. The Suez Crisis in November 1956 enabled him to pose as the champion of less developed, non-aligned states. Although his threat to sanction missile attacks on Britain, Israel and France was a bluff, it enabled him to take the credit for the failure for their defeat and the survival of Nasser in Egypt.

The division of Germany and the unsolved problem of Berlin remained a major destabilizing factor in Europe. The root of the problem was chronic economic weakness in the GDR that could perhaps be remedied by physically separating East and West Berlin to prevent the flight of skilled workers to the FRG. Khrushchev unsuccessfully attempted to pressure Britain, France and US into recognizing the legal existence of the GDR and agreeing to change the status of Berlin. When this failed, the Berlin Wall was built. The Wall led to the consolidation and, to some, the re-founding of the GDR.

Examination advice

How to answer 'to what extent' questions

The command term 'to what extent' is a popular one on IB exams. You are asked to evaluate one argument or idea over another, giving a final verdict as regarding extent. Stronger essays will also address more than one interpretation. This is often a good question in which to discuss how different historians have viewed an issue.

Example

> To what extent did the Suez Crisis of 1956 affect international relations?

1. To effectively address the question, it is important to note that the question asks you to decide the extent to which international relations were affected by the Suez Crisis. This means that you should consider more than just relations between the US and the Soviet Union, including, perhaps, relations between:

   - Britain and France and the US
   - Israel and Egypt
   - the Soviet Union and Egypt.

   While it may not be possible to address each of these it is important to consider several of them. Only after you have effectively discussed each of these relationships and how they were affected by the Suez Crisis can you state the extent to which international relations were affected.

2. Write a short outline in about five minutes. Be sure to address several different international relationships so that you are better able to make a judgement in your conclusion. For example:

> - *Relationships between the US and Britain/France:*
>   - *NATO alliance severely strained*
>   - *US condemns Britain/France/Israel action in Egypt in UN*
>   - *US forces Britain/France/Israel to withdraw*
>   - *France becomes less dependent on US*
>   - *US and Britain repair relations by agreeing to use Britain and US nuclear missile base*
> - *Hungary:*
>   - *Revolution crushed by Soviets*
>   - *US/NATO distracted by Suez Crisis and disunity*
> - *US/Soviet relations:*
>   - *Soviets support Middle East regimes such as Egypt at US expense:*
>   - *US and Britain send troops to Lebanon and Jordan to counter activities in region by Egypt*
>   - *Khrushchev began 'nuclear diplomacy' by threatening West with nuclear strikes as a negotiating method*

3. Your introduction should give a definition of the Suez Crisis, including participants, date and purpose of participants. This should be done with an economy of words and then a brief overview of the various international relationships you are going to discuss in the body of the essay. An example of a good introductory paragraph for this question is given below.

> The Suez Crisis of 1956 occurred when Britain and France secretly planned with Israel to take control of Egypt's Sinai Peninsula and the strategic Suez Canal. Britain and France wanted to remove Egypt's leader, Nasser, and restore the Suez Canal to their control (Nasser had nationalized it), while Israel wished to increase its territory. This short war on Egypt by these three aggressors had an impact on international relations. Britain and France, as well as Israel, were severely criticized by the US, forced to withdraw and co-operation within the NATO alliance was hindered. The distraction of NATO with internal divisions meant that the Soviets were able to defeat an anti-Soviet rebellion in Hungary without fear of Western intervention. US and Soviet relations, often already strained, were not affected in a significant way, although the Soviets emerged more confident with their perceived success in helping end the Crisis while gaining an important relationship with Egypt.

4. In the body of the essay, you need to discuss each of the points you raised in the introduction. Devote at least a paragraph for each one. It is important to fully address the impact on international relations of the Suez Crisis so that your conclusion is supported. An example of how one of the points could be addressed is given below.

> The Suez Crisis was initiated by NATO allies France and Britain in co-operation with Israel against Egypt and without the knowledge or approval of the US, practically the leader of NATO and supporter of Israel. US displeasure with its allies was clearly indicated when the US condemned the actions of its allies against Egypt publically at the United Nations. The US considered the actions of Britain and France to be more about maintaining their diminishing empires and less about overall international relations, which at that time involved a revolt in Hungary over Soviet control and a communist-inspired and supported war in Vietnam. Britain, France and Israel withdrew from

Egypt's territory, Egypt's leader Nasser was strengthened in Egypt and elsewhere so that soon Syria joined it to form the United Arab Republic in 1958 which in turn threatened Jordan and Lebanon, states friendly to the US and its European allies. The US and Britain soon repaired their relationship with a January 1957 treaty that allowed the US to station 60 nuclear missiles in Britain, while France worked to be less reliant on the US for military and economic assistance, yet remained within NATO. While the Suez Crisis strained relations between the US and its allies, this strain proved very temporary.

5. In the conclusion, be sure to state to what extent the Suez Crisis of 1956 affected international relations. An example of a good concluding paragraph is given below.

The Suez Crisis affected international relations to some extent. The US and its allies Britain, France and Israel had severely strained relations, but this proved temporary as Britain and France remained within NATO and dependent on US military and economic strength; Israel remained closely allied to the US as well. With this temporary rupture in relationships between Western military powers, the Soviets were able to crush a revolt in Hungary without having to be concerned with NATO's involvement, involvement that had clearly not been seriously contemplated by the US government or its allies. While the Soviets claimed a great diplomatic victory and their influence in the Middle East clearly increased, the relations between the Soviets and the West were not particularly disrupted and seemed to continue much as before. If any international relations were severely affected, it was the relations between Egypt and its Middle Eastern neighbours as Nasser and Egypt's prestige increased. Syria joined in union with Egypt in 1958 and Lebanon and Jordan reached out to the West to provide military support and protection while the newly proclaimed United Arab Republic remained dependent on Soviet assistance, bringing a new area of conflict into the Cold War. To some extent the Suez Crisis affected international relations.

6. Now try writing a complete answer to the question following the advice above.

Examination practice

Below are three exam-style questions for you to practise on this topic.

1. Evaluate the success of Khrushchev's foreign policy from 1953 to 1961.
   (For guidance on how to answer 'evaluate' questions, see page 98.)

2. Compare and contrast the foreign policies of Khrushchev and Eisenhower regarding Germany.
   (For guidance on how to answer 'compare and contrast' questions, see page 70.)

3. Analyse the importance of the Bandung Conference of 1955.
   (For guidance on how to answer 'analyse' questions, see page 36.)

Activities

1 Draw a summary diagram regarding the history of Germany, both the FRG and GDR, between 1945 and 1961. Use the summary diagram examples found in this book for guidance. This may be done using the textbox function on your word processing program, with artwork functions providing connectors of arrows and lines.

2 Discuss the following question in class: What was the importance of the Hungarian Uprising of 1956 for each of the following:

- Eastern Europe?
- NATO allies?
- Soviet Union?

3 Create a short-answer quiz with 30 questions regarding information located in this chapter. An example of this could be: Who was the leader of Egypt in the 1956 Suez Crisis? Quizzes should be exchanged and marked by classmates.

CHAPTER 6

The global Cold War, 1960–78

This chapter investigates the development of the Cold War outside Europe as it became a complex global confrontation. In the Middle East and Africa, the US, USSR and the PRC competed economically and politically to influence former European colonies. In Cuba, possibly the most dangerous crisis of the Cold War developed when the USSR supported Fidel Castro's revolutionary government and attempted to establish a nuclear missile base which would have made the US more vulnerable to Soviet attack. War also resumed in Vietnam where the US committed ever more forces in an unsuccessful attempt to defeat the Viet Cong communist guerrillas. The course of the Cold War was also altered by the bitter quarrel which developed between the USSR and the PRC.

You need to consider the following questions throughout this chapter:

✪ What were the reasons for the Sino-Soviet split?

✪ How successful was the US in excluding Soviet influence from Congo?

✪ Why did Soviet support for Castro provoke a major crisis with the US?

✪ Why was the US unable to prevent the spread of communism in Indochina?

✪ What were the results of US and USSR involvement in the Middle East from 1957 to 1979?

✪ How did the USSR become a successful counter-weight to US and western European influence in Angola and Ethiopia by 1978?

① The Sino-Soviet split

▶ *Key question: What were the reasons for the Sino-Soviet split?*

The late 1950s was an optimistic time for the Soviet leadership. The development of the ICBM, Sputnik and then the launching of the astronaut Yuri Gagarin into space to orbit the world aboard the *Vostok 1* spacecraft were all evidence of the remarkable technological progress the USSR had made since 1945. Living standards were improving and the **Virgin Lands Scheme** seemed to hold promise that famine was a thing of the past. Decolonization also created opportunities for the Soviet Union. Khrushchev and his advisors were convinced that new Third World countries would seek the protection of the Soviet bloc and develop into socialist societies; not to do so would make them vulnerable to their former colonial masters. Yet at the time when the communist world seemed to hold the initiative, relations between the PRC and USSR deteriorated to a point of open hostility.

  KEY TERM

Virgin Lands Scheme
Nikita Khrushchev's plan to increase the Soviet Union's agricultural production to alleviate the food shortages by bringing into cultivation previously uncultivated land.

Increasing tension, 1958–60

The Sino-Soviet split was caused by a mixture of both domestic and international factors, as well as by the simmering resentment in China of the long history of Russian imperialism which had encroached on its northern frontiers during the nineteenth and early twentieth centuries. Fundamentally, Mao perceived Khrushchev to be an appeaser of NATO and the US and, above all, a betrayer of the legacy of Stalin and Lenin. In return, the Soviet leadership was convinced that, under Mao, the PRC intended to displace the USSR as the leading communist state.

> **Why did mutual distrust between the party leadership of the PRC and USSR develop between 1958 and 1960?**

The 'Great Leap Forward', 1958–60

The year 1958 was a key year in the history of the PRC. Mao announced his revolutionary programme – the 'Great Leap Forward' – with plans to surpass Britain's economic output within fifteen years. He aimed to avoid the bottlenecks and bureaucracy which had slowed down the Soviet Five Year Plans and dramatically increase both industrial and agricultural production. The key to success, Mao believed, was to mobilize the population, primarily peasants. Private property was abolished and the Chinese peasantry placed into **communes**. The aim was to produce food for the cities and industrial centres outside the major cities. At the same time, large numbers of the population were mobilized to build dams and irrigation projects. In August, the PRC's Politburo decided that steel production should be doubled within the year by ordering the establishment of small backyard steel smelting furnaces in each commune and urban neighbourhood.

KEY TERM

Communes Communities of approximately 5000 households that organized and managed all resources within their control, including tools, seed, farmland and housing.

The 'Great Leap Forward' proved an economic disaster because crops were neglected as people concentrated on smelting and communes competed for what few resources were available. The lack of bureaucratic regulation led to vast regions starving, while the quality of most metals produced in these backyard furnaces was poor and not useful for industry. By 1961, at least 61 million people had died of overwork and starvation.

Opponents of the 'Great Leap Forward' were branded as being guilty of 'conservative and rightist tendencies'. Growing friction with the USSR was intensified when the Soviet economic advisors and technicians, who had arrived in 1956 to help the PRC industrialize, advised the PRC's government that the 'Great Leap Forward' was not practical and indeed harmful to the Chinese economy.

USSR accused of imperialism, 1958

Against the backdrop of the 'Great Leap Forward', relations between the PRC and the USSR steadily deteriorated. Attempts to co-operate in 1958 over the building of a long-wave radio receiving station in the PRC to enable the USSR to communicate with its submarines in the Pacific, as well as proposals for building a joint Chinese-Soviet submarine flotilla, ended in mutual recrimination. Mao was ready to accept Soviet assistance but would not agree either to share military bases or to operate joint naval units, which, he believed, were in reality plans to subordinate the PRC's armed forces to the USSR.

The Quemoy Crisis, 1958

In August 1958, the PRC began an intense bombardment of the Nationalist-controlled Quemoy Islands off Taiwan without initially consulting the USSR. US President Eisenhower responded by ordering the US Navy to escort supply ships from Taiwan to the islands, threatening to use nuclear weapons if the islands were invaded. Mao, however, had no plans for an invasion. By shelling Quemoy, he aimed to create a state of tension between the US and PRC which would rally the Chinese people behind his government and enable him to gain popular support for the 'Great Leap Forward'.

The Soviet government, alarmed that the Quemoy crisis would escalate into a major conflict, sent Foreign Minister Andrei Gromyko on a fact-finding mission to Beijing. Only when he was told that the shelling was intended to draw global attention to the Taiwan question and to distract the US from other parts of the world, particularly the Middle East, did the USSR publically support the PCR.

The Beijing meeting, October 1959

By autumn 1959, the differences between Beijing and Moscow were multiplying:

- In June, Khrushchev refused to assist the PRC any further with nuclear technology on the grounds that the US and USSR were discussing a possible ban on nuclear weapons at Geneva (see page 166).
- In April, tension increased between India and the PRC when the Indian government accepted the **Dalai Lama**'s exile government after the suppression by PRC troops of an anti-communist revolt in Tibet. This led to incidents along the disputed Sino-Indian Himalayan frontier and to the death of nine Indian frontier policemen on 9 October. The Soviets openly questioned the PRC's border claims.
- The 'Great Leap Forward' had failed, as Soviet economic advisors had forecast it would, while the Minister of War Peng Dehuai, a major critic of Mao's programme, was accused by Mao of being a Soviet agent.

In an attempt to heal the growing rift, Khrushchev visited Mao to mark the tenth anniversary of the PRC's founding in 1949. Far from restoring good relations between the two powers, the meeting on 2 October between the USSR's and PRC's delegations degenerated into a bitter exchange of insults.

KEY TERM

Dalai Lama Religious and political leader of Tibet and of Tibetan Buddhism.

Breakdown, 1964–69

Why did relations between the USSR and PRC continue to deteriorate between 1964 and 1969?

In July 1960, Khrushchev recalled the Soviet economic experts from the PRC. This gave Mao an excuse to make the Soviets the scapegoats for the failure of the Great Leap Forward, claiming that without their assistance the programme had failed. Mao exploited the conflict with the USSR to claim that his struggle to create communism in China was also a struggle to defend China from foreign enemies – the USSR and the US. Increasingly, he argued that the USSR had betrayed communism and had become a capitalist state. To prevent this happening in China, Mao insisted that **continuous revolution** was necessary.

With Khrushchev's fall from power in October 1964 (see page 233), there was initially some hope that better relations could be restored. In November, a mission led by Premier Zhou Enlai was sent to the USSR to improve Sino-Soviet relations, but it was unsuccessful, and allegedly the Soviet Defence Minister Marshall Rodion Malinowski actually urged Zhou Enlai to overthrow Mao.

The Cultural Revolution, 1966

In August 1966, Mao launched the **Cultural Revolution** which was meant to arouse the PRC's people to recapture the revolutionary enthusiasm of 1949 and to hunt down intellectuals and CCP officials allegedly guilty of 'revisionist' attitudes. Mao linked the fight against the 'revisionists' within China – those accused of revising the theory of Marxism–Leninism – with the propaganda against the 'revisionist' USSR, which was now regarded by himself and the CCP as the PRC's primary foe.

The Sino-Soviet border conflict, 1969

In the nineteenth century, the Russian Empire had forced the Chinese Empire to negotiate treaties which ceded several regions to Russia. After 1917, the USSR repudiated these treaties but never returned the territory. This was deeply resented by the PRC and contributed to the worsening relations between the two powers.

A major territorial dispute occurred in 1969, centred on the 52,000 square kilometres of Soviet-controlled land between the Xinjiang Uighur Autonomous region in western China and the Soviet-controlled region of Tajikistan. Each side massed hundreds of thousands of troops along the disputed border areas. In March 1969, two bloody conflicts erupted on Zhenbao Island, a small island on the Ussuri River, which marked the border between the PRC and the USSR. The island lay to the PRC side of the river, but was occupied by the Soviets. On the night of 1–2 March, a PRC force overwhelmed the Soviet garrison but was eventually driven off the island after a massive Soviet counter-attack. During the next few months, further clashes occurred along the frontier as both sides prepared for war (see page 237).

The tension was eased when the Soviet Premier Alexei Kosygin and Zhou Enlai met in September in Beijing and agreed to further talks in October which led to a truce along the borderlands. The border conflicts had a profound impact on the future course of the Cold War and led to both China and the USSR attempting to improve relations with the US. In 1972, Mao negotiated an understanding with the US directed against the USSR (see page 237). It was not until 1989, thirteen years after Mao's death in 1976, that normal relations were restored between the USSR and the PRC.

 **KEY TERM**

Continuous revolution
The conviction that revolution must be continuous since, if it is not going forward, it will inevitably go backwards.

Cultural Revolution A mass movement begun by Mao's supporters to purge the CCP and PRC society of those opposed to Mao's version of communism.

What information does Source A convey about the Zhenbao incident?

SOURCE A

PRC soldiers patrolling on Zhenbao Island, March 1969.

Reasons for the Sino-Soviet split, 1958–60

Soviet criticism of the 'Great Leap Forward'

Disagreement over Soviet plans for naval co-operation in the Pacific

The Quemoy Crisis, 1958

Soviet refusal to assist with development of PRC nuclear technology, 1959

Disagreement over Sino-Indian border dispute, 1959

Breakdown, 1964–69

PRC blames Soviets for failure of the 'Great Leap Forward'

USSR branded 'revisionist' during Cultural Revolution

Sino-Soviet border conflict, 1968

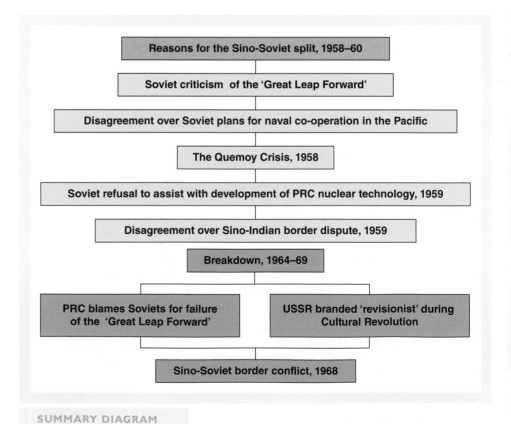

SUMMARY DIAGRAM

The Sino-Soviet split

The Congo Crisis, 1960–65

> ▶ *Key question: How successful was the US in excluding Soviet influence from Congo?*

By 1960, many of the European colonies in Africa had been granted independence. The end of European control in much of Africa created a political and economic vacuum which the PRC, the USSR and the US competed to fill.

Potentially one of the wealthiest and strategically important of the newly independent states in Africa was the former Belgian Congo. It was rich in copper and uranium deposits. In 1964, Mao was quoted as saying to a Chinese diplomat, 'If we can take the Congo, we can have all Africa'.

Independence, July 1960

Belgian authorities had done little to prepare the population for independence. When agitation started for independence in the late 1950s, there was no well-established professional elite that could unify and lead the whole country. The strongest organizations were regional and owed their allegiance to particular ethnic groups within the colony, of which there were more than two hundred. Only the Congolese National Movement (CNM) headed by Patrice Lumumba was able to mobilize a certain amount of support nationally. In the elections of May 1960, the CNM emerged as the largest party and, after the granting of independence in June, Lumumba was able to form a government.

> **Why did the granting of independence by Belgium lead to a prolonged crisis in Congo?**

Patrice Lumumba

Lumumba was a former postal clerk who became a leading figure in the Congolese trade union movement. Initially, he wanted to work closely with the Belgian authorities but he was imprisoned in 1956 on what was almost certainly a fabricated charge of stealing money from the post office. After his release from prison in 1957, his politics moved closer to the Non-Aligned Movement (see page 151). As Prime Minister, he was determined to make Congo genuinely independent of Belgian and Western business interests, and, to achieve that, he was ready to accept Soviet assistance – but not domination. In April 1959, he secretly contacted the Soviet ambassador in Brussels. A Belgian communist leader came to the conclusion after a five-hour meeting with Lumumba that 'conditions for the spreading of Marxism are more favourable in the Congo than in the other countries of Africa'.

Both Belgium and the US came to a similar conclusion. The head of the Union Minière, the Belgian company which controlled the mining of minerals in Congo, was convinced that once Lumumba was in power he would seek help from the Soviet bloc. To the US, Lumumba seemed to be a dangerous left-wing politician who would give the USSR, and possibly the PRC, access to Congo's immense natural wealth. In 1960, Eisenhower authorized the **CIA** to bribe key Congolese politicians in an unsuccessful attempt to prevent Lumumba coming to power. Once he became prime minister, the director of the CIA was convinced that he would be a greater threat to US interests than Fidel Castro in Cuba (see page 181).

The secession of Katanga, July 1960

After independence, Congo almost immediately disintegrated. The army mutinied in Leopoldville (Kinshasa) and began to threaten its Belgian officers and the expatriate non-African population. The South Kasai region broke away and established its own government, while the southern province of Katanga, which possessed more than half the country's mineral resources, immediately seceded on 11 July. Katanga was assisted by the Union Minière and Belgian troops still present in Congo during the hand-over of power. Moïse Tshombe, who was prepared to work closely with the Company, became, in effect, the **puppet ruler** of Katanga. His government was assisted financially by the Union Minière which in reality ruled the region.

UN intervention, July 1960

Lumumba appealed to the United Nations on 12 July for assistance to put down the mutinies, evict the remaining Belgian troops from the country and expel the **separatists** in Katanga. The United Nations Security Council, with the support of both the US and USSR, authorized the dispatch of a UN peacekeeping force under the direction of the UN Secretary-General Dag Hammarskjöld to keep order until the local security forces were strong enough to do the job by themselves. The UN Security Council demanded the withdrawal of Belgian troops from Congo but did not specifically condemn Belgium for aggression. When these troops merely withdrew into Katanga, the US, backed by Britain and France, who were also permanent members of the Security Council, was not ready to authorize the UN to take over Katanga or use force to evict Belgian troops.

Receiving no effective support from the UN, Lumumba turned to the USSR, informing Khrushchev in a telegram that he would ask the USSR to intervene 'should the Western camp not cease aggression against the sovereignty of the Congolese Republic'. Although the USSR was able to send some food and medical assistance, in reality there was little that it could do to help him. It was not equipped to intervene militarily in Africa. It had, as yet, no war ships that were capable of moving swiftly into areas of conflict and of launching amphibious landings, nor the airlift capacity that could fly in troops and supplies.

On 5 August, the USSR did demand Belgian withdrawal from Katanga and its reincorporation into Congo. In response, the Security Council, despite the objections by the Soviet ambassador, declared that the dispute with Katanga was an internal matter for Congo and that the UN could not be involved in the conflict. Hammarskjöld did, however, negotiate directly with Tshombe to secure the entry of UN troops into Katanga to replace Belgian troops, but they were not to be employed in support of Lumumba. By the end of August, US policy was to keep Katanga with its economic assets independent of the pro-Soviet Lumumba government in Congo.

 **KEY TERM**

Puppet ruler Ruler of a country controlled by another power.

Mobutu's seizure of power, September 1960

As the political and economic situation in Congo deteriorated, the US considered the possibility of armed intervention to pre-empt Soviet attempts to strengthen Lumumba and even planned his assassination. On 16 September, with US and Belgian support, General Joseph Mobutu, the Chief of Staff of the Congolese army, seized power in Congo and ended relations with the USSR. Under US pressure, the Soviet bloc and PRC embassies and advisors left Congo. Lumumba was placed under house arrest, but Deputy Prime Minister Antoine Gizenga managed to create a rival government in Stanleyville.

> What information is conveyed by Source B regarding the potential wealth of Congo? **?**

SOURCE B

Map of Congo after independence.

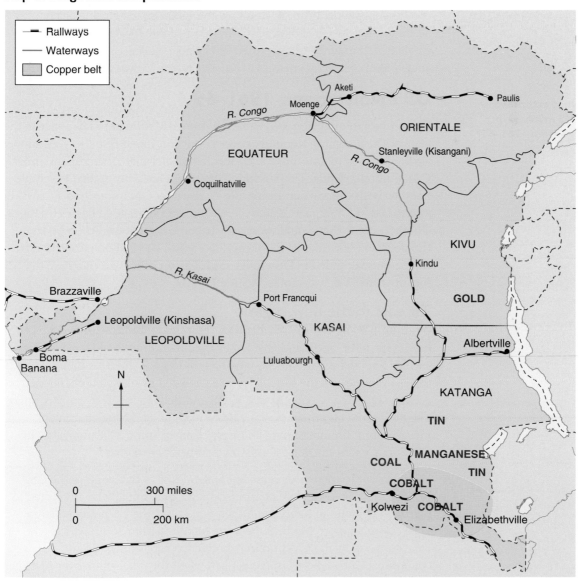

By October 1960, there were four different regimes in the Congo:

- Joseph Mobutu in Kinshasa, who was supported by the US and the Western powers
- Antoine Gizenga in Stanleyville, who was supported by the Soviet bloc, Cuba, Egypt, the Algerian FLN and most of the newly independent African nations
- Albert Kalonji in South Kasai, who achieved a precarious independence until December 1961, and
- Tshombe in Katanga, assisted by Belgium and Union Minière.

Lumumba's murder

Lumumba, who had escaped from house arrest, continued to enjoy the support of other independent African countries and called for an uprising against Mobutu. Both the US and Mobutu saw him as a threat who needed to be eliminated. Lumumba was captured by Congolese troops in December 1960 and handed over to his enemies in Katanga where he was brutally murdered.

To what extent was the US involved in Congo from 1961–65?

US involvement, 1961–65

Lumumba's murder removed the most immediate threat to US policy in the Congo. The incoming Kennedy government continued Eisenhower's support for the Mobutu regime, but forced it to install a civilian government under Cyrille Adoula. Under US pressure, Tshombe reluctantly agreed to reunite Katanga with Congo, but this occurred only after UN troops had successfully intervened in Katanga in January 1963, forcing Tshombe to flee to Rhodesia, a British colony that would eventually become Zimbabwe. Troops of the Congo Republic under Mobutu captured South Kasai after a four-month campaign that ended in December 1961. Once Congo was reunited, the UN security force was withdrawn by June 1964.

Threats to the new regime

By autumn 1964, Congo was again on the brink of collapse. It faced rebellions in the north and east led by the pro-Lumumba Marxist leaders such as Soumialot and Mulele, who had undergone guerrilla training in eastern Europe and the PRC. They were assisted by many independent African states that were opposed to US and Belgian involvement in Congo. The PRC sent equipment via Tanzania and Uganda, Soviet equipment moved south through Sudan, and Egypt trained some 2000 guerrillas. In addition, Cuba sent over 100 military instructors to assist.

US President Johnson was reluctant to send troops to Congo as the US became more involved in Vietnam (see page 202). Initially he attempted to persuade Belgium to intervene. When that failed, the US provided large-scale covert support. Mercenaries were recruited from South Africa, who were supplied by the CIA and transported in planes flown by anti-communist Cuban exiles. In November, when the rebels took over Kisangani (Stanleyville) and seized several hundred European hostages, US President Johnson agreed to the airlift of 500 Belgian paratroopers to rescue them.

By 1965, the rebellions had been defeated. On 25 November, Mobutu overthrew the civil government with the help of the CIA and established a military dictatorship. He stabilized Congo, remaining its dictator until 1997. The weakness of the country was revealed, however, when it was unable to defend itself from attacks from Angola in 1977–78 and had to be rescued by troops from Belgium and France, soon replaced by soldiers from Morocco and Senegal.

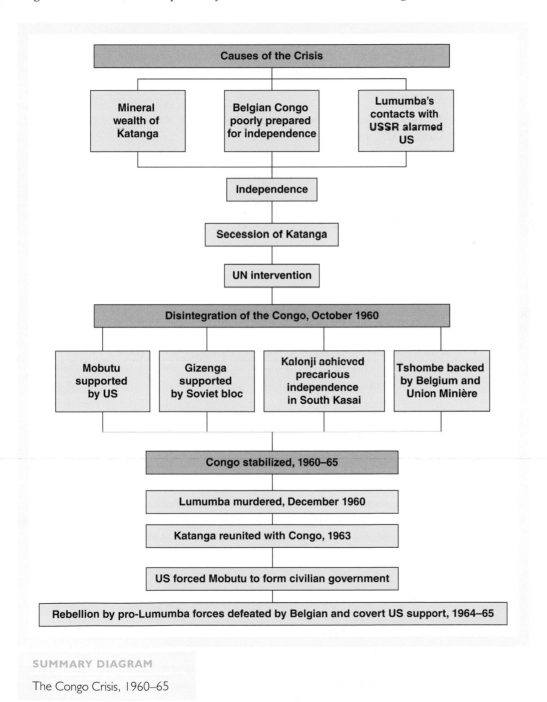

The Congo Crisis, 1960–65

③ The Cuban Missile Crisis, 1962

> ▶ **Key question:** *Why did Soviet support for Castro provoke a major crisis with the US?*

Although the Cuban Missile Crisis was a direct confrontation between the US and the USSR, involving neither NATO nor the Warsaw Pact, it had a profound impact on the Cold War both in Europe and throughout the world. Both sides came to the brink of war but a nuclear conflict was averted.

SOURCE C

? According to Source C, what was the cause of the Cuban Crisis?

An extract from *We Now Know* by John Gaddis, published by OUP, Oxford, UK, 1997, p. 261.

[The crisis over Cuba was] the only episode after World War II in which each of the major areas of Soviet–American competition intersected: the nuclear arms race to be sure, but also conflicting ideological aspirations, 'third world rivalries', relations with allies, the domestic political implications of foreign policy, the personalities of individual leaders. The crisis was a kind of funnel – a historical singularity if you like – into which everything suddenly tumbled and got mixed together. Fortunately no black hole lured at the other end …

What were the origins of the Cuban Missile Crisis?

Causes of the Crisis

KEY TERM

Guerrilla war A war fought by small groups of irregular troops. The term means 'little war' in Spanish.

In the 1950s, the Soviets accepted that South America was in the US sphere of interest. They had not protested, for example, when the CIA intervened in 1954 to topple the pro-communist President Jacobo Árbenz of Guatemala. The US's domination did, though, cause growing resentment among South American intellectuals and nationalists, and was one of the factors that influenced Fidel Castro to launch a **guerrilla war** against the government of Fulgencio Batista in Cuba in December 1956. By January 1959, contrary to expectations, his forces were able to take control of Cuba.

The Cuban Revolution

In 1959, Castro was certainly an anti-US Cuban nationalist, but not a communist. It was growing opposition from the Cuban middle classes to his economic policies and increasing US hostility to his attempt to adopt a policy of Non-Alignment in the Cold War that caused him to adopt Marxism–Leninism in order to address Cuba's economic needs and to achieve military protection from the US by forming a relationship with the Soviet Union. Friction with the US was also caused by his seizure of property and land owned by the major US firms.

As relations with the US deteriorated during the summer of 1959, Castro made contact with the Soviets and, in February 1960, he invited Deputy Chairman of the Soviet Council of Ministers, Anastas Mikoyan, to visit Havana, Cuba's capital. Mikoyan returned to Moscow with a glowing account of the Cuban Revolution which reminded him of the heroic early days of the Russian Revolution in 1917. In March 1960, Eisenhower ordered the CIA to begin equipping and training anti-Castro Cuban refugees for future operations against Castro. The US also put the Cuban economy under great pressure by no longer buying Cuban sugar or supplying Cuba with oil. In this increasingly tense situation, Khrushchev threatened in July 1960 to send Soviet troops to Cuba to defend the island if the US dared invade it. Khrushchev also suggested that the US should declare the end of the **Monroe Doctrine**.

The Bay of Pigs, April 1961

In April 1961, four months after Kennedy became US President, a force of about 1400 CIA-trained Cuban exiles landed at the Bay of Pigs south of Havana. It was hoped that this would trigger a popular uprising against Castro, but Castro, in anticipation of such a move, imprisoned thousands of suspects. At the last moment, Kennedy cancelled both bombing raids by US aircraft and a landing by US marines, thus dooming the invasion to failure. He feared that if US involvement became overt, Khrushchev would retaliate by causing a crisis in Berlin (see page 167). Deprived of US support, the Cuban exiles were rapidly defeated.

Although Khrushchev was delighted by the failure of the landing, he nevertheless saw it as a warning that the US would inevitably try again to topple Castro. In this he was correct. The CIA continued to devise plans for Castro's assassination and large-scale military manoeuvres took place in the Caribbean Sea in the spring and summer of 1962 in anticipation of an invasion.

The Soviet decision to place missiles on Cuba, 1962

In August 1962, a secret Soviet–Cuban Treaty was signed permitting the USSR to place missiles in Cuba. Over the next few weeks, the Soviets began secretly to deploy medium-range nuclear missiles in Cuba. These would be defended by 40,000 Soviet troops, anti-aircraft batteries, short-range battlefield rockets and MIG-21 fighter planes.

The key reasons for this highly dangerous operation were to:

- gain a base from which the US could be threatened by medium-range Soviet missiles
- correct the strategic imbalance caused by the construction of NATO missile bases in Turkey, which could reach the major industrial and population centres of the Soviet Union
- defend Cuba's socialist revolution, since the Soviets saw the revolution as a major success for Marxism–Leninism, and its defeat would, as Mikoyan told Castro, 'throw back the revolutionary movement in many countries'.

By 4 October, Soviet ships had brought enough nuclear warheads to equip at least 158 strategic and tactical nuclear missiles which could reach the majority of the US in a matter of minutes.

KEY TERM

Monroe Doctrine The doctrine formulated by President Monroe of the US (1817–25) that the European powers should not intervene in the affairs of North or South America.

What information is conveyed by Source D?

Map of Cuba and the Caribbean Sea region, 1959–62.

What information is conveyed by Source E about Khrushchev's decision to place missiles on Cuba?

An extract from *Khrushchev Remembers* by Nikita Khrushchev, translated and edited by Strobe Talbott, published by Little, Brown and Co., Boston, USA, 1971, p. 492.

We welcomed Castro's victory [in April 1961] of course, but at the same time we were quite certain that the invasion was only the beginning and that the Americans would not let Cuba alone … There are infinite opportunities for invasion, especially if the invader has naval artillery and air support.

The height of the Crisis, 14–28 October 1962

Why did the Cuban Crisis not result in war between the USA and the USSR?

On 14 October, a US U-2 spy plane discovered the missiles installations. President Kennedy was informed two days later and initially the news was kept from the US public. The options open to the US government were explored by a small crisis committee, the **ExComm**. They decided against:

- launching a surprise air attack on the missile installations in Cuba without any previous warning to the USSR, and
- appealing to the United Nations as the USSR had the right of veto as a permanent Security Council member.

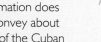 **KEY TERM**

ExComm The Executive Committee of the US National Security Council.

What information does Source F convey about the causes of the Cuban Missile Crisis?

SOURCE F

An aerial reconnaissance photograph showing a medium-range ballistic missile launch site in Cuba, October 1962.

ERECTOR ON LAUNCH PAD

MISSILE READY BLDGS

OXIDIZER VEHICLES

PROB HYDROGEN PEROXIDE TANKS

MISSILE READY BLDGS

FUELING VEHICLES

TENTS

ERECTOR ON LAUNCH PAD

MISSILE ON TRAILER

Instead, plans were created for a possible full-scale invasion of Cuba by US forces, but these would only be activated after the dispatch of an ultimatum to the USSR demanding that Soviet missiles be withdrawn from the island.

The quarantine zone

In the meantime, the US Navy established a so-called quarantine zone 1300 kilometres (800 miles) from Cuba's coast. Once they entered this area, Soviet ships would be stopped and searched for any weapons bound for Cuba. This was later reduced to 800 kilometres (500 miles).

On 22 October, Kennedy announced on US television the news of the existence of Soviet missiles in Cuba and of the quarantine zone. He also made it clear that if any nuclear missile was fired from Cuba, he would order a massive nuclear attack on the USSR. Initially, Khrushchev was determined to complete the missile sites in Cuba and he ordered Soviet ships to challenge the blockade. It now looked as though a naval confrontation was inevitable.

Soviet decision to withdraw the missiles

On 25 October, U. Thant, the acting Secretary-General of the United Nations, suggested a compromise: the USSR would withdraw its missiles from Cuba and in return the US would undertake not to invade it. Khrushchev adopted this proposal as his and communicated it to Kennedy the following day. His decision was influenced by the fact that the US had very visibly placed its air force at its highest readiness for war level since 1945, the end of the Second World War. A third of the US Strategic Air Command bombers had been put on airborne alert, the rest of the force was armed with nuclear bombs and dispersed to civilian airfields, and all available ICBMs were prepared for launching against Soviet targets.

However, the following day Khrushchev, in an attempt to avoid accusations of weakness from his critics in both the USSR and PRC, insisted, in a second message to Kennedy, that the removal of missiles from Cuba was dependent on the dismantling of NATO nuclear missile bases in Turkey. Kennedy responded to the first letter officially and ignored the second. He publically agreed to not invade Cuba, but secretly consented to remove the missiles from Turkey in the near future. He stressed, however, that if the Soviets made this offer public, it would be withdrawn.

Effectively this ended the crisis, and all the Soviet missiles and troops were withdrawn from Cuba by 20 November with NATO's missiles soon removed from Turkey.

SOURCE G

An extract from Khrushchev's message to Kennedy, 27 October 1962, from *Cuban Missile Crisis: The Essential Reference Guide*, edited by Priscilla Roberts, published by ABC-CLIO, Santa Barbara, California, USA, 2012, p. 213.

You are disturbed over Cuba. You say that this disturbs you because it is 90 miles by sea from the coast of the United States of America. But Turkey adjoins us … Do you consider, then, that you have the right to demand security for your own country and the removals of the weapons you call offensive, but do not accord the same right to us? You have placed destructive missile weapons, which you call offensive in Turkey, literally next door to us …

I think it would be possible to end this controversy quickly and normalize the situation …

I therefore make this proposal: We are willing to remove from Cuba the means which you regard as offensive … Your representatives will make a declaration to the effect that the United States, for its part, considering the uneasiness and anxiety of the Soviet state, will remove [the missiles] from Turkey …

> According to Source G, what were Khrushchev's motives for placing Soviet missiles in Cuba?

The aftermath of the Crisis

> **What were the consequences of the Cuban Missile Crisis?**

In the short term, US President Kennedy's prestige increased enormously. He was promoted as the one who had called Khrushchev's bluff. His concession that the Jupiter missiles would be withdrawn from Turkey in return for the removal of the missiles from Cuba remained a secret until after his death. Khrushchev's retreat met with bitter criticism from Mao and Castro, accusing him of surrendering to the US. It weakened his position within the USSR. Yet his fall in October 1964 (see page 233) was more the result of domestic politics and power struggles than a consequence of the Cuban Crisis.

Cuba

The Soviet decision to remove the missiles was seen as a betrayal by Castro and convinced him that Cuba would have to develop its own independent revolutionary strategy. By the mid-1960s, Castro actively assisted revolutionary movements in the Third World not only to support the spread of communism, but also to distract the US so that it would not renew pressure on Cuba.

An extract from a conversation between Castro and Anastas Mikoyan, 2 November 1962, from *The Global Cold War: Third World Interventions and the Making of Our Times* by Odd Arne Westad, Cambridge University Press, Cambridge, UK, 2005, p. 175.

Psychologically our people were not prepared for that [removal of Soviet missiles]. A feeling of deep disappointment, bitterness and pain has appeared, as if we were deprived of not only missiles, but of the very symbol of solidarity. Reports of missile launchers being dismantled and returned to the USSR at first seemed to our people to be an insolent lie. You know, the Cuban people were not aware of the agreement, were not aware that the missiles still belonged to the Soviet side. The Cuban people did not conceive of the juridical [legal] status of these weapons. They had become accustomed to the fact that the Soviet Union gave us weapons and that they became our property.

The USSR

The overwhelming superiority of the US in nuclear weapons, as shown during the nuclear crisis, came as a shock to the Soviet leadership. The USSR was determined to achieve parity in nuclear weapons with the US and began an ambitious programme for the construction of ICBMs (see page 236). The total command of the seas by the US which enabled it to establish so effectively the quarantine zone around Cuba also persuaded the USSR to build a large navy, which in the future would enable it to project its power globally.

Reduction in international tension

The Cuban Missile Crisis brought both the US and USSR to the brink of nuclear war. The crisis neither ended the Cold War nor stopped the nuclear arms race between the US and USSR, but it did lead to an understanding by both sides that nuclear war would lead to what became known as 'mutually assured destruction' or MAD. Increasingly, both sides began to give priority to plans for controlling the proliferation of nuclear weapons and their testing (see pages 232–236). In 1963, a **hotline** was established which linked the Soviet and US leaders. The intention behind this was that both leaders could directly contact each other instead of relying on contacts through the UN or their own diplomats, and therefore rapidly defuse crises that might lead to nuclear war.

KEY TERM

Hotline A direct communications link between US and Soviet leaders.

Causes

- Castro's revolution in Cuba

- Deterioration in US–Cuban relations

- Failure of Bay of Pigs invasion

- Secret Soviet-Cuban accord, August 1962: medium-range missiles installed and defended by Soviet troops

US reaction to discovery of Soviet missile pads, 14 October 1962
- Kennedy's ultimatum, 22 October
- Quarantine announced
- Threat of massive US retaliation if missiles are fired from Cuba

Khrushchev's reaction: two conflicting messages

1. Promised withdrawal from Cuba provided US does not invade Cuba

2. Withdrawal subject to later dismantling of US Jupiter missiles in Turkey

Kennedy's response
Accepted first publically,
but privately agreed to second

Consequences of Crisis

- Kennedy's prestige increased

- Khrushchev criticized by Mao, Castro and rivals in USSR

- Cuba developed revolutionary strategy in Third World, independent of USSR

- USSR determined to achieve nuclear parity with US and build surface fleet

- USSR and US agreed to hotline and plan to control proliferation of nuclear weapons

SUMMARY DIAGRAM

The Cuban Missile Crisis, 1962

Vietnam, 1954–75

> ▶ **Key question:** Why was the US unable to prevent the spread of communism in Indochina?

In many of the bitter local struggles that followed the collapse of the European empires, the US, PRC and USSR assisted rival politicians by means of arms deliveries and the dispatch of clandestine agents and military instructors. In South Vietnam, however, the US intervened directly to protect the regime from communist subversion orchestrated from North Vietnam. In response, both the USSR and the PRC aided the North Vietnamese and exploited US growing military involvement without themselves becoming directly involved.

Why was Diệm unable to consolidate his government in South Vietnam from 1960–64?

The growing crisis in Indochina, 1954–63

Although the US did not sign the Geneva Accords in 1954 that divided Vietnam at the 17th parallel (see page 133), it did issue a separate statement that it agreed with their general principles. Nevertheless, it was determined to avoid elections for a united Vietnamese parliament as stated in the Geneva Accords in case this resulted in a reunified, communist Vietnam. In an attempt to stop the spread of communism to southeast Asia, the US also established the Southeast Asian Treaty Organization (SEATO), as regional defence system, in September 1954. Its members were: US, Britain, France, Australia, New Zealand, Thailand, the Philippines and Pakistan. In practice, the alliance proved ineffective as its members were not legally obliged to assist each other militarily to prevent states from adopting communism.

Ngô Đình Diệm

In June 1954, with American support, Emperor Bao Đại (see page 130), appointed Ngô Đình Diệm as Prime Minister of South Vietnam, largely on the strength of his virulent anti-communism. Initially, he was able to consolidate his position in South Vietnam. He soon removed Bao Đại and declared South Vietnam a republic. For a short time, he seemed to enjoy the backing of the majority of the population and the US even discussed 'the Diệm miracle', but then rapidly Diệm lost support. He alienated key groups, particularly the majority Buddhists by favouring Roman Catholics who comprised 10 per cent of the population. Catholics were given preferential treatment in the allocation of posts in the army and the public service. He also did not carry out the promised programme of land reform which would have taken land away from the large landowners and redistributed it to the peasantry.

Formation of the National Liberation Front (NLF)

In 1957, communist leaders in the South called for preparations for an uprising and for intervention from the North, but initially North Vietnam, the USSR and PRC were opposed to this:

- Hồ Chí Minh (see page 128), was working to consolidate his own power in the North and introducing reforms aimed at ultimately creating a communist society.
- Khrushchev wanted *détente* with the West and did not wish to provoke another major crisis in Asia.
- Mao was absorbed with domestic reform and had no wish to risk another major confrontation with the USA so soon after the end of the Korean War.

However, by 1959 North Vietnam did decide to intervene in the South when it realized that Diệm's unpopularity created a favourable opportunity for action.

In spring 1959, it announced a resumption of the armed struggle against the South Vietnamese government and smuggled arms southwards along the newly constructed **Hồ Chí Minh Trail**. Hồ Chí Minh also sent many of the Viet Minh (see page 128) back to the South who had fled to the North after the division of Vietnam. In September 1960, the Viet Cong, the communist movement in South Vietnam, founded the National Front for the Liberation for Vietnam. This was an organization with a broad base led by the Viet Cong, which aimed at rallying all those opposed to Diệm's regime by promising reform and the creation of a united, independent Vietnam.

☞ KEY TERM

Hồ Chí Minh Trail An infiltration route of hundreds of kilometres that allowed the movement of troops and war material through neighbouring countries into South Vietnam.

US President Kennedy, 1960–63

Why did Kennedy's treatment of Laos and South Vietnam differ?

When Kennedy became US President in January 1961, he faced a deepening crisis not only in South Vietnam, but also in Laos. Both states faced growing communist threats, but Kennedy dealt with both crises differently.

Laos

It was decided at the Geneva Conference in 1954 that Laos should become an independent, non-communist neutral state, but the communist-supported Pathet Lao independence movement controlled large areas in the east of the country. At first, the government under Prince Souvanna Phouma attempted to conciliate the Pathet Lao, but in 1958 it was replaced by a more anti-communist administration. In turn, this was overthrown by a coup organized in December 1959 by Phoumi Nosavan who formed a regime that was even more hostile to the Pathet Lao. Rapidly, Laos degenerated into civil war:

- The Pathet Lao began guerrilla operations against the anti-communist government.

Map showing the Hồ Chí Minh Trail and significant places in the Vietnam War.

? What information about the Hồ Chí Minh Trail is conveyed by Source I?

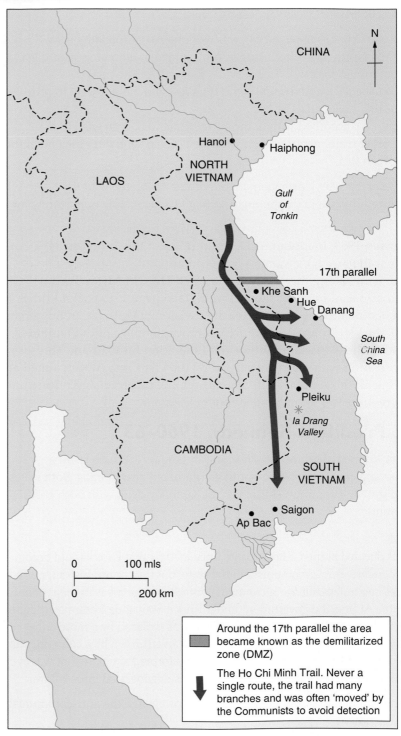

Around the 17th parallel the area became known as the demilitarized zone (DMZ)

The Ho Chi Minh Trail. Never a single route, the trail had many branches and was often 'moved' by the Communists to avoid detection

- In August 1960, Souvanna Phouma returned to power after another coup organized by a group of army officers.
- Phoumi Nosavan then rebelled against the new Souvanna Phouma government.

Increasingly, both the US and USSR were drawn into the civil war. Phoumi Nosavan was assisted by the US's CIA and military experts, while Souvanna Phouma turned to the Pathet Lao which received supplies from the USSR. Kennedy was determined to exclude the USSR from south-east Asia and, in April 1961, considered military intervention. With his attention on Berlin (see page 167) and faced with the threat of US military intervention in Laos, Khrushchev decided that Laos was of no strategic importance to the USSR and agreed to a diplomatic settlement of the conflict.

In April 1961, Kennedy agreed to a joint Soviet–British initiative to convene a conference at Geneva regarding Laos and accepted its recommendations in 1962 for creating a coalition government led by Souvanna Phouma in which the Pathet Lao would participate. While this prevented the civil war in Laos from escalating into a major conflict, low-key fighting continued. In April 1963, the Pathet Lao left the government and resumed guerrilla warfare.

North Vietnam tolerated the Souvanna Phouma government, but it insisted, contrary to the 1962 Geneva recommendations, on its right to use the Hồ Chí Minh trails through Laos. By 1969, it had 67,000 troops in Laos guarding the route to South Vietnam.

South Vietnam

By the autumn of 1961, the government in South Vietnam was in danger of collapse. The Viet Cong had seized control of a large number of villages and Diệm urged the US to provide more assistance. In response, Kennedy sent a mission under General Taylor who recommended the dispatch of more equipment to the South Vietnam's army, as well as a small force of 8000 US troops to help conduct military operations against the Viet Cong.

There were voices inside the US government urging negotiation with the Viet Cong. Averell Harriman, who represented the US at the Laos negotiations in Geneva, argued that, since Diệm was unpopular and the USSR interested in stabilizing the situation in south-east Asia, the US should reduce its military presence in South Vietnam and seek a settlement with North Vietnam. In contrast, Secretary of Defence Robert McNamara urged the dispatch 200,000 men to reinforce South Vietnam. Although Kennedy saw Vietnam as a test case for the US's ability to challenge communism, he rejected both the alternatives of either negotiating a peace settlement or deploying troops on a large scale, and, instead, adopted a more modest policy of increasing aid and the number of US military advisors.

The Battle of Ap Bac

For the first six months of 1962, the Diệm regime appeared, at last, to be making progress against the Viet Cong, but it soon became clear that the Viet Cong bases were almost impossible to locate in the impenetrable forests and swamps of South Vietnam. As soon as government troops had seized an area, the Viet Cong would re-conquer it after they had withdrawn. In January 1963, the weakness of the government troops was revealed when, near the village of Ap Bac, the South Vietnam army (AVRN), despite possessing overwhelming strength, failed to capture Viet Cong units and suffered 61 dead compared with only 3 Viet Cong casualties.

The fall of Diệm's government

Throughout 1963, control of South Vietnam by Diệm's government continued to deteriorate as it had no authority in many parts of the country. Diệm was bitterly unpopular as he continued to discriminate against the majority Buddhists. On 8 May 1963, government troops fired into a crowd of people celebrating Buddha's birthday because they had violated the law banning the flying of non-governmental flags. This provoked a wave of anger across the country which resulted in protest marches and even **self-immolations**.

KEY TERM

Self-immolations Burning oneself alive as a sacrifice and act of protest.

The US was concerned both by Diệm's lack of popular support and incompetence and by rumours that he and his brother, Ngô Đình Nhu, were considering negotiations with North Vietnam. The US calculated that the South was too weak to drive an advantageous deal with Hồ Chí Minh. By autumn 1963, Kennedy decided to back a coup mounted by the South Vietnamese army to remove Diệm. This took place on 1 November and both Diệm and his brother were murdered the next day. General Nguyện Khánh was installed as the new leader.

To what extent did the year 1963–64 mark an escalation in the Vietnam War?

President Johnson, November 1963–November 1964

President Kennedy was assassinated on 22 November 1963 and replaced by his Vice-President, Lyndon Johnson. Like Kennedy, Johnson attempted to pursue the objectives of winning the war without having to send large-scale American reinforcements to Vietnam. He wanted to avoid a massive military commitment before the presidential election in November 1964. On the other hand, he could not be seen to be too soft on the Viet Cong, otherwise his Republican rival in the Presidential elections, Barry Goldwater, would benefit. It was crucial, therefore, to encourage the new Khánh government and persuade it to fight the Viet Cong more vigorously.

SOURCE J

A Buddhist monk commits suicide in protest against the government's anti-Buddhists policies

What information does Source J convey about opposition Diệm in South Vietnam?

US search for allies

The US hoped to find allies in SEATO who would provide aid and at least token military contributions, but their only success was Australia which sent both troops and financial aid to South Vietnam. France, which still had strong links with South Vietnam, urged a political solution to the Vietnam conflict and, on 29 August 1963, French President de Gaulle called for a reunified Vietnam free of outside interference and made no secret of the fact that he thought armed intervention would be doomed to failure.

Britain was less openly critical of the US and needed to preserve good relations with the US for both military and economic reasons. Privately, however, British politicians were pessimistic about the success of any large-scale US military intervention. British Prime Minister Macmillan had a secret agreement with the US that he would not push for a negotiated settlement until the South Vietnam government enjoyed greater success against the Viet Cong.

The Tonkin Incidents, August 1964

In the meantime, Khánh pressed the US for more reinforcements and an expansion of the war to the north if these were not forthcoming. Khánh threatened to resign as South Vietnam's Prime Minister or negotiate a deal with the communists. It was in this tense atmosphere that the Tonkin Incidents occurred.

North Vietnamese patrol boats attacked a US destroyer, the *Maddox,* in the Gulf of Tonkin on 2 August. In response, the *Maddox* attacked and damaged two boats while sinking a third. Two days later, a second US destroyer, *C. Turner Joy,* responded to what its commander had thought to be another attack. In fact, there was no second attack. The alarm had most likely been caused by a false radar image. The incidents did, however, give Johnson the opportunity to order air strikes against selected North Vietnamese patrol boat bases and an oil depot. On 7 August, the US Congress, in an overwhelming vote, gave Johnson the authority 'to take all necessary measures' to defend US forces in south-east Asia in the so-called Gulf of Tonkin Resolution.

SOURCE K

What information is conveyed by Source K about US involvement in the Vietnam War?

An extract from the Gulf of Tonkin Resolution, 7 August 1964, quoted in 'The Avalon Project of the Lillian Goldman Law Library of Yale University', US at http://avalon.law.yale.edu/20th_century/tonkin-g.asp.

Whereas the United States is assisting the peoples of southeast Asia to protect their freedom and has no territorial, military or political ambition in that area, but desires only that these peoples should be left in peace to work out their destinies in their own way …

Now be it Resolved by the Senate and House of Representatives in Congress assembled that the Congress approves and supports the determination of the President, as Commander-in-Chief, to take all necessary measures to repel any armed attack against the forces of the United States and to prevent any further aggression.

How did PRC and Soviet policies towards Vietnam differ?

The USSR, the PRC and Vietnam, 1960–64

The Viet Cong insurgency occurred at a time of deepening tension between the USSR and PRC, preventing any effective diplomatic or military co-operation between the two powers.

The USSR

The USSR feared that any escalation of the conflict in Vietnam would only increase US and PRC involvement in the area. Like Britain and France, it favoured a diplomatic settlement that would create stability in the region. In January 1959, it had even suggested that both Vietnamese states should become members of the UN.

When the National Liberation Front (NLF) was created in South Vietnam and began its struggle against Diệm, Khrushchev reacted cautiously to requests for assistance, but between 1961 and 1965 the USSR did supply a limited amount of weapons. By 1964, however, Khrushchev was becoming increasingly impatient with North Vietnam. In the summer of 1964, an NLF delegation visited the Soviet Union. When the NLF argued that the fall of the Diệm government created opportunities for greater military action and asked for increased military aid, as well as the establishment of a permanent Soviet military mission in Hanoi, North Vietnam's capital, Khrushchev refused this outright. According to the British ambassador in Moscow: 'he had decided to have nothing to do with Vietnam … and virtually signed off' [sic].

PRC

The PRC, in the aftermath of the disastrous 'Great Leap Forward' (see page 177) and subsequent famine, was initially cautious about increasing its support for North Vietnam as this could lead to confrontation with the US. In May 1960, Zhou Enlai advised the leaders of North Vietnam to adopt a flexible approach to the South by combining political and military struggles. However, as US involvement in Vietnam intensified, the PRC increased its aid to North Vietnam. In July 1964, the PRC agreed to increase military and economic aid, train its pilots and, if the US attacked North Vietnam, provide support 'by all possible and necessary means'.

There were domestic reasons behind the PRC's new and more aggressive strategy towards the escalating conflict in Vietnam. Despite the failure of the 'Great Leap Forward' by 1961, Mao had not ended his intention of revolutionizing China's society. By creating the impression that the PRC was threatened by US military intervention in Vietnam, he could once again use the threat of external danger to quicken the pace of reform inside the PRC. At the same time, he could brand his critics as revisionist traitors and thereby strengthen his political position, which had been weakened by the debacle of the 'Great Leap Forward'.

Contrasting reactions to the Tonkin incidents

The PRC reacted promptly, but in a calculated way to the Tonkin incidents. The PRC–North Vietnam border was reinforced by over 400 aircraft. The intention was to deter the US from any further action in North Vietnam, rather than provoke open conflict.

The reaction of the PRC contrasted strongly with that of the Soviet Union, which remained, according to historian Ilya Gaiduk, 'for the most part a passive observer'. There were, however, complaints about the US's militancy in the Soviet press and Khrushchev did send Johnson a letter warning him about the dangers of war in Indochina.

The war escalates

By December 1964, the South Vietnam's army was in disarray and its morale low. US forces effectively took over the war from January 1965. The US began a sustained bombing campaign against North Vietnam, Operation 'Rolling Thunder', while by mid-May 1965, the number of US forces in Vietnam was increased to 47,000. There were over 500,000 US soldiers in South Vietnam a year later.

Despite their enormous destructive capability, US tactics were to prove ineffective against the Viet Cong, who were supplied with weapons and provisions transported down the Hồ Chí Minh trail. Eventually, supplies carried along this route were able to support some 170,000 Viet Cong guerrillas. The fields and dense jungles formed an ideal terrain for guerrilla fighting. The Viet Cong were able to ambush US and South Vietnamese forces regularly and with impunity, disappearing into the jungle immediately afterwards.

PRC assistance, 1965–70

Operation 'Rolling Thunder' and the large increases in US troops came as an unpleasant surprise to the PRC whose leaders, after the Tonkin Incidents, were initially convinced that the war would be confined to the intervention of US advisors and specialist units.

SOURCE L

According to Source L, what are the PRC's views on US involvement in South Vietnam?

An extract from Zhou Enlai's warning to the US while visiting Indonesia on 28 May 1965, quoted in *Mao's China* by Chen Jian, published by University of North Carolina Press, Chapel Hill, USA, 2001, p. 217.

(1) *China will not take the initiative to provoke war against the United States;*
(2) *China will honour what it has said;*
(3) *China is prepared; and*
(4) *If (the) United States bombs China that means bringing the war to China. The war has no boundary. This means two things. First you cannot say that only an air war on your part is allowed and the land war on my part is not allowed. Second, not only may you invade our territory, we may also fight a war abroad.*

In the summer of 1965, the PRC reached agreement with North Vietnam that the PRC's main role would be to guarantee material support and to defend the North so that North Vietnam could send as many men as possible to join the Viet Cong in the South. Unless US troops invaded the North, the PRC would not become directly involved in the war. From 1965 to 1969, the PRC's aid was substantial. Altogether, over 320,000 PRC troops served in North Vietnam and were engaged in the construction, maintenance and defence of transport links and important strategic targets.

This freed North Vietnamese troops for deployment in the South and deterred US expansion of the war into the North.

PRC limits aid

By 1969, several factors led to the PCR limiting aid to North Vietnam:

- The PRC was on the verge of economic and social collapse as a result of Mao's Cultural Revolution, which had not only destroyed his enemies, but much of the CCP and the government, as well as severely disrupting the economy.
- The relationship between the PRC and the USSR had deteriorated to the point where war between the two powers was possible (see page 179).
- The leadership of the PRC now perceived the USSR to be the major threat to the PRC and began to reconsider the role of the United States in China's security (see page 237).
- Closer relations between North Vietnam and the USSR (see below).

In July 1970 the last PRC troops returned home, although the PRC did continue to send weapons and other material assistance until the end of the war.

Soviet assistance

Khrushchev's overthrow in October 1964 led to closer links between the USSR and North Vietnam. Soviet Prime Minister Alexei Kosygin urged a *rapprochement* with the PRC and a more assertive policy against the US and NATO. Aid to North Vietnam was both an ideological duty (i.e. to help a communist state) and a response to US aggression. The USSR responded to the intensification of the US campaign against the Viet Cong by increasing its aid to North Vietnam. Between 1965 and 1967, it delivered about $670 million worth of goods and aid, including surface-to-air missiles, mainly for the defence of North Vietnamese cities against US air attack. It also sent some 12,000 military instructors to train North Vietnamese troops in the use of these missiles.

Kosygin visited the PRC in February 1965 in an attempt to co-ordinate supplies and aid toward North Vietnam. Although Zhou Enlai acknowledged that the positions of the PRC and USSR were 'either very close or coincidental', the PRC refused to join the Soviets in a joint condemnation of US aggression in Vietnam. Its distrust of the USSR ruled out the possibility of the two communist powers operating together to assist North Vietnam. Instead, each competed to be seen by the communist and Non-Aligned worlds as the more generous supplier of aid and arms to North Vietnam.

The Sino-Soviet split and North Vietnam

North Vietnam and the PRC entered the war as close allies, but became enemies at the war's end. The PRC hoped to exploit the war not only to emphasize that it, rather than the USSR, was the true centre of communism and global revolution, but also, as we have seen, to use the war to mobilize the population to support the Cultural Revolution. North Vietnam wanted first and foremost to reunite Vietnam. To them, the Sino-Soviet split was a distraction and they refused initially to take sides, while accepting help from both the USSR and the PRC.

North Vietnam–PRC friction

The PRC was increasingly disturbed by North Vietnam's assertion of its independence. For instance, when PRC military instructors first entered North Vietnam in August 1965, they were instructed not only to serve in a military role, but also to work as political agents to instruct the population in the benefits of communism as practised in the PRC. North Vietnamese authorities viewed this as interference in the internal politics of their country and rapidly stopped such activities. In March 1966, Mao was particularly annoyed when Lê Duẩn, the General Secretary of the Vietnamese Workers' Party, led a delegation to attend the Communist Party of the Soviet Union's Twenty-Third Congress, where he referred to the USSR as his 'second motherland'.

By 1968, there was clear evidence that North Vietnam was increasingly siding with the USSR. When a series of fights broke out between Chinese and Soviet military experts in Vietnam, the North Vietnamese authorities supported the Soviet experts. North Vietnam's growing military involvement and influence in Laos (see page 191) also caused suspicion between the PRC and North Vietnam since this threatened to create a pro-Soviet bloc of states on the PRC's south-western frontier. Although the PRC reduced its assistance to North Vietnam in 1969, there was no immediate break in relations between the two countries. It was only after Vietnam's invasion of Cambodia in 1979 (see page 206) that the PRC invaded North Vietnam as a punishment.

What difficulties did the US encounter in its attempts to end the war in Vietnam?

Negotiations to end the war, 1968–73

The US lost support for the war at home when public opinion turned against the conflict. Instrumental in this was the reporting by the US media of the **Tet Offensive** of January–February 1968 when South Vietnamese cities and military installations were attacked by the North Vietnamese and Viet Cong during the festival of Tết Nguyên Đán. That they managed to penetrate the US embassy compound was seized upon by the US and world media as evidence of US and South Vietnamese defeat. The fact that the offensive was halted with considerable loss of North Vietnamese and Viet Cong life was all but ignored. Facing violent student protest and a hostile media and public opinion, President Johnson stated that he would not campaign for re-election in November 1968 and began negotiations with North Vietnam for a ceasefire. This was initially unsuccessful as North Vietnam remained adamant that the US should withdraw its troops unconditionally.

KEY TERM

Tet Offensive North Vietnamese and Viet Cong offensive against South Vietnamese and US troops, which was launched despite an agreed truce during Tết Nguyên Đán, the Vietnamese New Year festival.

US President Nixon, 1968–72

Nixon's main aim, after his election in November 1968, was to end US involvement in Vietnam 'with honour' as quickly as possible, but this was a complex task. His National Security Advisor, Henry Kissinger, hoped to link peace in Vietnam with a *détente* with the USSR. He calculated that the USSR was so anxious to sign a treaty on Strategic Arms Limitation (see page 235) that it would put pressure on North Vietnam to come to the conference table.

This policy did not work. The USSR publically dismissed the attempt to link the situation in Vietnam with talks on Strategic Arms Limitation and went on to increase its military supplies to North Vietnam. In 1972, after the negotiation of the SALT I agreement (see page 236), the USSR informed the Soviet bloc and North Vietnam that it condemned US aggression in Vietnam. Neither did the Sino–US *rapprochement* (see page 237) help to end the Vietnam War as North Vietnam by 1969 was increasingly looking to the USSR for support and the PRC no longer had much influence on North Vietnam's leaders.

Withdrawal of American troops, 1972

Nixon's strategy was to carry out a policy of Vietnamization of the war, which meant transferring the burden of the land war to the South Vietnamese while withdrawing US troops. Increasingly, it was only US air power that prevented the defeat of South Vietnam. Nixon ordered the bombing of Viet Cong military bases and supply routes in Cambodia and sent troops over the border; large stocks of Viet Cong weapons were captured and pressure eased on South Vietnam as some 40,000 North Vietnamese troops had to be deployed in Cambodia to protect their installations and supplies.

In an attempt to reassure the US public that this was not a permanent escalation of the war, Nixon gave assurances that US troops would only advance 21 miles into Cambodia and would withdraw by the end of June. The US Congress remained unconvinced and responded by forbidding the future deployment of US troops in either Laos or Cambodia. Shortly before the last US troops evacuated Vietnam, the North launched a massive attack against the South in June 1972, which was halted with US air attacks which killed or wounded 50,000 North Vietnamese troops, preventing South Vietnam from being conquered. In August 1972, the last US soldier left Vietnam.

The Paris Peace Accords

In the end, the crucial factor leading to a peace agreement being signed in Paris was the realization by North Vietnam that US air power effectively prevented an immediate take-over of the South, despite the dominance of North Vietnamese forces on the ground. In another impressive display of

US air power, Nixon sent in waves of B-52 bombers in December 1972 against the Hanoi-Haiphong area in North Vietnam (see map, page 196), which used the new **'smart' bombs**, to target military installations with considerable effect.

On 27 January the Paris Peace Accords were at last signed:

- The US was to withdraw the last of their forces within 60 days.
- US prisoners-of-war would be released.
- A ceasefire was declared throughout Vietnam.
- The territorial integrity of the whole of Vietnam, according to the 1954 Geneva Agreement, would be recognized by the US.
- Elections were to be held in both North and South Vietnam.

In essence, as historian Norman Stone has observed, this peace agreement was a 'fraudulent face-saver for the Americans'. It did not halt the war. The North moved tanks and troops into the South in early 1975, and the US-trained South Vietnamese army was unable to stop them. By April 1975, Northern troops seized Saigon, the South's capital, and the US Embassy had to be evacuated by helicopter amid scenes of panic, which were shown around the world by television. The impression given was one of US defeat and humiliation. Vietnam was now a united, communist state.

T O K We know that treaties occur between various states throughout history. What gives a treaty validity and meaning? (History, Ethics, Language, Reason)

What were the international consequences of the US defeat in Vietnam?

 KEY TERM

'Smart' bombs Precision-guided bombs which enable a target to be hit accurately with the use of fewer and smaller bombs.

New Left The predominantly student left-wing movements that emerged in the US and Europe in the 1960s.

International consequences

North Vietnam's victory symbolized the success of a Third World revolution against the US. For both the Third World revolutionaries and the **New Left** in Europe, Vietnam and Cuba demonstrated the way ahead for victory against the US and Western capitalism. Communism was also triumphant in Laos and Cambodia.

Cambodia

In Cambodia, the communist Khmer Rouge party, led by Pol Pot, seized power in 1975 and established a regime whose policies resulted in the death of over 2 million of its citizens. In December 1978, in response to appeals from refugees and exiles that had created the Kampuchean United Front for National Salvation, Vietnam invaded, drove out Pol Pot and established a new regime: the People's Republic of Kampuchea.

Laos

Once South Vietnam fell to the North, Laos, as Khrushchev had already forecast in 1961, fell 'like a ripe apple'. In November 1975, the Pathet Lao took over Laos and established the Lao People's Democratic Republic. They permitted Vietnam to have military bases in the country and to send in political and economic advisors.

Vietnam's other neighbours

Yet, elsewhere, the US defeat did not lead to the 'domino effect' much feared by the US.

Indonesia

Indonesian President Ahmed Sukarno was one of the leaders of the Non-Aligned Movement (see page 151). When Malaysia was created by the British in 1963 by amalgamating their former colonial territories of Malaya, Singapore, Sarawak and Sabah, he was determined to destroy the Federation as it constituted a formidable barrier to Indonesian expansion. To the alarm of the US and Britain, he looked increasingly to the PRC for assistance and began to co-operate closely with the Indonesian Communist Party. This threat was removed as early as September 1965 when the Indonesian army seized power and forced Sukarno to resign two years later.

Thailand

North Vietnamese success in the war against the US encouraged the Communist Party of Thailand (CPT) to step up their campaign against government forces in Thailand. However, the Thai military was able to suppress the CPT to such an extent that only limited guerrilla action against US bases and Thai government installations was possible, and this with the assistance of the Khmer Rouge in neighbouring Cambodia. These limited attacks declined further once Vietnam's forces defeated the Khmer Rouge in 1979. The Thai government was also strengthened by a massive US aid programme.

Philippines

In the Philippines in 1970, the Communist Party launched a campaign against the dictatorship of Ferdinand Marcos, which was established in 1965. Although the Communists managed to create an army of some 20,000 guerrilla fighters by 1980, they failed to take power when the Marcos dictatorship collapsed in 1986.

The Creation of ASEAN

The stabilization of southeast Asia was also assisted by the formation of the anti-communist Association of Southeast Nations (ASEAN) in August 1967 by Indonesia, Malaysia, the Philippines, Singapore and Thailand. After the fall of Saigon, these states co-operated together closely to deter the spread of communism, primarily by sharing military intelligence.

The Vietnamese–Chinese War

After the end of the Vietnam War, relations between Vietnam and the PRC continued to deteriorate. In June 1978, Vietnam joined the Soviet economic bloc and in December invaded Cambodia. The new PRC leader, Deng Xiaoping (see page 276), alarmed by the threat of a strong pro-Soviet Vietnamese–Cambodian bloc on its frontier, decided to attack and intimidate Vietnam. It invaded northern Vietnam, and after a month's heavy fighting, withdrew claiming victory. In reality, this operation achieved little and it was not until 1989 that Vietnam withdrew its forces from Cambodia.

The US

Inevitably, the defeat in Vietnam, together with the **Watergate scandal**, did immense damage to US prestige and self-confidence, and made it reluctant to project its power in the years immediately after 1975. Nixon, Kissinger and, later, President Carter reduced direct US intervention in the Third World and instead attempted to use regional powers – Brazil, Turkey, South Africa, Iran and Indonesia – whose armed forces received aid and training, to contain communism in their regions. The humiliation of defeat disguised the fact that by 1979 the US was in fact winning the Cold War. In the Middle East, Egypt ended its close links with the USSR (see page 216), while the US's *rapprochement* with the PRC was a serious challenge to the USSR (see page 237).

KEY TERM

Watergate scandal On 17 June 1972, Republican Party officials broke into the headquarters of the opposition Democratic Party in the Watergate Building in Washington DC to find material which could be used to discredit Democrats. The break-in was discovered and eventually led to Nixon's resignation in 1974.

? What information does Source M contain about the results of US policy in Vietnam?

SOURCE M

US Embassy officials being evacuated by helicopter from Saigon, South Vietnam, April 1975.

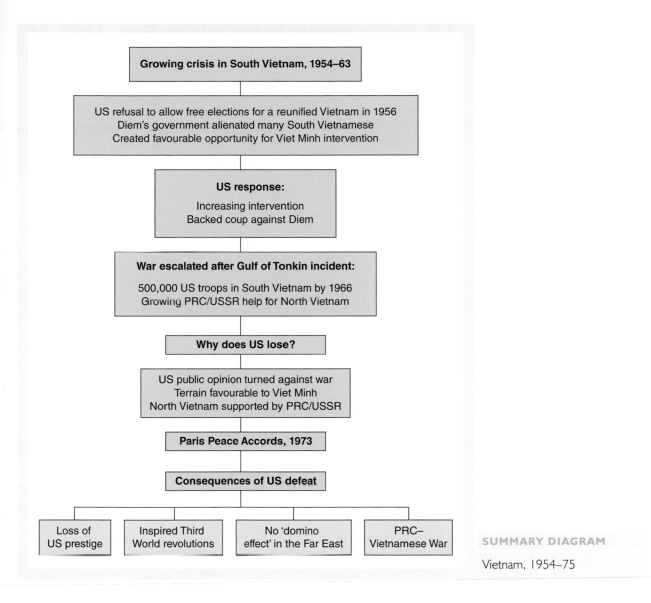

Growing crisis in South Vietnam, 1954–63

US refusal to allow free elections for a reunified Vietnam in 1956
Diem's government alienated many South Vietnamese
Created favourable opportunity for Viet Minh intervention

US response:

Increasing intervention
Backed coup against Diem

War escalated after Gulf of Tonkin incident:

500,000 US troops in South Vietnam by 1966
Growing PRC/USSR help for North Vietnam

Why does US lose?

US public opinion turned against war
Terrain favourable to Viet Minh
North Vietnam supported by PRC/USSR

Paris Peace Accords, 1973

Consequences of US defeat

| Loss of US prestige | Inspired Third World revolutions | No 'domino effect' in the Far East | PRC– Vietnamese War |

SUMMARY DIAGRAM

Vietnam, 1954–75

5 The Cold War in the Middle East, 1957–79

▶ *Key question: What were the results of US and USSR involvement in the Middle East from 1957 to 1979?*

The period 1957 to 1973 was one of acute crisis in the Middle East, involving two wars between the Arab states and Egypt with Israel in June 1967 and October 1973. While this bitter struggle was not in itself caused by the Cold War, it became influenced by the course of the global Cold War.

How successful was the US in limiting Soviet influence in the Middle East?

US–Soviet rivalry in the Middle East, 1957–66

The decline of British and French power in the region, accelerated by the Suez Crisis of 1956 (see page 155), created a political vacuum that both the US and USSR competed to fill. Immediately after the Suez War in 1956, the USSR promised to replace Egypt's lost armaments. The US responded by re-establishing close contact with Britain (see page 162) and by creating plans aimed at making the Middle East secure from communist penetration.

The Eisenhower Doctrine, 1957

In March 1957, US President Eisenhower gained approval from Congress for what became known as the 'Eisenhower Doctrine'. By this the US undertook to protect the territories and independence of any state threatened by communist aggression.

SOURCE N

How, according to Source N, would the US protect Middle Eastern states from communist aggression?

An extract from Eisenhower's message to the US Congress, 5 January, 1957 quoted in *The Cold War*, by E. Judge and J. Langdon, published by Prentice Hall, New Jersey, USA, 1999, p. 99.

The action which I propose would have the following features:

It would first of all authorize the United States to cooperate with and assist any nation or group of nations in the general area of the Middle East in the development of economic strength dedicated to the maintenance of national independence.

It would in the second place, authorize the Executive to undertake in the same region programs of military assistance and cooperation with any nation which desires such aid.

It would in the third place authorize such assistance and cooperation to include the employment of the armed forces of the United States to secure and protect the territorial integrity and political independence of such nations, requesting such aid.

The United Arab Republic

In 1954, the socialist and pan-Arab Ba'ath Party gained power in Syria. Unsuccessful attempts by Britain and the US to encourage its overthrow merely drove it closer to the USSR. In the summer of 1957, Syria managed to secure a massive military aid programme from the USSR. At the same time, Soviet experts were sent to reorganize its security services. This alarmed both the US and Syria's pro-Western neighbours who believed that Syria was now virtually a Soviet satellite. Turkey, Iraq, Jordan and Lebanon made plans, with US encouragement, to overthrow its government, but in the face of Soviet and Egyptian support for Syria backed down. In October, Egypt's President Nasser sent troops into Syria.

In November, a meeting of Syrian and Egyptian members of parliament recommended a federal union between the two countries. The plan was supported by the Syrian army for security reasons, but opposed by the country's communists as it would weaken Syria's links with the USSR. Nasser, with the covert support of the US, managed to out-manoeuvre the communists' efforts and the United Arab Republic was formed in January 1958. In 1961, Syria withdrew from the union but remained an ally of Egypt.

The Iraqi Revolution, July 1958

In July 1958, the Iraqi army mutinied and killed the King and Crown Prince of Iraq, as well as the Prime Minister, Nuri as-Said, and proclaimed a republic that looked to Nasser for support. This was a considerable blow to the West as Iraq had been a leading member of the Baghdad Pact (see page 126). Both the pro-Western regimes in Lebanon and Jordan felt threatened by the new Iraqi Republic and asked the US and Britain for immediate assistance. The US sent 14,000 troops to Lebanon and Britain 2200 paratroops to Jordan to assist King Hussein.

This show of strength alarmed Khrushchev who welcomed the Iraqi Revolution as a serious blow against Western influence in the Middle East. As a demonstration against Western intervention, the Soviets staged large-scale military manoeuvres in eastern Europe, but also advised Nasser not to provoke the West still further by intervening in Iraq. The Soviets called for a summit meeting on the Middle East, but the US, fearing that this would lead to an expansion of Soviet influence in this region, declined to participate. The demonstration of British and US military commitment to Lebanon and Jordan stabilized the region and soon troops from both countries were withdrawn.

Nasser leans towards the US

In September 1958, Iraq's pro-Nasser President Arif was ousted by Brigadier Abdul Karim Qassim who was closely allied with the Iraqi Communist Party. Khrushchev increasingly saw Qassim as a more reliable leader than Nasser and began to supply him with military aid. Nasser responded by persecuting the Egyptian Communist Party and, in an attempt to topple Qassim, by supporting an unsuccessful uprising against his regime in Mosul in the country's north. When Khrushchev criticized him for claiming to be a socialist but in reality attacking communists, Nasser accused the USSR of attempting to dictate to the United Arab Republic and, in protest, moved 250 Egyptian students studying in the Soviet Union to US universities in October 1958. Initially the US was concerned that Iraq would become a Soviet satellite, but Qassim avoided dependence on the Iraqi Communist Party by following Nasser's example and periodically persecuting it to show that he was the country's real authority.

What was the
significance of the
Six Day War for the
Middle East?

The Six Day War, June 1967

The main aim of the Arab states and Egypt was to remove Israel. The country's existence was seen by them as another form of European imperialism. They claimed it had been established at the expense of the Arabs in 1948, as well as being an illegal creation and a threat to regional security, as demonstrated by Israel's invasion of Egypt in 1956. These states welcomed Soviet assistance, but were not prepared to be dictated to by the USSR. The Soviets perceived the Arab–Israeli dispute to be an extension of the global Cold War and believed that Israel was merely an instrument of the United States. For the Soviets, Egypt was a valuable ally, particularly when it was strengthened by its close alliance with Syria.

The US, heavily involved in Vietnam, sought stability in the Middle East. By this they meant:

- creation of political regimes resistant to revolutionary change
- the blocking of Soviet influence
- economic prosperity based on capitalism, and
- Western access to the oil resources of the region.

To achieve this, US officials attempted to remain on friendly terms with both Israel and the Arab states. In 1964, President Johnson even briefly refused to supply Israel with weapons as this might trigger increased Soviet arms supplies to the other states.

Path to war, 1966–67

By early 1967, Israel was under increasing pressure from the new Ba'ath government in Syria. Its borders were shelled by Syria from the Golan Heights and Palestinian nationalists formed guerrilla groups that were armed and trained by the Syrian army, to carry out raids across the border. In response, the Israeli army urged its government to attack Syria.

On 16 May, the border tension escalated into a major crisis when Nasser expelled the UN Emergency Force which had patrolled the Sinai since 1957. Egyptian forces moved to occupy the territory evacuated by the UN. On 22 May, the crisis deepened still further when Nasser announced that Egypt would blockade the Straits of Tiran, preventing Israel from receiving ships in its southern port of Eilat, and seize cargoes bound for Israel. It was understood by Nasser and the other Arab leaders that a blockade and heightened state of tension would force Israel to mobilize its substantial armed forces and thus put a severe strain on Israel's economy. Nasser, facing economic stress at home as the result of military spending, increasing population and failed economic policies, sought renewed popularity with a demonstration of force; it is unclear if he intended actually to attack Israel in 1967.

US reaction

As tension mounted, the US attempted to find a means of avoiding war. It urged restraint on both Israel and Egypt. President Johnson appealed unsuccessfully to Nasser to lift the blockade and strongly advised Israel's Prime Minister Eshkol against taking any pre-emptive action. Johnson also appealed to the Soviets to use their influence with Nasser to prevent Egypt from attacking Israel. The US briefly considered requesting NATO forces to escort Israeli ships through the Straits of Tiran to protect them from Egypt. This idea was dropped as it would likely provoke the other Arab states and drive them closer to the Soviet Union.

By early June, it was clear that unless Egypt called off the blockade, Israel would attack Egypt, despite US objections.

SOURCE O

An extract from 'The Cold War and the Six Day War' by Peter L. Hahn in *The Cold War in the Middle East*, edited by N.J. Ashton, published by Routledge, London, UK, 2007, p. 25.

In several previous situations, most notably the Suez-Sinai War of 1956–57, Israeli leaders took action to defend the national interests in defiance of US advice. 'You should not assume that the United States can order Israel not to fight for what it considers to be its most vital interests', [US Secretary of State Dean] Rusk cabled US ambassadors on 3 June. '… The "holy war" psychology of the Arab world is matched by an apocalyptic psychology within Israel. Israel may make a decision that it must resort to force to protect its vital interests.'

What information is conveyed by Source O about the causes of the Arab–Israeli War of 1967?

The Israeli attack, 5 June

On 5 June, in a pre-emptive attack, Israel's air force destroyed the bulk of Egypt's aircraft while they were still on the ground. An hour later, Israel invaded Sinai and were able to destroy Egypt's tanks, trucks and soldiers with aircraft since Egypt no longer had an air force to protect them. By the following day, Sinai Peninsula was under Israel's control, with tens of thousands of Egyptian troops either captured, dead or trapped. When Jordan and Syria entered the war, Israel rapidly defeated their forces and occupied the West Bank, part of Jordan at the time, and Syria's Golan Heights. In response to urgent requests for help from Nasser, the Soviets airlifted spare parts for Egypt's tanks, provided air protection and manned anti-aircraft batteries along the Suez Canal.

The ceasefire, 8–10 June

Both the US and USSR attempted to bring about a rapid ceasefire. Johnson kept in direct touch with the Soviet Premier, Kosygin, using the hotline (see page 192). The United Nations Security Council agreed on a resolution demanding an immediate ceasefire. Soviet attempts to insist on an immediate Israeli withdrawal from Sinai were rejected. On 8 June, Nasser accepted an unconditional ceasefire and the next day an Israeli–Syrian

Arab–Israeli conflicts, 1967–73.

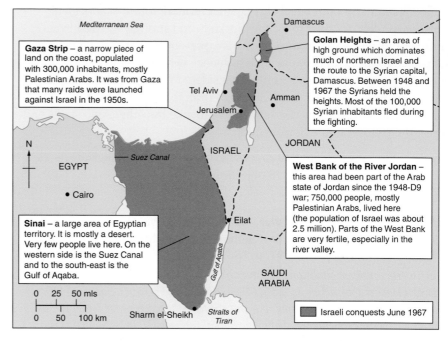

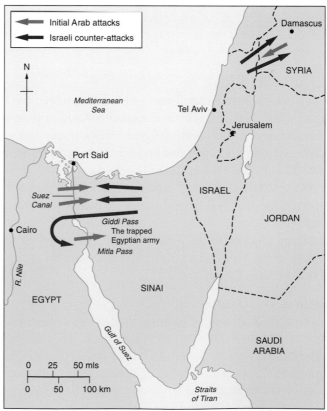

? What information about Arab–Israeli conflicts in 1967 and 1973 does Source P convey?

ceasefire was agreed as well, but did not take effect until the following day as both sides attempted to secure favourable positions before the fighting ended. At one stage, it seemed as if Israel would occupy a large portion of Syria. This possibility was met by a direct threat of Soviet intervention and successful US pressure on Israel to desist.

The aftermath

After the end of the war, the US hoped for a permanent peace between the Arab states and Egypt with Israel, but there were two major obstacles to this:

- Israel was determined to keep its large territorial gains.
- The USSR lost no time in rearming the Arab states and Egypt in order to preserve its relationship with them, Egypt in particular.

The October War, 1973

What was the result of the October War?

The Six Day War, as the 1967 conflict is often called, ended in a ceasefire and no peace treaty was signed. The Middle East remained one of the most sensitive areas in the Cold War. The USSR continued to supply arms to Egypt, Syria, and Iraq, while the US ensured that Israel received the most modern weapons to defend itself from the re-equipped Arab armies.

The War of Attrition, 1969–70

In 1969, Nasser launched what was called the War of Attrition: a series of artillery and commando attacks on Israeli positions, including commando operations into Israel itself, although most attacks-occurred in the Israeli-occupied Sinai Peninsula. Israel responded with counter attacks on Egypt while the Soviets sent artillery units, aircraft and military personnel to assist Egypt. Altogether, more than 20,000 Soviet servicemen served in Egypt from 1969 to 1970 while the Soviet Navy gained bases on the Red Sea and the Mediterranean coast. The effectiveness of Soviet aid persuaded Israel, under US pressure, to agree to a ceasefire in October 1970.

President Sadat

Nasser died in September 1970 and was replaced by Anwar El Sadat. The new Egyptian president was initially seen in both Egypt and abroad as a transitional figure, soon to be replaced by a more powerful politician. He was, however, a formidable statesman. His ultimate aim was to negotiate a peace treaty with Israel and the return of the territory including the Sinai Peninsula, that had been seized by Israel in 1967 back to their original owners. The key to success, he realized, was to persuade the US to pressure Israel to make concessions. In July 1972, he dismissed the 21,000 Soviet military advisors in the country after receiving a message from US President Nixon through the foreign minister of the Netherlands that he would make the achievement of peace in the Middle East a greater priority of US politics if Soviet personnel left Egypt.

When it emerged that Nixon, already weakened by the Watergate scandal (see page 208), was unable, or unwilling, to force Israel to make concessions, the only alternative left to Sadat for bringing Israel to the negotiating table was force. Sadat did not think that Israel would be completely defeated, but he calculated that a surprise attack, which would inflict some damage on Israeli forces, would make it more responsive to a comprehensive peace settlement.

The October War

On 6 October 1973, Egyptian troops successfully crossed the Suez Canal, defeating Israeli forces entrenched along its banks. Egypt's attack was a complete surprise as Israel did not expect Egypt to attack during Ramadan, a Muslim holy month of fasting, or during the Jewish festival of Yom Kippur. Israeli aircraft that attempted to penetrate Egypt's anti-aircraft defences along the Canal were shot down with surface-to-air missiles supplied by the Soviet Union. Once Egypt secured the eastern side of the Canal, its forces stopped in accordance with Sadat's plan. This was Israel's first major defeat since its independence, causing panic in Israel and alarm in the US. Syria soon joined the conflict to regain the Golan Heights, entering the Israeli-occupied area with large numbers of tanks. The US rapidly resupplied Israel with weapons and ammunition.

Once reinforced by the US, Israel counter-attacked on 11 October, destroying Syria's tanks with aircraft. To take pressure off Syria, Egypt moved a large army into the Sinai to threaten Israel's western border. Unsupported by anti-aircraft missiles, these troops were attacked by air and were soon encircled by Israeli troops who then crossed the Suez Canal. As the fighting continued, it was clear to both the US and the USSR that a ceasefire was required before they were pulled into a larger conflict in support of their allies. The United Nations Security Council ordered a ceasefire on 22 October; Israel initially ignored it to complete the encirclement of the Egyptian Third Army. In response, the Soviets threatened direct military intervention unless Israel complied, causing the US to put its military on a high state of alert. In response to this the Soviets announced that they would send troops into the region only with UN approval. On 26 October, most fighting ended and soon prisoners were exchanged, with Israeli troops moving back into Sinai, while Egypt's troops withdrew to the west side of the Canal.

Consequences

A consequence of the October War was that Egypt moved closer to the US to negotiate a settlement with Israel. In 1976, Sadat ended the 1971 friendship Treaty with the USSR. In 1977, after failing to get Israel to enter serious talks about the return of the Sinai Peninsula and the resolution of the Israeli–Egyptian conflict, he made the dramatic gesture of visiting Israel to speak to the Israeli parliament directly. This action stunned Israel, the Arab states, Egypt and much of the rest of the world as it was so unexpected, but it was a demonstration of Sadat's desire to resolve the conflict.

The USSR played no part in the preliminary negotiations of the 1979 Egypt–Israel Treaty and lost all influence over Egypt. The US, on the other hand, played a key role in negotiations. President Carter acted as mediator

between Sadat and Israeli Prime Minister Menachim Begin during talks at the US president's retreat, Camp David. The Camp David Accords, signed in 1979, normalized relations between Israel and Egypt and provided for the return of Sinai to Egypt.

The USSR, having been excluded from Egypt, concentrated its support on Syria and Iraq, both of which opposed Israel and US influence in the Middle East and increased aid to the **Palestinian Liberation Organization (PLO)**. Syria declined to negotiate with Israel, demanding simply that Israel should remove itself from the areas of Syria that it had occupied before any negotiations could commence.

🔑 KEY TERM

Palestine Liberation Organization (PLO) A Palestinian nationalist organization created in 1964 that operated as a political and paramilitary group.

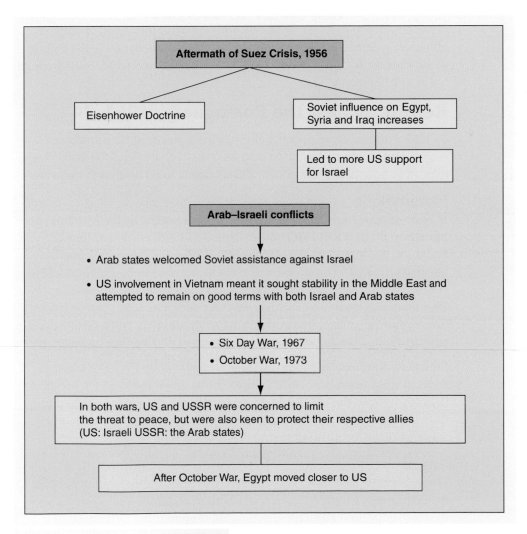

SUMMARY DIAGRAM

The Cold War in the Middle East, 1957–79

The Cold War in Africa, 1964–79

> ▶ **Key question:** What was the impact of the Cold War in Africa, 1964–79?

The struggles against colonialism predated the spread of the Cold War to southern Africa. However, as these struggles intensified, the Cold War conflict between the USSR, the PRC and the US helped influence both their course and outcome. By the mid-1970s, the liberation movements in Angola, Mozambique, Guinea-Bissau and Rhodesia (today's Zimbabwe) were becoming a focus for Cold War rivalry between the USSR and the USA.

The revolution in Ethiopia in 1974 toppled the pro-US Emperor Haile Selassie and also provided the USSR with opportunities for increasing its influence in Africa. In 1977, this led to the establishment of a leftist regime under Colonel Mengistu which relied on Soviet support to defend it from an invasion by Somalia.

> **How dependent on Soviet bloc aid were independence movements in Portuguese Africa?**

Revolts against the Portuguese, 1964–74

By 1965, Portugal faced major challenges to its power in Mozambique, Angola and Guinea-Bissau (see map on page 219) and found it increasingly difficult to finance and supply its military efforts to retain these territories.

Mozambique

In Mozambique, the war for independence was waged by the Mozambique Liberation Front, **FRELIMO**, under Eduardo Mondlane. It was formed across the border in Tanzania in September 1964 and began to launch guerrilla attacks on Portuguese targets in Mozambique. By 1967, over 20 per cent of Mozambique was controlled by FRELIMO. After Mondlane's assassination, possibly by Portugal's secret police, FRELIMO'S new leader, Samora Machel, intensified guerrilla operations, aiming particularly at terrorizing the Portuguese civilian population to destroy their morale.

Presidents Kennedy and Johnson were sympathetic to FRELIMO, but, as Portugal was a member of NATO, the US was unwilling to give it practical help. It was from the USSR and, to a lesser extent, the PRC, Cuba and the GDR that FRELIMO received shipments of weapons and instructions in subversion and political warfare.

Angola

The strength of FRELIMO lay in its ability to unite the opposition against the Portuguese. In Angola, which was both strategically and economically the most important Portuguese colony, there were three rival liberation movements divided both by ideology and ethnicity:

- The National Front for the Liberation of Angola (*Frente Nacional de Libertação de Angola* or FNLA), led by Holden Roberto, was strongly

 KEY TERM

FRELIMO *Frente de Libertação de Moçambique*, or Mozambique Liberation Front.

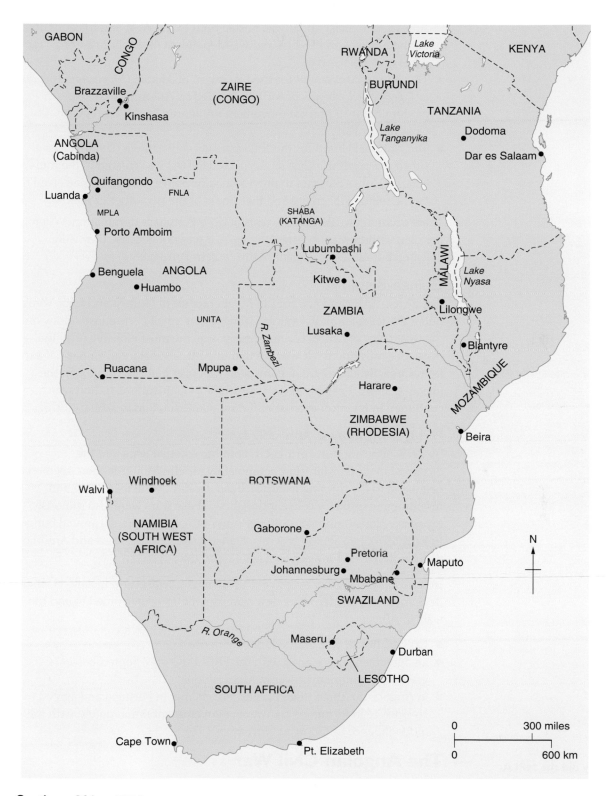

Southern Africa, 1974.

African nationalist and it was hostile both to the West and to communism but had links with the CIA and was dependent on Mobutu's Congo for bases and assistance.

- The Popular Movement for the Liberation of Angola (*Movimento Popular de Libertação de Angola* or MPLA), headed by Antonio Neto, was predominantly a Marxist movement influenced by the Portuguese Communist Party.
- The National Union for the Total Liberation of Angola (*União Nacional para a Independência Total de Angola* or UNITA) was created in the mid-1960s by Jonas Savimbi to provide an alternative to what he perceived to be the military inactivity and feebleness of the two other groups.

These divisions weakened the resistance to Portugal's domination. When Portugal withdrew from Angola in 1974, it was not because they were defeated but rather as a result of the coup in Portugal.

Guinea-Bissau

The PAIGC (African Party for the Independence of Guinea and Cape Verde), under the leadership of Amilcar Cabral, in the small Portuguese colony on the west coast of Africa, Guinea-Bissau, was the most effective of all the resistance movements. It was strengthened by a substantial amount of aid from Cuba. By early 1973, it controlled well over half the country. In the liberated areas, it established a competent civilian administration which continued to function even after Cabral's assassination in January 1973.

Portugal withdraws, April 1974

By 1973, opposition in Portugal to both the colonial wars and the dictatorship under Marcelo Caetano grew rapidly. Militarily there seemed to be no end to the fighting in Africa. Casualty rates were increasing and resentment of military conscription grew. These wars were also ruinously expensive, consuming some 40 per cent of the government's annual budget. In early 1974, two senior generals, Francisco de Costa Gomes and António de Spínola, called for a political solution to the conflicts.

In April 1974, the army staged a coup against Caetano and installed General de Spínola as President. The new government was determined to end the wars in Africa:

- Guinea-Bissau was granted independence
- an agreement was signed with the FRELIMO on 7 September 1974, granting it complete power in Mozambique
- in Angola, the three main parties' leaders met in Portugal and agreed to co-operate in forming a transitional government immediately, with full independence to follow in November 1974.

Why did the MPLA win the Angolan Civil War? $\rightarrow$

The Angolan Civil War

Civil war erupted in Angola soon after the meeting in Portugal between the rival groups.

US, PRC and South African aid, 1975

Having extracted itself from the Vietnam conflict, the US was not willing to become heavily involved in Angola, but it wished to avoid an MPLA victory that would allow the Soviets influence there. The US allocated $50 million for the recruiting of mercenaries and the training and equipping of FNLA/UNITA troops.

The PRC, also anxious to prevent Soviet domination of Angola, sent about 300 instructors to assist the FNLA.

South Africa, worried about the impact of the collapse of Portugal's empire on the borders of South African-occupied **Namibia**, decided in September 1975 to commit a force of 2500 regular troops to establish a buffer zone between Namibia and Angola which would help UNITA to establish secure bases from which to operate. This would also prevent raids across the frontier from the Namibian Liberation Movement (later **SWAPO**), which aimed for Namibian independence from South Africa.

MPLA's victory, 1976

Initially, South African intervention, together with Congo's refusal to allow Soviet assistance to flow through its territory, pushed the MPLA on the defensive. By mid-November, the UNITA army, led by South African troops, had almost reached Luanda, the capital of Angola. The MPLA was saved by large-scale Cuban intervention approved by the USSR. Altogether, the USSR transported 12,000 Cuban troops, along with tanks and missiles, to Angola. By December 1975, the Cubans had halted the South African/UNITA advance and inflicted two defeats on their forces.

Determined to prevent a growing US military interest in Angola which might escalate into a second Vietnam, the US Senate voted to block all funding for covert operations there. Deprived of US support, the South African government withdrew its troops from Angola. By March 1976, the MPLA was victorious.

The consequences

In the spring of 1976, the Soviet leaders were convinced that they had won the war in Angola. Soviet naval and air power had supported its allies in a brilliant logistical operation against the US-supported UNITA and FNLA and its ally South Africa. Together with the triumph of communism in Vietnam, the victory of the MPLA seemed to confirm that the newly independent states in the Third World were ready to embrace Soviet-style communism. The US, on the other hand, had suffered a defeat in the conflict over influence in the Third World. The failure in Angola strengthened the anti-interventionism sentiment in the US.

The victory of the MPLA in Angola and FRELIMO in Mozambique increased the pressure for African independence in Rhodesia (now Zimbabwe), which

KEY TERM

Namibia A former German colony which was entrusted to South Africa to govern under a 1919 League of Nations mandate; it became independent in 1991.

SWAPO Acronym for South West People's Organization which aimed to liberate Namibia from South African rule.

ANC Acronym for the African National Congress which aimed to end the rule of South Africa by those of European descent and the racist system that the South African government imposed on the African majority.

Soweto Uprising A protest on 16 June 1976 by at least 20,000 African students against the introduction of Afrikaans, the language of many European South Africans, as the sole language of educational instruction in schools; 700 protestors were killed and 4000 injured by government forces.

To what extent was Soviet intervention in Ethiopia successful?

KEY TERM

Separatists Those wishing to break away from an existing state to create an independent country.

Eritrea Formerly a colony of Italy, which became part of Ethiopia in 1951.

was ruled by Europeans who formed a small minority of the population. The Zimbabwe African National Union (ZANU) had guerrilla training bases in Mozambique, while the Zimbabwe African People's Union (ZAPU) was trained by Cuban instructors in Angola. By 1979, Rhodesian security forces had lost control of the countryside, and in 1980, Rhodesian Prime Minister Ian Smith agreed to majority African rule.

For South Africa, the victory of FRELIMO and the MPLA brought the Cold War to its borders. In Angola, training camps were created in 1976 where Soviet and Cuban instructors trained both **ANC** and SWAPO guerrillas. After the defeat of the **Soweto Uprising** in the summer of 1976, which was triggered by a police massacre of more than 40 school children at a protest meeting, the number of young South African refugees joining the ANC sharply increased.

By 1987, SWAPO attacks across the Angolan border into Namibia were increasing. To halt them and destroy the MPLA regime, the South African government launched another attack into Angola. Once again the MPLA was saved by Cuban forces that halted the South African advance. In response to the threat of Cuban assistance to guerrillas inside Namibia, the South Africans withdrew from Angola and signed a ceasefire agreement with SWAPO, leading to the granting of Namibian independence in 1991.

Ethiopia and the Horn of Africa

Ethiopia had a unique history in Africa. Apart from the Italian occupation 1936–41, the kingdom was the only African territory to escape being colonized by the European powers. By 1973, the government of Emperor Haile Selassie faced a growing challenge from the younger members of the Ethiopian professional classes and junior army officers who had been influenced by the radical student movements in western Europe and the US (see page 241).

By early 1974, the global oil crisis, which saw the price of oil quadruple in many countries, caused severe economic problems and social unrest in Ethiopia. In 1974, the army seized power in Ethiopia, and governed though the *Derg*, or Co-ordinating Committee. The Emperor was deposed and killed.

Haile Mengistu

By late 1974, Major Mengistu had emerged as the most radical left-wing member of the *Derg*, which was persuaded to back his ambitious plans for land reform, improving literacy and social equality in the countryside. These, however, rapidly ran into opposition from the local landlords. Other challenges came from **separatists** in **Eritrea**, left-wing dissenters and members of the old regime. In February 1977, Mengistu murdered most of his rivals in the *Derg* and seized sole power. He then proceeded to unleash what he described as the 'Red Terror', eliminating as many of regime's enemies as possible.

US reaction

During the 1960s, Haile Selassie had increasingly looked towards the US for economic and military aid, but in 1974, the US, enfeebled by the Watergate crisis (see page 208) and its defeat in Vietnam, did nothing to help him. The *Derg* wanted to lessen Ethiopia's economic and military dependence on the US. It suspected that the US was covertly assisting its internal enemies, and increasingly looked to the support of the USSR and the Soviet bloc in Europe. In April 1978, responding to CIA reports that Mengistu was preparing to remove US advisors from Ethiopia, President Carter pre-emptively recalled all US personnel in protest aganist the 'Red Terror'.

Soviet policy

Although approached with requests for aid and military assistance by the *Derg*, the USSR reacted cautiously. It was aware that the US in 1974–76 was still supplying Ethiopia with arms, while it was itself supplying Ethiopia's enemy, Somalia, with weapons. With the coup of February 1977, the attitude of the USSR changed. Mengistu convinced the Soviet ambassador that Ethiopia would be a potentially loyal regional ally. The USSR agreed immediately to send large arms shipments to Ethiopia. By mid-April, according to Western sources, more than a hundred tanks and armoured personnel carriers had already been delivered. For the USSR, the alliance with Ethiopia became its most ambitious intervention in Africa. It gave the USSR influence in the Indian Ocean and the Red Sea area through its access to Eritrean ports such as Assab and Massawa.

The Ogaden War, 1977–78

← **How successful was the USSR in Ethiopia?**

In the late nineteenth century, when the Somali territories were divided between Britain, France and Italy, Ethiopia acquired Ogaden. Once the British and Italian territories became independent in 1960, the two states merged and formed the new state of Somaliland and laid claim to Ogaden. In 1969, Major-General Siad Barre seized power. Barre turned to the USSR for military and economic assistance, but did not allow the Soviets to influence Somalia's internal politics.

In 1975, the Somali government established the Western Somali Liberation Front (WSLF) to conduct guerrilla operations within Ogaden against Ethiopia. From 1977 onwards, the WSLF was assisted by Somali troops who advanced into Eritrea. In early September, the important town of Jijiga fell to Somali forces.

The Horn of Africa 1973–78.

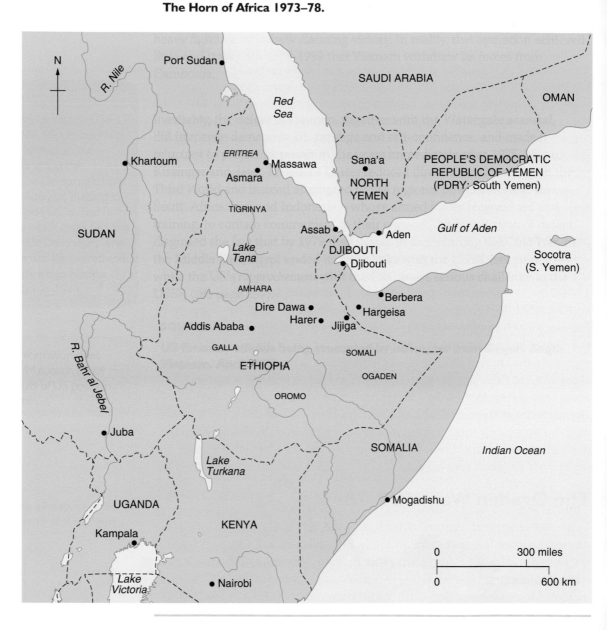

Soviet assistance

After initially unsuccessful attempts to mediate, the Soviets engaged in a large-scale operation to save the Ethiopian revolution. Between September 1977 and May 1978, they flew in $1 billion worth of military equipment to Ethiopia and 1000 military personnel to organize the counter-offensive against the Somalis. Fidel Castro also sent more than 11,000 troops from Cuba.

? What information does Source Q convey about the strategic importance of the Horn of Africa?

With Soviet aid, Ethiopian and Cuban troops recaptured Jijiga and defeated Somalia's army. The conventional war had now been won by Ethiopia, but WSLF guerrilla groups remained active in Ogaden until 1980.

Ethiopia's Marxist–Leninist revolution

The USSR had now become a major factor in African affairs. To many African leaders, the USSR was seen as a useful counter-weight to US and European influence. In Ethiopia, Mengistu attempted to rebuild Ethiopian society along Soviet lines. He was helped by thousands of experts from the Soviet bloc, the largest assistance programme the USSR had undertaken since helping China in the 1950s. Yet little progress was made, as:

- Mengistu had either murdered or driven into exile most Ethiopian Marxists
- peasants and workers proved unreceptive to the teachings of Soviet Marxism
- conflict continued with the Marxist-led Eritrean separatist movement and Soviet attempts to mediate satisfied neither side and failed to halt the conflict
- leftists were severely divided
- the introduction of intensive farming in the newly established collective farms led to soil erosion and widespread famine by 1984.

The impact on US–USSR relations

Large-scale Soviet intervention in Ethiopia threatened the policy of *détente* in Europe by antagonizing US President Carter's administration. The US Republicans' argument that the USSR was exploiting the spirit of *détente* to strengthen its position in Africa helped Ronald Reagan defeat Carter in the November 1980 presidential elections. It also led to increasing reluctance by the US Senate to ratify the SALT II treaty (see page 254).

SOURCE R

An extract from a speech by Ronald Reagan on 25 March 1978 quoted in *The Global Cold War: Third World Intervention and the Making of Our Times* by Odd Arne Westad, published by Cambridge University Press, UK, 2005, p. 283.

If the Soviets are successful – and it looks more and more as if they will be – then the entire Horn of Africa will be under their influence, if not their control. From there, they can threaten the sea lanes carrying oil to western Europe and the United States, if and when they choose. More immediately, control of the Horn of Africa would give Moscow the ability to destabilize those governments on the Arabian Peninsula which have proven themselves strongly anti-Communist [sic] … in a few years we may be faced with the prospect of a Soviet empire of protégés and dependencies stretching from Addis Ababa to Cape Town.

According to Source R, what are Reagan's views on Soviet influence in Africa?

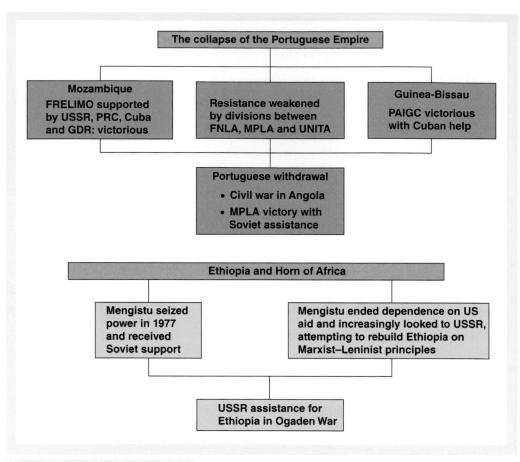

Chapter summary

The years 1960–78 saw an acceleration of the global Cold War. With the Sino-Soviet split there were two major communist powers competing against each other to win the support of Third World states and various liberation movements that were fighting to gain their independence from colonial powers. Both the USSR and the PRC assisted North Vietnam although they refused to co-operate with each other. By 1969, the two powers were on the brink of a major border conflict. Although a truce was arranged and war avoided, it was not until 1989 that normal relations were restored between the two communist states. The Sino-Soviet conflict ultimately altered the balance of the Cold War in favour of the US and its allies, although after the US defeat in Vietnam this was not immediately obvious.

While the US and USSR sought *détente* in Europe, they exploited local conflicts in Asia, Africa and the Middle East and fought what amounted to proxy wars against each other. The US, USSR and PRC each hoped to establish client regimes which would exclude their Cold War rivals. Initially the advantage lay with the US, which possessed far greater naval and air resources than the USSR. In the Congo, for instance, the US was able to marginalize Soviet influence and ensure that the pro-Western Mobutu replaced Lumumba.

In Cuba, the USSR was more successful in supporting Castro and was able to install medium-range nuclear missiles together with a Soviet garrison that could threaten the US. This ensured that the crisis was one of the most dangerous of the Cold War. War was avoided by Khrushchev's agreement to dismantle the missiles in exchange for a guarantee from Kennedy that the US would not invade Cuba as well as a promise that NATO's nuclear missiles would be removed from Turkey.

In South Vietnam, the US was unable to fight a war by proxy. The local forces were too weak to defeat communist infiltration from North Vietnam. Initially, the US sent only advisors and equipment, but in 1965 ground troops were dispatched; by 1966 their number had grown to over 500,000. The PRC and the USSR responded by assisting North Vietnam with military supplies, advisors and technical troops. After the propaganda success for the Viet Cong of the Tet Offensive in early 1968, US public opinion turned against the war, leaving President Nixon with little option but to withdraw US troops. The war was concluded with the Paris Peace Accords in 1973, but North Vietnamese troops seized all South Vietnam two years later, uniting the country.

In the Middle East, US policy in response to growing Soviet involvement was determined by the Eisenhower Doctrine. The US was ready to support Middle Eastern nationalism as long as it received no assistance from the USSR. However, as in Africa, it was not a region where the politics of the Cold War dominated. Egypt and the Arab states were more concerned about the challenge of Israel, and if necessary they would look to the USSR for the supply of weapons and expert instructors to defeat it in war. As a close ally of Israel, the US would not tolerate its defeat. Egypt and the Arab states fought two major wars against Israel in 1967 and 1973.

Both wars ended in an Israeli victory. The US and USSR cooperated briefly at the UN to arrange ceasefires. The USSR was not ready to tolerate the destruction of Egypt and Syria and threatened intervention in 1967 when Israel seemed poised to invade Syria, and in 1973 when the Israeli army ignored the UN ceasefire resolution. After 1967, the USSR immediately resupplied Egypt and Syria with weapons. The US won a major victory in the Cold War when President Sadat abrogated the Soviet Egyptian Friendship Treaty and looked to the US to assist in negotiating a peace treaty between Egypt and Israel. Once this was signed in 1979, Egypt became a key ally of the US in the Middle East.

The impact of losing the Vietnam War and the consequences of the Watergate scandal made the US less willing to intervene in other Third World struggles in Africa and allowed the USSR to strengthen its influence in Angola and Ethiopia. In both states, the USSR was able to marginalize US and PRC influence. With Cuban assistance it, helped the MPLA take control of Angola by 1976 and supported Mengistu in Ethiopia in a war in Ogaden. While the operations were a success for the Soviets, these were secured at the cost of further *détente* in Europe.

✅ Examination advice

How to answer 'why' questions

Questions that ask 'why' are prompting you to consider a variety of explanations. Each of these will need to be explained in full. It is also possible to question the question. This means that you can disagree with the basic premise of the question. In this case, you must present full counter-arguments and be prepared to expound on these.

Example

> **Why did the Soviet Union and the People's Republic of China develop mutual mistrust by mid-1969?**

1. In the case of this specific question, you should be prepared to write about several reasons that mistrust occurred between the Soviet Union and the People's Republic of China (PRC). While there may be obvious difficulties during a specific period of time, you may wish to consider long-term issues as well. It is important to provide supportive evidence and to understand that the question requires you to address the development of mistrust of both countries, not just the actions of one. An alternative approach to answering the question would be to challenge the question. You could take the point of view that there was no development of mistrust but that it always existed or perhaps that no mistrust existed between the two states. If you decide to challenge the question, provide detailed supporting evidence, perhaps referencing your answer to the views of specific historians that you may also wish to quote or paraphrase.

2. Take at least five minutes to write a short outline. Make a list of the main difficulties that caused these two states to develop mutual distrust. Choose the most critical events, making sure that your essay clearly explains why these were the most important. You may wish to develop your essay along thematic lines such as territorial disputes, the nature of their communist regimes and issues regarding the Third World. An example of an outline for this question might be:

Differing communist models
- *USSR: revolution by proletariat*
- *PRC: revolution by masses/peasants*
  - *Cultural Revolution versus dictatorship of proletariat*
- *Competition within Third World*
  - *Diplomacy and spread of particular model*

Imperialism
- *PRC views USSR as imperialist state/Russia*
  - *Border issues*
  - *USSR advises on economy/foreign policy*
    - *Great Leap Forward*
    - *Quemoy*
    - *Advisors ejected by PRC*
- *USSR views PRC as imperialistic*
  - *Tibet*
  - *India*

Weakening communism
- *USSR accused of capitalism and compromise by PRC*
- *PRC accused of provoking crises*
  - *Great Leap Forward*
  - *Border conflicts*
- *PRC accused of weakening Soviet military*
  - *Submarine radio antenna controversy*
- *USSR withdraws technological assistance*

3. In your introduction you should indicate how you will address the question. This will consist of stating that there was mutual distrust between the two states, if you are going to argue this, and then summarize the main points of your essay. You may wish to indicate which points are the most important.

There was mutual distrust between the Soviet Union and the People's Republic of China (PRC) that developed after 1949 and continued until 1969 when open conflict between the states occurred. In some ways, this distrust was unavoidable as each state followed its own form of communism although each claimed to represent what Marx and Lenin, two leading communists, intended. In addition to following, and advocating, different forms of communism, the PRC suspected the Soviet Union of continuing imperialism, something practised by Russia upon China, the two nations which the USSR and PRC developed from. The PRC remained suspicious of the USSR's intentions throughout the period, but specific actions on the part of both the USSR and the PRC increased with the PRC's conflicts with Taiwan, Tibet and India and the USSR's withdrawal of technical advisors and criticisms of China's leadership and their economic plans. There were several important reasons for mutual distrust to develop between the USSR and PRC.

4. Your essay will now explore the various issues that led to increased mistrust throughout the period. The outline above has been constructed thematically and the strongest argument is presented first: mistrust ultimately hinged on the differing forms of communism; you will need to start your essay with this issue.

5. Your conclusion will bring together your various arguments, restating your argument that there was, or was not, mutual distrust and the reasons for this mistrust. An example of a good conclusion is presented here:

> Mistrust certainly existed between the Soviet Union and the PRC after the PRC's creation in 1949. This mistrust, however, was based on each state's communist model as well as history. While the Soviet Union believed that the state should be managed by a dictatorship that would support, promote and build a proletarian state based on its industrial workers, the PRC believed that a communist society could only be formed through mass movements, such as the Great Leap Forward and the Cultural Revolution which necessarily meant that the PRC's model had to be based on peasants since they formed the vast majority of the population. The Soviet Union formed out of the Russian Empire which had taken control of some of China's territory in the nineteenth and early twentieth centuries, causing many in China to distrust Soviet motives and involvement in their state, the PRC, after 1949. While the PRC accused the Soviets of imperialism, they attacked neighbouring states or conquered areas that had formerly been part of China, such as Tibet, which the USSR criticized as imperialism, provoking unnecessary diplomatic crises. The continued breakdown of diplomacy and increased tensions eventually led to a short war between the two states in 1969, terminating practically all relations for the next twenty years.

6. Now try writing a complete answer to the question following the advice above.

Examination practice

Below are three exam-style questions for you to practise on this topic.

1. Analyse the importance of The Congo in the Cold War.
   (For guidance on how to answer 'analyse' questions, see page 38.)

2. To what extent were Soviet objectives obtained by the end of the Cuban Missile Crisis?
   (For guidance on how to answer 'to what extent' questions, see page 172.)

3. Explain the significance of the Vietnam War for both the United States and Vietnam by 1975.
   (For guidance on how to answer 'explain' questions, see page 134.)

 # Activities

1. Students should create six questions, each representing one of the formats presented in the examination practice at the end of the chapters in this book, using information from this chapter. Students should exchange questions and practise writing outlines and introductory paragraphs in timed exercises.

2. Choose one of the questions in Activity 1 and write a complete essay for homework. Students in class should mark the essay using the mark bands used to mark the official examination papers. Indicate where evidence is missing or incorrectly used, providing helpful comments on what information may have been more supportive. Give an overall mark. The teacher may wish to evaluate the student who did the marking instead of the student who wrote the essay in order to provide an incentive for accurate marking, or to evaluate both the writer and examiner.

3. Conduct independent research to determine the extent to which communism in the People's Republic of China differed from that of the Soviet Union. You may wish to review some of the works of Mao, Lenin, Marx, Stalin or various historians. This information may be compiled in the form of a chart or essay, perhaps tackling issues thematically in categories such as: agriculture and peasantry, industry and workers, role of women, role of army, nationalism, religion, and so forth.

CHAPTER 7

The politics of détente, 1963–79

This chapter investigates the period of *détente* and co-existence between NATO and the Warsaw Pact from the end of the Cuban Missile Crisis to the SALT II Agreement in 1979. Progress was made by the two superpowers towards controlling the proliferation of nuclear weapons. In Europe, through the development of FRG Chancellor Willy Brandt's *Ostpolitik*, the FRG recognized the GDR and effectively accepted territorial changes made in Poland and Czechoslovakia at Germany's cost in 1945. The Helsinki Accords of 1973 seemed to open a new era of peaceful co-existence between the US and its NATO allies and the USSR and the Warsaw Pact, although conflicts in Africa and the invasion of Afghanistan by the USSR (see chapter 8) demonstrated that *détente* was limited to Europe. The deterioration in Sino-Soviet relations led to a *rapprochement* between the US and PRC in 1972, which in turn encouraged the USSR to improve relations with the US. You need to consider the following questions throughout this chapter:

✪ To what extent did US–Soviet relations improve, 1963–72?

✪ How successful were NATO and the Warsaw Pact in achieving *détente* and co-existence in Europe from 1963 to 1969?

✪ How did the *Ostpolitik* contribute towards *détente* in Europe?

✪ To what extent could the Helsinki Accords be regarded as the final peace settlement of the Second World War in Europe?

 # US–Soviet relations, 1963–72

> ▶ *Key question: To what extent did US–Soviet relations improve, 1963–72?*

After the Cuban Missile Crisis, both the US and the USSR were ready to consider negotiations on arms control and to co-operate more closely to prevent a conflict between them and their allies in Europe. Progress towards this was hampered by the Vietnam War and the Soviet invasion of Czechoslovakia, but in late 1969 efforts resumed. In 1972, the leaders of both the US and USSR, Nixon and Brezhnev, signed the first Strategic Arms Limitation Treaty (SALT I) at a Moscow Summit.

Why did US–USSR relations improve in 1963?

Kennedy and Khrushchev, 1963

After the Cuban Missile Crisis which threatened to escalate into nuclear war between the US and USSR in 1962, Khrushchev indicated that he was willing to seek a broad understanding with the US for peaceful co-existence. Kennedy was receptive and responded with his 'Peace speech' (see Source A).

SOURCE A

Excerpt from US President Kennedy's speech at American University in Washington, D.C., USA on 10 June 1963 found at www.jfklibrary.org/ Research/Ready-Reference/JFK-Speeches/Commencement-Address-at-American-University-June-10-1963.aspx

In short, both the United States and its allies, and the Soviet Union and its allies, have a mutually deep interest in a just and genuine peace and in halting the arms race. Agreements to this end are in the interests of the Soviet Union as well as ours – and even the most hostile nations can be relied upon to accept and keep those treaty obligations, and only those treaty obligations, which are in their own interests … So let us not be blind to our differences – but let us also direct attention to our common interests, and the means by which those differences can be resolved. And if we cannot end now our differences, at least we can help make the world safe for diversity. For in the final analysis, our most basic common link is that we all inhabit this small planet. We'll breathe the same air. We all cherish our children's future. And we are all mortal …

According to Source A, why did Kennedy support *détente* with the USSR?

Khrushchev reacted favourably to this speech, calling it the best statement by any US President since Roosevelt, who was US President from 1933 to 1945. On 20 June 1963, the US and USSR agreed to install a direct communications link between the leaders of both the US and USSR. This would allow direct communication in times of crisis, instead of relying on intermediaries (see page 192).

(see page 192).

Nuclear Test Ban Treaty, 5 August 1963

Although Kennedy made a belligerent speech against communism at the Berlin Wall to a massive crowd of West Berliners, the US signed the Partial Nuclear Test Ban Treaty on 5 August, along with the USSR and Britain. This treaty banned nuclear tests in the atmosphere, under water and in outer space, but allowed nuclear explosions to continue underground. The treaty was not signed by France or the People's Republic of China (PRC); they were determined to develop their own independent nuclear weapons.

KEY TERM

Brezhnev, Leonid General Secretary of the Central Committee of the Communist Party of the Soviet Union, 1964–82.

Kosygin, Alexei Premier of the USSR, 1964–80.

Podgorny, Nikolai Chairman of the presidium of the Supreme Soviet, 1965–77.

Johnson and Brezhnev: *détente* stalls, 1964–69

Why was little progress made on arms reductions between 1964 and 1969?

With the assassination of Kennedy in November 1963 and Khrushchev's overthrow in October 1964, *détente* stalled. The new Soviet leadership, primarily **Brezhnev**, **Kosygin** and **Podgorny**, was initially paralysed by disagreements over defence and the economy. The escalating Vietnam War also made *détente* a more difficult policy for the USSR to pursue as this made its leaders vulnerable to accusations from the PRC that it was not fully supporting communists in Vietnam.

According to Source B, what is the impact of the Vietnam War on US–USSR détente?

TOK

Summits were held periodically during the Cold War. Why do we believe there is value in meeting people in person instead of communicating in others ways? (Human Sciences, Emotion, Sense perception, Language)

What information does Source C convey about the progress being made towards a US–Soviet détente?

SOURCE B

Excerpt from a Soviet Foreign Ministry memorandum to the Politburo on 13 January 1967, quoted in *In Confidence* by A. Dobrynin, Random House, New York, USA, 1995, p. 157.

As regards American aggression against Vietnam and its effect on bilateral relations, we should go on rendering comprehensive assistance to the DRV [Democratic Republic of North Vietnam] in consolidating its defense capacity to repulse aggression without getting directly involved in the war. We must give the Americans to understand that further escalation in the military actions against the DRV will compel the Soviet Union to render its assistance to this country on an ever growing scale … Nevertheless putting an end to the Vietnam conflict would undoubtedly have a positive effect on Soviet–American relations and open up new possibilities for solving certain international problems.

The Glassboro Summit, June 1967

In June 1967, in the immediate aftermath of the Six Day War, Kosygin attended the UN General Assembly's discussions on the Middle East. US President Johnson met him for talks at Glassboro, New Jersey, to discuss not only the Middle East and Vietnam but also the whole question of nuclear arms control. The discussions were frank and amiable, but inconclusive.

SOURCE C

Excerpt from the record of the conversation between US President Johnson and Soviet Premier Alexei Kosygin at Glassboro, 23 June 1967, from *Foreign Relations of the US, 1964-1968, Vol. XIV, Soviet Union, Document 229*, Washington, D.C., USA, 2001, p. 515.

Chairman Kosygin said that whenever we discussed any problem on a global scale, it seemed to him that there was complete agreement between the President's view and his own. We have the same goals, neither country wanted war and everything else the President had said he could endorse. However, it seemed to him that when we began to discuss specific problems and practical steps for their solution, then a great many difficulties and differences arose.

The Nuclear Non-Proliferation Treaty, July 1968

The way to further progress on nuclear arms control was opened by Johnson's decision in March 1968 to suspend bombing over most of North Vietnam and to begin peace talks in Paris in May (see page 204). In July, the Nuclear Non-Proliferation Treaty was signed by Britain, the US and USSR. They agreed not to transfer nuclear weapons to other countries or to assist other states to manufacture them. In November 1969, they were joined by West Germany. Both France and the PRC signed only in 1993.

The Soviet invasion of Czechoslovakia

The Soviet invasion of Czechoslovakia in August 1968 (see page 246) briefly interrupted the progress towards a Soviet–US détente. Johnson, who had been invited to Moscow in early October, cancelled the visit and warned the USSR against intervention in Romania and Yugoslavia. However, secretly both sides assured each other that the Czechoslovakian crisis represented only a temporary delay in *détente* negotiations. In November, talks on Strategic Arms Limitation (SALT I) began in Vienna, Austria and Helsinki, Finland.

Nixon and *détente*

When Richard Nixon became US President in January 1969, his stated main objective was to withdraw US forces from Vietnam. He hoped to make progress in the SALT talks, dependent on Soviet willingness to put pressure on North Vietnam to end the war, but the USSR dismissed any linkage between the two. The Soviets were not ready to put pressure on a friendly country to achieve an arms agreement. It was only when the second round of negotiations began in Vienna on 16 April 1970 that a comprehensive formula for arms limitation was agreed.

The ABM challenge

The US had been alarmed by both the Soviet deployment of **anti-ballistic missiles** (ABM) around Moscow from 1963 onwards and the increase of anti-aircraft defences. President Johnson feared that the effective development of the ABM system by the USSR would upset the nuclear balance of power between the US and USSR afforded by the doctrine of Mutual Assured Destruction (see page 192). This might tempt the USSR to risk a surprise attack on the US if it was convinced that its own defences were effective.

The US countered this by developing **multiple independently targeted re-entry vehicles** (MIRVS). These were missiles that carried up to twelve nuclear warheads, each being released in the upper atmosphere to attack a different target, making Soviet defences less likely to succeed since they would have twelve targets instead of just a single missile with a single warhead. Johnson hoped that this threat would cause the Soviets to agree to ban ABMs. At Glassboro, Kosygin initially rejected such a ban on the grounds that the ABMs were defensive weapons and therefore could hardly trigger the outbreak of war. However, by the time the SALT talks began in November 1969, Soviet leaders agreed that the question of ABM limitation should be included in the SALT talks, fearing that the US might develop a more effective ABM system to counter Soviet nuclear missiles.

The SALT negotiations, April 1970–May 1972

The crucial issue during these talks was the Soviet demand that the term 'strategic arms' should cover all systems capable of launching any type of attacks on the USSR, both nuclear and conventional warheads. This would include all US missile launching systems in Europe and at sea. In the end, compromise was reached when the US made an agreement on limiting ABMs conditional on the USSR freezing the number of ICBMs at their

How successful was the US in restricting ABM (anti-ballistic missile) development?

KEY TERM

Anti-ballistic missiles Missiles designed to destroy enemy missiles.

Multiple independently targeted re-entry vehicles Missiles capable of carrying multiple nuclear warheads, each destined for a different target.

existing level, which would still favour the US. President Nixon was determined that if the US made concessions on its ABM defensive system, then the USSR should decrease it offensive capacities. On 26 May, Nixon and Brezhnev signed both the ABM and SALT I Treaties.

Treaty on the Limitation of Anti-ballistic Missile Systems, 26 May 1972

This treaty allowed both countries to deploy two fixed, ground-based defence sites of 100 missile interceptors each. One site was permitted to protect each national capital, while the second site could be deployed to protect an intercontinental ballistic missile (ICBM) field base.

Strategic Arms Limitation Treaty (SALT I), 26 May 1972

The SALT I Treaty included:

- a five-year freeze on the construction of missile launchers
- a freeze on construction of intercontinental and submarine-launched ballistic missiles.

New submarine-launched ballistic missile (SLBM) launchers and modern ballistic submarines could only be constructed after the same number of older launchers had been dismantled.

SOURCE D

? What information does Source D convey about the US–USSR arms race?

Numbers of US and Soviet nuclear launchers and warheads, 1962–80, from *The Cold War* by M. Walker, Vintage, London, 1993, p. 214.

Year	US		USSR	
	Launchers	Warheads	Launchers	Warheads
1962	1653	3267	235	481
1964	2021	4180	425	771
1966	2139	4607	570	954
1968	2191	4839	1206	1605
1970	2100	4960	1835	2216
1972	2167	7601	2207	2573
1974	2106	9324	2423	2795
1976	2092	10436	2545	3477
1978	2086	10832	2557	5516
1980	2022	10608	2545	7480

What impact did the **PRC-US** *rapprochement* have on USSR–US relations?

PRC–US *rapprochement*, 1972

Détente in Europe took place against the background of tensions between the USSR and the PRC while the US and the PRC had developed a *rapprochement*. By 1968, the Sino-Soviet alliance was in ruins. This weakened the global position of the Soviet Union and encouraged the Soviets to be more active in seeking *détente* with NATO and the US. If war with the US were to break out, the USSR could now no longer rely on the support of the PRC. At the same time, Sino-Soviet hostility strengthened the US just when it was facing defeat in Vietnam, as its two great communist enemies were now divided by mutual hostility.

Throughout the summer of 1969, relations between the USSR and PRC continued to deteriorate. On 13 August, in a major clash in Xinjiang Province, a PRC brigade of over a thousand men was annihilated by Soviet troops. The PRC retaliated by declaring a general mobilization along the border with the USSR and Mongolia. A few days later, a diplomat at the Soviet Embassy in the US, almost certainly with the knowledge of Brezhnev, startled the US government when he asked a US official what the US response would be if the USSR made a pre-emptive strike against the PRC's nuclear installations. US President Nixon made it clear to his cabinet that the US would not allow the PRC to be 'smashed' in a war between the PRC and the Soviet Union.

Tensions eased in early September after talks between Kosygin and Zhou Enlai in Beijing where it was agreed that a PRC–Soviet conflict would only benefit the US (see page 179). However, in late 1969 and early 1970, friendly diplomatic contacts between the PRC and the US began for the first time. In May 1971, the US Secretary of State Henry Kissinger flew to the PRC in secrecy to make arrangements for a visit by Nixon to China. This took place in February 1972, with the US and PRC governments declaring that:

- neither the PRC nor the US would 'seek hegemony in the Asia–Pacific region and each is opposed to efforts by any other country [i.e. the USSR] to establish such hegemony'
- the future of Taiwan should be settled peacefully. The US would end the patrols of its navy through the Taiwan straits (see page 178) on the understanding that the PRC would not invade the island.

This declaration was a major blow for the USSR. Nevertheless, the Soviets hoped to prevent an alliance between the US and the PRC by improving relations with the US.

The Moscow Summit, May 1972

In the summer of 1971, the USSR rejected the US proposal for a summit in the autumn and, instead, delayed until May 1972 in the hope of extracting further concessions from the US in the peace talks with North Vietnam and the SALT negotiations. This enabled Nixon's successful visit to the PRC to come first and so strengthen the US negotiating position in Moscow. In March, the Moscow Summit was nearly cancelled by the USSR to protest against the US bombing of North Vietnam (see page 205). In the end, the Soviet Politburo decided to hold the summit after all, as the advantages of *détente* with the US would go some way to balance the US–PRC *rapprochement*.

<aside>What was achieved at the Moscow Summit?</aside>

Results of the Summit

The May 1972 meeting was a success for both participants:

- The ABM and Arms Limitation Treaties were signed (see above).
- Brezhnev agreed to discuss with the North Vietnamese government the latest US proposals for peace in Vietnam.
- The US agreed to allow the USSR to purchase grain and to expand bilateral trade, resulting in the Soviet–US Trade Agreement of October 1972.
- Both agreed to hold a conference on European security, which the USSR had long wanted.

The summit concluded with the 'Basic Principle of Relations' which historian Raymond Gartoff calls 'a charter for *détente*':

SOURCE E

? What information does Source E convey about the US–Soviet *détente*?

Excerpt from *Basic Principles of Relations between the United States and the Soviet Union*, Moscow, 29 May 1972, from www.ioc.u-tokyo.ac. jp/~worldjpn/documents/texts/docs/19720529.O1E.html.

The United States of America and the Union of Soviet Socialist Republics … have agreed as follows:

First … differences in ideology and in the social systems of the USA and the USSR are not obstacles to the bilateral principles of sovereignty, equality, non-interference in internal affairs and mutual advantage.

Second. The USA and the USSR attach major importance to preventing the development of situations capable of causing a dangerous exacerbation of their relations. Therefore, they will do their utmost to avoid military confrontations and to prevent the outbreak of nuclear war. They will always exercise restraint in their mutual relations, and will be prepared to negotiate and settle differences by peaceful means. Discussions and negotiations on outstanding issues will be conducted in a spirit of reciprocity, mutual accommodation and mutual benefit …

Fifth. The USA and the USSR reaffirm their readiness to continue the practice of exchanging views on problems of mutual interest …

Sixth. The Parties will continue their efforts to limit armaments on a bilateral as well as on a multilateral basis …

The USA and the USSR regard as the ultimate objective of their efforts the achievement of general and complete disarmament and the establishment of an effective system of international security in accordance with the purposes and principles of the United Nations.

Seventh. The USA and the USSR regard commercial and economic ties as an important and necessary element in the strengthening of their bilateral relations …

Eighth. The two sides consider it timely and useful to develop mutual contacts and cooperation in the fields of science and technology …

Conflicting interpretations of *détente*

← **How different were the US and Soviet interpretations of *détente*?**

The US and USSR hoped to achieve different results from the Moscow Summit. They both supported *détente* in the belief that it would be in their own interests. The USSR hoped to:

- stabilize the arms race once it had achieved approximate parity in nuclear weapons with the US; the Soviets wanted to reduce expenditure on nuclear weapons and found it increasingly difficult to keep up with the US technologically
- strengthen *détente* and **Ostpolitik** (see below) in Europe with the aim of gaining legal recognition from the US and NATO of the GDR and of Poland's and Czechoslovakia's post-1945 frontiers
- encourage East–West trade, which would give Soviet and eastern European economies access to Western technology and finance
- neutralize the threat of a US–PRC alliance by giving the US and NATO states reasons to maintain good relations with the USSR.

> **KEY TERM**
>
> **Ostpolitik** West Germany's policy towards eastern Europe, which involved recognition of the GDR and the post-war boundaries of eastern Europe.

The US in its turn hoped that *détente* with the USSR would:

- strengthen its relations with its NATO allies, especially the FRG, which were actively seeking *détente* in the form of the new *Ostpolitik* with the USSR and its Warsaw Pact Allies (see page 247)
- facilitate a settlement in Vietnam which would allow a withdrawal without major embarrassment
- halt the escalating arms race
- create a new international order which, through *détente*, arms control and trade, would discourage the USSR from undermining NATO and the US.

Conclusion

Détente between the US and USSR did not end the Cold War. While it created a new framework for US–USSR relations, both sides believed that it could be exploited to the disadvantage of the other.

SOURCE F

Excerpt from US Secretary of State Kissinger's briefing to US President Nixon before the Moscow Summit as quoted in J.P.D. Dunabin, *The Cold War*, Pearson/Longman, 2008, p. 372.

(Nixon's underlinings are shown.)

[Brezhnev] sees the US at once as a rival, mortal threat, model, source of assistance and partner in physical survival ... he no doubt wants to go down in history as the leader who brought peace and a better life to Russia [sic]. This requires conciliatory and cooperative policies towards us. Yet he remains a convinced Communist who sees politics as a struggle with an ultimate winner; he intends the Soviet Union to be that winner ...

> According to Source F, what was the US government's goal with *détente*? ?

Almost certainly Brezhnev continues to defend his détente policies in Politburo debates in terms of a historic conflict with us as the main capitalist country and of the ultimate advantages that will accrue to the USSR in this conflict. Brezhnev's gamble is that as these policies gather momentum, their effects will not undermine the very system from which Brezhnev draws his power and legitimacy. Our goal on the other hand is to achieve precisely such effects over the long run …

Kennedy and Khruschev, 1963
• Hotline
• Nuclear Test Ban Treaty
Johnson and Brezhnev, 1964–69
• *Détente* stalled because of Vietnam conflict, 1964–67
• Glassboro summit, 1967
• Nuclear Non-proliferation Treaty, 1968
• Talks on SALT began, November 1968
Nixon and Brezhnev
• Treaty on Limitation of Anti-ballistic Missile Systems, May 1972
• SALT I, May 1972
• Moscow Summit, May 1972: 'the charter for *détente*'

SUMMARY DIAGRAM

US–Soviet relations, 1963–72

2 *Détente* in Europe, 1963–69

> ▶ *Key question*: How successful were NATO and the Warsaw Pact in achieving détente *and co-existence in Europe over the period 1963–69?*

The peaceful resolution of the Cuban Missile Crisis in 1962 and the stabilizing effect of the Berlin Wall on the GDR laid the foundations for a new period of stability in both eastern and western Europe. Instead of confrontation, both blocs moved slowly towards accommodation with each other.

Détente and western Europe, 1963–68

How did western European states attempt to pursue a policy of *détente* with the USSR, 1963–68?

In western Europe, a number of factors combined to loosen the close links between the US and the leading NATO states forged in the early days of the Cold War:

- The economies of France, the FRG and Italy were doing well and no longer needed US economic assistance.
- The Test Ban Treaty of 1963 and the Nuclear Non-proliferation Treaty in 1968 were welcomed in western Europe, but essentially they assumed a world divided into two blocs led by their respective superpower. There were growing doubts, especially in France and to a lesser extent in the

FRG, whether the US would risk a nuclear war to defend western Europe from a Soviet attack.

- The US involvement in Vietnam was also criticized by the western European states who rejected US President Johnson's argument that the war was vital to confront communism and prevent its adoption by other states. Despite the fact that the US had committed some 300,000 troops to protect western Europe since 1947, no western European state sent troops to Vietnam.
- By 1968, the Vietnam War was causing growing hostility to the US as a result of what appeared to be its ineffective but often ruthless military tactics, losing its position as the moral leader of the West.
- A wave of student protests swept through western European universities aimed principally at US involvement in Vietnam.

France, 1963–69

French President de Gaulle took the lead in the attack on US influence in western Europe. After the Cuban Missile Crisis in 1962, he believed that the threat from the USSR in Europe was receding. He now saw French participation in a US-dominated NATO as the main threat to French national independence. In January 1963, the US refused to share its nuclear technology with France, but by the Nassau Agreement of December 1962 agreed to supply Polaris missiles to the UK. In protest, de Gaulle vetoed Britain's application to join the EEC (see page 162) on the grounds that Britain was still too dependent on the US. De Gaulle also denounced the 1963 Test Ban Treaty with the argument that France must be able to defend itself. Three years later, he both withdrew French forces from NATO and removed its headquarters from Paris, although he declared that France would still come to the help of any NATO member subject to unprovoked aggression.

De Gaulle also resented the power in Europe of big US multinational corporations, fearing their economic take-over of western European industries. He therefore worked to weaken the US dollar at a time when the US was starting to feel the financial pressure of the costs of the Vietnam War. Between 1965 and 1968, France converted large number of paper dollars, held in the French banks at the internationally agreed rate of $3.5 per ounce, into gold. By doing this, he diminished US gold reserves.

De Gaulle's concept of détente

De Gaulle aimed to achieve *détente* with the Warsaw Pact by following two separate policies:

- Improving relations with the USSR.
- Establishing relations with the individual members of the Warsaw Pact and encouraging them to imitate French national assertion by making themselves more independent of the USSR.

Despite his aim of undermining the unity of the Warsaw Pact, the USSR appreciated the disruption he caused in NATO and his hostility towards the

US. He was invited to visit the USSR in 1966, where, after a tour, he signed a joint declaration which provided for a permanent communications link between the French and Soviet governments and for a Franco-Soviet Commission to expand Franco-Soviet contacts. In December, Kosygin visited France and, together with de Gaulle, called for a European conference to examine the problems of security and the possibilities of European co-operation. Ultimately, this prepared the way for the Conference on Security and Co-operation in Europe in 1973 (see page 251).

In 1967–68, de Gaulle visited Poland and Romania. In both countries he announced that European states should liberate themselves from the 'bloc mentality' of the Cold War. He also praised President Ceaușescu of Romania for asserting his independence from the USSR (see page 245), which he compared to the way France had distanced itself from the US.

FRG: The beginnings of *Ostpolitik*

De Gaulle's determination to follow an independent policy towards the USSR and Warsaw bloc countries, as well as the development of *détente* between the US and USSR, created a new situation for the FRG. During the 1950s, Chancellor Adenauer followed a rigid policy of refusing to recognize the GDR. In 1955, in what became known as the Hallstein Doctrine (see page 147), the FRG undertook to sever diplomatic relations with any country that recognized the GDR. Increasingly this policy was becoming counter-productive. In 1965, for example, a visit to the Middle East by Ulbricht, the GDR leader, led to ten states recognizing the GDR and ending diplomatic relations with the FRG.

Gradually during the 1960s, the FRG began to abandon the Hallstein Doctrine and reconsider its policy towards the GDR and the Soviet bloc. A key figure in developing what became known as *Ostpolitik* was Willy Brandt, the Social Democratic (SPD) Mayor of West Berlin. As early as December 1963, he negotiated directly with East Berlin, and by agreeing to refer to it as the 'GDR capital', he secured for eighteen days the right of West Berliners to visit their relatives in East Berlin.

Ostpolitik began to take a more definite shape when the **Grand Coalition** under Kurt Kiesinger was formed in December 1966 with Willy Brandt as Foreign Secretary. The Coalition established **trade missions** in Yugoslavia and Romania and made an agreement with Czechoslovakia whereby both countries could open consulates in each other's territory. In April 1967, Kiesinger presented the GDR with several practical proposals for improving inter-German trade, communications and contacts between relatives separated by the division of Germany. This was supplemented by an invitation from the SPD to the SED (see page 50) for talks between the two parties.

At first, these initiatives were ignored by the SED. The GDR's leader, Walther Ulbricht, went out of his way to dismiss compromise and to argue that unity was only possible between two socialist Germanys. The USSR also initially took a sceptical view of *Ostpolitik* as it feared that the FRG sought to undermine the Warsaw Pact.

NATO and *détente*

← How did **NATO** adapt to *détente*?

France's departure from NATO's military organization and growing divisions between the US and western Europe threatened the unity of NATO. If it were to survive in an age of *détente*, it would have to adapt.

The US and NATO, 1963–69

Given the economic prosperity of the western European states, their refusal to assist the US in Vietnam, and the hostility of de Gaulle, there were increasing demands in the US that NATO states should be prepared to assume a greater role in the defence of western Europe. Indeed, in 1967 US Senator Michael Mansfield suggested in the US Senate that there should be drastic cuts in US defence spending in western Europe which would have led to the withdrawal of 50 per cent of US troops. This attracted the support of nearly half the Senate. Although President Johnson did cut troop numbers in Europe from 392,000 to 285,000 between 1965 and 1970, he managed to keep the NATO alliance intact despite France's withdrawal.

The US was waging a major war in Vietnam, yet in Europe it supported *détente,* and in 1968 started arms control negotiations with the USSR (see page 234). To Johnson, these two apparently contradictory positions could be reconciled with each other. In Vietnam, he argued that the US was fighting to show that aggression should not succeed, while in Europe it was seeking to create a climate of co-operation and *détente*, which would eliminate the threat of nuclear war.

The Harmel Report and NATO

France's withdrawal from NATO's military organization threw it into turmoil. NATO'S headquarters was moved to Brussels and all NATO troops had to leave France. The danger for the alliance was that other countries, particularly the FRG, might follow France's lead, build their own nuclear deterrent and withdraw from NATO. Already in 1963–64 the FRG had demanded a greater say in NATO's nuclear strategy. The US attempted to satisfy it by proposing an allied nuclear force – the Multilateral Force (MLF) – which would consist of nuclear armed submarines with multinational crews. This was dropped when neither France nor Britain were willing to participate as they preferred to develop their own nuclear weapons.

After the lack of agreement on the MLF, France's withdrawal from NATO and growing differences between the US and the western European states, there were fears that unless NATO adjusted its aims and organization to take account of the new mood of *détente*, it might break up in 1969 when the original treaty of 1949 came up for renewal. In December 1966, Belgium's

Foreign Minister Pierre Harmel proposed that NATO should reconsider both its military and political role in Europe.

In December 1967, Harmel and NATO officials produced a report that stated NATO's role was not only to defend western Europe, but also to reach a *détente* with Warsaw Pact states. The Harmel Report redefined NATO's role in the age of *détente* and prevented the political tensions resulting from the Vietnam War from destroying the NATO alliance.

? What information does Source G convey about the role of NATO in the period of *détente* in Europe?

SOURCE G

Excerpt from 'The Report of the North Atlantic Council: The Future Tasks of the Alliance (Harmel Report)', 13 December 1967, from www.nato.int/cps/en/natolive/topics_67927.htm

Since the North Atlantic treaty was signed in 1949, the international situation has changed significantly and the political tasks of the Alliance have assumed a new dimension. Amongst other developments, the Alliance has played a major part in stopping Communist expansion in Europe; the USSR has become one of the two world super powers but the Communist world is no longer monolithic; the Soviet doctrine of 'peaceful co-existence' has changed the nature of the confrontation with the west but not the basic problem …

The Atlantic Alliance has two main functions. Its first main function is to maintain adequate military strength and political solidarity to defend the territory of member states …

… the second function of the Alliance … [is] to pursue the search for progress towards a more stable relationship in which the underlying political issues can be solved. Military security and a policy of détente are not contradictory but complementary. Collective defence is a stabilising factor in world politics. It is the necessary condition for effective policies directed towards a greater relaxation of tensions. The way to peace and stability in Europe rests in particular on the use of the Alliance constructively in the interests of détente. The participation of the USSR and USA will be necessary to achieve a settlement of the political problems in Europe.

Divisions within the Warsaw Pact

To what extent was the Warsaw Pact divided during the period 1963 to 1969?

The growing atmosphere of *détente* and the Sino-Soviet split all combined to weaken Soviet control over eastern Europe and provide some opportunities for these states to pursue independent policies.

Albania

Albania's leader Enver Hoxha drew closer to the PRC for a number of reasons. He:

- rejected COMECON plans for the integration of the Albanian economy into the Soviet bloc
- opposed the improvement in relations between Yugoslavia and the USSR
- was hostile to the USSR's policy of *détente* with the US

- increasingly saw Maoism as the model for Albania and launched his own Cultural Revolution in February 1967
- withdrew Albania from the Warsaw Pact after the invasion of Czechoslovakia (see below).

By successfully disobeying the USSR and effectively freeing itself from the Soviet bloc, Albania created a precedent for the other states to follow.

Romania

Romania's Nicolae Ceauşescu also used the Sino-Soviet split to strengthen Romania's own version of communism. It was generally in the Soviet model, but also nationalist, and asserted Romania's economic, political and cultural independence from the USSR. With some support from Poland and Bulgaria, it forced the USSR to abandon plans for economic integration in the Eastern bloc. Although it did not leave the Warsaw Pact, in 1964 it did not allow the Pact to hold manoeuvres in Romania and in 1968 did not participate in the invasion of Czechoslovakia.

Bulgaria

Todor Zhivkov, Bulgaria's communist leader, remained a close ally of the USSR. He survived the fall of Khrushchev and strengthened his position at home by purging his opponents. He supported Brezhnev's policy of *détente* and frequently acted as a diplomatic channel for contacts between the USSR and NATO.

Poland

In October 1956, Gomułka saved Poland from Soviet intervention by assuring Khrushchev that he would take measures to protect Polish communism (see page 147). In effect, Gomułka had managed to achieve a special status for Poland. Its agriculture, in contrast to the rest of the Soviet bloc, was not collectivized; it received aid from the US for the purchase of grain and its volume of trade with the West was the highest in the Warsaw Pact. This was tolerated by the USSR as the price for maintaining communism in Poland.

Hungary

After the suppression of the revolt in Hungary in November 1956 (see page 154), the Hungarian government under János Kádár made no attempt to distance itself from the USSR. It followed Soviet directives on foreign policy and *détente* and was a loyal member of the Warsaw Pact. Kádár did, however, follow an independent economic policy in an attempt to win support for his regime by establishing the New Economic Mechanism in January 1968. This abandoned central planning and encouraged enterprises to make their own economic decisions.

Czechoslovakia: the Prague Spring

The Soviet government's efforts to consolidate its control over eastern Europe and to co-ordinate the foreign and military policies of the Warsaw Pact suffered a serious setback when, in January 1968, Alexander Dubček became the First Secretary of the Czech Communist Party. Like Nagy in Hungary in 1956 (see page 154), he attempted to create a socialist system that would be based on the consent of the people, rather than forced on them by the USSR as had been the case in eastern Europe since the late 1940s.

In April 1968, he unveiled his programme for democratic change and modernization of the economy which marked the start of what was called the **Prague Spring**. In April, the Czech Communist Party announced a programme for 'a new profoundly democratic model of Czechoslovak socialism conforming to Czechoslovak conditions'. Like Gorbachev later in the USSR (see page 270), Dubček wanted to preserve socialism, but increasingly public opinion began to press for the creation of a democracy based on the Western model. In June, he abolished censorship, leading to a flood of anti-Soviet propaganda being published.

Inevitably these developments worried Brezhnev and other Warsaw Pact leaders as they threatened to undermine communist governments throughout the region.

KEY TERM

Prague Spring A period of political and economic reforms initiated in Czechoslovakia in 1968 that included multi-party elections, freedom of speech and press, as well as reducing government control of the economy.

? According to Source H, how did leaders from other Warsaw Pact states react to Dubček's reforms in Czechoslovakia?

SOURCE H

Excerpt from minutes of the meeting in Warsaw of Communist Party leaders from Bulgaria, Poland, the GDR, Hungary and the USSR on 15 July 1968, from *The Czechoslovak Crisis, 1968*, edited by Rhodes James, Weidenfeld and Nicolson, London, UK, 1969, p. 168.

Dubcek [sic] was warned that:

We are deeply disturbed by the course of events in your country. The offensive reaction, backed by imperialism, against your party and the foundations of the Czechoslovakian Socialist Republic, threatens … to push your country from the road of Socialism, and thereby threatens the interest of the entire socialist system …

We cannot reconcile ourselves … with the fact of hostile forces pushing your country off the road of socialism and creating a threat of tearing away Czechoslovakia from the socialist community. This is NO longer only your concern. This is the common concern of all Communists and workers' parties and of states united by alliance co-operation and friendship …

Although Dubček reluctantly agreed to restore censorship, Brezhnev had no confidence that he would succeed and, during the night of 20–21 August, twenty divisions of Warsaw Pact troops invaded Czechoslovakia. The Soviets at first hoped to form a new pro-Soviet Czechoslovakian government but when this proved impossible because no politicians were ready to serve in it, they negotiated a compromise agreement with Dubček. He and his colleagues would remain in office, but would cancel all the reforms that had led to the 'Prague Spring'.

In April 1969, Dubček resigned and was replaced by Gustáv Husák. In November, Brezhnev defended the invasion by again stressing that any threat to socialism in a Warsaw Pact country was also a threat to its allies. To counter this, collective intervention, as happened in Czechoslovakia, would be justified, which became known as the Brezhnev Doctrine.

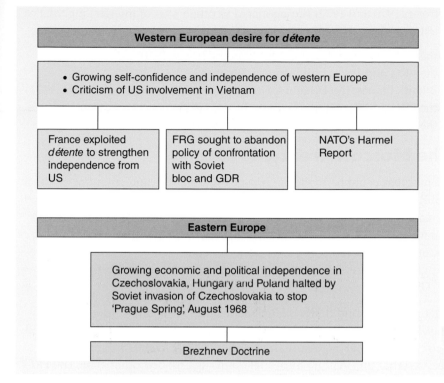

Détente in Europe, 1963–69

 # Ostpolitik

▶ **Key question:** *How did the* Ostpolitik *contribute towards* détente *in Europe?*

The invasion of Czechoslovakia was, as France's Prime Minister Michel Debré stated, 'a traffic accident on the road to *détente*'. It slowed down, but did not halt progress. The election of Richard Nixon to the US Presidency in November 1968 and of Willy Brandt to the West German Chancellorship in October 1969, with a mandate for his *Ostpolitik* policy, were soon to give it fresh impetus. By recognizing the GDR as a legal state and accepting the post-1945 Polish and Czechoslovakian frontiers, the FRG accepted political reality. At the same time, by improving relations between the two Germanys, Brandt hoped to begin a political process that would gradually end in the reunification of Germany. He reassured the US and his NATO allies that the FRG did not intend to withdraw from NATO or the **European Community**, thus gaining their support.

 **KEY TERM**

European Community
The European Economic Community (EEC) had changed its name to the European Community (EC).

Between 1970 and 1972, he negotiated a complex set of interlocking treaties marking a major turning point in the Cold War. These were between:

- the FRG and Soviet Union (the Moscow Treaty, 1970)
- the FRG and Poland (the Warsaw Treaty, 1970)
- Britain, France, the US and USSR (the Four-Power Treaty on Berlin, 1971)
- the FRG and the GDR (the Basic Treaty, 1972)
- the FRG and Czechoslovakia (the Prague Treaty, 1973).

Why can the Moscow Treaty be called 'the foundation stone of Ostpolitik'?

The Moscow Treaty, 1970

No progress could be made in *Ostpolitik* without the agreement of the USSR. The FRG's signature of the Nuclear Non-proliferation Treaty in 1969, its readiness to increase technological and economic links with the USSR and willingness to agree to a European security conference which the Soviets hoped would confirm its post-war control of eastern Europe, were all preliminary concessions that helped to pave the way for a treaty with the USSR.

After prolonged and difficult negotiations, the 'foundation stone of *Ostpolitik*', as the historian A.J. Nicholls calls the Moscow Treaty, was signed on 12 August 1970 by Brandt and Brezhnev. In this, the USSR and FRG declared that they had no territorial claims against any other state. The FRG recognized the 'non-violability' of both Poland's western frontier and the inner German frontier. In a second part of the treaty, the FRG committed itself to negotiating treaties with Poland, the GDR and Czechoslovakia. The FRG agreed to abandon the Hallstein Doctrine and accept that both Germanys would eventually become members of the United Nations.

The FRG also presented Brezhnev with a 'letter on German unity'. This stressed the FRG's right to work towards a state of peace in Europe in which 'the German people regains its unity in free self-determination'. Similarly, the term '**inviolable**' as applied to the Oder–Neisse line and the inner German frontier, rather than the preferred Soviet word '**immutable**', arguably kept the door open for a later peaceful revision of the frontier. Finally, the ratification of the treaty was made dependent on a Four-Power Agreement over Berlin.

The Warsaw and Prague Treaties

Negotiations with Poland ran parallel with the Moscow talks and were completed in December 1970. Both Poland and the FRG recognized that they had no territorial demands on each other and that the Oder–Neisse line was 'inviolable'. Trade and financial assistance from the FRG were to be increased, while the ethnic Germans still within Poland were to be allowed to leave for West Germany if they desired.

In June 1973, the Prague Treaty was initialled (agreed) with Czechoslovakia, but not finally ratified by the FRG's parliament until January 1974. It:

- revoked the Munich Treaty of 1938 which had awarded the Sudetenland to Germany (see page 15).

 KEY TERM

Inviolable Not to be attacked or violated.

Immutable Unchangeable.

- acknowledged the inviolability of the FRG-Czechoslovakian common borders and renounced all territorial claims.
- allowed the emigration of any Czechoslovaks to the FRG who had German citizenship, about 10,000 people.

SOURCE I

Picture of Willy Brandt kneeling in atonement on the site of the Warsaw Ghetto, 1970.

What message does Source I convey about Brandt's policy towards Poland?

Four-Power negotiations over Berlin

To what extent did the Four-Power Treaty on Berlin solve the Berlin problem?

In March 1970, Four Power discussions began on the difficult problem of access to West Berlin. The involvement of Britain, France and the US in these negotiations sent signals to both NATO and the Warsaw Pact that *Ostpolitik* would not lead to a weakening of the FRG's links with the West. The NATO allies wanted a settlement underwritten by the USSR that would finally confirm West Berlin's political links with the FRG and guarantee its freedom of access through the GDR to the FRG.

At first, the Soviets attempted to avoid making too many concessions, but both their desire for a general European security conference and their reluctance to challenge US President Nixon at a time when he was planning to improve relations with PRC made them more responsive to Western demands.

The Four-Power Treaty on Berlin, signed on 3 September 1971, was, to quote the historians L. Bark and D.R. Gress, a 'milestone in the history of divided Berlin and divided Germany'.

The Soviets conceded three vital principles:

- unimpeded traffic between West Berlin and the FRG
- recognition of West Berlin's ties with the FRG
- the right of West Berliners to visit East Berlin.

In return Britain, France and the US agreed that the Western sectors of Berlin were not legally part of the FRG, even if in practice they had been since West Berlin adopted the FRG's constitution in 1950.

To what extent was the Basic Treaty a victory for the GDR and USSR?

GDR–FRG negotiations

Once the Moscow Treaty and the agreement on Berlin had been signed, the way was open for direct negotiations between the GDR and FRG. For the GDR, an agreement with the FRG was not without risk. If successful, it would undoubtedly secure the state international recognition, but risked closer contact with the **magnetic social and economic forces of the West**. In July 1970, Brezhnev stressed to the somewhat sceptical Erich Honecker, who had just replaced Ulbricht as the GDR leader, the key advantages of the treaty for the GDR in that '[i]ts frontiers, its existence will be confirmed for all the world to see …' However, he also warned him that Brandt was aiming ultimately at the '**Social Democratization**' of the GDR; or in other words, gradually, through contacts and co-operation, turning the GDR into a Social Democratic country similar to the FRG. Brezhnev warned: 'It … must not come to a process of *rapprochement* between the FRG and the GDR … Concentrate everything on the all-sided strengthening of the GDR, as you call it.'

Initially, a series of technical agreements on **transit traffic**, the rights of West Berliners to visit East Berlin, and on postal communications were concluded.

The Basic Treaty

The two states then moved on to negotiate the more crucial Basic Treaty which was signed in December 1972. In it, the FRG recognized the GDR as an equal and sovereign state and also accepted that both states should be represented at the United Nations. The FRG did, however, stress that it still considered the people of the GDR to have a common German citizenship, and in a 'Letter Concerning German Unity' which it presented to East Berlin, it repeated its determination to work peacefully for German reunification.

The existence of the two Germanys now seemed to be a permanent fact confirmed by treaty. The two German states joined the United Nations in 1973. Nothing, however, had changed the essential vulnerability of the GDR. Economically it was still far behind the FRG. At most, the majority of its population tolerated the regime but if given a chance would most likely vote for a united Germany. As the events of 1989 were to demonstrate, its very existence in the last resort depended on Soviet support.

KEY TERM

Magnetic social and economic forces of the West Brandt believed that the economy and way of life in West Germany was so strong that ultimately it would excert a magnet-like attraction on the GDR and lead to unification.

Social Democratization Converting the communist SED into a more moderate Western-style Social Democratic Party like the SPD in the FRG.

Transit traffic Traffic crossing through another state.

Willy Brandt needed to secure approval from the USA, USSR and NATO
Moscow Treaty, August 1970: FRG committed itself to recognizing post-1945 frontiers
Berlin Treaty signed by the four occupying powers, September 1971: unimpeded transit rights to West Berlin recognized
Treaties with Poland, December 1970, and with Czechoslovakia, June 1973, confirmed 1945 borders
The Basic Treaty, December 1972: FRG gave up Hallstein Doctrine and recognized GDR

SUMMARY DIAGRAM

Ostpolitik

 # Helsinki Accords and SALT II, 1975–79

▶ **Key question:** *To what extent could the Helsinki Accords be regarded as the final peace settlement of the First World War in Europe?*

In July 1973, the Conference on Security and Co-operation began in Helsinki, Finland. One journalist, Robert Hutchings, has called it the 'centrepiece of Soviet and East European diplomacy' in the 1970s. Essentially the USSR wanted to persuade the West to recognize as permanent the territorial and political division of Europe made at Yalta (see pages 32–35), while increasing economic, scientific and technological co-operation. It was anxious to exploit Western scientific knowledge and technology to modernize its economy.

The US initially consented to the conference in return for a Soviet agreement on Berlin and the opening of negotiations in Vienna, Austria, on mutual reductions of troops and armaments in central Europe. The preparatory talks for the Helsinki conference began in late 1972, when the agenda of the conference was finally agreed on. Detailed negotiations concluded with a summit consisting of the leaders of 35 countries in Helsinki in July and August 1975.

NATO states at the NATO Council Meeting of 9–10 December 1971 decided that the agenda should be widened to include the 'freer movement of people, information and ideas between the Soviet and Western bloc'. During the Helsinki meeting, foreign ministers of the NATO states were determined to extract from the USSR concessions on **human rights**. Initially, the USSR tried with great effort to avoid making these concessions, but finally Brezhnev

 **KEY TERM**

Human rights Basic rights such as personal liberty and freedom from repression.

agreed in order to gain acceptance of the legality of the communist post-war regimes and their frontiers in eastern Europe by NATO. He was reassured by Gromyko that such concessions in reality represented no threat to the USSR. In time, however, they would help bring about fundamental changes in the Soviet bloc and lead to a loosening of Soviet control over the satellites (see chapter 8). The subsequent Helsinki Accords marked the high point of *détente* and was signed on 1 August 1975 by 33 European states, Canada and the USA.

Terms of the Helsinki Accords

The Accords were divided into three sections, or 'baskets' as they were called:

- 'Basket one' dealt with European security and established guiding principles for inter-state relationships. The principles included the settlement of disputes, non-interference in internal affairs of other states and the 'inviolability' of frontiers. Brezhnev had hoped initially that he would be able to negotiate a peace treaty permanently guaranteeing the new post-war frontiers, but under West German pressure, US Secretary of State Henry Kissinger managed to persuade the Soviets to accept the eventual possibility of a 'peaceful change to frontiers'.
- 'Basket two' concerned promoting co-operation in economics, science, technology and environmental issues.
- 'Basket three' called for 'co-operation in humanitarian and other fields'. This meant expanding trade, tourism and cultural contacts between the two blocs, as well as promoting the reunion of families split by the Iron Curtain.

There was to be a follow-up conference two years later to work out further measures for European security and co-operation.

SOURCE J

Excerpt from 'Declaration of Principles Guiding Relations between Participating States', 1 August 1975, from www.hri.org/docs/Helsinki75.html

VII. Respect for human rights and fundamental freedoms, including the freedom of thought, conscience, religion or belief

The participating States will respect human rights and fundamental freedoms, including the freedom of thought, conscience, religion or belief, for all without distinction as to race, sex, language or religion.

They will promote and encourage the effective exercise of civil, political, economic, social, cultural and other rights and freedoms all of which derive from the inherent dignity of the human person and are essential for his free and full development.

Within this framework the participating States will recognize and respect the freedom of the individual to profess and practice, alone or in community with others, religion or belief acting in accordance with the dictates of his own conscience.

The participating States on whose territory national minorities exist will respect the right of persons belonging to such minorities to equality before the law, will

? What information does Source J convey about the provisions made for safeguarding human rights by the Helsinki Accords?

afford them the full opportunity for the actual enjoyment of human rights and fundamental freedoms and will, in this manner, protect their legitimate interests in this sphere.

The participating States recognize the universal significance of human rights and fundamental freedoms, respect for which is an essential factor for the peace, justice and well-being necessary to ensure the development of friendly relations and co-operation among themselves as among all States …

They confirm the right of the individual to know and act upon his rights and duties in this field …

The SALT II Agreement

What delayed the conclusion and then ratification of the SALT II Agreement?

In 1973, talks began in Vienna to explore the potential of reducing military forces and armaments in Europe. The talks aimed to create stability in central Europe by negotiating a mutually balanced programme of arms reduction. For Nixon, another important reason for the negotiations was to deter demands from Congress for unilateral US troop reductions in western Europe (see page 243). The negotiations rapidly became bogged down in complex detail, but continued without any conclusions for years.

In view of this deadlock, the hope for securing military stability between NATO and the Warsaw Pact came to focus on reductions in nuclear rather than conventional weapons. Negotiations began in Geneva in September 1973. Both sides attempted to ensure that any agreement would give them the advantage over the other, and progress was also slowed by the Watergate scandal (see page 208) which forced Nixon to resign in August 1974.

The Vladivostok Summit, November 1974

Nixon's successor, President Gerald Ford, did manage to make progress at the Vladivostok Summit in November 1974. He and Brezhnev agreed that by 1985 the two countries would reach a state of numerical equality in the deployment of missile launchers and bombers. Disagreement on technical details and criticism once again delayed the signature of the SALT II Agreement until after the US Presidential elections.

President Carter

Initially, the new US President Jimmy Carter demanded far greater mutual arms reductions. The Soviet Union rejected this outright, but by February 1977 the numerical limits proposed by both sides were close to those ultimately agreed upon.

The worsening international climate (see chapter 8), the problems of how to monitor whether both sides were carrying out the agreement, the issues over the maximum number of warheads per missile and the deployment of new missile types delayed the signing of the agreement until June 1979.

The SALT II Agreement

The key terms of the SALT II agreement were:

- a limit of 2400 warheads was placed on the overall number of strategic missiles and bombers each side could possess.
- of these, 1320 missiles could have multiple warheads
- negotiations for further 'significant and substantial reductions' were to take place.

Non-ratification of SALT II by the US

Many Senators, as well as the US military, were highly critical of SALT II. They felt that too much had been conceded to the USSR at a time when it was strengthening its position in Africa (see chapter 6). In January 1980, President Carter decided not to submit it to the Senate in protest over the Soviet invasion of Afghanistan (see page 264).

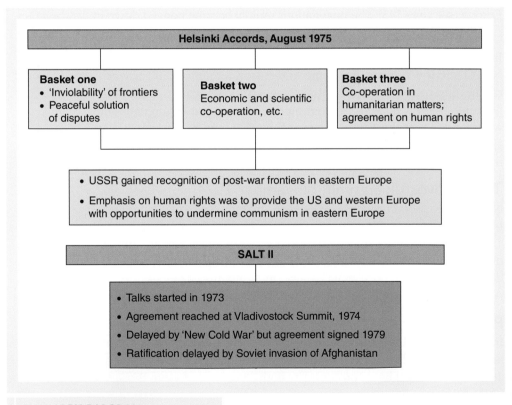

Helsinki Accords and SALT II, 1975–79

Chapter summary

The years from 1963 to 1979 were a period of *détente* in Europe. The US, distracted by the Vietnam War, wanted a stable Europe, while the USSR was facing a growing challenge from the PRC and hoped to consolidate gains made in eastern Europe in 1945. The European allies of both the USSR and the US increasingly exploited these superpower concerns to pursue more independent policies. France wanted to end the powerful grip of the two superpowers on Europe, while the West Germans wanted to normalize relations with the GDR.

In the Soviet bloc, the Soviet satellite states also exploited *détente* and the Sino-Soviet split to gain a greater independence from the USSR. Albania openly sided with the PRC, Romania followed a more nationalist policy, Hungary experimented with economic reform, while Poland maintained the autonomy it had gained in October 1956. It was in Czechoslovakia, however, that demands for economic and political reform threatened to go beyond what the USSR could tolerate, leading to the intervention by Warsaw Pact troops in August 1968.

This did not stop both the development of *détente* in Europe and between the US and USSR, but it showed its limits.

Between 1963 and 1979, *détente* took the following forms:

- The realization of Brandt's *Ostpolitik*.
- The interlocking treaties between the FRG, and the USSR, Czechoslovakia, Poland and the GDR, recognizing the frontier of 1945 and the legal existence of the GDR, 1970–72.
- The Four-Power Treaty on Berlin of 3 September 1971 regulated the status of Berlin, which had caused two major crises (1948–49 and 1958–61).
- The three 'baskets' of the Helsinki Accords of 1975.
- The treaties controlling the development of nuclear weapons.

The following treaties were also signed:

- The Test Ban Treaty of 1963.
- The Non-proliferation Treaty of 1968.
- SALT I Agreement, 1974.
- SALT II Agreement 1979, although this was not ratified by the US.

A consequence of deteriorating Sino-Soviet relations was the US–PRC *rapprochement* of 1972, making the USSR more determined to secure *détente* with the US.

✓ Examination advice

How to answer 'assess' questions

Questions that ask you to 'assess' are similar to those which ask you to 'evaluate' (see page 96). You must make judgements to support with evidence and explanations. It is important for you to demonstrate why your own assessment is better than alternative ones.

Example

> **Assess the reasons for improved relations between the US and the USSR from 1963 to 1972.**

1. To address this question, you will need to discuss the status of relations between the US and the USSR before 1963 so that it is clear that relations improved over the next ten years. This should be done briefly. You will also need to explain why relations between the two countries improved during the period 1963 to 1972, probably from the perspective of each of these nations in addition to those reasons they had in common. Be sure to focus on only the more important reasons, explaining why those are the most important. Stronger candidates might successfully challenge the question by stating, and providing supportive evidence, that relations actually did not improve, but essentially remained the same or similar to the previous decade or decades.

2. First, take at least five minutes to write a short outline.

Pre-1963 tensions
- *Problems over Germany/Europe*
- *Two alliance systems*
- *Growing nuclear arsenals, expense*

Cuban Missile Crisis
- *Nuclear war averted*
- *Missiles in Turkey and Cuba*

Split between USSR and PRC
- *Borders*
- *Ideology*
- *Third World*
- *Soviet fear of US–PRC alliance, PRC need for trade and better relations with US over USSR*

Weakened NATO and Warsaw Pact
- *NATO problems with France*
- *Warsaw Pact problems with Poland/Romania, etc.*

US and Soviet political motives
- *Soviets: recognize post-1945 Europe borders, expand trade*
- *US: undermine communism through negotiations*

Conclusion: There were several reasons for détente during the period 1963 to 1972 and not just for pre-1963, but ones that developed in this period and were ongoing.

3. Your introduction should briefly summarize the points you will make in your essay and state your answer.

The US and the USSR had improved relations from 1963 to 1972. This followed a period from the Second World War in 1945 until the Cuban Missile Crisis in 1962 during which the Soviet Union installed pro-Soviet, communist governments in eastern and central Europe and assisted in most of China becoming a communist state, while the US worked to limit the expansion of communism through the Marshall Plan and war, specifically the Korean War. Both the US and the Soviet Union developed and stockpiled nuclear weapons and military alliances, NATO and the Warsaw Pact respectively. Relations improved starting in 1963 as a result of the Cuban Missile Crisis which narrowly averted a nuclear war as well as a desire on both sides to reduce military expenditure. Both military alliances were weakened with internal divisions, meaning reduced tensions reduced the possibility of conflict for which they were not prepared, and the Soviets hoped that improved relations would not only help improve their economy, but also prevent an alliance between the US and the People's Republic of China. Finally, the US may have wished for improved relations as part of an overall strategy to weaken the Soviet Union generally.

4. Your essay will probably review the three strongest reasons that there were improved relations between the two superpowers during the stated time period. It may be that you are able to discuss a reason in one paragraph, but do not be afraid of using two paragraphs for one reason especially if one paragraph deals with the Soviet Union and another the US. Be sure to include supportive evidence and dates when possible. Avoid sweeping generalizations and over-simplification. Paragraphs of this essay may read as follows:

Both the US and USSR wished to reduce military tensions as a result of weakened alliances. While the Soviet Union and the People's Republic of China were not part of a formal alliance system, it was assumed in the 1950s that if either were threatened, the other would come to its aid; both co-operated somewhat during the Korean War and the Soviets provided various advisors to the PRC until the late 1950s. By the late 1950s and certainly during the 1960s, there were major tensions between the Soviets and the PRC, with Mao openly criticizing Khrushchev's conclusion of the Cuban Missile Crisis, with the Soviets criticizing the PRC's conflict with India and, finally, with the two countries fighting on the PRC's western border. The Soviets were so perturbed by the PRC that they even asked the US what its response would be if they attacked PRC nuclear installations in a pre-emptory attack.

While the Soviets may have been afraid of a PRC nuclear attack on the USSR, they were certainly concerned about a possible alliance against them between the PRC and the USA. In order to deter the US from more than diplomatically recognizing the PRC, such as forming an alliance, the Soviets worked to give the US a reason to not form further, stronger alliances against the USSR and its allies. They specifically agreed to various treaties and summits in the late 1960s and early 1970s, such as the Moscow Summit of 1972 when the Anti-ballistic Missile Systems and Strategic Arms Limitations Treaties were signed reducing various types of weapons and therefore the threat of war and the need for strengthened or expanded alliances.

5. Your conclusion will summarize your argument and clearly state your answer to the question.

Relations between the US and the USSR improved from 1963 to 1972. This was the result of the fear of nuclear war triggered by the Cuban Missile Crisis and the lack of communication between the two superpowers which had contributed to it. While both countries wished to reduce military expenditure, both also wished to avoid conflict as a result of weakened alliance systems. While the Soviets wanted legal recognition of Europe's borders after 1945 so that tensions could be reduced and trade increased to help their economy, some in the US government hoped that by negotiating with the capitalist, democratic US, the Soviet communist government would be undermined by the contradiction of a communist state working with a capitalistic one. There were several reasons for détente during the period 1963 to 1972 and not just for the pre-1963 period, but ones that developed in this period and were ongoing.

6. Now try writing a complete answer to the question following the advice above.

Examination practice

Below are three exam-style questions for you to practise on this topic.

1. Explain the significance of Ostpolitik for both West Germany and the Soviet Union?
   (For guidance on how to answer 'explain' questions, see page 134.)

2. To what extent did relations between the US and the USSR improve between 1972 and the end of 1979?
   (For guidance on how to answer 'to what extent' questions, see page 172.)

3. Explain the importance of Europe in relations between the US and the USSR between 1963 and 1979.
   (For guidance on how to answer 'explain' questions, see page 134.)

Activities

1 Divide the class into several groups. Have each group make a series of ten cards, each with a different reason for *détente* between the US and USSR. Each group should then place these cards in order from the strongest to the weakest reasons for *détente* and then present to the other groups their listing and arguments. The class should create an overall, ordered list of reasons for *détente* based on these discussions and debate.

2 Using information from this and other chapters, students should compare and contrast Soviet actions in Hungary in 1956 and the Czechoslovakia in 1968.

3 It is critical for students to understand that history is the interpretation of evidence, hence the reasons there are so many views of different events. In pairs, they should explain why the following statements are true in 200 words or less:

   • 'The greatest threat to the Soviet Union was the People's Republic of China.'
   • 'The greatest threat to the Soviet Union was its economy.'
   • 'The greatest threat to the Soviet Union was the United States and western Europe.'
   • 'The greatest threat to the Soviet Union was eastern Europe.'

CHAPTER 8

The end of the Cold War

This chapter investigates the outbreak and course of what some historians refer to as the 'New Cold War'. It explores the cost and failure of Soviet policies and the eventual collapse of the USSR. It also reviews the decline of the Soviet and COMECON economies and the impact of Gorbachev's policies of *glasnost* and *perestroika*. You need to consider the following questions throughout the chapter:

✪ How was the USSR weakened by the 'New Cold War' from 1976 to 1985?

✪ Why did Gorbachev improve relations with the US and the PRC between 1985 and 1989?

✪ Why did communism collapse in eastern and south-eastern Europe between 1989 and 1990?

✪ Why was Gorbachev unable to prevent the disintegration of the USSR?

1 'New Cold War', 1976–85

▶ **Key question:** *How was the USSR weakened by the 'New Cold War from 1976 to 1985?*

A new period of competition between the Soviet and Western blocs began in 1976. This included a renewed arms race, the Soviet invasion of Afghanistan, and various crises in eastern Europe. *Détente* essentially ended and by the end of 1980, US–Soviet relations had deteriorated to a level not experienced since the early 1960s.

SOURCE A

? What information does Source A convey about the reasons for the collapse of superpower *détente*?

An excerpt from 'The collapse of superpower détente, 1975–1980' by Olav Njølstad in *The Cambridge History of The Cold War*, Vol. III, edited by M. Leffler and O. Westad, Cambridge University Press, Cambridge, UK, 2010, p. 135

The collapse of superpower détente *did not happen overnight. Nor was it caused by a single, overwhelming destructive force, like an earthquake or tsunami. Rather it was a slow, eroding process, in which multiple events and forces added strength to one another and gradually tore apart the delicate fabric of lofty ideas, pragmatic assumptions and half sincere obligations associated with* détente.

What caused the weakening of the *détente* between the USSR and the Western powers in Europe?

→ The weakening of *détente* in Europe

The first blow to the Helsinki spirit occurred when the Soviet Union placed SS-20 medium-range nuclear missiles in central Europe in 1976. These weapons could reach targets between 600 and 5000 kilometres away, threatening all NATO states in Europe. This threat alarmed NATO and the organization initiated a policy that if an arms agreement could not be reached with the Soviets, the US would deploy 552 Pershing and other nuclear-equipped missiles in Europe by 1983.

This agreement, however, was difficult to reach as the Soviet Union had invaded Afghanistan (see below). In November 1981, US President Reagan suggested that both sides destroy their *existing* medium-range nuclear weapons, but the Soviets immediately rejected this as a one-sided gesture that would require them to destroy their weapons, while the US had not yet deployed its up-to-date missiles. The Soviets also hoped that growing opposition to the deployment of nuclear weapons in western Europe would prevent their eventual deployment, so disarmament talks regarding medium-range missiles could only undo a Soviet military advantage.

SOURCE B

Demonstrations against deployment of missiles in West Germany, June 1982. The slogan reads: 'Work instead of rockets'.

What information is conveyed by Source B that is important for historians? **?**

Despite continued protest, however, the US-supplied missiles were installed between 1983 and 1987 in the FRG, Britain, Belgium, the Netherlands and Italy, eliminating any Soviet strategic advantage.

What impact did the invasion of Afghanistan have on the outbreak of the 'New Cold War'?

The invasion of Afghanistan

The Soviet invasion of Afghanistan in 1979 finally ended US–Soviet *détente*.

Communist coup in Afghanistan, April 1978

In 1973, Afghan Prime Minister Mohammed Daoud Khan seized power from his cousin King Zahir Shah. Afghanistan had remained a Non-Aligned state, but the USSR enjoyed greater influence there than any other power as a result of aid it had granted the country. Daoud attempted to modernize both the economy and society, but met with opposition from traditional, conservative Afghan leaders, including the Muslim religious authorities; the reforms were perceived as an attack on ethnic and religious traditions. He wished to develop agriculture, build modern roads and establish a strong centralized state. At the same time, Daoud was criticized by Afghan communists for not modernizing the country more rapidly.

In April 1978, Daoud's government was overthrown by the Afghan Communist Party, which was composed of two rival groups: the *Parcham* and the *Khalq*. The communists embarked on a radical new reform programme, accompanied by widespread repression which provoked opposition from conservative Muslims in the countryside. Their attempts to modernize agriculture by seizing land from the peasantry was deeply unpopular. The USSR increased financial and military assistance to the government, but as yet did not send any troops

Reasons for Soviet intervention

By November 1979, the USSR came to the conclusion that if the communist regime was to survive in Afghanistan, the unpopular President Hafizullah Amin of the *Khalq* faction of the Communist Party would have to be removed. Not only was his government unstable, there were also growing fears that he would turn to the US government for assistance, potentially creating a US ally on the Soviet Union's southern border.

The USSR also wanted to prevent Afghanistan falling under the control of a conservative Islamic government. It believed that an Islamic-controlled Afghanistan, together with the Islamic regime already established in Iran in 1979, threatened to spread Islamic militancy to the Soviet Union's central Asian republics.

Soviet military operations

Between 24 and 27 December 1979, 50,000 Soviet troops were flown into Kabul, the capital of Afghanistan; there were 100,000 Soviet troops stationed in the country within months. On 27 December, Soviet soldiers attacked the presidential palace, executed Amin, and replaced him with his *Parcham* rival Babrak Kamal. The Soviets aimed to crush the Muslim fundamentalist rebels and stabilize the government so that they could rapidly withdraw within a few weeks.

Soviet forces were able to occupy Kabul and all the other major cities, but they encountered two major military problems:

- The Afghan army disintegrated, leaving Soviet forces to conduct all military actions and secure the country.
- Babrak Kamal did not have the support of the Afghan people who felt that he worked for the foreign Soviets, not Afghans, leading them to support Muslim fundamentalist guerrilla fighters known as the *mujahedin* who wished to establish an Islamic government for the country.

SOURCE C

Map of the Soviet invasion of Afghanistan, 1979.

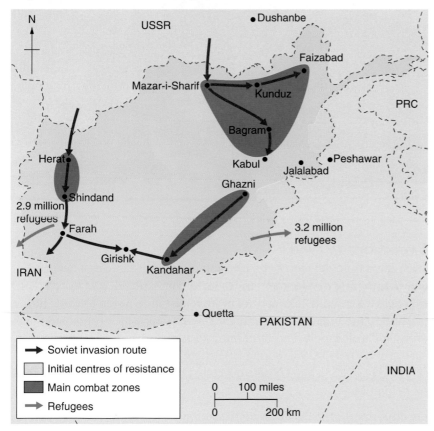

What information does Source C convey about the Soviet invasion of Afghanistan?

Faced by up to 200,000 *mujahedin* guerrillas, the Soviet military controlled only one-fifth of the country; both sides committed atrocities. By 1985, it was clear that the war could not be won by the Soviets as they faced seven different *mujahedin* factions who had headquarters in mountainous areas along the border with Pakistan. The constant conflict demoralized Soviet forces and became a substantial financial strain on the Soviet Union.

Mujahedin resistance fighters posing for a photo on a captured army lorry.

US reaction, 1979–87

The US government believed the invasion of Afghanistan was a new and highly threatening development in Soviet foreign policy. It was feared that the Soviets intended to take control of Afghanistan as a step towards further expansion to the Indian Ocean and the Persian Gulf which contained much of the world's oil supply. President Jimmy Carter responded by banning grain exports to the USSR and the US Senate refused to ratify the SALT II Treaty (see page 253). The US also boycotted the 1980 Olympic Games that were held in Moscow.

More importantly, the US financed the supply of weapons to the Afghan *mujahedin* with money distributed through agencies in neighbouring Pakistan. By 1985, the US was also co-operating closely with conservative, Islamic states such as Saudi Arabia to obtain even more funding for weapons. In 1986, US President Ronald Reagan decided to send the *mujahedin* new lightweight ground-to-air missiles, rapidly diminishing Soviet air superiority, and allowing the guerrillas the benefit of US satellite and communications information.

? Of what importance is source D to the historian?

People's Republic of China

The PRC denounced the invasion of Afghanistan, cancelled the Sino-Soviet talks which were due to start in 1980, and increased the supply of arms to the guerrillas in the country. The invasion also brought the PRC closer to the US. In May 1980, the PRC Minister of Defence Geng Biao visited the US, which soon approved the export of 400 items of advanced military technology to the mujahedin.

Western Europe

The FRG, France, Britain and the other western European states condemned the invasion of Afghanistan at the United Nations, but were unwilling to let it destroy the *détente* that *Ostpolitik* had created in Europe. Many Europeans argued that the Soviet invasion of Afghanistan was no different from the invasion of Czechoslovakia in 1968 (see page 246). In both situations, the USSR acted to preserve communist governments in neighbouring states.

Solidarity in Poland, 1980–82

Apart from the USSR Poland was militarily the most important country in the Soviet bloc because:

- it was the geographical link between the Soviet Union and the GDR through which any attack on the West, or from it, would occur
- it provided one-third of all eastern European armed forces in the Warsaw Pact.

Poland was also important because it had the largest population of any Soviet bloc state other than the USSR and was heavily industrialized, making it important economically. Poland's communist government, however, failed to find effective solutions to the country's economic and political problems.

The Baltic Crisis, 1970–71

Unlike the other states in COMECON, Poland's agriculture was not collectivized (see page 245). While this protected the small-scale farmer, the communist government did not encourage the development of capitalist agricultural policies that would have encouraged more production for more profits. Consequently, farms remained small and inefficient.

By 1970, the government had decided to encourage better farming practices and more food production by increasing the price of food so that farmers would gain more profit. A 30 per cent rise in food prices was announced in 1970, leading to strikes in the shipyards of Gdańsk, Gdynia, and Szczecin, as well as political demonstrations and attacks on Communist Party offices. Altogether, 45 demonstrators and police were killed. The Soviet government recommended the replacement of Gomułka by Edward Gierek. Peace was restored by freezing food prices at their

> **What was the significance of Solidarity for Cold War relations?**

former levels and securing a substantial loan from the USSR to alleviate economic stress in the country.

June 1976 riots

Over the next five years Gierek attempted to make the Polish economy more competitive. He borrowed large sums from western Europe to pay for imported Western technology. He hoped that Poland would be able to produce goods that it could sell to the West and so earn **hard currency** to repay the loans. By 1975, however, it was clear Poland was becoming ever more indebted. Once again, the government responded by increasing food prices in June 1976 – this time by 60 per cent. This again triggered riots throughout the country and again the government was forced to retreat on the issue. The riots also led to the formation of the **Workers' Defence Committee**.

? What information does Source E convey about Poland's economy?

SOURCE E

Statistics of Poland's trade balance from 1950–76 in millions of convertible złoty, from *God's Playground A History of Poland*, Vol II by Norman Davies, Oxford University Press, Oxford, UK, 2005, p. 448.

Date	Import	Export	Balance
1950	2673	2357	-137
1965	9361	8911	-450
1971	16,151	15,489	-662
1976	46,100	36,600	-9500

Political opposition

In 1975, Gierek attempted to reform the constitution to give the central ministries more effective power over Poland's provinces and also to confirm the leading role of the Polish United Workers' Party (**PUWP**). This was seen by many Poles as an effort to tighten the grip of the party on Poland and led to a new wave of opposition to the government:

- Exploiting Basket three of the Helsinki Final Act (see page 252), groups dedicated to the defence of human rights were established.
- Around twenty underground newspapers and periodicals were secretly published and circulated to communicate ideas and information outside of government channels.

Opposition groups extended their activities within Poland and made contact with sympathizers abroad while facing repression by the police. In May 1979, the newly installed Roman Catholic Pope, John Paul II, who was from Poland, visited his home country. Huge crowds greeted him and his popularity in the face of a theoretically atheist government demonstrated further disconnection between Poland's citizens and their government.

The emergence of Solidarity (Solidarność)

By mid-1980, Poland faced a major economic crisis. The constant rise of oil inflated prices (see page 271) and an economic recession in the West meant that Poland had no market for its exports. Additionally, the government had failed in its programme to modernize the economy and make it more competitive with western European states.

In August 1980, strikes erupted throughout the country when the government once again, without any previous warning, announced major increases in the price of food. In Gdańsk, 20,000 workers under the leadership of trade union activist Lech Wałęsa barricaded themselves in to the Lenin Shipyards. Although they reached agreement with management on their own local issues, they refused to end the strike until strikes elsewhere in Poland had been similarly resolved. It was this action which gave birth to the Solidarność, or Solidarity, Movement, which challenged the monopoly of power enjoyed by the PUWP.

The government made far-reaching economic and political concessions and in August recognized Solidarity as an independent trade union. At first, it tried to claim that this concession only applied to Gdańsk, but this provoked a wave of labour unrest culminating in the threat of a national strike. On 31 August, the Gdańsk Agreement was signed between Solidarity and the government:

- Solidarity was recognized as an independent and self-governing trade union.
- The right to strike, freedom of speech and access to the media were guaranteed.
- Solidarity recognized the leading role of the PUWP.

By December 1981, membership of Solidarity had risen to nearly 8 million. It attracted members from every section of society and became a mass movement more popular than the PUWP. It also received the enthusiastic support of the Catholic Church, another rival organization to the communist government.

Threat of Soviet intervention, December 1980

Brezhnev and other Warsaw Pact leaders urged the new Polish Prime Minister, Stanisław Kania, who had replaced Gierek, to crush the 'anti-Socialist opposition forces'. The GDR's Honecker wanted Brezhnev to send in troops.

SOURCE F

An excerpt from a translation by M. Kramer of a letter from Honecker to Brezhnev, 28 November 1980, quoted in *CWIHP (Cold War International History Project)*, Bulletin 5, p. 124, Wilson centre, Washington, 1995.

According to information we have received through various channels, counter-revolutionary forces in the People's Republic of Poland are on constant offensive, any delay in acting against them would mean death – the death of socialist Poland.

> According to Source F, why does Honecker consider Solidarity to be a great threat?

Warsaw Pact forces were mobilized in early December, but at the last moment intervention was cancelled as Kania convinced Brezhnev that he could restore order without assistance. US warnings against the use of force may have also helped.

Martial law, 1981

Throughout 1981, Poland's economy remained in crisis and rationing began. Negotiations between the PUWP, Solidarity and the Catholic Church to form a three-sided council of national reconciliation failed. The threat of Soviet intervention again arose, but in December Brezhnev agreed to a declaration of **martial law** by General Wojciech Jaruzelski, Kania's successor. This led to:

- the arrest of Solidarity's leadership
- the use of soldiers to end strikes
- Poland's army ruling the state
- the outlawing of Solidarity in October 1982.

Jaruzelski's action gave the PUWP a chance to consolidate its position in Poland.

US and NATO reaction

Both the US and the western European members of NATO condemned the declaration of martial law in Poland. There were, however, significant differences between them. The US urged tough sanctions against the USSR and the cancellation of a planned Soviet gas line to western Europe. Western European leaders rejected this, as their states were in need of fuel, but agreed to the further restrictions on advanced technology exports to the Soviet bloc.

How bad were US–USSR relations between 1981 and 1984?

Years of tension, 1981–84

In January 1981, Ronald Reagan became the US President. Between 1981 and 1983, he adopted an uncompromising line towards the USSR. This approach included:

- hostile speeches about the USSR and communism
- a massive increase in US armaments that absorbed 30 per cent of all government spending between 1981 and 1985
- the rejection of the SALT II Treaty
- the deployment of missiles in western Europe
- support for the *mujahedin* in Afghanistan.

Yuri Andropov

In November 1982, Brezhnev died and was replaced by Yuri Andropov. In 1983, Reagan announced the Strategic Defence Initiative (SDI), also commonly called 'Star Wars' which was meant to be an anti-ballistic missile shield composed of nuclear missiles and laser-armed satellites that would

SOURCE G

An excerpt from President Reagan's speech to Britain's Houses of Parliament, 8 June 1982. Quoted from: www.reagan.utexas.edu/archives/ speeches/1982/60882a.htm

I have discussed on other occasions, including my address on May 9th, the elements of Western policies toward the Soviet Union to safeguard our interests and protect the peace. What I am describing now is a plan and a hope for the long term – the march of freedom and democracy which will leave Marxism-Leninism on the ash-heap of history as it has left other tyrannies which stifle the freedom and muzzle the self-expression of the people. And that's why we must continue our efforts to strengthen NATO even as we move forward with our Zero-Option initiative in the negotiations on intermediate-range forces [see page 261] and our proposal for a one-third reduction in strategic ballistic missile warheads.

Our military strength is a prerequisite to peace, but let it be clear we maintain this strength in the hope it will never be used, for the ultimate determinant in the struggle that's now going on in the world will not be bombs and rockets, but a test of wills and ideas, a trial of spiritual resolve, the values we hold, the beliefs we cherish, the ideals to which we are dedicated.

The British people know that, given strong leadership, time and a little bit of hope, the forces of good ultimately rally and triumph over evil.

> What information does Source G convey about US President Reagan's policy towards the USSR?

protect the US from attack. This essentially meant that if ever fully deployed, SDI would make obsolete the Soviet Union's ability to threaten the US, while, without this defence, the Soviet Union would remain vulnerable to attack by the US. The ramifications of this were tremendous for international diplomacy and threatened potentially to end the balance of power between the two superpowers in favour of the US.

On 1 September 1983, tension between the US and USSR was further increased when a Soviet fighter aircraft destroyed a South Korean passenger aircraft, killing all 269 people on board, including 61 US citizens. The USSR refused to accept any responsibility, leading Reagan to describe the incident as 'an act of unprecedented barbarism'. Andropov responded that his government felt that it could no longer do business with the US. In November 1983, relations were so poor that Andropov feared that an annually scheduled NATO military exercise might be a cover for a nuclear attack on the USSR.

Reduced tensions, 1984–85

> **Why did tension begin to lessen in 1984–85?**

At the end of 1983, Reagan and his advisors came to the conclusion that relations with the USSR needed to be improved. This was partially the result of a more confident US government that had now gained military dominance over the Soviets, especially in terms of technology. More importantly, perhaps, was the appeal of the US's European allies that the US should be less aggressive and avoid provoking a war. Tensions with the Soviet Union between September and December 1983 convinced Reagan that the danger of war between the two superpowers was a real possibility and one that should be avoided if possible.

Konstantin Chernenko

The Soviet response to Reagan's diplomatic initiatives was delayed by the death of Andropov in February 1984. His successor, Konstantin Chernenko, was a cautious and elderly Soviet politician, but did agree to reopen arms negotiations for the Strategic Arms Reduction Treaty (START). These negotiations had ended earlier when the US installed nuclear missiles in western Europe, starting in 1983 (see page 261). The renewed negotiations began in March 1985, the month that Chernenko died and was replaced by Mikhail Gorbachev.

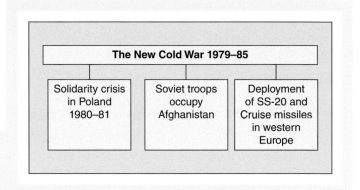

SUMMARY DIAGRAM

The 'New Cold War', 1979–85

Mikhail Gorbachev and renewed *détente*, 1985–89

▶ **Key question:** Why did Gorbachev improve relations with the US and the PRC between 1985 and 1989?

When Gorbachev became General-Secretary of the Communist Party, he appeared a youthful and dynamic leader in contrast to his elderly, ill predecessors. His great aim was to modernize the USSR, and two key terms, *glasnost* and *perestroika*, set the tone for his reforms.

Gorbachev realized that the ultimate survival of the USSR depended on ending the Cold War and reforming the economy. He inherited a very difficult situation:

● The collapse of *détente* in the late 1970s between the US and USSR led to a new and expensive arms race which the USSR could not financially afford.

- The war in Afghanistan drained resources and had little chance of success.
- The Soviet economy was hampered by inefficiency, corruption and lack of technology.

USSR's economic weakness

In 1990, Gorbachev told the Lithuanian Communist Party that 'it is politics that follows economics and not *vice versa* [the other way round]'. It was the economic weakness of the USSR and the COMECON states that was a key factor in the collapse of communism and the disintegration of the USSR by 1991. Yet until at least 1960, the Soviet economy had performed relatively well. Similarly, when the COMECON states adopted the Soviet economic model, they too experienced rapid industrialization and impressive growth in their heavy industries until the 1960s. One reason for this was that the main industrial technology of the time was based on large productive units, such as car and tractor factories, and heavy industry, particularly coal and steel. These functioned effectively as large units controlled by a central planning system which set targets for production and maintained and managed Five Year Plans.

By the 1960s, the Soviet **command economy** had become very bureaucratic and inflexible. The system functioned well when it concentrated on a particular target, such as war production or post-Second World War recovery, but it was poor at adapting to supplying at competitive prices the multitude of consumer goods which were available to the capitalist states. In the early 1960s, Soviet economist Yevsei Liberman and Ota Šikin from Czechoslovakia put forward ideas for decentralizing the economy to allow decisions of production, design and pricing, etc., to be taken by local factory managers. In Czechoslovakia, these ideas began to be realized between 1965 and 1968:

- Greater freedom was given to the factory managers.
- Business taxes were reduced to encourage production.
- Wage differentiation between skilled and unskilled workers was introduced.
- Wholesale prices were determined by the market.

After the termination of the Prague Spring (see page 246), economic experiments aimed at modernization and increased economic competitiveness in the Soviet bloc were discouraged for fear that they might lead to growing demands for political concessions.

The 1970s

The 1970s were a period of great economic change and crisis for capitalist economies in the Western bloc. After the October War in 1973 (see page 215), oil prices were quadrupled by the Organization of Petroleum Exporting Countries (OPEC) in just a few months in protest against the West's support of Israel. This weakened the western economies and fuelled inflation. At the same time, the old coal and steel industries were contracting in western Europe and unemployment was growing. Western

←
How serious were the economic problems facing the Soviet economy, 1960–85?

🔑 **KEY TERM**

Command economy An economy where supply and pricing are regulated by the government rather than market forces such as demand, and in which all the larger industries and businesses are controlled centrally by the state.

Europe and the US responded to this challenge by modernizing and adapting their economies to take advantage of developing new industries and technologies.

By contrast, the USSR and COMECON continued with centralized governmental control of their economies, emphasizing heavy industry such as coal and steel. For a short time, this appeared to work well. *Détente* and *Ostpolitik* opened the way for generous Western loans to COMECON members. The USSR was also well placed to exploit the global oil crisis by selling its oil at a high price to the West, allowing them to import from the West. From July 1975 onwards, the USSR increased charges on oil exported to eastern Europe by 30 per cent on the assumption that Western loans would make the extra payment by their allies possible.

SOURCE H

Total indebtedness to the West (in millions of US dollars) of GDR, Poland and USSR.

	1975	1980	1985	1989
GDR	5,188	13,896	13,234	20,600
Poland	8,388	24,128	29,300	41,400
USSR	10,577	23,512	25,177	52,392

Source: Table from *Dissolution: The Crisis of Communism and the End of East Germany* by C.S. Maier, Princeton University Press, Princeton, USA, 1997, p. 63.

? What information does Source H convey about the debts of the USSR, Poland and the GDR to the West?

1980–85

COMECON states negotiated loans with the West on the assumption that this money would enable them to modernize their economies. By 1980, it was increasingly clear that the USSR and eastern Europe had failed to develop the new industries based on information technology. They had amassed huge debt that had to be paid back with interest at the end of ten years to western European and US banks. At the same time, oil prices on the international market fell from $35 to $16 a barrel, resulting in a disastrous decline in the income for the Soviet Union.

This was the bleak economic scenario that confronted Gorbachev when he came to power in 1985 and contributed to the collapse of the Soviet Union and communism in eastern Europe.

How did Gorbachev re-establish *détente*?

Détente renegotiated, 1985–88

While Gorbachev wanted to prevent the introduction of the US's SDI, he hoped to achieve even more. He was determined to end the Cold War as it was too costly and prevented the implementation of *perestroika* and *glasnost*. He aimed to reform the Soviet economy fundamentally and liberalize its political system. Unlike Stalin, Khrushchev and Brezhnev,

SOURCE I

An excerpt from Soviet periodical *Novy Mir*, No. 6, by Nikolai Shmelevin, 1987, quoted in *Gorbachev* by Martin McCauley, published by Longman, UK, 1998, p. 68.

At present our economy is characterized by shortages imbalances … unmanageable, and almost unplannable … Industry now rejects up to 80 per cent of technical decisions and inventions … the working masses have reached a state of almost total lack of interest in … honest labour… Apathy, indifference, thieving… have become mass phenomena, with simultaneous aggressive envy towards those who are capable of earning. There have appeared signs of … physical degradation of a large part of the population, through drunkenness and idleness. Finally there is disbelief in the officially announced objectives and purposes, in the very possibility of a more rational economic and social organization of life. Clearly, all this cannot be quickly overcome – years, perhaps generations, will be needed.

What information does Source I convey about the state of the Soviet economy in 1987?

he did not conduct Soviet foreign policy according to the Marxist–Leninist revolutionary ideology (see page 9); he no longer emphasized that communism would eventually triumph over the capitalist West. Instead, he worked towards achieving international co-operation and a real co-existence between the two hitherto rival systems whose values and principles would in time converge rather than conflict. It is, however, important to remember, as historian Jonathan Haslam has pointed out, that Gorbachev fundamentally 'sought to improve the Soviet system, not destroy it'.

Although the decision had been taken to renew arms talks only months before Gorbachev came to power, he quickly indicated that he was determined to negotiate major reductions in nuclear weapons. Quite apart from the economic benefits for the USSR, he also believed that a conciliatory Soviet policy would undermine the apparently bellicose Reagan and appeal to those in western Europe and the US who desired *détente*. That Reagan also wanted a renewal of *détente* was not yet clear to Gorbachev (see page 269).

In April 1985, Gorbachev halted the installation of further SS-20 missiles in eastern Europe, and in October began to reduce the total number deployed. He failed at the Reykjavik Summit in Iceland in 1986 to persuade President Reagan to stop SDI development in return for the negotiation of arms control treaties. However, such was his wish to end the arms race, that he accepted unconditionally a NATO plan for a total withdrawal of medium-range missiles by both sides in Europe at the Washington Summit in December 1987.

An excerpt from a memorandum for Gorbachev from one of his advisors, Alexander Yakovlev, December 1986, quoted in 'Svetlana Savranskaya, Alexander Yakovlev and the Roots of Soviet Reforms', *National Security Archive Electronic Briefing Book*, No. 168, Doc. 3, 2005 George Washington University, Washington, US, www.gwu.edu/~nsarchiv/ NSAEBB/NSAEBB168/yakovlev03.pdf

We have created an extremely important and effective breach head for our offensive against Reagan ... Today we should expand it ... into ... an offensive against the position of the far right ... of the active proponents of the arms race in general, while at the same time ensuring opportunities for cooperation with moderate conservative and liberal groups within the US and Western Europe.

... Under the current correlation of forces, the USSR is confronting the USA not only in the international arena but also inside the US itself. Of course we cannot elect a 'good' President for ourselves. However, we can protect ourselves from the worst. Today this would mean: to increase pressure on Reagan and the circles standing behind him...

Human rights, 1986–88

In May 1986, Gorbachev informed his diplomats at a meeting at the Soviet Ministry of Foreign Affairs that the USSR would now consider 'Basket three' of the Helsinki Accords on human rights as important. This declaration led to:

- prominent Soviet dissident Andrei Sakharov being allowed to return to Moscow from exile in the city of Gorky in December 1986
- the release of more dissidents from prison in 1987 and 1988
- Soviet Jews being allowed to emigrate to Israel more easily
- foreign government media, such as the US's Voice of America and Britain's BBC Foreign Service radio-transmitted news, being permitted to broadcast freely within the USSR.

By 1988–89 these concessions had helped create a new climate of intellectual and cultural freedom never before experienced in the USSR (see page 293).

Global *détente*

During the 1980s, there were four main areas of **proxy conflict** where the US and USSR supported opposing sides:

- Afghanistan
- Cambodia
- Nicaragua
- Angola.

Afghanistan

Gorbachev realized that Soviet policy had failed in Afghanistan (see page 264) and in November 1986 decided that Soviet troops, regardless of the consequences within Afghanistan, would have to be withdrawn as soon as possible. The Soviets replaced Afghan President Babrak Karmal with Mohammed Najibullah, who, they believed, would be able to form a government of national unity that could negotiate a peace between the various factions fighting in Afghanistan. In April 1988 agreements were signed in Geneva, Switzerland between Pakistan and Afghanistan, with the USSR and US as sponsors. These consisted of:

- a bilateral agreement between Pakistan and Afghanistan that neither state would interfere in the internal affairs of the other
- neither state would allow militant groups, hostile to the other state, to train within their territory
- Afghan refugees in Pakistan would be permitted to return to Afghanistan
- the withdrawal of Soviet troops from Afghanistan would begin on 15 May 1988 and end by 15 February 1989.

The agreements did not bring peace to Afghanistan. The *mujahedin*, who were not represented at Geneva, fought on, while the USSR continued to give financial assistance and arms to Najibullah's forces. As long as this continued, the US gave financial and military support to the *mujahedin*. Fighting continued at varying levels in Afghanistan after the collapse of the Soviet Union and into the current period.

Cambodia

In 1979 Vietnam, supported by the USSR, invaded Cambodia and overthrew the Khmer Rouge regime (see page 207), establishing the pro-Vietnam People's Republic of Kampuchea (PRK). Vietnamese military units remained in Cambodia to support the new republic. The extension of Vietnamese influence into Cambodia was opposed by the PRC, the US and the ASEAN (see page 207) states, which supplied resistance groups operating against the PRK. These hoped to restore the Khmer Rouge, which was recognized by the UN as the legal government of Cambodia, to power.

Gorbachev was ready to collaborate with both the US and PRC to find a solution to the Cambodian problem. Just before his visit to Beijing in May 1989 (see page 277), where he hoped to end the division between the PRC and the USSR, he successfully pressured Vietnam to withdraw its troops from Cambodia. This did not lead to immediate peace, but a ceasefire between the PRK and rebels was negotiated in 1991 by the UN Security Council with active US and USSR assistance.

Nicaragua

In July 1979, the Marxist-leaning Sandinista political party came to power in Nicaragua after the overthrow of the country's US-backed leader Anastasio Somoza Debayle, and supported rebel activity in nearby El Salvador. In 1981, Sandinista leaders visited the USSR and succeeded in persuading the Soviets to send military equipment to Nicaragua.

This alarmed the US, which became increasingly worried about communist influence in central America. US troops invaded the island state of Grenada in the Caribbean Sea in October 1983, overthrowing a communist regime established there in 1979 and launched a covert war against the Sandinista government of Nicaragua. US President Reagan's government equipped and supplied anti-Sandinista rebels, collectively referred to as the *Contras*, despite the US Senate's decision to prohibit the funding of this. This defiance of the Senate led to a major political scandal and subsequent investigations which weakened Reagan's government. In 1988, both the US and USSR supported a plan drawn up by the Central American states that ended foreign assistance to all fighting groups and called for free elections to resolve the Nicaraguan Civil War.

Angola and Namibia, 1988

In 1987, fighting increased in Angola between the Movement for the Liberation of Angola (MPLA) and the South African-backed UNITA (see page 222). MPLA's defeat was swiftly followed by the advance of South African troops into the country, but this was halted by intervention of cuban airpower. Both the US and USSR pressured Cuba, Angola and South Africa to agree to a ceasefire and the withdrawal of Cuban troops. In December 1988, South Africa agreed to implement UN Resolution 435 which called for the independence of Namibia, a huge region on Angola's southern border that was administered by South Africa.

Ethiopia

Gorbachev continued to send financial aid to assist the Mengistu regime (see page 222) in Ethiopia until 1989. In early 1990, due to the financial crisis triggered by the collapse in the prices of its coffee exports, Mengistu turned to the US for financial aid, but in May 1991 he was ousted in a coup led by his anti-Marxist opponents. Little attention was given to Ethiopia in the final years of the Soviet Union's existence.

→ **What factors made the end of PRC–Soviet dispute possible?**

PRC–Soviet relations, 1976–89

After Mao's death on 9 September 1976, the **Gang of Four**, headed by Mao's widow, was soon removed from power. Deng Xiaoping, with the support of the army and the majority of the Chinese Communist Party's officials, emerged as the PRC's new leader by 1978.

KEY TERM

Gang of Four The four senior Communist politicians who led the PRC immediately after Mao's death.

Deng's policies

Deng abandoned Mao's policies of 'class struggle' and 'continuous revolution' (see page 179) which had led to a stagnated economy and political chaos in various periods of Mao's rule. Instead, Deng aimed to improve the PRC's economy and thereby strengthen the CCP which would benefit from the country's prosperity and rising standards of living. To accomplish this, he encouraged the adaptation of capitalist methods of production and allowed the market to determine which products were produced and to set prices. This was accompanied by modest political liberalization which allowed more open political discussion and the election of local officials, while maintaining the CCP as the ruling organization.

US–PRC co-operation

Deng's new economic reforms of the late 1970s occurred at the same time as Soviet–US relations began to deteriorate after the Helsinki Conference. Both states appreciated the advantages of closer co-operation. For the US this would help contain the growing Soviet threat while the PRC would use this relationship to further isolate the USSR and gain access to modern technology from the US. On 1 January 1979, the PRC and the US announced the restoration of formal diplomatic relations.

SOURCE K

An excerpt from 'China and the Cold War after Mao' by Chen Jian, edited by M. Leffler and O.A. Westad in _The Cambridge History of the Cold War_, Vol III published by Cambridge University Press, Cambridge, UK, 2010, p. 195.

By the mid-1980s, the Soviet Union was a superpower in decline, and China contributed in crucial ways to Moscow's problems. In a strategic sense, Beijing's partnership with Washington and its continued confrontation with Moscow completely altered the balance of power between the two superpowers. More importantly, China's market orientated reforms destroyed Moscow's claims that Communism remained a viable alternative to capitalism. Beijing's repudiation of the Soviet model discouraged other Third World countries from thinking that Communism could serve as an exemplary model for achieving modernity. Since the Cold War from its inception had been a global struggle between two contrasting ideological and social systems, the new course embraced by China obscured the distinctions between the two sides and favoured the capitalist world. The Soviet Union and its allies found it increasingly more difficult to sustain the course of the Cold War.

What information does Source K convey about the impact on the course of the Cold War of the Sino-Soviet split?

End of the PRC–Soviet dispute

Soviet withdrawal from Afghanistan and Vietnamese troops from Cambodia, coupled with the reduction of Soviet troops along the PRC-Soviet frontier, cleared the way for improving relations between the PRC and the USSR. In May 1989, after a summit meeting in Beijing between Gorbachev and the PRC leadership, relations were fully restored. This was partly the result of Gorbachev's announcement that there would only be 120,000 Soviet troops stationed along the lengthy border between the two states, reducing the PRC's fears of an attack.

Tiananmen Square

Gorbachev's visit to Beijing in 1989 was overshadowed by the PRC's own political crisis. _Glasnost_ and _perestroika_ in the USSR had inspired chinese students and intellectuals who wanted political reform in addition to the economic ones. On his arrival at Beijing, Gorbachev was greeted by hundreds of thousands of students. The day after Gorbachev left Beijing, the

PRC government declared martial law and forcibly cleared demonstrators from Tiananmen Square, with many killed. This incident served as a warning that while the PRC intended to modernize its economy, the rule of the CCP was not to be challenged and that any attempt to alter the political system would be met with deadly force if necessary. In essence, all reforms would be imposed by the leaders and not result from popular movements or demonstrations.

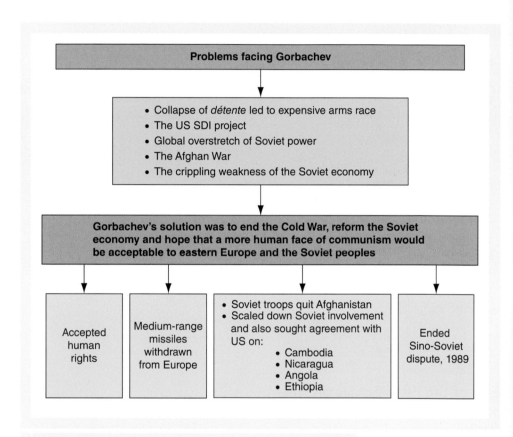

SUMMARY DIAGRAM

Mikhail Gorbachev and the creation of a new détente, 1985–89

3 The collapse of communism in eastern Europe, 1989–90

▶ *Key question: Why did communism collapse in eastern and south-eastern Europe between 1989 and 1990?*

By withdrawing from Afghanistan and Africa, Gorbachev re-focused Soviet policy on Europe. He hoped to safeguard Soviet security in Europe through a policy of political co-operation and negotiation rather than force. Indeed, in July 1988, he effectively dismissed the Brezhnev Doctrine (see page 246).

SOURCE L

An excerpt from Gorbachev's speech on 6 July 1988 to the Council of Europe, quoted in http://chnm.gmu.edu/1989/archive/files/gorbachev-speech-7-6-89_e3ccb87237.pdf

There are no 'bystanders' nor can there be any in peace building in Europe: all are equal partners here and everyone, including neutral and non-aligned countries bears his share of responsibility.

The philosophy of the concept of a common European home here rules out the possibility of an armed clash, all possibility of an armed clash and the very possibility of the use of force, above all military force by an alliance against another alliance, inside alliance, or whatever it might be.

> To what extent does
> Source L indicate that
> Gorbachev has rejected
> the Brezhnev Doctrine? **?**

By 1989, Gorbachev encouraged communist eastern European states to reform economically and to liberalize politically, but it was initially unclear how far the reform process would be allowed to go. At first, Gorbachev, both in the USSR and the eastern European states, was ready to make limited political concessions, so long as the communists remained in a dominant position.

Eastern and south-eastern Europe was divided into three loose groups:

- In Poland, Hungary and Bulgaria, governments were ready to contemplate at least limited political and economic reform as long as communists remained in overall control.
- In the GDR, Czechoslovakia, Romania and Albania, governments were unwilling to experiment with political or economic reform and were compelled to reform by the dramatic events occurring in the GDR.
- Yugoslavia, even before the collapse of communism in eastern Europe, was facing major challenges with nationalism which would ultimately tear it apart.

Developments in Poland, Hungary and Bulgaria, 1988–89

The political changes in Poland, Hungary and Bulgaria have been described as 'negotiated revolutions'. What is meant by this is that the revolutionary changes that occurred in these countries were introduced with the support of the ruling communists and decided upon before the opening of the Berlin Wall.

Poland

With Poland's economy increasingly indebted (see Source H, page 272), the ruling leader General Jaruzelski was forced once again to introduce price rises up to 200 per cent in 1988. This, coupled with other issues such as endemic corruption throughout the government and the industries it controlled, led to a series of strikes throughout the nation, forcing the government to legalize Solidarity again and enter into negotiations with this group. This was not opposed by the Soviets and soon negotiations began between the government, the Catholic Church and Solidarity.

All sides agreed at this point that relations with the USSR and the Warsaw Pact could not be discussed as they did not wish to provoke a military intervention. Neither did Solidarity challenge the dominance of the communists in Poland. On 7 April 1989, the Round Table Agreements were signed between the three groups. Solidarity was recognized not just as a trade union, but also as a political party. A new constitution was also created. This allowed Solidarity to compete for 35 per cent of seats in the lower house of parliament, the Sejm, with 65 per cent reserved for communists (PUWP). The upper house of the Sejm would be elected in free elections and both houses would elect the President of Poland.

Gorbachev welcomed this agreement as he felt that it safeguarded communist power. At the same time, there were sufficient political concessions to please the West and encourage it to increase its financial assistance to Poland.

In the first round of the elections on 4 June, Solidarity won 92 out of the 100 seats in the Sejm's upper house and 160 of the 161 seats in the lower house for which they were allowed to compete. Two weeks later, communists won all the seats reserved for them, but only 25 per cent of eligible voters voted. As there was dissent within the Communist Party regarding the inclusion of Solidarity in a possible government, it was decided that Solidarity would form the government and that the communists would hold a minority of ministerial positions. On 18 August, Solidarity led a coalition government that contained only four communists.

Significantly Gorbachev made it clear on 16 August that the USSR would not intervene to reinforce an unpopular communist regime. However, at the time it was still not obvious that a major turning point had been reached. Communists still controlled the Ministries of Defence, Interior, Transportation and Foreign Trade, while Jaruzelski remained President. Solidarity declared that Poland would remain a member of the Warsaw Pact.

Only with the collapse of communist rule in the GDR and Czechoslovakia (see below) did Solidarity remove communists from control of the army and police. In January 1990, the PUWP was dissolved and reformed as the Social Democrat Party. Jaruzelski resigned in November 1990 and Lech Wałęsa of Solidarity was elected President.

Hungary

From the 1960s onwards, Hungary's leader János Kádár pursued a policy tolerant of criticism as long as the legitimacy of the communist regime was not undermined. At the same time, he allowed the development of minor capitalism within the Hungarian economy. The USSR tolerated this as Kádár remained loyal to the Warsaw Pact. By 1987, criticism of both the economy and the government was growing. Living standards declined and the country's debts to the West were the highest in eastern Europe. Corruption existed throughout the government: wasting public money and placing associates and families of officials into important positions.

In May 1988, responding to the atmosphere created by Gorbachev's *perestroika* and *glasnost*, the Hungarian Socialist Workers' Party (**MSZMP**) replaced Kádár with Károly Grósz, a committed reformer. In February 1989, the Party accepted that Hungary would have to become a multi-party democracy to prevent a revolution. When Grósz visited the USSR in March 1989, Gorbachev's advisor, Aleksandr Iakovlev, welcomed these reforms as evidence that the MSZMP could stay in power by winning popular support rather than through force. Gorbachev was more ambiguous. Although he, too, welcomed the developments in Hungary, he emphasized that the dominant position of socialism in Hungary should not be threatened (see Source M, page 282).

In June, following Poland's example, 'round table' talks began between the government and the opposition groups, ending in agreement that free parliamentary elections were to be held in March and April 1990. The Party leaders accepted this because they were convinced that, having seized the initiative to reform, the Hungarian Socialist Workers' Party would emerge as the dominant force in the new parliament and safeguard socialism in Hungary. The Party attempted to transform itself into a Western-style socialist party later in the year and changed its name to the Hungarian Socialist Party (HSP), but in the elections in March 1990, it won less than 11 per cent of the vote and did not take part in the next government.

> **⚷ KEY TERM**
>
> **MSZMP (Magyar Szocialista Munkáspárt)**
> The Hungarian Socialist Workers' Party, the Communist Party in Hungary between 1956 and 1989.

What information does Source M convey about Gorbachev's views on Hungarian political reforms?

SOURCE M

Excerpt from Document No 3 'Memorandum of Conversation between M.S. Gorbachev and HSWP [Hungarian Socialist Workers' Party] General Secretary Károly Grósz, 23-24 March 1989. Quoted from: *Cold War International History Bulletin*, **Issue 12/13, Autumn/Winter 2001, p. 78, Wilson Centre, Washington, www.coldwar.hu/html/en/publications/pol_trans.pdf**

Comrade Grósz informed the negotiators about the Hungarian situation. He said that the events in Hungary have accelerated lately. Their direction is according to our intentions, while the pace is somewhat disconcerting. Comrade Grósz emphasized that we wish to retain political power and find a solution to our problems by political means, avoiding armed conflict.

We have a good chance for reaching our goals. People are afraid of a possible armed conflict. Workers, peasants and professionals want to work and live in peace and security …

… Comrade Gorbachev has recently analyzed the 1968 events in Czechoslovakia [see page 246], and they continue to maintain that what happened there was a counter revolution … the Dubček regime was unable to prevent counter-revolutionary forces from gaining ground through them …

Comrade Gorbachev emphasized that we clearly have to draw boundaries, thinking about others and ourselves at the same time. Democracy is much needed and interests have to be harmonized. The limit, however, is the safe keeping of socialism and assurance of stability.

Bulgaria

By 1989, the ruling Bulgarian Communist Party had been led by Todor Zhivkov for 35 years. Zhivkov had made many enemies in the Party through his radical administrative reforms which had led to the termination of the careers of around 30,000 government officials. He had also promoted his family into positions of authority for which they were not qualified: his daughter was a member of the Politburo until her death and his son-in-law headed the Olympic committee and was chairman of the government's television company. Those whom Zhivkov favoured in the Party were allowed to shop in special stores which stocked imported Western goods, have access to the best education, receive up to 500 per cent more salary than other officials and so forth; cronyism was one of the main features of his rule. Zhikov also launched a programme of 'Bulgarianization' which had led to the expulsion of some 200,000 ethnic Turks from Bulgaria. This resulted in widespread international condemnation.

The Bulgarian Foreign Minister Petar Mladenov confidentially informed Gorbachev in July 1989 that he intended 'to carry out a change of direction in Bulgaria' which Gorbachev did not oppose. Mladenov gained the backing of the Deputy Prime Minister and Minister of Defence and on 9 November forced Zhivkov to resign. As in Poland and Hungary, talks were held with emerging opposition groups and free elections were promised for June 1990. The

Bulgarian Communist Party transformed itself into a socialist party and was successful in winning the elections with a majority of 52.75 per cent. In 1991, when elections based on the new constitution took place, it was defeated.

The GDR on the brink of collapse

However inevitable it might seem in retrospect, the collapse of the GDR was not anticipated in the Soviet Union, in the FRG or any other Western state. German unification was not, as proponents of *Ostpolitik* envisaged, a gradual knitting together of the two states but rather, to quote historian Tim Garton Ash, a sudden 'hurtling and hurling together sanctioned by great power negotiations'.

> **To what extent was it the desire for reunification with the FRG that brought the GDR to the brink of collapse?**

The GDR in the 1970s

In the 1970s, diplomatic recognition by the West (see page 250) gave the GDR international legitimacy, which it had hitherto lacked. As a result of the Berlin Wall (see page 168), which prevented emigration to the FRG, the majority of East Germans had little option but to come to terms with the regime. Acceptance was also assisted in the 1970s by full employment and the production of more consumer goods such as refrigerators, washing machines and cars. In March 1978, the regime was further strengthened when Protestant churches recognized that they had to work within a socialist society and in return received a degree of toleration from the government.

Protest movements

Ostpolitik and the implications for human rights in the Helsinki Accords (see page 252) increased popular demands for closer contact with the FRG and a more liberal regime. By the autumn of 1987, *Stasi* (secret police) reports reached Honecker and showed that protest movements were growing and beginning to present a real challenge to the government. At the same time, the deteriorating economy, crippled by debt (see Source H, page 272) had discredited the regime. Honecker's response was a determined, but unsuccessful, attempt to stamp out the dissent.

SOURCE N

An excerpt from *Dissolution*, by C.S. Maier, Princeton University Press, Princeton, USA, 1997, p. 106.

By September 1987, the Stasi *reported: 'Frequently workers are demanding to be kept informed about emerging problems and their solutions. In part this is tied to the question of whether the party and state leadership actually know the real solution'. When they got the chance to talk with West German visitors, East Germans deprecated the productive capacity of their own economy … 'To an increasing extent manifestations of indifference and even resignation are evident' … Comparisons between the level of consumption in the GDR and FRG drawn by East German citizens returning from allowed family visits 'glorified' the West …*

> What information does Source N convey about dissent in the GDR in September 1987?

Popularity of visits to FRG

In 1986, short visits to the FRG to see friends and relatives were made possible, provided a return to the GDR was guaranteed. This meant that a close relative would have to be left behind in the GDR, who in the event of non-return could be arrested. Visits proved increasingly popular, but at the same time the conditions attached to them emphasized the lack of freedom for GDR citizens. It was to be the issue of the right to free travel and emigration to the FRG that brought about the terminal crisis of the GDR.

SOURCE O

A table indicating numbers of visitors from the GDR to the FRG. The statistics are drawn from *Dissolution*, by C.S. Maier, Princeton University Press, Princeton, USA, 1997, p. 128, and *East Germany in Comparative Perspective*, by D.Childs and T. Baylis, Routledge, London, 1989, p.5.

Year	No. of visitors to FRG
1985	66,000
1986	573,000
1987	2,475,804
1988	2,790,582

? What information does Source O convey about relations between the GDR and FRG by 1988?

Hungary opens its border

On 2 May 1989, Hungary began to dismantle the barriers along its frontier with Austria, a neutral state. Hungary did not originally intend to allow citizens from other Warsaw Pact states to travel through it to Austria, but in July, thousands of East Germans, who were allowed to visit Warsaw Pact countries without permits, travelled to Hungary hoping to cross into Austria. Initially the East Germans were refused permission to cross into Austria. In response, a group of 200 East Germans broke into the West German embassy in Budapest on 7 August and occupied its gardens in a successful attempt to force the FRG to intervene on their behalf with Hungarian and Austrian authorities. On 11 September, Austria agreed to accept those East Germans in Hungary and within three days, 18,000 people came across the border.

Growing unrest in the GDR

In the meantime, more GDR citizens besieged the FRG embassy in Prague, Czechoslovakia. By early September, 3500 were encamped in the embassy grounds. The Czechoslovak government was not prepared to open its borders with the FRG, but also refused to use force against the East Germans.

Unwilling to force a confrontation on the eve of the celebration of the 40th anniversary of the founding of the GDR which Gorbachev would attend, Honecker granted those GDR citizens in Czechoslovakia exit visas to the West, but insisted that they would have to travel back through the GDR to the FRG in locked trains after which the Czechoslovak–GDR frontier would be closed. There was no chance of keeping these events secret from the rest of the population of the GDR who watched developments on West German television stations. Once the route the trains were taking to the West German frontier became known, large crowds demonstrated along the routes. At Dresden station on 7 October, a crowd of 10,000 attempted to storm the station and board the trains to the FRG.

The Leipzig demonstrations, 25 September to 16 October

On four successive Mondays between 25 September and 16 October, large but peaceful demonstrations took place in Leipzig in the GDR. Protestors sang protest songs and shouted out such slogans as 'We are the people' and 'We are staying here' by which they meant they would push for reform within the GDR rather than emigrate to the West. Although there were clashes between the police and demonstrators, the regime did not use force on a large scale to clear the streets. This restraint set a precedent that was followed all over the GDR in the coming weeks. This non-violent approach by the government was the result of:

- disciplined, non-violent demonstrators
- a deeply divided Politburo that was unsure of what approach was needed and of the loyalty of its policemen and the factory militias
- knowledge that no help could be expected from the Soviet Union to reinforce the government's authority
- a statement by Gorbachev during a visit to East Berlin on 6 and 7 October when he indicated that reforms were needed by stating 'life punishes latecomers'.

On 17 and 18 October, frustration in the Politburo with Honecker's stubborn refusal to reform and resolve the crisis spreading in the GDR led to his replacement by Egon Krenz, the former Head of Security and Youth Affairs. Krenz immediately announced policy changes but these were all designed to protect the SED's monopoly of power. There were, for instance, to be elections on the basis of the existing constitution which could only result in confirming the leading role of the SED, the GDR's communist party. At local level, however, SED leaders were already negotiating concessions with Protestant church leaders.

The Berlin Wall opens

In the absence of any effective restraints by the police or the army, crowds of demonstrators continued to grow in the cities. On 4 November, half a million congregated in East Berlin to demand further reform and the right to travel abroad. Two days later, a proposal was made by Krenz's government to issue permits for travel up to 30 days per year, but this was rejected by the *Volkskammer*, the GDR's parliament, as insufficient. On 9 November, a more sweeping concession was made which granted all GDR citizens with passports the right to an exit visa valid for any border crossing, including entry into West Berlin. Initially, this was supposed to take effect from the morning of 10 November, but it was announced prematurely in a press conference on the evening of the 9th, and that night border guards, facing a crowd of 20,000, opened up the crossing points through the Wall and into West Berlin.

Consequences of 9 November

The opening of the Berlin Wall had immediate consequences for Czechoslovakia and Romania.

> What was the significance of the opening of the Berlin Wall for Czechoslovakia and Romania?

The 'Velvet Revolution': Czechoslovakia

In 1989, Czechoslovakia was still controlled by those who had called for the suppression of the Prague Spring (see page 246). Opposition was limited to small groups such as Charter 77 led by Václav Havel, which attempted to monitor the government's compliance with the Helsinki Accords. However, the changes in Poland and Hungary in the summer of 1989 did impact on the situation in Czechoslovakia:

- Prime Minister Ladislav Adamec announced economic reforms, which were similar to those introduced during the Prague Spring, but they were not accompanied by political reforms.
- The number of opposition groups increased to nearly 40.
- On 21 August 1989, the 21st anniversary of the Prague Spring, 10,000 demonstrators chanted slogans such as 'Long live Poland' and 'Long live Dubček'.

After the Berlin Wall was opened up in the GDR, the political situation changed dramatically. A demonstration officially called to honour the death of a student killed by Germany in the Second World War escalated and turned into a mass protest against the government. This triggered a series of events known as the Velvet Revolution:

- On 19 November twelve opposition groups formed the Civic Forum.
- A series of large demonstrations of up to 750,000 people forced Adamec to open talks with the Civic Forum.
- Adamec offered 5 out of 21 cabinet seats to non-communists, but this offer was soon dropped.
- On 7 December Adamec resigned and non-communists formed a new government with a minority of communist members.
- On 29 December, the Parliament elected Václav Havel as President.

Havel and Civic Forum persuaded the USSR to withdraw its troops from the country while agreeing to remain part of the Warsaw Pact. Once it became clear that the two German states would reunite (see page 288), Czechoslovakia, with Poland and Hungary, pressed for its dissolution.

Romania

The opening of the Berlin Wall and the Velvet Revolution provided the Romanians with an opportunity to oust their communist leader: Nicolae Ceaușescu. Ceaușescu's economic policies – specifically, borrowing huge sums from Western states which then necessitated food and fuel shortages as these products were exported to pay back the loans – as well as corruption, such as promoting members of his family into positions of authority (one of his brothers was a general and another a high-level diplomat) and building a 1,100-room palace, caused significant opposition to emerge against him from within and without the government.

Gorbachev had been informed of plans to overthrow him as early as November 1988, and agreed, provided that the Romanian Communist Party was left as the dominant force in the country. The first revolts against the regime broke out in the largely ethnic Hungarian city of Timișoara near the Hungarian border and spread to Bucharest, Romania's capital, on 21 December. Once it became clear that the army had sided with the people against Ceaușescu's secret police, he fled the capital. He was soon arrested by the army and executed with his wife on 25 December.

The National Salvation Front (NSF) was formed on 22 December by Silviu Brucan, a former ambassador to the US, who was under house arrest on the orders of Ceaușescu, General Militaru and Ion Iliescu, a leading communist. After talks with opposition groups, the NSF established a Council for National Unity and held elections for a new government in May 1990. The NSF managed to win a majority in the elections and Iliescu was elected President. The success of the NSF was an example of what Gorbachev hoped a reformed communist party could achieve. Romania remained a reliable member of the Warsaw Pact until its dissolution in 1991.

Yugoslavia and Albania

Yugoslavia

After the expulsion of Yugoslavia from Cominform in 1948 (see page 95), it followed a different pattern from the other communist states in eastern and south-eastern Europe. It had more contact with the West and, in the 1960s and 1970s, allowed greater cultural and intellectual freedom than other communist states. However, Yugoslavia faced growing economic and political problems that were to destroy it by 1990. It was heavily dependent on foreign investment and by 1989 inflation had reached almost 300 per cent annually.

The economic problems worsened relations between the nationalities that formed the Yugoslav state. The prestige of President Tito managed to keep ethnic rivalries in check, but after his death in 1980, leaders of the Yugoslav Federation increasingly used nationalism to strengthen their own political position. In the Soviet bloc, people's dissatisfaction with governments led to demands for democratic reform and the overthrow of communism. In Yugoslavia this was channelled into increasing ethnic rivalries.

Influenced by the events in eastern Europe, the Communist Party's leading role in Yugoslavia was removed by the Federal Prime Minister Ante Marković from the constitution in January 1990 and multi-party federal elections were announced. These, however, only took place at state level beginning with the northern state of Slovenia in April 1990. Each election brought to power nationalists and soon each Yugoslav state demanded independence, leading to the dismemberment of the country into newly independent rival states and war. Successively, Slovenia, Croatia, Bosnia and Herzegovina, Macedonia, Kosovo and Crna Gora, also known as Montenegro, declared their independence from Yugoslavia between 1991 and 2006. All but Macedonia and Crna Gora fought wars to achieve independence, with the most brutal being the war in Bosnia and Herzegovina between 1992 and 1995 in which 100,000 people were killed, millions displaced and most cities heavily destroyed.

> **To what extent was the collapse of communism in Albania and Yugoslavia a consequence of the events in eastern Europe in 1989?**

Albania

Under Enver Hoxha, Albania ended relations with the USSR in 1961 and followed a strict Stalinist interpretation of communism. On Hoxha's death in 1985, Ramiz Alia initially continued the same policies, but in February 1989 announced a limited reform programme based on Gorbachev's *perestroika*. Ceaușescu's fall in Romania led to anti-communist unrest and riots in the capital city of Tirana. This pushed the government into announcing further reforms for fear of a larger revolt:

- The economy was partly decentralized.
- A new electoral law was announced, allowing multi-candidate, but not multi-party, elections in 1991.

After demonstrations in December 1990, Alia agreed to the legalization of political parties and to delay the elections until March 1991. In these elections, the former Communist Party, now renamed the Socialist Party of Albania, won the majority of seats. It briefly formed a government and Alia was elected President in May, but after a general strike in June, it resigned. A multi-party Government of National Stability came into power. In 1992, in new elections, the Democratic Party won by a sizeable margin of votes and Alia resigned as President in favour of Sali Ram Berisha.

How was Germany reunified? →

Unification of Germany

On 13 November, Prime Minister Egon Krenz was replaced by Hans Modrow, the Dresden Communist Party Secretary. Modrow agreed on 22 November to an initiative first put forward by the Protestant churches for a dialogue with opposition groups. At the first meeting in December, he agreed that free elections should be held in the GDR. When these took place on 18 March, Communists took only 16.4 per cent of the votes, while the pro-German unity party, the Christian Democratic Union (CDU) won 40.8 per cent of the vote. This effectively marked the end of communism in the GDR and made unification with the FRG more likely.

The future of Germany remained undecided. At first, the USSR, Britain and France did not want a reunited Germany. FRG Chancellor Helmut Kohl proposed only a loose confederation which would gradually develop into a political union or federation. Nevertheless, the strength of East German public opinion in the winter of 1989–90 convinced him that unity was the only option. The division of Germany marked the beginning of the Cold War; its reunification marked the end.

Bonn-Moscow-Washington talks

Kohl could not reunify Germany without the agreement of the USSR, the US and Germany's main western European allies, Britain and France. However, only the USSR and the US had the power to prevent it. Thus, the real negotiations were between the FRG, USSR and US. At first, Gorbachev was opposed to the dissolution of the GDR, and in December 1989 promised that

SOURCE P

GDR troops starting to demolish the Berlin Wall, February 1990.

What message does Source P imply about the future of Germany? **?**

he would 'see to it that no harm comes to the GDR'. Yet by the end of January, his support for the GDR ebbed rapidly. On 10 February, he told Kohl in Moscow that the Germans themselves should decide on the question of German unity. In Ottawa, Canada, four days later, US President Bush also agreed and outlined a formula for proceeding with the negotiations: 'two-plus-four talks'. This would involve both Germanys and the four former occupying powers which still had **residual rights** in Berlin (see page 81).

In a series of negotiations in the summer of 1990 agreement on German unity was reached. The USSR was persuaded to agree to the reunification of Germany and Germany's membership in NATO by generous loans which Gorbachev hoped would facilitate the modernization of the Soviet economy. Opposition in the West, particularly in Britain and France, was also overcome by Kohl's insistence on a united Germany's continued membership of NATO and the European Community.

On 12 September, the Two-Plus-Four Treaty was signed in Moscow. It was in effect a peace treaty ending the partition of Germany, as it terminated the residual rights of the former occupying powers in Germany and committed the new state to recognizing the Oder–Neisse border with Poland. At midnight on 2 October 1990, the GDR was integrated into the FRG and a reunited Germany came into existence.

**KEY TERM**

Residual rights The remaining privileges from 1945 that the four occupying powers of Britain, France the US and USSR still enjoyed in the FRG.

To what extent did
the Paris agreements
signal the end of the
Cold War?

Concluding the Cold War in Europe

After agreement on German reunification, the Cold War was effectively ended
by decisions taken in Paris in November 1990. Representatives of NATO and the
Warsaw Pact, which was dissolved in July 1991, met in Paris to sign the Treaty on
Conventional Armed Forces in Europe. It provided for the equal reduction of
conventional weapons in both eastern and western Europe, agreed on a process
of inspection and verification and declared that the countries signing the pact
were 'no longer adversaries'. The participants of the conference also produced
the Charter of Paris for a New Europe. This established a secretariat to organize
annual meetings at head of government level and for the creation of a Conflict
Prevention Centre in Vienna to advise on conflict avoidance.

? What information is
conveyed by Source Q?

SOURCE Q

Map of the new Europe, 1991

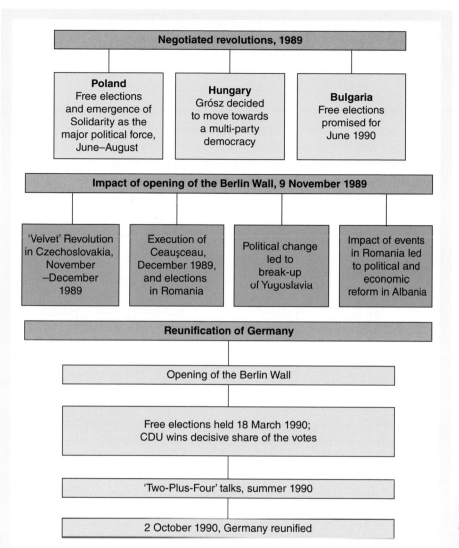

Negotiated revolutions, 1989

Poland
Free elections and emergence of Solidarity as the major political force, June–August

Hungary
Grósz decided to move towards a multi-party democracy

Bulgaria
Free elections promised for June 1990

Impact of opening of the Berlin Wall, 9 November 1989

'Velvet' Revolution in Czechoslovakia, November –December 1989

Execution of Ceauşceau, December 1989, and elections in Romania

Political change led to break-up of Yugoslavia

Impact of events in Romania led to political and economic reform in Albania

Reunification of Germany

Opening of the Berlin Wall

Free elections held 18 March 1990; CDU wins decisive share of the votes

'Two-Plus-Four' talks, summer 1990

2 October 1990, Germany reunified

SUMMARY DIAGRAM

The collapse of communism in eastern Europe, 1989–91

Collapse of the USSR

> **Key question:** Why was Gorbachev unable to prevent the disintegration of the USSR?

The collapse of Soviet power in eastern Europe in 1989–90 and then the disintegration of the USSR itself in 1991 came as a surprise to governments worldwide, including that of the Soviet Union. The emergence of the USSR as one of the world's two superpowers in 1945 after its defeat of Germany disguised the essential weaknesses of the USSR during the early post-war years:

- The Cold War meant massive expenditure on armaments, while also limiting trade and aid from the West.
- Large armies were maintained in eastern Europe and COMECON economies were heavily subsidized between 1956 and 1970, again causing a massive drain on the economy.
- The USSR had limited access to many of the world's raw materials until the 1970s as a result of the cold war.
- Many ethnic groups, including the formerly independent Baltic states, wished to have either more or total independence.

By the 1970s, the USSR appeared to be in a much stronger position. Its nuclear weaponry rivalled that of the US and its NATO partners and had acknowledged in the Helsinki Accords the post-war borders in eastern and central Europe. The USSR had also profited from the fall of the European colonial empires to intervene in post-colonial conflicts in Africa and Asia, as well as gain access to emerging markets and raw materials. However, within the USSR the economy stagnated and communism began to lose its appeal for many.

→ Gorbachev's reforms

How did Gorbachev's various reforms affect the USSR?

Initially Gorbachev aimed to reform the economy by:

- increasing investment in technology
- restructuring the economy so it was less centralized – *perestroika*
- giving workers greater freedom and incentives to encourage them to work harder.

Glasnost

To win the support of the people for his reforms, Gorbachev realized that a policy of openness or *glasnost* had to be followed. In other words, economic and political issues needed to be debated openly. From the spring of 1986 onwards, state censorship of the media was progressively eased and reception of foreign broadcasts was allowed. This ensured that the disaster at the Chernobyl nuclear power station in 1986 received major international publicity, as did Soviet failures in the Afghanistan war. In this new climate, investigative journalism, hitherto unknown in the USSR, played a key role in exposing the corruption of the Communist Party elite with their subsidized shops, chauffeur-driven cars and other benefits. All of this did much irreparably to damage the image of the Party in the eyes of many.

Climax of *glasnost*

The years 1988–89 were the high points of *glasnost*. New political organizations were established, such as the **Democratic Union**, and books by former dissidents were published. Religion, too, was tolerated. Churches, mosques and synagogues were reopened and for the first time in Soviet history religious texts and books were openly on sale in the shops. There was also a sudden appearance of uncensored newspapers and journals. In May 1989, the USSR Congress of People's Deputies was elected in what were the first contested national elections organized by the Communists. Although the Congress was no parliament, many different strands of public opinion were represented in it, and it had complete freedom to debate and criticize the government's policies. It also had the task of selecting the members for the new Supreme Soviet.

In February 1990, the cancellation of Article 6 of the old Soviet Constitution, which guaranteed the Communist Party a leading role in the USSR, destroyed the whole foundation on which the USSR's government existed. Party officials now had to have the backing of over 50 per cent of the electorate to remain in office, and in the March elections most long-term officials were rejected. Gorbachev was elected the first executive President of the USSR.

Growing economic crisis

By 1989, it was clear that *perestroika* had not managed to resolve the country's economic difficulties. The USSR's budget revenue steadily declined, while inflation rose. The consequences of this were that there was a growing shortage of goods and a fall in living standards.

SOURCE R

Soviet state deficit in billions of roubles. Information from *Gorbachev*, by M. McCauley, published by Longman, Harlow, UK, 1998, p. 114.

1985	37
1986	47.9
1987	57.1
1988	90.1
1989	100

> What information does Source R convey about the Soviet economy, 1985–89?

The nationalities problem

The USSR was a federation of fifteen republics in which the Russian Soviet Federative Socialist Republic (RSFSR) was by far the largest state. *Perestroika*, *glasnost* and the collapse of communism in eastern Europe led to a re-awakening of nationalism in many constituent republic states that were part of the USSR and felt dominated by ethnic Russians. The collapse of the Soviet economy also removed any remaining incentive to remain within the USSR.

> To what extent was nationalism a factor in the disintegration of the USSR?

KEY TERM

Democratic Union The first opposition party to the CPSU (Communist Party of the Soviet Union), set up in 1988.

The Baltic states

Estonia, Latvia and Lithuania had been parts of the Russian Empire until the collapse of Russia in the First World War, when they gained temporary independence. They were absorbed by the Soviet Union in 1940, occupied by Germany from 1941 to 1944, and then again merged with the Soviet Union. *Glasnost* and *perestroika* encouraged reformers and nationalists to press for independence. In 1988, so-called Popular Fronts, which were coalitions of reformers, formed in all three republics:

- The Latvian People's Front demanded autonomy within the USSR.
- The Reform Movement of Lithuania, or Sajūdis, announced its 'moral independence' from the USSR.
- The Estonian Popular Front issued a declaration of no confidence in the USSR.

SOURCE S

What information does Source S convey about the ethnic composition and structure of the USSR?

Republics of the USSR from *Soviet Politics in Perspective*, by Richard Sakwa, published by Routledge, London, UK, 1998, pp. 242–250.

Republic	Population of republic (000s) 1979	1989	% urban 1979	Titular nationality (1989)	Russian (1989)
Soviet Union	262,436	286,717	67	–	51.4
Russian SFSR	137,551	147,386	74	81.3	81.3
Ukrainian SSR	49,755	51,704	68	72.7	22.1
Byelorussian SSR	9560	10,200	67	77.9	13.2
Moldavian SSR	3947	4341	47	64.5	13.0
Azerbaijan SSR	6028	7029	54	82.7	5.6
Georgian SSR	5015	5449	57	70.1	6.3
Armenian SSR	3031	3283	68	93.3	1.6
Uzbek SSR	15,391	19,906	42	71.4	8.3
Kazakh SSR	14,685	16,538	57	39.7	37.8
Tajik SSR	3801	5112	33	62.3	7.6
Kirghiz SSR	3529	4291	38	52.4	21.5
Turkmen SSR	2759	3534	45	72.0	9.5
Lithuanian SSR	3398	3690	68	79.6	9.4
Latvian SSR	2521	2681	72	52.0	34.0
Estonian SSR	1466	1573	71	61.5	30.3

In February 1990, local elections were held throughout the USSR and pro-independence candidates won in the three Baltic republics. In March, Lithuania and Estonia declared their independence and Latvia followed in May. They were given encouragement and support by Solidarity in Poland.

Gorbachev's reaction

Initially Gorbachev reacted strongly against the independence movements in the Baltic. He was determined to keep the USSR together at all costs. He imposed an economic blockade on Lithuania in April 1990 and in January 1991 Soviet troops entered all three Baltic states on the pretext of searching for military deserters. In Vilnius, Lithuania, they seized the radio and television centre, killing thirteen civilians, but encountered massive public demonstrations and were forced to withdraw. On 11 January, US President Bush contacted Gorbachev and expressed his concern. The violence only served to strengthen the determination of the nationalists to gain independence.

Transcaucasia and Central Asian Republics

Glasnost had also encouraged the emergence of historic ethnic conflicts in Georgia, Armenia and Azerbaijan, as well as in the central Asian republics of Kazakhstan and Uzbekistan.

Armenian–Azerbaijan conflict

The most serious conflict occurred in the southern Caucasus region and involved Christian Armenia and Muslim Azerbaijan. The Nagorno-Karabakh district, populated by Armenians, was claimed by Armenia but had been granted to Azerbaijan by Stalin in 1923. It was divided from Armenia by a thin strip of land. *Glasnost* encouraged the Armenians to hold rallies during the winter of 1987–88 and demand its return. In February 1988, after a week of growing demonstrations in Stepanakert, the capital of Nagorno-Karabakh, Nagorno-Karabakh voted to merge with Armenia. After this was vetoed by Gorbachev, anti-Armenian riots erupted in Azerbaijan and 32 people were killed in Stepanakert.

Gorbachev removed the leaders in both Republics, but his failure to find a solution to the Nagorno-Karabakh issue led to growing nationalism in both Armenia and Azerbaijan:

- In early 1988, leading Armenian intellectuals and nationalists formed the Karabakh Committee to lead and organize a campaign for the return of Karabakh to Armenia.
- In May 1989, the anti-communist **Pan-Armenian** National Movement was founded, aiming for Armenia's complete independence from the USSR.
- In June 1988, the Supreme Soviet in Armenia, contrary to Gorbachev's wishes, decided to support the demand for the return of Nagorno-Karabakh to Armenia.
- In opposition to this, the Popular Front of Azerbaijan was formed in July 1988, which aimed at independence from the USSR and retention of Nagorno-Karabak.

Blockade of Armenia

In July 1988, Nagorno-Karabakh was temporarily placed under direct rule of the central government in Moscow. In an attempt to find a lasting solution, Gorbachev allowed the USSR's Supreme Soviet to decide on the region's

The Cold War is held to have ended with the collapse of the Soviet Union, yet communist states exist in the world today, such as the People's Republic of China, Cuba, and North Korea, and continue to influence international diplomacy. What determines the end of some historical event? (History, Language, Reason)

KEY TERM

Pan-Armenian All or the whole of Armenia.

future. This, however, merely voted in November 1989 to return Nagorno-Karabakh to Azerbaijani control. In defiance of this vote, the Armenian Supreme Soviet decided to ignore the decision and integrate the territory into Armenia. In response, the Azerbaijan Popular Front organized a rail blockade of Armenia which led to shortages of petrol and food. It also held a series of demonstrations in Baku, Azerbaijan's capital, which rapidly degenerated into riots against the local Armenians – at least 91 were killed. On 19 January, the Azerbaijan Popular Front declared a state of emergency and the following day, its members seized government and Communist Party buildings.

Gorbachev responded by declaring martial law and sent Soviet troops to restore the government. Late at night on 19 January 1990, 26,000 Soviet troops entered Baku, smashing through barricades established by the Popular Front and attacking protestors, killing over 130. While the army gained control of Baku, it alienated Azerbaijan. Most of the population of Baku attended the mass funerals of the victims. Thousands of Communist Party members publically burned their party cards.

Georgia

The independence movements in the Baltic and Transcaucasia inspired similar movements in Georgia. On 7–8 April 1989, troops were sent onto the streets of Tbilisi, Georgia, after more than 100,000 people gathered in front of government offices and the Communist Party headquarters and called for Georgia's independence. Nineteen people were killed and more than 200 wounded. This radicalized Georgian politics, leading many to believe that independence was preferable to continued Soviet rule.

The Central Asian Republics

In Kazakhstan and Uzbekistan, Gorbachev's attempt to purge the local Communist Party organizations of corrupt officials triggered a nationalist backlash that ultimately resulted in both republics voting to leave the USSR. In 1986, Gorbachev replaced the ethnic Kazakh leader of the local branch of the Communist Party with a Russian. This was seen by the local population as humiliating and evidence of further ethnic Russian domination. On 16 December, rioting broke out in cities across the republic. The government arrested thousands in a brutal crackdown.

In neighbouring Uzbekistan, Gorbachev's attempts were equally clumsy. Over 18,000 Uzbek Communist Party members were dismissed and mostly replaced with ethnic Russian officials, who knew little of the country or the language, triggering rising nationalism which agitated for ethnic Uzbek rule and independence.

Why did the western republics and Russia declare themselves independent?

The western republics and Russia

In Belarus, Moldavia and Ukraine, demands for independence were strongest in those areas which had been annexed by the Soviet Union between 1939 and 1940.

Moldavia

The Democratic Movement of Moldova was created in 1988 to campaign initially for greater cultural independence from the USSR. This took the form of demands for the revival of Moldavian traditions and the recognition of Moldavian as the official language. In May 1989, inspired by events in the Baltic, the Popular Front of Moldavia was founded. It successfully persuaded the Moldavian Supreme Soviet to adopt a new language law on 31 August 1989 which made Moldavian the official state language. In March 1990, it became the largest party in the elections for the Supreme Soviet.

Ukraine

The key to the future of the USSR was Ukraine, its second largest republic. If Ukraine chose independence, the USSR would be doomed. Lvov, in western Ukraine, became the centre of protests which demanded greater toleration for Ukrainian Christians and culture. Initially, local communist authorities attempted to end demonstrations, but that became much more difficult when the republic-wide Ukrainian Popular Front Movement, also known as *Rukh*, was created in 1989. In October 1990, *Rukh* declared that its principal goal was no longer autonomy within the USSR, but compete independence.

Belarus

Again inspired by the Baltic Popular Fronts, the Belarus Popular Front was established in 1988 as both a political party and a cultural movement demanding democracy and independence for Belarus. The discovery of mass graves in woods outside Minsk, the capital, of those executed by the Soviet government added momentum to the pro-democracy and pro-independence movement in the republic. It was argued that in the future only complete independence from the USSR would protect Belarus from a recurrence of such atrocities.

Russia

Elections took place to the **Russian Federation Congress of People's Deputies** in March and April 1990 and gave a majority to reformers. It was realized that the old USSR in the form that it had existed since the early 1920s was doomed. Gorbachev's rival, Boris Yeltsin, emerged as the leading politician in Russia and was elected chairman of the Congress. On 12 June, the Congress declared that Russia was a sovereign state and that its laws took precedence over those made by the overall union, the USSR. The term 'sovereign' asserted the moral right of the republic to self-determination. It did not necessarily rule out the possibility of voluntarily negotiating a new federation.

'The summer of sovereignty'

Elections also took place in the other republics during March and April 1990 for all the republics' Supreme Soviets. All followed Russia's example in declaring their sovereignty. The exception was Latvia, which already claimed to be independent.

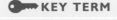 KEY TERM

Russian Federation Congress of People's Deputies The Russian parliament in the era of the Soviet Union.

The end of the USSR

These declarations of independence prompted Gorbachev to create a draft of the new Union Treaty in November 1990. In March 1991, a referendum was held on the question of creating a new union formed by the former members of the USSR. Soviet citizens were asked whether they supported the creation of a 'renewed federation of equal sovereign republics'. The referendum was boycotted by the Baltic republics, Moldavia, Georgia and Armenia, but in the other republics it was supported by 74 per cent of voters.

Gorbachev under threat

Gorbachev faced opposition from two quarters:

- Communists in the army, Party and the KGB.
- Reformers led by Boris Yeltsin, who in June 1991 became the first directly elected President of Russia.

Gorbachev was in an increasingly vulnerable position. Unlike Yeltsin, he had not been democratically elected nor did he have a secure power base. He was still President of the nearly defunct USSR.

The coup of 18–19 August 1991

On 18 August, just two days before the Union Treaty was to come into effect, leading communists, who were opposed to change, made one last attempt to save the old USSR. They launched an abortive coup in Moscow while Gorbachev was on holiday. There was no public backing for the rebels and the coup collapsed. Yeltsin played a key role in rallying the crowds in Moscow against the coup and was able to emerge as the saviour of the new Russia. Gorbachev was sidelined as he was on holiday in the Crimea and Yeltsin was seen as the hero who saved Russia from a military coup. The once all-powerful Communist Party was made illegal in Russia in August.

The consequences

The nine republics that had agreed to the Union Treaty now refused to implement it. Gorbachev attempted to draft a new treaty, but this too was rejected by all the republics. The final blow to the USSR came when the Ukraine decided on complete independence from the USSR after holding a referendum in December 1991.

In December, the Ukraine, Russia and Belarus established the **Commonwealth of Independent States (CIS)** which was then joined on 21 December 1991 by eight additional former Soviet Republics – Armenia, Azerbaijan, Kazakhstan, Kyrgyzstan, Moldova, Turkmenistan, Tajikistan, and Uzbekistan. Georgia joined two years later, in December 1993. On 25 December 1991, Gorbachev resigned and on 31 December, the USSR ceased to exist.

KEY TERM

Commonwealth of Independent States (CIS) A voluntary organization eventually of twelve of the successor states of the USSR. Any decision made by it was not binding on its members.

SOURCE T

Successor states of the USSR

What information does Source T convey about the collapse of the USSR?

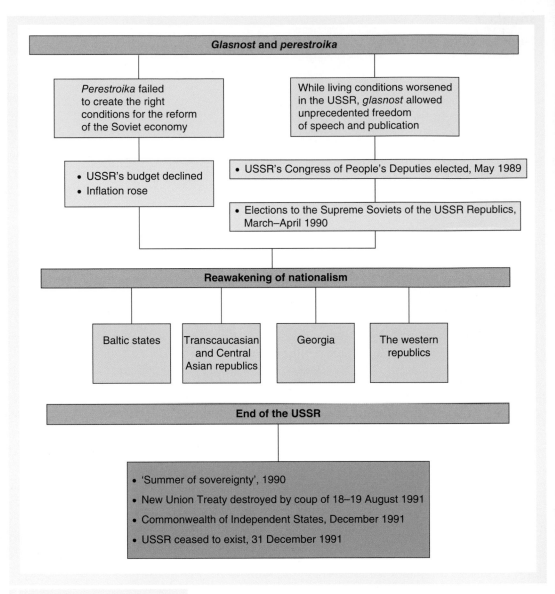

SUMMARY DIAGRAM

Collapse of the USSR

Chapter summary

In the late 1970s and early 1980s, the USSR appeared to be at the height of its power:

- It had a large army and had developed an air force and navy that could operate globally.
- It was politically, economically and militarily active in Angola, the Horn of Africa and elsewhere in the developing world.
- It was challenging the Western bloc by installing SS-20 medium-range nuclear missiles in eastern Europe.
- In Poland, it was instrumental in forcing General Jaruzelski to declare martial law to crush Solidarity.
- It invaded Afghanistan in December 1979 to maintain a communist regime there.

Yet beneath this impressive surface, its centralized command economy was in rapid decline. It had squandered enormous sums on armaments and failed to restructure itself to face the economic challenges of the 1970s and 1980s. It was weakened by the renewed arms race and the Afghan war, and could no longer afford to enforce the Brezhnev Doctrine.

Gorbachev thus had little option but to seek Western financial assistance and try to modernize the Soviet economy by the partial introduction of free market principles, thereby implicitly admitting that the Soviet model of communism had failed to achieve the promised utopian society. He hoped that a reformed and economically strengthened USSR would be able to forge new links of genuine friendship with eastern European states which would still willingly remain communist. This, however, was a miscalculation, except possibly for a time in Romania and Bulgaria:

- The GDR collapsed and German unification took place on the FRG's terms.
- In Poland, Solidarity became the dominant political force.
- In Hungary and Czechoslovakia, communist regimes collapsed.
- In Romania, a revolution overthrew Nicolae Ceaușescu, although in the subsequent election the reformed Communist Party, the National Salvation Front (NSF), regained power.
- In Bulgaria, the Communist Party transformed itself into a socialist party and was successful in winning elections with a small majority.
- In Albania, the Communist Party renamed itself and maintained its power until 1992.
- Yugoslavia dissolved into several non-communist successor states.

Gorbachev did not foresee that dissatisfaction with communism and Soviet rule would spread to the USSR. The liberation of eastern Europe from communism set precedents for the republics of the USSR. Weakened by economic crisis, the USSR had little to offer them. The Baltic republics, the Transcaucasian and central Asian republics, as well as Moldavia, Belarus, Ukraine and, finally, Russia itself, decided to abandon the USSR and communism. In December 1991, the USSR was replaced by the establishment of the Commonwealth of Independent States and Gorbachev was forced to resign. The Cold War had ended.

✓ Examination advice

How to answer 'identify' questions

When answering questions with the command term 'identify', you should present several possibilities and discuss their relative importance.

Example

> Identify the reasons for the collapse of communism in eastern Europe, excluding the Soviet Union.

1. The command term identify requests that you single out specific reasons for communism's collapse in eastern Europe. Please note that the word 'reasons' is plural, so you are expected to state several reasons. The question does not limit your answers to short-term or long-term ones, so you have a lot of possibilities to consider. You should clearly state in your answer which reasons are the more significant ones and explain your judgements.

2. Take at least five minutes to write a short outline. An example of a focused outline to this question might be:

- Growing nationalism
  - Poland, Baltic states, central Asia, Transcaucasia
- Economic stress, lack of consumer goods
  - Rising costs of living/food, inefficient industries, lack of technology
- Corruption
  - Nepotism, cronyism
- Collapse of Brezhnev Doctrine and Soviet weakness
  - Perestroika, glasnost, Poland, GDR, Baltic Popular Fronts

3. In your introduction, set out your key points about why communism ended in eastern Europe. An example of a good introductory paragraph for this question is given below.

Communist governments in eastern Europe collapsed relatively rapidly in 1989 and 1990. There were several reasons for this rapid change of government. In many states in eastern Europe, there was growing nationalism, such as that in Poland and the various Baltic states. Communism opposed nationalism, promoting instead the unity of the world's workers as opposed to ethnic or nationalistic connections between people. Closely connected to the rise of nationalism was the reality that communism, more or less imposed by the Soviet Union on

*many eastern European states after the Second World War, had failed
to advance eastern Europe economically. Single-party rule by
communist parties in the various states of the region had led to
nepotism and cronyism where corruption was rampant. This brought
with it financial waste, but also promotion and special benefits were
denied to most of the states' citizens. Finally, and perhaps most
importantly, and certainly connected with the other points made
above, the apparent lack of Soviet determination to support unpopular,
failing regimes by Gorbachev, the Soviet Union's leader in the late
1980s, meant that governments and politicians opted to transform in
order to survive or prevent violent revolution.*

4. For each of the main points you have outlined and mentioned in the
   introduction, you should be able to write two to three paragraphs that
   contain supporting evidence. Be sure to remain focused on the region of
   eastern Europe and to indicate which factors were related to other factors and
   which of these have greater significance than others. An example of how one
   of the key points could be expanded into a paragraph is given below.

*Perhaps most importantly, the Soviet Union's leader from 1985,
Mikhail Gorbachev, clearly indicated that the Soviet Union would
not intervene to support communist governments in eastern Europe.
In a July 1988 speech, a year before communist regimes began to fall
or transform in Europe, Gorbachev stated to the Council of Europe
that there would be no military force used to resolve problems. This
necessarily meant a rejection of former Soviet leader Brezhnev's
doctrine that communist regimes would be reinforced with Soviet or
Warsaw Pact military power if necessary; this had been demonstrated
during the Prague Spring in 1968. By stating that military force
would not be used, governments understood that they were essentially
on their own and would have to resolve their own difficulties.
Unsure of the loyalties of their soldiers or police, who also suffered
from rising food and fuel costs, and aware that growing nationalism
might also appeal to these people, governments faced the choice of
transforming into something new, perhaps even democratic systems,
or holding onto power at whatever costs. In almost all cases,
transformation into new parties, introduction of governing reforms
and elections in which there were multi-party options was the norm.*

5. In the final paragraph, you should tie your essay together and state your conclusion. Do not raise new points here and do not introduce material that extends past the collapse of communism in eastern Europe. An example of a good concluding paragraph is given below.

> Single-party, communist governments in eastern European states began transforming in 1989. The process had begun earlier with the inability of these governments to modernize their economics and become more competitive in the international market. Borrowing funds from capitalist countries meant massive debt and eventually higher costs of living in order to return the money borrowed, with interest. Industries and government were inefficient and wasteful as the result of corruption in which officials required bribes to function and unqualified people were promoted on the basis of party membership or other subjective factors. The result of economic stress was the formation of groups, such as Solidarity in Poland or Popular Front groups in the Baltic republics, all of which desired reform of their governments to address the needs of people; these later developed into independence movements once it was clear that the Soviet Union would not move to militarily support communist governments outside the Soviet Union. Gorbachev was unwilling, or unable, to use military force and therefore abandoned the Brezhnev Doctrine that had enforced communist rule in the region. Without the threat of Soviet military assistance, communist parties in eastern Europe understood that they had little alternative other than to transform into new parties in multi-party, democratic systems if they wished to prevent violent revolution against their unpopular regimes which had failed to deliver promised social, political and economic equality that was at the core of communist philosophy.

6. Now try writing a complete answer to the question following the advice above.

Examination practice

Below are three exam-style questions for you to practise on this topic.

1. Assess the importance of *glasnost* in causing the collapse of communist governments in eastern Europe between in 1989 and 1991?
(For guidance on how to answer 'assess' questions, see page 256)

2. Why, and with what results, was there renewal of detente between 1985 and 1989?
(For guidance on how to answer 'why' questions, see page 228)

3. To what extent were Gorbachev's political and economic policies responsible for the end of the Soviet Union in 1991?
(For guidance on how to answer 'to what extent' questions, see page 172)

Activities

I Create a chart in which each country in eastern Europe in 1989, excluding the Soviet Union, is listed along the side. Make a list of categories along the top which you will use to compare and contrast the experiences of each of these states. Categories might be:

- member of the Warsaw Pact (yes/no)
- date communist rule ended
- old/new name of former ruling party
- peaceful transition (yes/no)
- name of previous occupation of first president in democratic system, and so forth.

Now compare results with your class and create an overall work which can be used for examination review.

2 Make flashcards with the names of various political parties, figures, events on one side with explanations or definitions of these on the other. Use these as either examination review or to develop a game which tests your knowledge.

3 Cartoons are an interesting and often entertaining form of news or propaganda. Locate cartoons concerning the collapse of communism in eastern Europe and the Soviet Union. There are many internet sites which may be consulted, including www.cartoons.ac.uk, which is maintained by the University of Kent in the United Kingdom. Try to find cartoons from the US, Britain, eastern European states, and the Soviet Union; a balanced perspective is important. Discuss the imagery as a class as well as the meaning and message of the cartoons. Extend this by deciding which cartoons portrayed events or individuals most accurately in retrospect.

Glossary

Airlift The transport of food and supplies by aircraft to a besieged area.

Allied Control Commissions These were set up in each occupied territory, including Germany. They initially administered a particular territory in the name of the Allies.

Allied powers Commonly referred to as the Allies during the Second World War, this group first consisted of Poland, France, Britain and others, with the Soviet Union and the United States joining in 1941.

Allies In the First World War, an alliance between Britain, France, the US, Japan, China and others, including Russia until 1917.

ANC Acronym for the African National Congress which aimed to end the rule of South Africa by those of European descent and the racist system that the South African government imposed on the African majority.

Anglo-French Guarantee Britain and France guaranteed Polish independence, in the hope of preventing a German invasion of Poland.

Anti-ballistic missiles Missiles designed to destroy enemy missiles.

Appease To conciliate a potential aggressor by making concessions.

Armistice The official agreement of the suspension of fighting between two or more powers.

Arrow Cross Party A Hungarian ultra-nationalist political party that supported Germany in the Second World War.

Article 99 of the UN Charter 'The Secretary-General may bring to the attention of the Security Council any matter which in his opinion may threaten the maintenance of international peace and security.'

Asian defence perimeter A line through east and south-east Asia which the US was willing to defend against any other nation.

Atlantic Charter A statement of fundamental principles for the post-war world. The most important of these were: free trade, no more territorial annexation by Britain or the USA, and the right of people to choose their own governments.

Autarchic economy An economy that is self-sufficient and protected from outside competition.

Axis The alliance in the Second World War that eventually consisted of Germany, Italy, Japan, Slovakia, Hungary, Bulgaria, and Romania, as well as several states created in conquered areas.

Balance of payments The difference between the earnings of exports and the cost of imports.

Bank of Emission The bank responsible for the issue of a currency.

Benelux states Belgium, the Netherlands and Luxemburg.

Berlin's open frontier There was no physical barrier between communist East Berlin and capitalist and democratic West Berlin.

Bilateral Between two states.

Biological warfare A form of warfare in which bacteria and viruses are used against enemy armies and civilians.

Bolshevik Party The Russian Communist Party which seized power in a revolution in October 1917.

Bourgeoisie The middle class, particularly those with business interests, whom Marx believed benefited most from the existing capitalist economic system.

Brezhnev, Leonid General Secretary of the Central Committee of the Communist Party of the Soviet Union, 1964–82.

Capitalism An economic system in which the production of goods and their distribution depends on the investment of private capital with minimal government regulation and involvement.

CCP Chinese Communist Party led by Mao.

CENTO Central Treaty Organization, also known as Baghdad Pact, formed in 1955 by Iran, Iraq, Pakistan, Turkey and UK; it was dissolved in 1979.

Christian Democrats Moderately conservative political party seeking to apply Christian principles to governing the country.

CIA The Central Intelligence Agency was established by the US in 1947 to conduct counter-intelligence operations outside the United States.

Collective security An agreement between nations that an aggressive act towards one nation will be treated as an aggressive act towards all nations under the agreement.

Collectivization of agriculture Abolishing private farms in favour of large, state-owned farms where peasants worked together.

Cominform The Communist Information Bureau established in 1947 to exchange information among nine eastern European countries and co-ordinate their activities.

Comintern A communist organization set up in Moscow in 1919 to co-ordinate the efforts of communists around the world to achieve a worldwide revolution.

Command economy An economy where supply and pricing are regulated by the government rather than market forces such as demand, and in which all the larger industries and businesses are controlled centrally by the state.

Commonwealth of Independent States (CIS) A voluntary organization eventually of twelve of the successor states of the USSR. Any decision made by it was not binding on its members.

Commonwealth Organization of states formerly part of the British Empire.

Communes Communities of approximately 5000 households that organized and managed all resources within their control, including tools, seed, farmland and housing.

Communism A political and economic system in which all private ownership of property is abolished along with all economic and social class divisions.

Confederation A grouping of states in which each state retains its sovereignty; looser than a federation.

Consultative Council A council on which the member states of the Brussels Pact were represented.

Continuous revolution The conviction that revolution must be continuous, since if it is not going forward it will inevitably go backwards.

Cultural Revolution A mass movement begun by Mao's supporters to purge the CCP and PRC society of those opposed to Mao's version of communism.

Customs union An area of free trade.

Dalai Lama Religious and political leader of Tibet and of Tibetan Buddhism.

Dardanelles Strait connecting the Mediterranean and Aegean Seas with the Black Sea, separating Europe from Asia Minor.

De-Stalinization The attempts to liberalize the USSR after the death of Stalin in 1953.

Decolonization Granting of independence to colonies.

Democratic Union The first opposition party to the CPSU, set up in 1988.

Denazification The process of removing Nazi Party ideology, propaganda, symbols, and adherents from all aspects of German life.

Détente A state of lessened tension or growing relaxation between two states.

Dictatorship of the proletariat A term used by Marx to suggest that, following the overthrow of the bourgeoisie, government would be carried out by and on behalf of the working class.

Doctrine of containment A policy of halting the USSR's advance into western Europe. It did not envisage actually removing Soviet control of eastern Europe.

Domino effect The belief that the fall of one state to communism would result in a chain reaction leading to the fall of other neighbouring states.

Dutch East Indies A Dutch colony that became Indonesia.

Economic nationalism An economy in which every effort is made to keep out foreign goods.

Eritrea Formerly a colony of Italy, which became part of Ethiopia in 1951.

European Community The European Economic Community (EEC) had changed its name to the European Community (EC).

ExComm The Executive Committee of the US National Security Council.

Federal A country formed of several different states that have considerable autonomy in domestic affairs.

Federal Republic of Germany (FRG) Capitalist state established in western Germany in 1949 following the Berlin Blockade, which involved amalgamating the British, US and French zones of occupation.

Five Year Plan Plan to modernize and expand the economy over a five-year period.

Four-Power Control Under the joint control of the four occupying powers: Britain, France, the US and USSR.

Fourteen Points A list of points drawn up by US President Woodrow Wilson on which the peace settlement at the end of the First World War was based.

Free city Self-governing and independent city-state.

Free French The French who supported de Gaulle after the fall of France in June 1940, when he established his headquarters in London.

FRELIMO *Frente de Libertação de Moçambique*, or Mozambique Liberation Front.

French Indochina A French colony consisting of today's Laos, Cambodia, and Vietnam.

Gang of Four The four senior Communist politicians who led the PRC immediately after Mao's death.

German Democratic Republic (GDR) Communist state set up in eastern Germany in 1949 following the Berlin Blockade.

Glasnost Openness regarding the USSR's economic and political systems, including public discussion and debate.

Grand Coalition Coalition between West Germany's two biggest parties: SPD and CDU.

Guerrilla groups Fighters who oppose an occupying force using tactics such as sabotage and assassination.

Guerrilla war A war fought by small groups of irregular troops. The term means 'little war' in Spanish.

Guns and butter Phrase used initially in the US press in 1917 to describe the production of nitrates both for peaceful and military purposes; now usually used to describe the situation when a country's economy can finance both increased military and consumer goods production.

Hard currency A globally traded currency such as the dollar, usually from a highly industrialized country.

High Commission The civilian body charged with the task of defending the interests of the Western allies in Germany.

Hồ Chí Minh Trail An infiltration route of hundreds of kilometres that allowed the movement of troops and war material through neighbouring countries into South Vietnam.

Hotline A direct communications link between US and Soviet leaders.

Human rights Basic rights such as personal liberty and freedom from repression.

Hydrogen bomb A nuclear bomb hundreds of times more powerful than an atomic bomb.

Immutable Unchangeable.

Intercontinental ballistic missiles (ICBM) Missiles capable of carrying nuclear warheads and reaching great distances.

Intermediate-range ballistic missiles (IRBM) Missiles capable of carrying nuclear warheads and travelling up to 5000 kilometres in distance.

International Ruhr Authority Established how much coal and steel the Germans should produce and ensured that a percentage of its production should be made available to its western neighbours. It was replaced in 1951 by the European Coal and Steel Community.

Inviolable Not to be attacked or violated.

Isolation A situation in which a state has no alliances or close diplomatic contacts with other states.

Joint Chiefs of Staff Committee of senior military officers who advise the US government on military matters.

KMT (Kuomintang) Chinese Nationalist Party led by Chiang Kai-shek.

Kosygin, Alexei Premier of the USSR, 1964–80.

Land corridors Roads, railways and canals, which the USSR had agreed could be used to supply West Berlin in 1945.

League of Nations International organization established after the First World War to resolve conflicts between nations to prevent war.

Lebensraum Literally living space. Territory for the resettlement of Germans in the USSR and eastern Europe.

Left-wing Liberal, socialist or communist.

Lend-lease The US programme begun in March 1941 that gave over $50 billion ($650 billion in today's terms) of war supplies to Allied nations.

The Long March A retreat by the Chinese Communist Party from southern to north-western China, covering 12,500 kilometres in approximately one year, and in which 90 per cent of all participants died.

Magnetic social and economic forces of the West Brandt believed that the economy and way of life in West Germany was so strong that ultimately it would exert a magnet-like attraction on the GDR and lead to unification.

Manchuria A region in the far north-east of China, occupied by the Japanese in 1931 until the end of the Second World War.

Marshall Plan US economic aid programme for post-war western Europe, also known as Marshall Aid.

Martial law Military rule involving the suspension of normal civilian government.

Marxism–Leninism Doctrines of Marx which were built upon by Lenin.

Military Governor The head of a zone of occupation in Germany.

Militia Part-time military reservists.

Monroe Doctrine The doctrine formulated by President Monroe of the USA (1817–25) that the European powers should not intervene in the affairs of North or South America.

MSZMP (Magyar Szocialista Munkáspárt) The Hungarian Socialist Workers' Party, the Communist Party in Hungary between 1956 and 1989.

Multiple independently targeted re-entry vehicles Missiles capable of carrying multiple nuclear warheads, each destined for a different target.

Munich Agreement An agreement between Britain, France, Italy and Germany that the Sudetenland region of Czechoslovakia would become part of Germany.

Namibia A former German colony which was entrusted to South Africa to govern under a 1919 League of Nations mandate; it became independent in 1991.

Nationalist Someone devoted to the interests and culture of their nation, often leading to the belief that certain nationalities are superior to others.

Nationalist China The regions of China controlled by the Nationalist Party of China led by General Chiang Kai-shek.

Nationalize A state take-over of privately owned industries, banks, and other parts of the economy.

New Left The predominantly student left-wing movements that emerged in the US and Europe in the 1960s.

NKVD Soviet security organization responsible for enforcing obedience to the government and eliminating opposition.

Non-Aligned Movement (NAM) Organization of states committed to not joining either the Western or Soviet blocs during the Cold War, founded in Belgrade in 1961 and based on the principles agreed at the Bandung Conference.

Nuclear diplomacy Negotiations and diplomacy supported by the threat of nuclear weapons.

Occupation Statute A treaty defining the rights of Britain, France and the USA in West Germany.

Ostpolitik West Germany's policy towards eastern Europe, which involved recognition of the GDR and the post-war boundaries of eastern Europe.

Palestine Liberation Organization (PLO) A Palestinian nationalist organization created in 1964 that operated as a political and paramilitary group.

Pan-Armenian All or the whole of Armenia.

Paramilitary police force Police force that is armed with machine guns and armoured cars.

Paris Peace Conference The peace conference held in Paris in 1919–20 to deal with defeated Germany and her allies. It resulted in the Treaties of Versailles, St. Germain, Neuilly and Sèvres.

Parliamentary government A government responsible to and elected by parliament.

Partisan groups Resistance fighters or guerrillas in German- and Italian-occupied Europe.

Pathet Lao Independence movement in Laos, supported by the Viet Minh.

Perestroika Transformation or restructuring of the Communist Party to make it more responsive to the needs of the people.

Podgorny, Nikolai Chairman of the presidium of the Supreme Soviet, 1965–77.

Polish Home Army The Polish nationalist resistance group that fought German occupation during the Second World War.

Politburo The Political Bureau of the Central Committee of the Communist Party.

Prague Spring A period of political and economic reforms initiated in Czechoslovakia in 1968 that included multi-party elections, freedom of speech and press, as well as reducing government control of the economy.

Presidium Soviet inner council or cabinet.

Proletariat Marx's term for industrial working-class labourers, primarily factory workers.

Provisional government A temporary government in office until an election can take place.

Proxy conflict A war in which greater powers use third parties as substitutes for fighting each other directly.

Puppet government Government that operates at the will of and for the benefit of another government.

Puppet ruler Ruler of a country controlled by another power.

PUWP The Polish United Workers Party, the Communist Party in Poland between 1948 and 1989.

Ratify When an international treaty has been signed, it can come into effect only after the parliaments of the signatory states have ratified (i.e. approved) it.

Red Army The army of the USSR.

Reichsmark German currency before 1948; it lost most of its value after Germany's defeat in the Second World War.

Reparations Materials, equipment or money taken from a defeated power to make good the damage of war.

Representative government A government based on an elected majority.

The Republican Party One of the two main US political parties.

Residual rights The remaining privileges from 1945 that the four occupying powers of Britain, France the US and USSR still enjoyed in the FRG.

Revisionist In the sense of historians, someone who revises the traditional or orthodox interpretation of events and often contradicts it.

Ruhr The centre of the German coal and steel industries and at that time the greatest industrial region in Europe.

Russian Federation Congress of People's Deputies The Russian parliament in the era of the Soviet Union.

Secretary of State The US foreign minister.

Self-determination Giving nations and nationalities the right to be independent and to form their own governments.

Self-immolation Burning oneself alive as a sacrifice and act of protest.

Separatists Those wishing to break away from an existing state to create an independent country.

'Smart' bombs Precision-guided bombs which enable a target to be hit accurately with the use of fewer and smaller bombs.

Social Democratization Converting the communist SED into a more moderate Western-style Social Democratic Party like the SPD in the FRG.

Sovereignty National political independence.

Soviet bloc A group of states in eastern Europe controlled by the USSR.

Soviet Union See **USSR**.

Sovietization Reconstructing a state according to the Soviet model.

Soweto Uprising A protest on 16 June 1976 by at least 20,000 African students against the introduction of Afrikaans, the language of many European South Africans, as the sole language of educational instruction in schools; 700 protestors were killed and 4000 injured by government forces.

Spheres of interest Areas where one power is able to exercise a dominant influence.

Sputnik Russian for 'fellow traveller', or supporter of the USSR, and the name of the world's first artificial satellite placed in the Earth's orbit.

Stalin cult The propaganda campaign vaunting Stalin as the great ruler and saviour of the USSR.

Suez Canal Canal located in Egypt connecting the Mediterranean and Red Seas.

Supranational Transcending national limits.

Supreme Soviet Set up in 1936 by Stalin. It consisted of two bodies: the Soviet of the USSR and the Soviet of Nationalities. Each Soviet republic had a Supreme Soviet or parliament, as did the overall USSR.

SWAPO Acronym for South West People's Organization which aimed to liberate Namibia from South African rule.

Tactical nuclear weapons Small-scale nuclear weapons that can be used in the battlefield.

Tariffs Taxes placed on imported goods to protect the home economy.

Tet Offensive North Vietnamese and Viet Cong offensive against South Vietnamese and US troops, which was launched despite an agreed truce during Tết Nguyên Đán, the Vietnamese New Year festival.

Third World Developing states, many of which had been colonies or under the control of predominately European states.

Titoism Communism as defined by Tito in Yugoslavia.

Trade embargo A suspension of trade.

Trade missions Organizations to promote trade between states.

Trade surplus The situation that occurs when a country sells more than it buys from other countries it trades with.

Transit traffic Traffic crossing through another state.

Trusteeship Responsibility for the government and welfare of a state handed over temporarily to other powers.

USSR Union of Soviet Socialist Republics, the name given to communist Russia and states under its control from 1922, also known as the Soviet Union.

Viet Minh 'League for the Independence of Vietnam' (English translation).

Virgin Lands Scheme Nikita Khrushchev's plan to increase the Soviet Union's agricultural production to alleviate the food shortages by bringing into cultivation previously uncultivated land.

Watergate scandal On 17 June 1972, Republican Party officials broke into the headquarters of the opposition Democratic Party in the Watergate Building in Washington DC to find material which could be used to discredit Democrats. The break-in was discovered and eventually led to Nixon's resignation in 1974.

Western bloc An alliance of western European states and the USA.

Western European integration The process of creating a Western Europe that was united politically, economically and militarily.

Workers' Defence Committee A body created to give aid to those arrested by the communist authorities and also to help their families.

World Bank International financial institution that provides loans to developing countries for large-scale engineering projects.

Yugoslavia In 1918, the kingdom of Serbs, Croats and Slovenes was formed. In 1929, it officially became Yugoslavia. The Serbs were the dominating nationality within this state.

Zionism A form of Jewish nationalism that supported the foundation of a Jewish state in the historic land of Israel.

Timeline

1917	**October** Russian Revolution
1918	**April** Wilson's Fourteen Points
1919	**March** Comintern set up
1922	USSR created
1925	**March** Chiang Kai-shek became the leader of Nationalist China
1939	**September** Britain and France declared war on Germany
	Hitler and Stalin partitioned Poland
	November Stalin attacked Finland and annexed territories along the Soviet border
1941	**June** Germany invaded USSR
	December Japan bombed Pearl Harbor
1943	**November–December** Tehran Conference
1944	**June** Allied forces invaded France
	July Red Army entered central Poland
1945	**February 4–11** Yalta Conference
	May Unconditional German surrender
	July–August Potsdam Conference
	August USSR declared war on Japan
	US dropped A-bombs on Hiroshima and Nagasaki
	Japan surrendered and occupied by US
1946	**March** Churchill's Iron Curtain speech
	June CCP–GMD civil war resumes in China
	November Guerrilla warfare begins in Vietnam

1947	**March** Truman Doctrine announced
	June Marshall Aid Programme announced
	October Cominform founded
1948	**June** London Six Power Conference recommended calling of a West German Constituent Assembly
	Currency reform in Western zones
	Berlin Blockade began
1949	**April** NATO set up
	May USSR lifted Berlin Blockade
	FRG approved by western Allies
	August USSR successfully tests A-bomb
	October GDR set up
	People's Republic of China proclaimed
1950	**February** USSR–PRC Treaty
	June Outbreak of Korean War
	October PRC enters Korean War
1951	**April** European Coal and Steel Community treaty (Schuman Plan)
	September Peace treaty signed with Japan
1952	**May** European Defence Community (EDC) Treaty signed in Paris
1953	**March** Stalin died
	June Strikes and riots in the GDR
	July Korean War ended
1954	**May** French defeated by Viet Minh at Điện Biên Phủ
	July Geneva Agreements on Vietnam
1955	**April** Bandung Conference
	May The FRG became a sovereign state and joined NATO
	Warsaw Pact signed
	July Geneva Summit

1956	**February** Khrushchev attacked Stalin's record at 20th Party Congress
	October–November Suez Crisis
	Hungarian Uprising defeated
1957	**March** Eisenhower Doctrine approved by Congress
	August USSR fired first ICBM
1958	**November** Berlin Crisis began
1959	**January** Castro set up a revolutionary government in Cuba
1960	**May** US U-2 spy plane shot down over USSR
	June Belgian Congo gained independence
	July Soviet experts recalled from PCR
	Katanga secedes from Congo
1961	**April** Bay of Pigs incident
	August Border between East and West Berlin closed. Construction of Berlin Wall began
1962	**October** Cuban Missile Crisis
1963	**August** Test Ban Treaty
1964	**August** Gulf of Tonkin incident
	October Fall of Khrushchev
1965	**February** US bombing of North Vietnam began
	November Mobutu established military dictatorship in Congo
1967	**June** Six Day War in Middle East
	Glassboro Summit
	December Harmel report
1968	**January** Tet Offensive in South Vietnam
	August Soviet invasion of Czechoslovakia
1969	**March** USSR–PCR border conflict
	July Non-proliferation Treaty

1970	**August** USSR–FRG Moscow Treaty
	December Warsaw Treaty
1971	**September** Four-Power Treaty on Berlin
1972	**May** SALT I
	Moscow Summit
	December Basic Treaty between FRG and GDR
1973	**January** Paris Peace Accords signed between US and North Vietnam
	October The October War
1974	**April** Military coup in Portugal
	September Mozambique gained independence
1975	**April** North Vietnam occupied South Vietnam
	August Helsinki Final Act
	November Angola gained independence
1976	**March** Victory of MPLA in Angola
	September Death of Mao
1977	**February** Mengistu seized power in Ethiopia
1978	**March** With Soviet and Cuban help Ethiopia recaptured Jijiga from Somali forces
1979	**December** NATO decision to install Cruise and Pershing missiles in western Europe in the event of no arms agreement with USSR
	Soviet invasion of Afghanistan
1980	**May** Gen Biao, PRC's defence minister, visited US
	November Reagan elected President of US
1981	**December** Martial law declared in Poland
1983	**March** Reagan announced development of SDI

1985	**March** Gorbachev became USSR Party Leader
1986	**October** USSR–US summit at Reykjavik
1987	**December** Gorbachev signed treaty banning Intermediate nuclear missiles (INF)
1988	**April** Geneva Accords signed between Pakistan and Afghanistan with the USSR and US as guarantors
1989	**February** Soviet troops withdrawn from Afghanistan **April** Tbilisi killings in Georgia **May** PCR–USSR relations normalized **June** Elections in Poland **September** Hungary allowed GDR citizens through frontier to Austria **November** Berlin Wall breached **December** Ceaușescu executed
1990	**May** Latvian Supreme Soviet announced its aim to achieve independence **October** Germany reunified **November** Treaty on Conventional Forces in Europe
1991	**January** Soviet forces intervened in the Baltic Republics **March** Referendum on future of USSR **August** Failure of attempted military coup in USSR **December** Commonwealth of Independent States founded USSR formally dissolved

Further reading

Studies covering the whole of the Cold War, 1945–91

S.R. Ashton, *In Search of* Détente: *The Politics of East–West Relations since 1945*, Macmillan, 1989
It was published just before the Cold War ended, but it is nevertheless a useful survey, particularly on *détente*.

J.P.D. Dunbabin, *The Cold War. The Great Powers and their Allies*, second edition, Pearson Education 2008
A detailed study of the global Cold War. It is arguably the most precise and detailed one volume history of the Cold War in English.

J.L. Gaddis, *The Cold War*, Allen Lane, 2005
A helpful and readable synthesis of the Cold War.

M. Leffler and O.A. Westad (editors), *The Cambridge History of the Cold War*, Vol. I *Origins*, Vol. II *Crises and Détentes*, Vol. III *Endings*, Cambridge University Press, 2010
The three volumes contain chapters on all aspects of the global Cold War written by experts. The chapters can be informative, although not easy to read.

J.W. Mason, *The Cold War, 1945–91*, Routledge, 1996
An excellent introductory survey of just 75 pages. It covers the Cold War in both Europe and Asia.

N. Stone, *The Atlantic and its Enemies*, Penguin, 2011
A witty and wide-ranging book on the global Cold War.

M. Walker, *The Cold War*, Vintage, 1994
A readable, journalistic study of the whole Cold War. It covers all aspects of this struggle and contains much useful information.

Historiography and problems of the Cold War

J.L. Gaddis, *We Know Now: Rethinking Cold War History*, Oxford University Press, 1997
This puts the Cold War into its global context and assesses the changing interpretations and explanations of the Cold War.

K. Larres and A. Lane, *The Cold War*: *The Essential Readings*, Blackwell, 2001
Contains some interesting articles and extracts from leading Cold War historians.

O.A. Westad, *Reviewing the Cold War: Approaches, Interpretations, Theory*, Frank Cass, 2000
Brings together the often conflicting views of historians on the Cold War.

The origins of the Cold War up to 1953

J.L. Gaddis, *The United States and the Origins of the Cold War, 1941–1947*, Columbia University Press, 2000
A study of US policy towards the USSR, 1941–47.

M.P. Leffler and D.S. Painter, *Origins of the Cold War*, Routledge, 1994
Focuses on the global origins of the Cold War and through the contributions of historians introduces readers to a variety of views on the Cold War.

W. Loth, *Die Teilung der Welt. Geschichte des Kalten Krieges, 1941–1955*, Deutsche Taschenbuch Verlag, 2000
A German analysis of the origins of the Cold War.

M. McCauley, *The Origins of the Cold War, 1941–49*, second edition, Longman, 1995
A clear and well-explained introduction to the causes and early stages of the Cold War.

D. Reynolds (editor), *The Origins of the Cold War in Europe: International Perspectives*, Yale University Press, 1994
An informative survey of the historiography and the international historical debates on the Cold War covering the period 1945–55.

D. Yergin, *Shattered Peace: The Origins of the Cold War and the National Security State*, Houghton Mifflin, 1977
A revisionist study of the US's involvement in the Cold War in Europe.

Europe during the Cold War

J. Laver, *The Eastern and Central European States, 1945–92*, Hodder & Stoughton, 1999
Provides a clear guide to the eastern European states.

G. Swain and N. Swain, *Eastern Europe since 1945*, Macmillan, 1993
A fuller study of the same subject.

J.F. Young, *Cold War Europe, 1945–91*, second edition, Arnold, 1996
An informative chapter on the Cold War and *détente* and then further useful chapters on European integration, eastern Europe, the USSR and the main western European states.

Studies of Cold War Germany

M. Fulbrook, *Anatomy of a Dictatorship: Inside the GDR, 1949–1989*, Oxford University Press, 1995
An informative study of the GDR based on primary sources.

W. Loth, *Stalin's Unwanted Child. The Soviet Union, the German Question and the Founding of the GDR*, Macmillan, 1998
An interesting study which argues that Stalin did not intend the division of Germany.

D.G. Williamson, *Germany from Defeat to Partition, 1945–1961*, Pearson Education, 2001
Covers the occupation and division of Germany.

The USSR and the Cold War

J. Haslam, *Russia's Cold War From the October Revolution to the Fall of the Wall,*
Yale University Press, 2011
A study of Soviet foreign policy and its formulation during the Cold War.

M. McCauley, *The Khrushchev Era*, 1953–1964, Longman, 1995
A concise study of this dramatic period.

M. McCauley, *Gorbachev*, Longman, 1998
A biography of Gorbachev and particularly useful for the years 1989–91.

R. Pearson, *The Rise and Fall of the Soviet Empire*, Palgrave/Macmillan, 2002
An excellent but brief study of the USSR, 1945–91.

G. Roberts, *The Soviet Union in World Politics: Coexistence, Revolution and Cold
War, 1945–91*, Routledge, 1999
A brief but comprehensive survey of Soviet foreign policy during this period.

Vladislav Zubok and Constantine Pleshakov, *Inside the Kremlin's Cold War:
From Stalin to Khrushchev*, Harvard University Press, 1996
Important reading for an understanding of Soviet policy during the early Cold
War years up to 1964.

The Third World and the Cold War

N.J. Ashton (editor), *The Cold War in the Middle East*, Routledge, 2007
A collection of informative essays on the Middle East and the Cold War.

O.A. Westad, *The Global Cold War*, Cambridge University Press, 2007
By far the best study of the impact of the Cold War on the Third World.

China

J. Chang and J. Haliday, *Mao: The Unknown Story,* Jonathan Cape,
A lengthy, comprehensive biography.

S.N. Goncharov, J.W. Lewis and Xue Litai, *Uncertain Partners*, Stanford
University Press, 1993
Very helpful on Sino-Soviet relations and the Korean War as well as having a
useful selection of sources.

C. Jian, *Mao's China and the Cold War*, North Carolina Press, 2001
Essential reading for understanding China during the Cold War.

M. Lynch, *Mao*, Routledge, 2004
A concise biography with useful information on the Chinese Civil War.

The Vietnam War

F. Logevall, *The Origins of the Vietnam War*, Pearson, 2001
A helpful guide to the causes of the war up to 1965.

R.D. Schulzinger, *A Time for War: The United States and Vietnam, 1941–1975,*
Oxford University Press, 1997
A good general account of the US and the Vietnam War.

Détente and *Ostpolitik*

T. Garton Ash, *In Europe's Name: Germany and the Divided Continent*,
Jonathan Cape, 1993
A very useful guide to *Ostpolitik* and the reunification of Germany.

O. Bange and G. Niedhart (editors), *Helsinki, 1975 and the Transformation of Europe*, Berghahn Books, 2008
Useful for understanding the impact of the Helsinki Final Act on the Cold War.

M. Bowker and P. Williams, *Superpower* Détente: *A Reappraisal*, Sage, 1988
Gives a full account of *détente* in the 1970s.

The end of the Cold War

T. Garton Ash, *We the People – The Revolution of 1990*, Penguin, 1990
A journalist's account of the collapse of Communism in eastern Europe.

R. Garthoff, *The Great Transition: American–Soviet Relations and the End of the Cold War*, Brookings Institution, 1994
A difficult but important book on the end of the Cold War.

M. Hogan (editor), *The End of the Cold War, its Meanings and Implications*,
Cambridge University Press, 1992
Contains some excellent but difficult essays on the reasons for the end of the Cold War.

C. S. Maier, *Dissolution,* Princeton University Press, 1997
An interesting account of the collapse of the GDR.

Internet sources

http://cwihp.si.edu
The Cold War International History Project Bulletin (CWIHP, Woodrow Wilson International Center for Scholars, Washington DC). CWIHP has published hundreds of articles and documents from eastern European and Soviet archives. Its aim is 'to disseminate new information and perspectives on Cold War history emerging from previously inaccessible archives'. It has become a major source for Cold War studies.

www.gwu.edu/~nsarchiv/NSAEBB
National Security Archive Electronic Briefing Books provide online access to critical declassified records on issues including U.S. national security and foreign policy. These include, for example, CIA reports as well as translated Soviet documents.

www.fordham.edu/halsall/mod/modsbook.asp
Fordham University's Internet Modern History Sourcebook: Contains some material relevant to the Cold War.

www.historyplace.com/index.html
The History Place: US perspectives of twentieth-century history, which include the Cold War years.

Internal assessment

The internal assessment is an historical investigation on a historical topic that is required of all IB History students. This book has many key and leading questions which may be adapted for use as a research question for your internal assessment. In addition to those, you may wish to consider questions such as these:

Origins of the Cold War

1 Was the Yalta Conference more responsible for the Cold War than the Potsdam Conference?
2 How different were Soviet war aims to those of Britain in the Second World War?
3 In what ways and for what reasons was the future of eastern Europe responsible for the Cold War?
4 Why was no single peace treaty agreed upon by the Allies regarding the outcome of the Second World War?
5 How did Soviet atomic bomb development differ from that of the United States?

Germany in the Cold War

1 How did the economy of western Germany differ from that of eastern Germany between 1945 and 1950?
2 Did visual art and music develop differently in eastern and western Berlin during the Cold War up to 1949?
3 What was the effect of the Marshall Plan on western Germany compared to France?
4 To what extent were former Nazi government officials involved in the formation of governments in eastern and western Germany after the Second World War?
5 In what ways and for what reasons did Soviet cartoons depict international tensions over Germany after the Second World War until the formation of the German Democratic Republic?

The Cold War in Europe

1 To what extent was Yugoslavia's governing structure different from those of other communist states in central and eastern Europe?
2 How did the economic plans of the GDR and Poland compare in the 1960s?
3 Why did COMECON fail to bring prosperity to Hungary?
4 What was the experience of Bulgaria's Jews compared to those Jews living in Romania during the Cold War?
5 How did government propaganda in Albania differ from that of Yugoslavia?

The Cold War in Asia

1 Why did the Soviet Union not support North Korea militarily during the Korean War?
2 How did communism in the People's Republic of China differ from communism adopted in Vietnam by 1975?
3 Were there any provinces in the People's Republic of China that were successful during Mao's Great Leap Forward?
4 How were traditional forms of music affected by the implementation of communism in south-east Asia?
5 How did the experiences of minority groups in Laos differ from the experiences of minorities in the People's Republic of China?

Cold War Crises

1 How were Egyptian Jews affected by the Suez Crisis?
2 To what extent was the Berlin Crisis the result of US domestic politics?
3 Why did the North Atlantic Treaty Organization not intervene in the Hungarian Crisis in 1956?
4 What was the economic effect of the Berlin Wall on East Berlin?
5 What was the response of South American states towards Castro's regime after the Cuban Missile Crisis?

End of the Cold War

1 Why did the Soviet government choose Mikhail Gorbachev to lead the Soviet Union from 1985?
2 How did the policy of *perestroika* affect North Korea?
3 What was the economic impact of the collapse of COMECON on Cuba's economy?
4 To what extent was the Roman Catholic Church involved in the removal of Poland's communist government?
5 How did the goals of the Popular Fronts of the three Baltic republics differ?

Index